The Finnish Political System

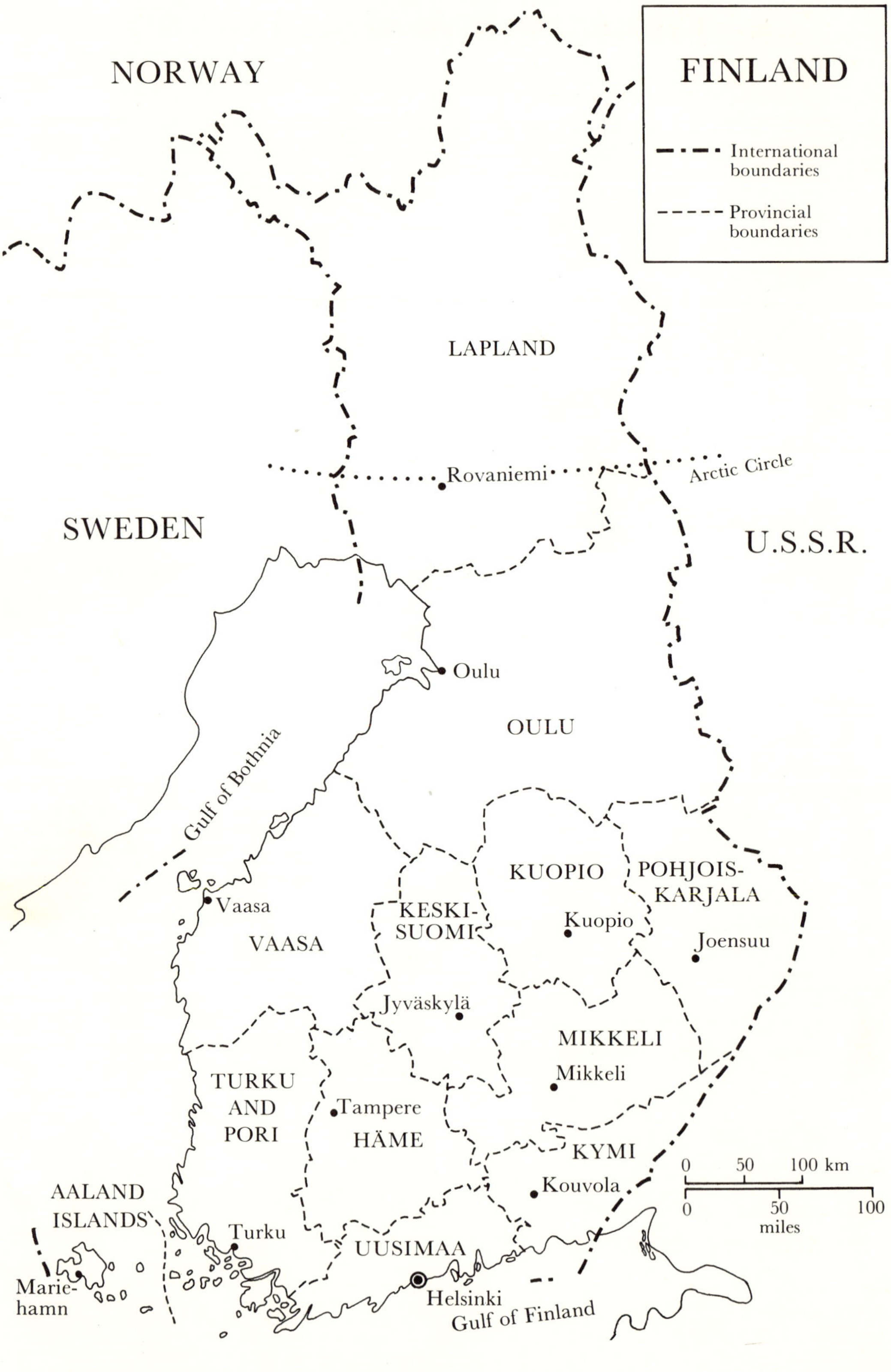
FINLAND
International boundaries
Provincial boundaries
NORWAY
SWEDEN
U.S.S.R.
LAPLAND
Rovaniemi
Arctic Circle
Oulu
OULU
Gulf of Bothnia
Vaasa
VAASA
KESKI-SUOMI
KUOPIO
Kuopio
POHJOIS-KARJALA
Joensuu
Jyväskylä
MIKKELI
Mikkeli
TURKU AND PORI
Tampere
HÄME
KYMI
Kouvola
AALAND ISLANDS
Turku
Marie-hamn
UUSIMAA
Helsinki
Gulf of Finland
0 50 100 km
0 50 100
miles

The Finnish Political System

Jaakko Nousiainen

Translated by John H. Hodgson

Harvard University Press Cambridge, Massachusetts 1971

Distributed in Great Britain by Oxford University Press, London

Based on the third Finnish edition, 1967

Library of Congress Catalog Card Number 76–120320

SBN 674-30211-7

Printed in the United States of America

Preface

This book was originally written for Finnish students, as an introduction to their own system of government and politics. The significance of an English edition lies in the fact that literature about Finnish political life in the widely known languages of the world has to date consisted either of general treatments from a historical or legalistic perspective, or of specialized studies. My work should be seen in light of its original purpose, to provide students with basic knowledge of both the constitutional norm structure and actual political activity. This study provides broad coverage of the institutions and processes in Finnish political life without relying on one perspective and without placing particular emphasis on certain sectors of activity. As such, it perhaps deals more with the central parts of the system than with a comparative interpretation of the system in its entirety. Comparison would necessitate including a great quantity of additional information for foreign readers concerning, for example, the historical and geographic background, the social and economic surroundings, and the political culture of Finnish society; these matters are the subjects of study in certain specialized works, some of which are included in the list of supplementary readings.

The translation is based on the third edition of the Finnish text, which appeared in 1967. In a number of places minor deletions have been made and in others more current information has been added.

I want to express particular gratitude to the translator of this book, Professor John H. Hodgson, whose familiarity with the Finnish language and with Finnish politics has resulted in an exact and fluent translation. I would also like to thank Professor Sven Lindman for his assistance in the resolution of certain terminological questions.

J. N.

Turku
December 1969

Contents

Part One — Political Forces

I — The Structure of Finnish Society 3

II — Political Parties 19

III — Pressure Groups 101

IV — The Press 130

Part Two — Governmental Institutions

V — Finland's Constitution 145

VI — Parliament 159

VII — The President of the Republic and the State Council 214

VIII — Parliamentarism 253

IX — The Bureaucracy and Administration of Law 282

X — Communal Self-Government 312

XI — Self-Government in the Aaland Islands 345

Part Three — The System in Operation

XII — Foreign Policy and the Conduct of Foreign Affairs 357

XIII — National Defense 382

XIV — National Fiscal Policy 393

XV — Social Policy 413

Supplementary Readings, by Chapter 435

Index 447

Tables

1. Population by age brackets, 1850–1960 5
2. Educational level of fifteen-year olds, 1960 7
3. Total population and urban population, 1960 8
4. Population by occupation, 1960 9
5. Changes in occupational structure, 1880–1960 13
6. Gross domestic product by occupations, 1950, 1958, 1963 16
7. Social stratification of society, 1940, 1950, 1960 17
8. Party percentage of popular vote in parliamentary elections, 1907–1970 40–41
9. Party percentage by electoral district in parliamentary election, 1966 45
10. Voters grouped by social class and party preference, 1958 46
11. Party membership in 1965, votes received in 1966, and party membership as a percentage of votes received 57
12. Organizational representation in parliamentary groups elected in 1951 123
13. Daily press by party affiliation, 1965 133
14. Electoral districts, 1966 parliamentary election 164
15. Voter turnout in parliamentary elections, 1907–1970 175
16. Parliamentary seats by party, 1907–1970 180–181
17. Occupational groupings of members of Parliament elected 1945–1958 182
18. Social stratification of members of Parliament elected 1945–1958 183
19. Private member legislative bills before Parliament, 1954–1957 198
20. Matters before Parliament and their resolution, 1962–1965 212
21. Voter turnout in presidential elections, 1925–1968 216
22. Percentage by party of votes cast in presidential elections and votes cast in previous parliamentary elections 218
23. Voting intentions of individuals by party preference and social class, 1956 presidential election 221
24. Cabinets and their political composition, 1917–1970 262–265
25. Bourgeois and leftist majorities in communal councils by province following 1964 communal elections 320
26. Communal revenues, 1964 334
27. Communal expenditures, 1964 336
28. State budget revenues, 1963, 1964, 1965 399

29. State budget expenditures, 1963, 1964, 1965 401
30. State budget expenditures by function, 1964 402
31. National debt, 1938–1964 403
32. Appropriations requested in private member bills and approved by Parliament, 1954–1957 406
33. National budget, 1967 408

Part One Political Forces

1 The Structure of Finnish Society

POPULATION

Population and Density. The first statistical information about the population of Finland dates back some four hundred years to the tax lists of the governments of Gustavus Vasa, John III, and Gustavus Adolphus; some of the lists were so detailed that it has been possible to make definite conclusions about the population of the nation in those times. It is estimated that Finland's population in 1610–1620 was around four hundred thousand and in the middle of the century around four hundred and fifty thousand. Exact information about the population and population changes has been available since the middle of the eighteenth century, at which time the maintenance of regular population statistics based on church records was begun.

The growth of the population really began in the relatively peaceful conditions of the latter half of the eighteenth century. During the early part of the century the population had not increased at all; in fact, it had decreased because of wars, territorial losses, starvation, and epidemics. The population figure reached one million in 1812, when the Viipuri province, the so-called "Old Finland," was returned to Finland. From this point on the population has always doubled in sixty-five to seventy years, demonstrating that the development has continued rather evenly. The population rose to two million in 1879, to three million in 1912, and to four million in 1950; at the census of 1960 the exact figure was 4,446,200. A slowdown in this development during the present century is due to great population losses during the wars and to a decline in the birthrate and in emigration abroad. The birthrate in Finland, however, is still at such a level that there is no fear in the immediate future of an end to the population growth, particularly as the deathrate can be expected to continue declining slightly. Projections are that the Finnish population will be 4.9 million in 1970, and 5.1 million in 1975.

In terms of area Finland is one of Europe's largest countries but in terms of population one of the smallest. Population density is relatively low (on the average, only 15.1 people per square kilometer in 1964); but the density in various parts of the country is quite different so that the average figure gives an incomplete picture. More than three-fifths of the population live in the six southernmost provinces, whose surface area is only a little more than one-quarter of the country's total area. In 1964 there were 93.3 residents in Uusimaa province per square kilometer, 30.5 in the province of Turku and Pori, and 36.3 in Häme province, but in Oulu province there were only 7.4 and in Lapland province only 2.3. A factor influencing the figures for population and surface area in the different provinces is, of course, the degree to which there are large cities in each province. If only the rural communes are examined, the discrepancy in numbers becomes smaller, although the former characteristics are generally retained. So long as the primary occupations, agriculture and forestry, are in a leading position, the division of the population in different parts of the country is determined by external factors such as climate and soil. Because of this one finds that population centers are concentrated in the southern and western parts of the country and that as one travels further north the centers become more sparse. In an industrializing society certain factors such as raw materials, availability of power and labor, transportation facilities, and market conditions influence the territorial location of industries and, consequently, of population; thus, as industrialization has expanded, population density has grown in many areas which previously were sparsely inhabited.

Sex and Age. According to statistics, 100 girls are born for every 105–106 boys. This does not, however, mean that there are more men than women in Finland: the deathrate for men of all ages is greater than for women. From this it follows that the number of men and women at the marrying age is fairly even and that in the oldest age brackets women are in the clear majority. In the 1960 census 51.8 percent of the total population were women, 48.2 percent men. The surplus of women was 161,700, and for every 1,000 women there were 930 men. In addition to the fact that the natural deathrate varies in

Table 1. Population by age brackets, 1850–1960

Year	0–14 Percent	15–64 Percent	65–—— Percent
1850	34.5	61.1	4.4
1900	35.0	59.6	5.4
1920	33.4	60.7	5.9
1940	26.9	66.7	6.4
1950	30.0	63.3	6.7
1960	30.1	62.4	7.4

Source: Statistical Yearbook of Finland 1965, tables 15 and 31 (Helsinki: Tilastollinen päätoimisto, 1966), pp. 26–27, 45.

different sex groups, wars more than any other factor have influenced the numerical relationship between the male and female population, resulting in fundamental changes. The loss of population during turbulent times has affected men primarily, so that the female surplus has grown greatly during wartimes (for example, 1788–1790, 1808–1809, 1918, 1939–1944) only to decline again slowly during long periods of peace. The female surplus is not evenly spread out over the whole country, but is concentrated in the southern part and, as a rule, in cities and other population centers; but the northern provinces of Oulu and Lapland remain predominantly male.

Focusing on the ability to work and on productivity, it is customary to divide the population into three broad age groups: children under fifteen years of age, people in the "productive" age group fifteen to sixty-four, and people sixty-five and older. The development of this structure is clear from Table 1. The age structure of the population has developed in one decided direction: the percentage of children and young people has dropped, whereas the percentage of older people has shown continual growth. Between the years 1950 and 1960 the economically active population grew by only 2.5 percent, whereas the growth of the total population was 10.3 percent. This development, according to projected estimates, will continue as a result primarily of two phenomena: a decline in the birth rate and an increase in life expectancy. In time, one can expect these changes in the age structure to influence greatly the economic, social, and cultural life of the nation.

Language, Religion, and Education. The linguistic duality of the population has left a visible imprint on the course of development in different areas of Finnish life. Social position of the two population groups has for a long time stirred up conflicts and created tension; it was in fact the take-off point for party activity in the second half ot the nineteenth century. The areas inhabited by the Swedish-speaking population, which have remained approximately the same since the Middle Ages, are located in the southern and western parts of the country along the coastline; they are the Pohjanmaa coast on both sides of Vaasa, the Aaland Islands, the Turku coastline with its islands, and the Uusimaa coastline from the Swedish-speaking area of Turku east to Kymijoki. Since the turn of the century and up to the 1950's, the absolute number of Swedish-speaking Finns has slowly grown, but in percentage terms there has been a significant drop. In 1900 12.9 percent of the total population were Swedish-speaking, in 1930 10.1 percent, and in 1960 only 7.4 percent. Fundamental provisions regarding the position of the two languages and the two language groups are found in the Constitution, according to which "Finnish and Swedish are the national languages of the republic" and in which it is affirmed that "the cultural and economic needs of the Finnish and Swedish-speaking population will be satisfied by the state on the basis of equality" (paragraph 14).

With respect to religion, the Finnish nation is from a formal point of view unified: in 1960 92.4 percent of the population belonged to the Lutheran church. By comparison, religious minorities remain very small: in 1960 1.4 percent of the population belonged to the Greek Orthodox church, and 0.6 percent supported other faiths. Those on the civil register, outside the church, were 5.5 percent. In these circumstances, and given no sharp conflicts between the faiths, religious factors in Finnish political life do not have the significance they possess in certain Central European countries like France, where religious differences in certain places are extremely sharp and can influence political behavior decisively. Revivalist movements within church circles in Finland may, however, have some political consequences in this respect.[1]

As educational institutions have become more widespread and school attendance compulsory, literacy as a measure of the general educational level of a country has lost its meaning. Practically speaking, one can say that in Finland the entire adult population —except for the mentally retarded and some of the blind—are

1. See Erik Allardt, *Social struktur och politisk aktivitet* (Borgå, 1956), pp. 96–105.

Table 2. Educational level of fifteen-year olds, 1960

Without a junior high school course or college entrance examination	2,738,162	% 88.2
With a junior high school course	234,753	7.6
With a college entrance examination	130,353	4.2

Source: Official Statistics of Finland VI C:193, General Census of Population 1960 VIII, table 3 (Helsinki: Tilastollinen päätoimisto, 1964), p. 12.

able to read and write. By examining the educational level of the population in the light of available statistics (Table 2), this picture becomes clearer.

In 1964, of children subject to compulsory education (ages 7–15), only 130 children out of 793,721 dropped out of school. There were 573,851 children in primary school, 161,072 in secondary school, and 5,857 in other schools. During the 1964–1965 school year there were in all some 258,000 students in secondary schools and 35,900 at universities and higher professional schools.

Countryside and Cities. During the last several generations the urbanization of society has progressed very rapidly. In 1880 only 8.4 percent of the population lived in cities and towns; twenty years later the figure had risen to 12.5 percent, within forty years it was up to 16.1 percent, and in 1940 it was 26.8 percent. According to the 1960 census, the rounded population of cities and towns was 1.7 million people—38.4 percent of Finland's total population—and the population of the rural communes was 2.7 million. The main reasons for the absolute and relative growth of the urban population, tied as it is to developments in the country's occupational structure, have been migration from the countryside and territorial incorporations; the natural population increase in cities is smaller than in the countryside, and changes from one form of communal government to another have not had a decisive impact in this respect. In spite of the fact that the absolute growth of the rural population came to a halt in the 1930's, Finland is nonetheless still one of Europe's most rural countries.

These figures, based on administrative divisions, do not give a complete and correct picture of the population's division into urban and rural areas. The fact is that in rural communal areas there are also numerous residential concentrations—suburbs, industrial communities, villages, harbors, garrisons, clusters of summer cottages—which are by nature urban areas and whose population consequently, in residential terms, is closer to the urban than to the actual rural population. In conjunction with the 1950 census, information was also gathered about population centers with more than five hundred people located in rural communes; when this information was added to the figure for the population of cities and towns, the urban share of the total population rose to two-fifths. Ten years later statistical information was gathered on another basis regarding urbanization that included all building clusters where there were at least two hundred residents and where the distance between buildings in general did not exceed two hundred meters. By this method the breakdown in Table 3 emerged.

Table 3. Total population and urban population, 1960

Area	Total population	Urban population	Urban population as percent of total population
Whole country	4,446,222	2,486,737	55.9
Cities and towns	1,707,049	1,651,956	96.7
Rural communes	2,739,173	834,781	30.5

Source: Official Statistics of Finland VI C:103, General Census of Population 1960 II, table 1 (Helsinki: Tilastollinen päätoimisto, 1963), p. 2.

There are, of course, wide variations in the urban population in different parts of the country. The percentage of the total population living in cities and towns in 1960 in Uusimaa province was about two-thirds and in Häme province about one-half, but it was less than one-fifth, for example, in the provinces of Northern Karelia and Oulu.

OCCUPATIONAL CLASSIFICATION AND CLASS DISTRIBUTION

The members of a society can be divided into groups in many different ways, for example, on the basis of population factors as already discussed. From the political point of view, the most important and most interesting division is without question that by occupation and social class. It is a fact, namely, that in a multiparty country such as Finland the opposition of social classes has a greater influence on the birth of party groupings than any other social antagonism. Political measures affect in the same way people who are in the same economic and social position, and so these people are also inclined to react similarly to those measures.

Occupational Structure. In analyzing the population's occupational groupings information from the 1960 census, summarized in Table 4, is useful. It should be emphasized that the statistics do not show the professions of individuals; they show, rather, only to which occupational branch that enterprise belongs in whose employ the individuals

Table 4. Population by occupation, 1960

Occupation	Number	Percent
Agriculture and forestry	1,408,240	31.7
Industry	916,816	20.6
Construction	456,140	10.3
Commerce	393,149	8.8
Transport and communications	299,458	6.7
Services	481,560	10.8
Unknown	12,722	0.3
Economically inactive	478,137	10.8
Total	4,446,222	100.0

Source: Official Statistics of Finland VI C:103, General Census of Population 1960 IV, table 1 (Helsinki: Tilastollinen päätoimisto, 1963), pp. 2–3.

are; individuals with the same profession can therefore be in very different occupational branches.

The table shows that almost one-third of the population still earns its living from agriculture and forestry. This large occupational group is disparate in composition: in addition to the largest individual branches, agriculture and forestry, it includes truck farming, the tending of reindeer and fur-bearing animals, and hunting and fishing. The farm population in 1960 numbered 1,119,000, or 25 percent of the country's entire population. In spite of the noticeable development of industrial occupations Finland has remained, in contrast to most Western European countries, an agrarian nation. In many industrialized countries the agrarian share of the total population is under 10 percent.

Of those economically active in agriculture, accounting for about 51 percent of the total number working in this occupational branch, there were 274,000 independent farmers and 32,000 farm laborers in 1960. The relationship between these two groups indicates indirectly the small scale of Finnish agriculture. Of all farms in 1950, 26.6 percent consisted of plots under 2 hectares and 27.8 percent of plots 2–5 hectares in size.

The forestry population accounted for 257,000 people, or 5.8 percent of the total population, in 1960. An overwhelming number of people working in forestry were lumbermen, either "full-time," without land, or, typical of Finnish conditions, small farmer-lumbermen for whom it is sometimes difficult to decide the correct occupational branch. Small farmers have been included statistically in the forestry group if they have been engaged in forestry work for at least four months out of the year.

It is customary to contrast industrial occupations, which include industry and handicrafts, commerce, transportation and communications, with agriculture and forestry. The great structural change in contemporary Finnish society has resulted in an expansion of these occupations at the expense of agriculture, and in many respects it has meant a lifting of the industrial labor force to a commanding position in society. As society industrializes, this population group has shown the most rapid growth; and its significance and influence rest upon, besides its great numbers, its relative homogeneity, strong sense of togetherness, good organization, and political alertness. In 1960 the industrial labor force, including construction work but excluding lumbering and logging, numbered approximately 500,000—much greater already than the number of farmers and farm laborers. Although the industrial labor force seems as a whole to be unified in structure, closer examination reveals many different groups within that category that differ from each other in terms of professional skills, working conditions, job hazards, and general social position. Thus one can discover certain regular differences between these groups in political behavior, particularly with respect to the support divided between the Social Democrats and the Communists.

The aforementioned number of workers in the industrial labor force is divided by major branch of industry as follows: 146,000 workers in construction, 97,000 in the metals industry, 83,000 in the wood-processing industry, 64,000 in the textile, footwear, and clothing industry, 39,000 in the food, beverages, and tobacco industry, and 5,000 in mining and quarrying.

Compared with the laborers, other industrial and construction groups—employers and the self-employed, as well as managers and salaried employees—are small; at the 1960 census there were 42,000 of the former and 94,000 of the latter. The share of salaried employees as a percentage of the population in occupational branches has, however, risen quickly. Both groups are, socially speaking, very disunited. Industrial salaried employees include office personnel as well as foremen, engineers, and persons in other supervisory capacities. Some of these by virtue of their position are comparable to the workers; others are closer to the employers. But characteristic of Finnish conditions is the fact that salaried employees—up to foremen and office personnel—have wanted to remain outside the trade union movement, recognizing and emphasizing their different social positions and political affiliations. In the category of employers and self-employed there are, both, a handful of industrial and company magnates and modest-living handicraft workers who practice their professions alone, without hired labor.

Commerce, and transportation and communications, have both developed in recent decades at a very rapid rate. In the field of commerce in 1960 there were 30,000 self-employed, 155,000 managers and salaried employees, and 43,000 workers, whereas in the field of transportation and communications the comparable figures were 24,000, 35,000, and 69,000. In the former occupational branch, office and sales personnel were the largest group; in the latter, however, the largest group consisted of actual laborers, of whom a substantial number worked for the state railways, post office, and telegraph and thus were in a special position when compared with those in the service of private employers. Among the self-employed in transportation and communications, owners of buses and trucks were the dominant group.

That population group which makes up the "services" category is the most heterogeneous of all in terms of social structure. It includes the military establishment, state and communal government services, the school system, religious congregations, public health and sanitary services, social services, organizational activities, and artistic and recreational institutions. Both civil servants and the self-employed have increased greatly during the last 50 years; this is demonstrated by the fact that in 1910 only about 4 percent of the country's total population belonged to the service category. On one hand there is a greater need than ever before for people in public service (in health and sanitation, social work, and education, for example); on the other hand, as the standard of living rises and as society develops, the demand in "private markets" for service personnel has become brisker and more varied.

Included in the last two occupational groups are, among others, individuals for whom it is impossible to establish an occupational branch: individuals who are economically inactive; people formerly in a profession; students; people living from capital, interest, and savings; prisoners and institutional cases.

Great territorial differences are also observable in the occupational structure. Industrial and service occupations have spread in southern and southwestern Finland much more rapidly than elsewhere in the country: the industrial population, not including construction work, was in 1960 about 25 percent of the population in the province of Uusimaa and in Turku and Pori province, and about 30 percent in Häme province, but it was only 10–12 percent in the provinces of Northern Karelia, Oulu, and Lapland. This is tied in with another phenomenon, the urbanization of industry; in 1960 about one-third of the city and town population, but only about one-eighth of the rural communal population, worked in the industrial sector.

Changes in Occupational Structure. In order to give depth to the profile above of the occupational structure of Finnish society in the middle of the twentieth century, the same occupational groups should be examined over time. In this way one can form an impression of the historical development from which contemporary society has received its characteristic features, and of the directions in which society continues to change. Twentieth-century society is very dynamic; during half a century fundamental structural changes have occurred and are occurring that are illuminated by Table 5. The figures are not in all respects comparable, and, for the years before 1950, when information was based on church records, they are not entirely accurate; but they provide an adequate general picture of the development.

The earlier mentioned phenomenon of agriculture giving up more and more, over the decades, its ruling position is the most significant and most apparent of the really great changes which have taken place

Table 5. Changes in occupational structure, 1880–1960

Year	Agriculture	Industry	Transportation/Communications	Commerce	Others
1880	1,590[a]	135	42	21	273
1920	2,061	419	104	106	415
1930	2,074	510	128	145	523
1940	2,014	664	172	188	658
1950	1,674	1,177	242	277	659
1960	1,408	1,373	299	393	972
1880	77.1[b]	6.5	2.1	1.0	13.3
1920	66.4	13.5	3.3	3.4	13.3
1930	61.4	15.1	3.8	4.3	15.4
1940	54.5	18.0	4.6	5.1	17.8
1950	41.5	29.2	6.0	6.9	16.4
1960	31.7	30.9	6.7	8.8	21.9

Source: Statistical Yearbook of Finland, table 21 (1952), table 24 (1961), table 24 (1962) (Helsinki: Tilastollinen päätoimisto, 1953, 1962, 1963), pp. 28–29, 26–39, 36–37.

[a] By thousands of persons.

[b] By percent.

in Finnish occupations during the last two or three generations. Migration from the countryside to population centers has been a flight from agriculture to the sectors of industry and services. The country's population doubled between the years 1880 and 1950, whereas the agricultural population at these two points in time was almost the same—although the percentage of the total population was dropping all the time. The absolute number of people earning a living from agriculture and forestry was still growing until the mid-1930's, when a peak of about 2,100,000 people was reached; but during the following two decades a decrease of almost comparable size took place. The present farm population is approximately the same as it was a hundred years ago. And the speed of this development shows no signs of abating; on the contrary, it has grown more intense, as Table 5 demonstrates. The special conditions following the Second World War contributed to this flight from agriculture and to the urbanization of the population; a relatively large number of the Karelian refugees found their way into population centers and industrial occupations.

Industrial and other "city occupations" have thus drawn from the countryside, in large numbers, the landless population, and agriculture has had to adjust to new circumstances. Through mechanization and rationalization an effort has been made to reduce the need for labor, and by utilizing modern methods of crop and animal care a growth in agricultural production has even been possible. At the same time there has been an attempt to encourage intensive land settlement so that as large a part of the farm population as possible can be induced to remain in the sector of original occupation. As a result of the freeing of the crofters (1918) and the voluntary and legislated land-settlement programs, a typical phenomenon of Finland has developed—a large number of small farmers whose incomes come only partially from farming and who are thus forced to find work beyond the confines of their plots and to depend on state aid. These sorts of measures have not been able to change the direction of development, nor have they prevented the flight from the countryside, but apparently they have to some degree slowed it down. A sure guarantee that the present direction, leading to a reduction of the relative number and significance of the agricultural population, will in any event continue are the opinions of both the economic experts and the political groups that continued improvement in the population's standard of living and the maintenance of a high level of employment presuppose a brisk development of industry.

By 1960 the growing industrial and construction population had almost reached the decreasing agricultural population in numbers; industry is becoming the country's new chief occupation. But significant structural changes have also occurred within this occupation. The fact that about two-thirds of the 1944–1952 war reparations to the Soviet Union came from the metals industry meant a sudden expansion of that industry. In fact, in 1960 the metals industry was already a greater employer of labor than the wood-processing industry. Other domestic branches of industry (food, chemicals) have also shown rapid development.

The greatest growth of all, however, is occurring in the service occupations, namely in commerce, transportation and communications, and regular services; on the basis of the experience of more developed Western countries one can predict that in time they will, taken as a whole, become the largest occupational group. Although the number of people working in agriculture and forestry declined from 1950 to 1960 by nearly 200,000 and the number in industry grew by only 36,000, there was an increase of 76,000 in commerce, 22,000 in transportation and communications, and 75,000 in services.

One should also take note of a feature that is significant from the point of view of the political behavior of citizens and that is connected with the changing pattern of occupational groupings—a feature familiar in the more industrialized nations. In industry and construction, as well as in the service occupations, the strongest growth is in office personnel; as far as workers are concerned, growth has been considerably slower, and the self-employed share of the labor force shows an outright decline. Office personnel and managers increased in the above mentioned decade by 136,000 (by 43 percent), and in 1960 they comprised 22 percent of the working population. The addition for laborers was 47,000 (6 percent), or 43 percent of the working population. This development has thus meant a considerable strengthening of the middle class.

Occupations and National Income. The division of the population into occupational branches does not, of course, reveal their relative significance in the national economy. Table 6, showing different occupations as a share of the value of total production in specific years, amplifies that picture. After the Second World War, industry and construction became more important than agriculture and forestry; the latter's share in the national income, it can be observed, is considerably smaller than its share in the population, which indicates relatively low productivity.

Social Classes. In Finland, some principles of social stratification have been formulated in connection with a number of field research projects, but a complete picture is still not possible. Until now the statistical divisions encompassing the whole society, the foundation for which is the researcher's knowledge of the structure of Finnish society, have emanated from a grouping by professions. On this basis Heikki Waris carried out a general classification drawing upon 1940 population statistics; Nieminen and Rauhala did the same thing, drawing upon information from the 1950 and 1960 censuses (see Table 7). As Waris notes, "Finnish society is in structure decisively a society of workers and farmers, of physical laborers."[2] In numbers

2. Heikki Waris, *Suomalaisen yhteiskunnan rakenne*, 2nd ed. (Helsinki: Otava, 1952), p. 185. All translations of quoted matter originally in Finnish are mine unless otherwise noted (JHH).

Table 6. Gross domestic product by occupations, 1950, 1958, 1963

Occupation	Millions of marks			Percent		
	1950	1958	1963	1950	1958	1963
Agriculture and forestry	1,234.3	2,382.2	3,397.7	25.9	20.7	18.3
Industry	1,451.2	3,351.3	5,472.6	30.4	29.1	29.5
Construction	472.1	1,098.6	1,754.6	9.9	9.5	9.5
Transportation and communications	307.7	831.4	1,311.3	6.5	7.2	7.1
Commerce	587.1	1,363.0	2,393.1	12.3	11.8	12.9
General government	416.5	1,156.9	1,981.4	8.7	10.1	10.7
Other services	300.5	1,323.2	2,222.0	6.3	11.5	12.0
Total	4,769.4	11,506.6	18,532.7	100.0	99.9	100.0

Source: Statistical Yearbook of Finland 1965, table 247 (Helsinki: Tilastollinen päätoimisto, 1966). p. 252.

Table 7. Social stratification of society, 1940, 1950, 1960

Class	Thousands			Percent		
	1940	1950	1960	1940	1950	1960
Workers	921	854	881	62	55	51
Farmers	356	311	280	24	20	16
Middle class	163	342	518	11	22	30
Upper class	45	46	52	3	3	3
Total	1,485	1,553	1,731	100	100	100

Source: Urho Rauhala, "Yhteiskuntaluokka," *Yhteiskuntatieteiden käsikirja* (Helsinki: Otava, 1964), II, 1006–1011.

the working class (which according to established practice includes people with job contracts, particularly physical laborers) is by far the largest. Remaining outside of this definition are those employed in industry and business, as well as the vast majority of state and communal functionaries, who are considered—and who consider themselves as—members of the middle class. This class is perhaps the most heterogeneous and loosest in the sense that it is very difficult to define its limits. Two main groups can be singled out: the old middle class formed by the self-employed; and the new middle class formed by employees such as state and communal functionaries and employees of industry and commerce.

Above the middle class and behind a very ill-defined boundary is the upper class, whose characteristic feature is "a feeling of social security and independence based on economic independence or a highly developed sense of awareness."[3] Coming from agriculture, there are large landowners in this class; from industry and commerce, independent industrialists and managers and well-to-do private merchants; from the service occupations, the highest functionaries, especially those self-employed who have had an academic education.

Characteristic of Finland, as of the other Nordic countries, is the fact that the majority of independent farmers are not included in the aforementioned groups, but, rather, that they form a social class separate from the rest of society and unified by their own agricultural traditions, way of life, and outlook upon the world. On one hand,

3. *Ibid.*, p. 181.

large scale farmers can be considered members of the upper class; on the other hand, the boundary between farmers and workers is, as far as the small farmer-lumberers are concerned, blurred. But otherwise there is a clear differentiation between the independent farmer and the middle class, composed mostly of those in industrial occupations —a significant fact in the historical development of the country's party life.

The three divisions in Table 7 may not be comparable in any large degree, since in 1940 heads of households were classified but ten and twenty years later the working population was classified; at all dates there were many estimates, and a rather large number of individuals were left unclassified. Likewise, the nomenclature for occupational branches and professions had changed somewhat, and the statistical data was from the outset of a different nature. However, one can perhaps venture from these figures the conclusion that during the decades in question the middle class became stronger at the expense of the workers and the farmers.

Support for the correctness of this class division is to be found in a comparison, based on election statistics, of the relative strength of the political groupings. In the 1945 parliamentary election the workers' parties together received 48.6 percent of the popular vote, the Agrarian party 21.3 percent, and the other three parties together 28.6 percent. In the 1951 election the corresponding figures were 48.1, 23.2, and 27.9 percent. To a degree the divisions resemble each other, but, since the formation of political opinion is tied to many other factors besides economic and social interests, the relative strength between parties cannot depict with exactness the class divisions of society. Naturally the kinds of differences in electoral participation between the different social groups are also influential. It is significant, however, that as far as the farm population is concerned the correlation is the clearest of all.

II Political Parties

THE PARTY SYSTEM AND THE DEVELOPMENT OF PARTIES

The Development of Party Life. Before a closer examination of the structure, aims, and relations of Finnish parties can be made, the development of party life in Finland must be briefly summarized and light shed on the bases of party groupings.

Searching for the first signs of participation by Finns in party life, one can go back in time to the period of Swedish power, to the "Era of Freedom" in the eighteenth century, when primitive party activity in Stockholm was practiced in groups formed by members of Parliament. The first party forms in Finland that were distinctly Finnish appeared on the political scene in the second half of the nineteenth century, when the four-estate Diet (nobility, clergy, burghers, peasants) began to meet again after a pause of some fifty years and as political, economic, and cultural life generally became more lively. Language and the nationality question were the earliest bases for party groupings. An initiating force, stemming from the influence of J. V. Snellman (a key figure behind the development of Finnish nationalism in the nineteenth century), was the Finnish movement—a linguistic-political radicalism which took on practical political goals and which in attempting to achieve these goals formed in the 1860's the country's first party grouping, the Finnish party. This was a clear-cut linguistic party which sought to raise the Finnish language to its rightful position as an official and cultural language; already during that decade it had a majority among the farmers and clergy in Parliament. One of the most prominent leaders of this Finnish-minded movement in the nineteenth century was the professor and senator Yrjö Sakari Yrjö-Koskinen.

The increasing language struggle gave birth to the Swedish party as a counterweight to the Finnish movement; the spiritual base for this party was the notion, as interpreted by A. O. Freudenthal and others, of a Finnish-Swedish nationality concept, and the party took firm shape in the 1870's and early 1880's. In a quickly bypassed intermediary stage, an attempt was made with the formation of the Liberal party to cut across the language barrier. In 1880 the Liberals published a program that was mainly the work of Leo Mechelin and that was the first real party program; it did not, however, stir up much interest among the Finnish-language people. Snellman, among others, was sharply critical. The Liberal group soon fell apart and most of its members joined the ranks of the Swedish party.

Another stage of development in party life began around the turn of the century when the language question became less important and two other serious problems, the social question and relations with Russia, came to the forefront. Social points of view did, it is true, have significance even earlier as a factor separating parties: the Finnish-language people also tried to see the Finnish movement as a social movement. They sought to appear as reform-minded individuals attempting to raise the economic, social, and educational level of the nation—although the Finnish party did not have a common line in matters other than the language question—while the Swedish party, in a defensive position, took the stand of aristocratic, conservative liberalism. As early as the 1880's, there appeared within the Finnish party an opposition group formed by the "youth" that was more liberal socially but less flexible on the language question and that adopted its own program in the 1894 general congress. From this a Finnish liberal party could soon have developed if events of the "years of frost" (Russification, 1899–1905) had not intervened, causing the united Finnish party to split on other grounds—grounds involving the Russian question.

How one should react to Tsarist oppression became during the years of frost a watershed in political life. The Swedish party supported passive resistance, whereas the Finnish party split, following previous divisions, into two major parts: the Old Finns and the Young Finns. The party leadership represented in the Senate, along with most of the Old Finns, wanted to meet oppression with a flexible defense—with a policy of compromise; those who supported passive resistance joined the Young Finns and founded the Constitutional-Finnish Minded party in 1902. The Constitutionalists did not, however, form a tight party until 1906. They cooperated in defense of the country's rights with the Swedish-speaking Finns; representatives of both groups led the country in the Mechelin constitutional Senate of 1905–1908, while the Old Finns went into opposition as a result of reductions in tension following the 1905 general strike. They were united only by similar views on methods in the constitutional struggle and by distrust of compromise tactics; they differed greatly in terms of social and linguistic programs. Leaders of the Old Finns, in addition to Yrjö-Koskinen, included J. R. Danielson-Kalmari and E. G. Palmen; Young Finn leaders included P. E. Svinhufvud and K. J. Ståhlberg; and leaders of the Swedish-speaking Finns included Leo Mechelin and R. A. Wrede.

During the eventful 1880's the first rise of the labor movement also occurred. In this so-called Wright period, the first labor associations were founded on the initiative of individuals who, like Victor Julius von Wright, belonged to the bourgeoisie and were interested in improving the position of the lower classes; these associations functioned as subordinate units of the Finnish-speaking parties. However, by the turn of the century socialist ideas had become widely, though still somewhat superficially, known in Finland; a result was that the workers broke from the guardianship of the bourgeoisie and began independent action under socialist slogans. At the congress of labor associations held in Turku in 1899 the Finnish Labor party was formed, and four years later, at the Forssa party congress, it adopted a purely socialist program based on the teachings of Marx, on the 1891 Erfurt program of the German Social Democratic party, and on the program of the Austrian Social Democratic party; it also changed its name to the Finnish Social Democratic party (Suomen sosialidemokraattinen puolue). During the first phase of activity, up until the general strike of 1905, the main emphasis was on political indoctrination and external pressure; the party sought to raise the class consciousness and activity of the workers and at the same time it struggled against the four-estate Diet and practiced effective agitation on behalf of electoral reform. The golden age of the party began after the election in 1907 of eighty of its representatives to the first unicameral legislature.

With its broad organization, program, and rules, the Social Democratic party was in fact the country's first modern party organization. Other political bodies were at this time still haphazard, almost unorganized groups formed without mass support by the political leadership. Jussi Teljo has characterized these first party groups as follows:

Parties were not founded by an explicit decision; rather, they were formed slowly and almost unnoticed as individuals interested in politics and characterized by likemindedness came together around newspapers and politicians representing a definite line of thought. As ill-defined and loose unions, the parties were devoid of a tight organization and a detailed program; there were no lasting, continually acting party organizations, and the ideas and goals of the parties were defined in accordance with the direction set by their most prestigious leaders and newspapers. Later some sort of party congresses began to be held, but the participants were invited personally by the party leaders and were not elected by party members.[1]

As J. K. Paasikivi mentions in his memoirs concerning the years of Russian oppression, the Finnish party at the turn of the century still did not have an elected leadership, excluding the fact that a delegation was elected for the duration of Parliament to outline the group's general policy. And in 1904–1905 the preparation of a practical program for the party was opposed, on the ground that it was purportedly by resting on a detailed program that the liberal party had died twenty years before.[2] In the years preceding the general strike there were already signs of party cohesion, but it was only the achievement of a universal and equal vote that turned these bourgeois groups around 1905–1908 into organizationally and programatically modern party organizations. All in all, their early history fits rather well into the general scheme of parties in the nineteenth century as presented by Duverger.[3]

Because the activity of the Swedish party had slackened considerably during the first period of Russian oppression and because the 1906 electoral reform demanded an intensification of party work, the question of a reorganization of party activity was brought forth and discussed by Swedish-speaking Finns. On May 20 and 21, 1906, at a congress held in Helsinki, the Swedish People's party (Svenska folkpartiet) was founded. The new party was to bring under one banner, irrespective of social classes, the entire Swedish-speaking population in the country. In order to keep the party together, it was decided that concrete demands in the program should concern

1. Jussi Teljo, *Suomen valtioelämän murros 1905–1908* (Porvoo: WSOY, 1949), p. 31.
2. *Paasikiven muistelmia sortovuosilta*, (Porvoo, 1957), I, 185–186.
3. Maurice Duverger, *Les partis politiques*, 4th ed. (Paris, 1961), pp. 2–8.

only national matters that were of importance to the Swedish-speaking population and that within the party it would be possible to form factions acting on behalf of their own special programs. Organized in this fashion, the party gained the approval of the country's Swedish-speaking population; it was successful in obtaining their support, with the exception of the organized Social Democrats, for its candidates at election time.

Of the old parties, the Swedish People's party was the only one to appear at this time with a program based almost exclusively on the language and nationality question. With an eye on forthcoming elections to the unicameral Parliament, the Old and Young Finns approved quite similar economic and social reform programs. The radical social program of the Finnish party, through which it hoped to compete with the Socialists for the favor of the greatly increased electorate, attracted special attention. In the 1907 election the party fared much better than the Young Finn party (59 seats compared with 26). Relations with Russia—the compromise policy—caused difficulties for the Finnish party, however, until new Russification measures drove all of Finland's parties into national opposition.

In the early stage of party formation the Finnish movement united the Finnish-speaking rural laborers with a part of the upper class in the name of elevating the Finnish language and Finnish culture; but as the language question became less important the conflict between these groups became vividly apparent and found political expression with the formation (little by little, in many general congresses during the years 1906–1908) of the Agrarian party (Maalaisliitto). The October 1906 congress in Seinäjoki is considered the founding congress of the party. In the 1907 election, however, the Agrarian party was still composed of two groups: the Etelä-Pohjanmaa Young Finn Agrarian party, formed by Santeri Alkio and others, was still separate from the party itself. It was not until the January 1908 congress in Tampere that this group joined the national organization, and final unification of the programs occurred at the end of the same year. In terms of ideals, the party began strictly on the basis of Finnish nationality. Significant for its future development was the fact that the core of the party consisted not of well-to-do farmers, who to a great degree were still tied to the Finnish parties, but rather of small farmers in Pohjanmaa and Karelia. Like the Social Democratic party, the Agrarian party was also formed to defend the interests of certain social groups against ruling groups—the city civil servants, employers, and the self-employed. In 1907 the party had nine seats in Parliament, and this figure grew quickly to forty-two in 1919.

With good reason one can state that the beginning of modern party life in Finland began with the change caused by electoral and parliamentary reform. During the following decade, however, the possibility of parties leading political activity in the country was still limited because the "home government" Senate continued to be, for the most part, controlled by the Russians. Especially during the world war, when the tempo of Russification and infringement on Finnish rights increased, party activity was muted; more important were certain secret "clubs" and "leagues."

Because of the Civil War (1918) and the struggles over Finland's form of government, momentous changes in party structure occurred as the country became independent. As far as the bourgeoisie was concerned, the question of form of government became a decisive line of demarcation. For the Agrarian party and the Swedish People's party the answer was clear and somehow unanimous: the former supported a republic, the latter a monarchy. The Finnish parties, however, split and their supporters divided into new parties that were fundamentally different. In the Young Finn party the monarchists led by Svinhufvud, and the republicans led by Ståhlberg, drifted apart. The conflict ended when the latter met with the leaders of the small people's party and the republican group which had left the Finnish party; on December 8, 1918, they founded the National Progressive party (Kansallinen edistyspuolue). The Old Finnish party received its successor on December 9, 1918, in the form of the National Coalition party (Kansallinen kokoomus), around which gathered the core of Old Finns, who supported attempts to establish a monarchy, and Young Finns who had joined this core. From the party's name it becomes clear that the aim was to replace the defunct parties with a broad organization of "forces to preserve society."

The question of whether a president or a king should be head of state was not the only factor separating the parties—with the defeat of Germany, this question was in fact soon struck from the agenda. The Finnish party, whose heir the Coalition party considered itself, had been more conservative than the Young Finnish party, which left a certain residue as an inheritance for the program of the Coalition party. And doubtless the monarchists were, in general outlook, more to the right than the republicans. Only after the form of government question had been settled, however, did the ideological foundations of these parties clearly take shape. The Coalition party from the 1920's began to adopt ideals characteristic of modern conservatism: its goal was to unite citizens in defense of the inherited social order and strong government, whereas the Progressive party, led to a degree by Ståhlberg, started off in a more liberal and more democratic direction and represented in its practical policies a more conciliatory attitude regarding problems following the Civil War.

The Social Democratic party, whose leadership in 1917 had passed to revolutionary radicals, was struck down in the Civil War. But the party began to function again in the fall of 1918, under the leadership of moderate leaders like Väinö Tanner and others who had remained on the sidelines during the revolt, and it was able in the election of 1919 to win eighty seats in Parliament. The new program was structured on principles of Western social democracy: recognition of peaceful, parliamentary development and condemnation of violent revolutionary activity. The decisive showdown with radicals of the left occurred at the 1919 party congress, where the Communists remained a clear minority.

As early as August 1918, the leaders of the revolt who had fled to Russia founded the Finnish Communist party (Suomen kommunistinen puolue, SKP) in Moscow. In Finland leftwing opposition broke with the Social Democratic party by founding, in May 1920, the Socialist Workers' party of Finland, which, however, was immediately broken up after it had resolved to join the Third International. But the party was formed again in June with the same name. According to the program, it sought to destroy bourgeois state machinery and to turn Finland into a Soviet state. In August 1923 the Kallio Cabinet imprisoned leading Communist figures including the entire parliamentary group, and the party, like its newspapers, was suppressed. The extreme left then participated in elections by forming election blocs of Socialist workers and small farmers. Public activity by the Communists was choked off completely in the early 1930's as a result of the Lapua movement.

In 1933, acting jointly with the Coalition party, the People's Patriotic Movement (Isänmaallinen kansanliike, IKL)—born in 1932 as a result of domestic turmoil—took part in a parliamentary election for the first time. It had taken its credo from the totalitarian ideologies of Central and Southern Europe, and in the domestic struggle it represented positions which were extreme and which in their most radical form were undemocratic. The party received fourteen seats in Parliament, mostly at the expense of the Coalition party; when examining mass support, one can probably consider the party an offshoot of the Coalition party. Initially the Coalition party felt great sympathy for the Lapua movement, but in the mid-1930's it renounced its ties with the IKL and set as its goal the rejection of "fascist efforts." The IKL was suppressed in 1944 in accordance with the Armistice Agreement.

The end of the Second World War meant a regrouping within the left and a new crisis in the Social Democratic party. In October 1944 the Communist party was registered in Finland as a legal association. An opposition that had developed within the Social Democratic party during the war, and which ended up outside the party, began to seek cooperation with the Communists; the result was the formation on October 29, 1944, of the Finnish People's Democratic League (Suomen kansan demokraattinen liitto, SKDL). The purpose was to form not a new party, but rather a political organization for cooperation that could be joined, irrespective of party affiliation, by individuals and organizations approving of the principles and goals of the League. The following became member organizations of the League: the Finnish Communist party, the Finnish Women's Democratic League, the League of Finnish Comradely Associations, the Academic Socialist Society, and the Socialist Unity party (formed in 1946 by leftwing Socialists). The latter decided in 1955 to resign from the League; this decision meant, in fact, dissolution of the party. The cooperative nature of the SKDL was most apparent during its first four years of activity; following the electoral defeat of 1948 and the subsequent opposition stance of the People's Democrats, the League began to resemble a party and to change into a "shirt-tail" organization of the Communist party after the latter turned out to be the only party organization desirous of cooperation. The Social Democratic party has reported that in the years 1944–1948 it lost to the SKDL a total of 105 local associations whose general membership was around 3,000.[4] This figure does not, of course, reveal the actual loss in membership.

Over the decades the support base for the Progressive party has shrunk continually; in 1948 it received somewhat less than 75,000 votes and 5 seats in Parliament. In this situation it was decided in 1951 to put an end to the party, and on February 3, 1951, at a con-

4. *Suomen sosialidemokraattinen työväenliike 1899–1949* (Helsinki, 1949), p. 364.

gress in Helsinki, the Finnish People's party (Suomen kansanpuolue) was founded in its stead. This party took as its ideological base the liberal Finnish world outlook of its predecessor, but at the same time it tried to gather more effectively the political strength of center groups which had supported several different parties.

The Social Democratic party hardly had time to recover from the postwar crisis when it was again faced with internal conflicts and dissension. In the mid-1950's an open power struggle began between an opposition group led by the party secretary Väinö Leskinen and called the "Leskinens" and a group led by the party chairman Emil Skog called the "Skogs." When the opposition became a majority and gained control of the party leadership at the April 1957 party congress, the minority organized itself and began independent action within the party. Mediation attempts failed, and the conflict reached a climax in autumn 1958, when three minority members elected to Parliament on their own lists formed, as "independent Social Democrats" joined later by eleven Social Democrats, the "parliamentary group of the Social Democratic opposition." In early 1959 the party leadership began extensive expulsion measures against the "rebellious" members and sections, and in the spring of the same year the opposition organized as a party—the Social Democratic League of Workers and Small Farmers (Työväen ja pienviljelijäin sosialidemokraattinen liitto, TPSL). It is difficult for an outside observer to identify the most important causes of the split. Differences of opinion seem, in any event, to have spread in terms of the program. The minority that split from the party has for tactical reasons attempted to appear with clearly leftwing slogans, sharply attacking rightwing "big capital" and the Social Democratic majority group, which it considers to have given up the principles adopted by the party.

As the structure of society quickly changed, the Agrarian party began in earnest, in the 1960's, to broaden its sphere of influence outside the ever-decreasing agricultural population. The first important phase was the adoption in 1962 of a new principle and action program; three years later, the final step was taken when the name of the organization was changed to the Center party (Keskustapuolue). At the same time, the small center groups saw that intensified competition necessitated more effective action. By a decision of December 29, 1965, the Finnish People's party and the League of Independents merged into the Liberal People's party (Liberaalinen kansanpuolue), which with its slogans of social liberalism appeals most to society's center groups.

Party System. From the above sketch it is apparent that the most important factors influencing the development of parties over time have been crucial, fundamental questions that have often had decisive importance for the existence of the whole nation, and that the shaping of party groupings is tied organically to different phases of the country's political and social development. One can consider Finland's Scandinavian-type multiparty system quite natural because it fits rather well the structure of Finnish society. Its foundation is a three-fold division: conservatives-liberals-socialists. The use of these labels does not, however, mean that there is only, or even primarily, a division caused by great ideological forces. In general it is very difficult to classify parties according to whether the forces and needs which influenced their birth and which have maintained them are by nature "spiritual" or material; as pointed out in the discussion of social classes, a competition seemingly carried out in the name even of "spiritual" efforts is in fact largely a competition between social strata over economic benefits and social position. Rudolf Heberle calls attention to that paradoxical situation in which the correlation between social classes and parties is most clearly seen in countries where social and political questions of principle separate parties from each other.[5] Since the 1800's conservatism has above all been a political movement of the upper class, which has been in a position of leadership economically and socially, and socialism a political movement of the working class; liberalism has received its strongest support from middle-class groups between these two. Local conditions in different countries have, of course, given their own nuances to these movements.

Since the birth of modern parties, socialism in Finland has been represented by the Social Democratic party, liberalism by the Progressive party, and conservatism by the National Coalition party. A place in this initial scheme was soon taken by the Agrarian party, an organization whose birth was dependent upon a political movement composed primarily of the agricultural landowning class. Finally, the labor movement has divided politically into two parts, the Social Democratic and the Communist movements. The

5. Rudolf Heberle, *Social Movements* (New York, 1951), pp. 164–165; see also Onni Rantala, *Konservatismi ja sen kannattajat* (Tampere: Tammi, 1960), pp. 42–43.

country's linguistic and nationality division still lends additional hues to party conditions, with the Swedish minority defending its position through the help of a party which was formed especially on these grounds. Thus the parties are in close contact with the population's economic and social structure and with the great political ideological currents; this serves to keep party divisions sharp and gives a certain intensity to the country's party life. However, parties in Finland still do not seem to have achieved the level of stability found in many other Western democracies that have reached a high degree of industrialization. Factors causing this instability may perhaps be sought, on one hand, in the nature of the development of society—its relatively tardy development—and, on the other, in the political situations of past and present. The fact that a system kept in motion by these political forces sometimes functions rather imperfectly and with many disturbances, especially when compared, for example, with the Scandinavian countries, is probably not a result of the structure of parties and the party system, but rather a result of functional factors, of the relationship between parties and party tactics—a result of special features to be discussed later in this chapter.

During the period of Finnish independence, five or six sizeable national parties playing a visible role in parliamentary and related activity have operated simultaneously. In the mid-1960's these parties were the National Coalition party, the Swedish People's party, the Liberal People's party, the Center party, the Finnish Social Democratic party, and the Finnish People's Democratic League. In addition to these parliamentary parties there were also the Social Democratic League (seven seats) and the Finnish Rural party (one seat).

In examination of ideological lines and practical activity the parties customarily fall into two large fronts, the bourgeois and the leftist (more correctly socialist) groups. This traditional division, which is probably based on the original and differing notions held by parties about the superiority of one economic system over another, is still in force; but in terms of general politics one should view it as partially obsolescent and even misleading because it is no longer the major basis for division. Socialism and socialization appear in the ideology of the Social Democratic party in a much watered-down form when compared with the original version; and in practical politics—trying with the aid of partial reforms to promote economic and social development—the party acts much like the bourgeois groups. The bourgeois parties, for their part, hardly constitute a unified grouping: the Center party and the People's parties strongly prefer not to call themselves "bourgeois," and the Agrarian party–Center party and the Coalition party, in particular, view each other with much distrust. The parties become large groups with conflicting opinions on many questions which are independent of each other, and these different divisions do not always coincide with each other—they break down, in part, as borders intersect. It is just this sort of combination of opposing forces that, in a sense, is the foundation of a multiparty system. On many primary questions the division into bourgeois parties and leftist parties is consequently devoid of practical significance. One of the clearest and most visible examples of other bases for division is the attitude taken toward the political order and parliamentary democracy; here one finds the Communists on one side, all other parties on the other.

With the passage of decades, a scheme based on the conflict between the bourgeoisie and the leftists has gradually become murky. The point of departure, as the period of independence began, was the deep chasm which developed between the victorious bourgeoisie and the defeated workers in the Civil War, even though the battle line in the war did not follow precisely that social division of classes. Göran von Bonsdorff has called the period up to the mid-1930's a period of bourgeois cooperation; the Social Democrats, on one hand, were inclined toward a voluntary withdrawal, and the center groups, on the other hand, in spite of their disenchantment with the right were nonetheless more desirous of cooperation with it than with the left. In the 1920's the Social Democrats still clung to their theory of class struggle, and in the party congress of 1919 they decided that ministerial socialism—the acceptance of Cabinet responsibility—would be permissible only in exceptional situations. The power of decision on this matter would rest with a party congress or a majority of the party members. During the period of centrist politics, 1919–1924, the Social Democrats drew somewhat closer to the center, but the party again became isolated during the bourgeois coalition governments which followed—a fact which, together with the example of the Scandinavian countries and the United Kingdom, precipitated a re-examination of the question of cooperation and Cabinet membership. In 1926 Cabinet participation was made permissible in completely normal situations, provided that the party council and the parliamentary group should first give their approval by a two-thirds majority vote. The next decade was an important period of growing maturity for the party: a rejection of theoretical dogma and an attachment to the Scandinavian parliamentary viewpoint. Because the Agrarian party was also ready for a drawing together, it was possible for the first time since independence to cross the border separating Socialists and the bourgeoisie and to form a coalition Cabinet (1937).

The leftist direction following the Second World War meant not only an increase in the influence and "Cabinet respectability" of working-class parties, but also a broad reappraisal by the center of its attitude toward the right and the left. The situation with respect to the right became strained, since an attempt was made to place major responsibility for wartime policies on the shoulders of the right; after the Communists became part of the opposition, cooperation with the Coalition party was avoided for reasons of foreign policy balance. The "left center"—the Social Democratic party—stepped forward in cooperative efforts with the "bourgeois center." During the confused parliamentary situation of 1957–1960, traditional party lines were badly shaken. The Coalition party and the Social Democratic party moved closer to each other, whereas the Agrarian party sought cooperation with the left Social Democratic opposition group (which had become independent in 1957) and even with the People's Democrats in the framework of a general coalition government. Thus there was not much left of the bourgeois and left fronts. In the early 1960's the situation again changed somewhat with leftist parties joining in opposition to the bourgeois governments.

In many cases one can perhaps depict political reality better with a three-class division, right-center-left, than with a dichotomy between the bourgeoisie and the socialists. In any event, it appears that in at least some periods—for example, the early 1920's and the 1950's—center party tactics of a sort have been dominant. Future research will determine whether one can speak of centerism as an ideological phenomenon. In practice this division, too, needs further investigation: the Coalition party should without dispute be considered part of the right and the workers' parties part of the left, but opinions vary greatly with respect to the other parties. Olavi Borg has affirmed that these concepts describing party groupings, although they reveal certain significant political differences, are nonetheless ill-defined and in popular speech are used with many different meanings—for example, depending upon whether they are used to characterize an entire party continuum, or individual parties, or internal opinions within parties.[6]

In a content analysis of party programs, Borg has attempted to define more exactly the ideological foundations, or the traditional right-left extension. He concludes that, with respect to questions concerning a group's general functional orientation and especially its attitude toward society, parties can be scaled from right to left on the level of ideologies. With respect to many special questions of importance, however, the notion of the existence of a straight scale is imprecise and even erroneous. Likewise, the usual two-fold grouping of parties does not hold for all questions; and besides, the border is not constant but fluctuates according to the issue at hand. In examining ideologies as entire systems, it was found that the similarity between party ideologies was greatest among the Coalition and Finnish People's parties, whereas the Swedish People's party was most clearly a special type.[7] Pertti Pesonen in his 1958 study of Tampere examined the distances between parties as seen by their supporters. At this level there was not much left of the bourgeois-socialist grouping. An inquiry about the superiority of parties showed that the People's Democratic League was a great distance from the other groups. Most People's Democrats, it is true, considered one or the other of the Social Democratic parties the second best party, but only one of ten Social Democrats chose the SKDL. Taken as a whole it was the most objectionable party for Social Democrats and for others, too. On the other hand, a great many city Agrarians, members of the people's parties, and Coalition party members placed the Social Democratic party in a secondary spot.[8]

An analysis of parliamentary voting by Pekka Nyholm shows, however, that when examined at another level the bourgeois-left dichotomy is still a watershed in political behavior that must be taken into account. During the 1948–1951 period a total of 194 (49 percent) of the 396 open votes in the plenary sessions of Parliament revealed a division which saw on one side majorities of the Agrarian and Coalition groups and on the other side majorities of the Social Democratic and SKDL groups. Furthermore, group cohesion in this sort of

6. Olavi Borg, "Monipuoluejärjestelmän ideologisten peruserojen kuvaamisesta," *Politiikka*, 5, no. 1 (1963), 1–13.

7. Olavi Borg, *Suomen puolueideologiat* (Vammala, 1964), pp. 262–269.

8. Pertti Pesonen, *An Election in Finland* (New Haven, 1968), pp. 140–143.

voting was above average. In an interpretation of these results one must, of course, consider the prevailing parliamentary situation. First, for almost two years the Social Democrats had ruled as a single party, followed by what can best be described as an Agrarian-led center minority coalition government. In the Parliament elected in 1954, when cooperation existed between the Agrarian party and Social Democrats, the importance of this dichotomy was much smaller: only 10.9 percent of the votes revealed the bourgeois-left opposition.[9] One must also note that in communal politics, especially in the most remote rural areas, this dividing line still seems to reflect to a large extent the reality of the situation.

Small Parties. In addition to the parliamentary parties which have been mentioned, there have been many smaller groups which over the decades have participated in political competition but whose significance has nonetheless been rather small. They have appeared either on a completely new basis outside the old parties or as offshoots of them, but they have usually died quickly without being able to attract the continued mass support necessary for longevity. In 1907–1919 there was the Christian Workers' League, which at its peak in 1909 received somewhat less than three percent of the popular vote. During this period it managed to send to Parliament sometimes one, sometimes two, representatives. In the 1917 election the People's party appeared as a new group; it received considerable support in central Finland and had a total of five seats in Parliament. But the following year it merged with the Progressive party. The same name was used in two elections, 1933 and 1936, by a group seeking to compete with the Agrarian party for votes in northern Finland; in the former election it received two seats, in the latter one. The Small Farmers' party was much longer-lived, for it participated in elections with its own candidates during the years 1929–1951. By 1945, however, it had lost all importance. Its center of strength was Oulu province, and during its peak period in 1933 it received 3.4 percent of the total popular vote in the country and three seats in Parliament. Until the beginning of the 1950's the Swedish Left, a separate group on the fringes of the Swedish People's party, participated in most elections jointly with the mother party. In 1930 and in 1945 it was able to elect one of its

9. Pekka Nyholm, *Suomen eduskuntaryhmien koheesio vuosien 1948–1951 vaalikaudella ja vuoden 1954 valtiopäivillä* (Helsinki, 1961), pp. 55–62, 134–137.

own representatives. The League of Liberals, formed in 1951 when the Progressive party was breaking up, has generally concluded election blocs with the Coalition party. It was not until 1962 that it proclaimed itself a party, after having elected one of its own men to Parliament; but three years later it became part of a new Liberal People's party. The Social Democratic League, formed in 1959, had a rather broad parliamentary base following the election of 1958; in that election the party opposition, it is true, managed to elect only three representatives on their own lists, but after the election they were joined by eleven representatives elected on Social Democratic lists. In 1962 their number of representatives in Parliament fell to two, only to rise again four years later to seven as a result of successful election blocs. Finally one must mention the Finnish Rural party (until 1966 the party of the small farmers), which split from the Agrarian party; in 1966, in its second attempt, the party was able to elect its leader Veikko Vennamo to Parliament.

Special Features of the Party System. Characteristic of Finnish party life has been the central position, and in certain periods the ruling position, of the large Agrarian party. This phenomenon deserves attention in that one discovers, when examining party conditions in different countries, that strong farmer parties are a rarity. This is because there is no real "farmer class"; within the agricultural population there is constant conflict between landowners and landless, between large farmers and small farmers. Thus the formation of an agrarian party is difficult, and flight from it to the left and to the right is natural. The agrarian proletariat feels a strong attraction to socialist and communist movements, so that the farmer parties often remain small conservative groups. The Scandinavian countries are a significant exception to this general pattern, for it has been possible in these countries to found and maintain independent farmer parties. Searching for an explanation of this phenomenon, Duverger points to historical factors. He explains that in Scandinavia the general conflict between conservatism and liberalism became in the nineteenth century a conflict between the cities and the countryside; politically the countryside was on the left, the cities on the right.[10] It should be noted that the founding of the Agrarian party came at a time when the tie between the rural "toilers" and the overwhelmingly civil servant upper class had been broken—as the language

10. Duverger, *Les partis politiques*, pp. 266–267.

question faded at the turn of the century—and the conflict between these two groups had become apparent. Also of significance may be the fact that the agricultural population in the Scandinavian countries has been more unified in structure than is true for many Central European nations.

Also requiring explanation is the fact that the Agrarian-Center party in Finland has grown large, while similar groups in Sweden and Norway, for example, have remained small. The reasons are numerous as well as complicated. The answer can perhaps be found in the general structure of Finnish society (the relative delay in the advent of modern industrialization), in the internal structure of the agricultural population, in the phases of political history which have given direction to party development, and in the party's own tactical behavior. The Agrarian party rested from the outset on the support of small farmers; this, too, determined the direction later taken by the party. Without a doubt it has followed the development visible in other countries, and against this background one can perhaps examine its new ideological and practical orientation. All in all, it may be that in this respect better points of comparison with Finland are to be found in certain Eastern European countries—where, formerly, large peasant parties existed—than in Scandinavia.

In the political life of industrializing Western societies, one sees over time a consistent movement to the left. This leftism can take many different forms; it may mean an adjustment by all or most parties to changing circumstances, assisted by gradual shifts in positions, or it may mean a strengthening of those parties—at the expense of others—which clearly fly the leftist banner. The latter path has been followed in the Scandinavian countries, where the united labor parties have risen to a leading position, even to a point where they are majority parties holding power. From this point of view, Finnish party conditions are characterized by the labor movement's relative weakness and factionalization. Finnish politics over the decades can be labeled "bourgeois" because the center of gravity of parliamentary (and, in general, also nonparliamentary) power has been on this side of the front. The electoral reform augured well for Social Democrats; their number of representatives rose quickly from eighty to ninety, and in 1916, though under exceptional conditions to be sure, they received an absolute majority in Parliament with one hundred and three seats, forming one of Europe's strongest socialist parties. As a result of different factors—including the Civil War, the split within the labor movement, discrimination against the left, agricultural reforms, the rise of the Agrarian party—there was a shift from this direction to another, and even after the Second World War the bourgeoisie still was able to preserve a slight majority in Parliament. It may be that here, too, the Scandinavian countries, which differ from Finland in social structure and political traditions, are not the best source of comparison; in any case, one can probably say that in terms of social structure there are in Finland at least as many conditions favoring socialism. Significant in this respect is the fact that the Agrarian-Center party has received its support from the lower income groups in agriculture, and, in general, in the countryside and has thus gathered into its fold people whom one can suppose would support the leftwing parties if another party scheme were used. On the other hand, the spread of Social Democracy into the middle class has been made difficult by the traditional effort of state and communal administrative personnel, of lower-salaried employees of commerce, industry, transportation and communications, and of small employers and self-employed to emphasize and raise their own social position by detaching themselves from the workers and by avoiding participation in their political and trade union movements. At this time it is difficult to say whether the impressive election victory of the Social Democrats in 1966 indicated a more lasting reorientation of opinions or whether it was a temporary counter-reaction caused by the situation that had prevailed for some ten years. In any case, it put the Social Democratic party into an undisputed ruling position, and cooperation with the People's Democrats, which was born of a mutual desire, opened up new possibilities for carrying out leftwing policies in the country with the support of a parliamentary majority.

Finally, the split within the labor movement gives a degree of uniqueness to party conditions in Finland and weakens in a basic way the left's ability to act, especially in the field of politics. The mass support for Communism in Finland has been explained in many different ways: some have gone back into history and have tried to find in past events and conditions the causes for the radicalism of the workers; others have focused on the country's geopolitical position as Russia's neighbor; some call attention to the present economic situation or institutional factors, to the ways in which political power is exercised; certain sociological works explain "backwoods Communism" as an expressive action, a protest stemming from the limitations on political and social participation. It is evident that all these factors make up the causal equation of Communism, but it is difficult to say in what proportions. It is not possible to treat this question at length, but attention should be called to the interesting though perhaps a bit shaky comparisons made by Lipset between stable Western democratic systems and unstable democratic and dictatorial systems. He refers to the economic level of development and to factors which determine the legitimacy of a political system: in other words, to factors which determine to what degree large social groups accept existing rules for the attainment of power.[11]

Still characteristic of Finnish party life are a rather great permanence of party strength, a sharpness of party lines, and a vehemence in the struggle for power. The country's major parties have long been tightly-knit organizations which act independently, are suspicious of each other, and find it impossible to consider any other group a trustworthy ally even within the framework of brief Cabinet cooperation, not to speak of a longer relationship involving trust. Certain historical factors have undoubtedly had an influence in this respect. Unlike her western neighbor Sweden, Finland has not been able to enjoy an uninterrupted, lengthy period of peaceful parliamentary development that would have lowered social barriers and educated individuals and parties in democratic patterns of thought based on cooperation and a desire to compromise. An open struggle against foreign oppression, a Civil War, a semifascist attempt at revolution, and two wars against a foreign power, as well as certain less severe periods of internal crisis—all experienced within a relatively short period—have kept Finnish society divided, preserved a certain mentality of violence, and tied individuals to parties around questions of fundamental significance for the life of the whole nation. The conflicts between social classes and between parties are consequently deep; parties and political life have not achieved that level of stability which exists in many other Western democracies.

But behind the party struggle one can also see other factors even closer in time and more clearly recognizable. In general the relative strength of parties changes slowly, but if the changes are tied to shifts in the structure of the electorate, one can be sure that they are of a lasting nature. In Finland today there is still a rapid process of development, which means an expansion of industrial occupations at

11. Seymour Martin Lipset, *Political Man* (New York, 1960), chaps. ii and iii.

the expense of agriculture and forestry. One may expect this change in the population's occupational and social structure to bring about significant changes in party structure, and these expectations help shape party life. Uncertain about the future, parties are trying to strengthen their positions, which serves to sharpen stances, to draw parties away from each other, and to emphasize efforts aimed at securing the greatest economic advantages possible for one's own group.

Parties and the Constitution. Finland's fundamental laws belong to those older constitutional documents that do not heed the existence of parties and that are totally silent about participation of parties in political decision-making. It may be that the original basis for this line of reasoning is traceable to the old Rousseauan notions about parties as nests of selfish, special interests destroying a nation's unity, and to the political theory notion of postrevolutionary France that power should be wielded only by institutions set forth in the constitution, with no role for groups in an intermediary position between the citizens and those institutions. Parties in Finland are consequently civil organizations whose activity is bound only by liberal rules of general legislation pertaining to associations. Since parties are not recognized, the state does not supervise or restrict their activity in any special way. As examples of instances when extremely sharp measures were taken against parties, one can mention the end of open activity by the Communists in the 1920's and 1930's as well as the suppression of the IKL after the Second World War.

But since party organizations and parliamentary groups are a fact, they have in practice been given de facto recognition. Proportional voting in general elections and within Parliament is based on the existence of parties. The position of party groups as the basic units of parliamentary activity is demonstrated by the group seating arrangement in plenary sessions, by the designation of meeting rooms for parliamentary groups, and by the granting to "official" representatives of groups the right to speak first in some of the most important debates. It should also be noted that the Finnish president, following established practice, begins the process of forming a new government by consulting the chairmen of the party groups.[12]

12. See Nyholm, *Suomen eduskuntaryhmien koheesio*, pp. 10–11.

MASS SUPPORT AND MEMBERSHIP

Relative Strength of the Parties. General elections can be considered an important measure of citizen opinion on major political issues that indicates the degree of support received by the various parties. Parliamentary elections are the best measure of this formation of opinion, for here party politics appear in their most naked form. In this respect there are certain disturbing factors about presidential and communal elections: personal characteristics of presidential candidates in the former instance and a blurring of party lines in the latter due to local election blocs. Parliamentary elections are thus a better indicator of party support within the nation.

Table 8 shows party strength in parliamentary elections during the period of the unicameral legislature. The general features of development in the table are tied to the broad changes in party life discussed above. Insofar as economic and social factors, that is, conflicts between social classes, have pushed their way forward in political life and have become primary bases for party grouping, parties which began on other grounds have lost support to new, "class-oriented" parties. Support for the Old Finn party fell continuously in 1907–1916, perhaps in part—in spite of the fact that in 1907 it adopted a stand far to the left in social questions—because of its attitude, at variance with views held in the other parties, on the question of Russification. The Finnish party's successor, the Coalition party, has experienced slight ups and downs over the decades, but in general its position remains the same. In 1962 the party's relative share of the vote was almost the same as in 1919. In the 1930's, when the bourgeoisie closed ranks in its struggle against the Communists, the right experienced a significant rise in strength; but it was the IKL, not the Coalition party, which benefited from this. Characteristic of the Young Finnish party until 1917 was the stability of its support base; the Progressive party, however, was not able to preserve this base and began in the 1920's to shrink hopelessly and to move toward final destruction. As is often the case with ideological center parties, this one was not able to prevent its supporters from fleeing to both the right and the left. With the passage of years the city population's share of the party's electorate grew many times over, which shows that the party was not so successful as the Coalition party in preserving its support among the farmers. The political influence of the Progressive party depended throughout most of its life, and especially

Table 8. Party percentage of popular vote in parliamentary elections, 1907–1970

Year	Party												
	Finnish party;[a] National Coalition party[b]	IKL[b]	Young Finnish party;[a] Progressive party	Finnish People's party; Liberal People's party	Swedish People's party	Agrarian party; Center party	Small Farmers' party; Finnish Farmers' party	Christian Workers' League	Social Democratic party	Social Democratic League[c]	Socialist Workers' party; SKDL	Others[d]	Total
1907	27.3	–	13.6	–	12.6	5.8	–	1.6	37.0	–	–	2.1	100.0
1908	25.4	–	14.2	–	12.8	6.4	–	2.3	38.4	–	–	0.5	100.0
1909	23.6	–	14.5	–	12.3	6.7	–	2.8	39.9	–	–	0.2	100.0
1910	22.1	–	14.4	–	13.5	7.6	–	2.2	40.0	–	–	0.2	100.0
1911	21.7	–	14.9	–	13.3	7.8	–	2.2	40.0	–	–	0.1	100.0
1913	19.9	–	14.1	–	13.1	7.8	–	1.8	43.1	–	–	0.2	100.0
1916	17.6	–	12.4	–	11.8	9.0	–	1.8	47.3	–	–	0.1	100.0
1917		–		–	10.9	12.4	–	1.6	44.8	–	–	0.2	100.0
1919	15.7	–	12.8	–	12.1	19.7	–	1.5	38.0	–	–	0.2	100.0
1922	18.1	–	9.2	–	12.4	20.3	–	–	25.1	–	14.8	0.1	100.0

1924	19.0	–	9.1	–	12.0	20.3	–	–	29.0	–	10.4	0.2	100.0
1927	17.7	–	6.8	–	12.2	22.5	–	–	28.3	–	12.1	0.4	100.0
1929	14.5	–	5.6	–	11.4	26.1	1.1	–	27.4	–	13.5	0.4	100.0
1930	18.1	–	5.8	–	10.0	27.3	1.8	–	34.2	–	1.0	1.8	100.0
1933	16.9		7.4	–	10.4	22.6	3.4	–	37.3	–	–	2.0	100.0
1936	10.4	8.3	6.3	–	11.2	22.4	2.0	–	38.6	–	–	0.8	100.0
1939	13.6	6.6	4.8	–	9.6	22.9	2.1	–	39.8	–	–	0.6	100.0
1945	15.0	–	5.2	–	7.9	21.3	1.2	–	25.1	–	23.5	0.8	100.0
1948	17.1	–	3.9	–	7.7	24.2	0.3	–	26.3	–	20.0	0.5	100.0
1951	14.6	–	–	5.7	7.6	23.2	0.3	–	26.5	–	21.6	0.5	100.0
1954	12.8	–	–	7.9	7.0	24.1	–	–	26.2	–	21.6	0.4	100.0
1958	15.3	–	–	5.9	6.7	23.1	–	–	23.2	1.7	23.2	0.9	100.0
1962	15.0	–	–	6.3	6.4	23.0	2.2	–	19.5	4.4	22.0	1.2	100.0
1966	13.8	–	–	6.5	6.0	21.2	1.0	–	27.2	2.6	21.2	0.5	100.0
1970	18.0	–	–	6.0	5.7	17.1	10.5	–	23.4	1.4	16.6	1.3	100.0

Source: Official Statistics of Finland, ser. XXIX 1–14, A:15–29 (Helsinki: Keisarillisen Senaatin kirjapaino, Valtioneuvoston kirjapaino, Valtion painatuskeskus, 1909–1967).

[a] In 1917 the Finnish, the Young Finnish, and the People's parties formed an election bloc and together received 30.1 percent of the vote.

[b] Included in the Coalition party vote of 1933 are IKL votes received in joint election blocs.

[c] The Social Democratic opposition in the 1958 election.

[d] Included in the "others" category are votes received by the people's party (1933 and 1936) and by the League of Liberals, as well as votes received by the Swedish left in 1930, 1939, and 1945 (otherwise they are considered part of the vote for the Swedish People's party); the "others" category also includes write-ins.

in later years, more on the personal role played by its leaders than on mass strength: in 1948 it received only 73,400 votes. In its first two elections the Finnish People's party was successful, since it was able by 1954 to double, mostly at the expense of the Coalition party, the relative number of votes received by the Progressive party in its last election. In 1958 the party suffered a clear defeat, but four years later it again increased its support in both absolute and relative terms.

The third of these old groupings is the Swedish People's party. Its support base is constantly, yet very slowly, declining: 12.6 percent in 1907, 6.0 percent in 1966. A natural explanation for the steady decline is, of course, the fact that Swedish-speaking Finns, who support the party, are shrinking as a share of the total population. Another probable factor is the fact that after the Second World War there seems to have been a movement of Swedish-speaking voters to the Social Democratic and Communist parties. Furthermore, with the passage of time the difference in electoral participation between the Swedish-speaking and Finnish-speaking population has leveled off.

The Agrarian party participated in the 1907 election as a small party, and in terms of mass support it remained a small party until the country became independent. In 1919 there was a sudden growth from 12 percent to 20 percent, following which the party's relative share of the popular vote has been 20–24 percent except for the years of crisis in 1929–1930, when support for the Agrarian party was at its highest point.

The support curve for Social Democrats has gone up and down, depending upon the government's attitude toward organizational and election activity of the extreme left. Even in the first unicameral parliamentary election the Social Democratic party was able to obtain 37 percent of the vote and 80 seats, and during the next decade the united workers' front became still broader. There was a strong conviction among workers during these years that social and economic conditions could be improved through parliamentary action, and so they were very active at the polls. The party was weakened in the 1920's by the aftermath of the Civil War, the split within the labor movement, and the competition from Communists; even in the 1930's, when electoral activity by the Communists had been proscribed, the party was not able to recapture its previous position. Statistics show that many radical leftists preferred to abstain rather than cast a ballot for the Social Democrats. The extreme left's rapid march forward after the Second World War, with new slogans of a people's democracy, again drew many supporters away from the Social Democratic party. Strong support for Communism is a permanent phenomenon in Finland; thus Finland, like France and Italy, is one of Western Europe's "reddest" countries. After 1945 Communism increased its strength only temporarily in many European countries, while in Finland its mass support has remained almost the same over the 1945–1966 period. Some research, for example my work on the province of Kuopio, demonstrates that certain differences exist between various occupational groups. In many industrial centers the support for Communism rose abruptly right after the war, only to fall again in the next election; but in some isolated rural communities, where opinions change more slowly, it was not until the 1948 and 1951 elections that Communism gained a firm foothold.

In the second half of the 1950's the Social Democrats had special difficulties emanating from internal squabbles and the situation with respect to foreign policy. The splitting off of the left wing caused the party's share of the popular vote in 1962 to drop to 19.5 percent, the smallest figure since 1907. However, a counterattack occurred 4 years later when the mother party gained its broadest support ever, about 645,000 votes.

At this point it should be noted that, although a party's influence in political life is essentially dependent on how many voting citizens give it mandates to act on their behalf, influence is not directly proportional to the extensiveness of mass support. It is determined by many other factors, such as the position of the party in the party continuum and the general political situation. The significance of the former factor is shown by the ever-important position held throughout the period of independence by parties of the center. Since Finnish political life demands cooperation between many parties, the center groups understandably occupy a key position whether politics lean to the right or to the left. One leading force has been the Agrarian party, which only rarely and for short periods of time has been forced into the background. As pointed out earlier, so long as it was difficult to achieve cooperation across the bourgeois-left boundary the Social Democratic party remained isolated and was able only under exceptional circumstances to influence Cabinet policy directly. Both parties on the extremities, the Coalition party and the Communists, have suffered because of their position. Strong support for the Coalition party among society's influential upper class and among the great industrial interests, however, has increased the actual political influence of the right independently of Cabinet representation. As examples of the significance of the situation variable, one can refer to the 1920's and 1930's, when rightwing politics were favored; the crisis of adaption following the Second World War, which meant a radical shift to the left in the center of gravity; and the period since 1957, which has been called the "period of Agrarian party hegemony."

The Basis of Mass Support. In general terms, the territorial division of party support is as follows. The Swedish People's party understandably receives its support from a restricted number of unified territories, from the Aaland Islands and from Swedish communities located on the country's southern and western coastline. In 1966 the party received 53 percent of its votes in Helsinki and Uusimaa and 34 percent from the electoral district of Vaasa province. Mass support for the Coalition and Liberal People's parties is concentrated in population centers around the country; about one-half of those who vote for the Coalition party and about two-thirds of those who vote for the Liberal People's party live in cities and towns. The Coalition party receives support from the farming population mainly in the country's more prosperous western and southern sections. In addition to Helsinki, this party's strongest areas are Häme province, the northern part of Turku province, the southern part of Vaasa province, and Kymi province. The Center party is spread rather evenly over the countryside: only in Häme province, Helsinki, and Uusimaa—and excluding, of course, the Aaland Islands—is its share of the vote appreciably less than the average for the entire country. The party is especially strong among voters in the north, in the provinces of Oulu and Lapland (38.3 percent and 33.6 percent in 1966), as well as in southeast Finland, in many agricultural communes located in the provinces of Mikkeli and Kymi. When the Social Democratic share of the vote in different electoral districts (multimember constituencies) and communes is examined, it becomes clear that one area of support has been the country's southern and central section—a square with corners approximately at Helsinki, Pori, Kajaani, and Ilomantsi. In the coastal communities of Pohjanmaa the relative vote is smaller; in addition, Pohjois-Savo, which is in the square, remains outside the Social Democratic sphere of influence.

Table 9. Party percentage by electoral district in parliamentary election, 1966

Electoral district	Coalition party	Swedish People's party	Liberal People's party	Center party	Farmers' party	Social Democratic party	TPSL	SKDL	Others
Helsinki	18.3	12.9	12.0	2.8	–	32.5	2.5	18.2	0.8
Uusimaa province	9.7	16.7	7.6	10.4	0.5	33.8	3.0	17.9	0.4
Turku, South	12.9	6.3	9.5	18.0	–	26.9	2.2	24.2	0.0
Turku, North	15.9	–	3.3	24.4	0.8	29.3	0.9	24.4	0.9
Aaland Islands	–	96.3	–	–	–	–	–	3.7	0.0
Häme, South	18.7	–	7.8	16.3	0.5	32.4	3.9	19.6	0.8
Häme, North	21.9	–	4.8	9.8	0.3	33.9	3.0	26.3	0.0
Kymi province	15.3	–	7.2	22.7	0.5	37.2	4.0	12.1	1.0
Mikkeli province	10.6	–	4.8	33.8	0.8	30.6	5.4	12.4	1.6
Northern Karelia province	10.8	–	6.2	29.2	3.5	31.1	2.6	16.5	0.0
Kuopio province	12.2	–	3.5	28.5	6.8	17.5	2.3	29.1	0.0
Keski-Suomi province	10.4	–	5.7	26.6	0.5	28.6	6.2	22.0	0.0
Vaasa province	14.1	20.9	1.0	29.4	1.4	16.8	0.6	15.3	0.6
Oulu province	8.6	–	5.4	38.3	1.4	13.4	0.7	31.9	0.3
Lapland province	8.0	–	7.8	33.6	–	14.4	1.1	35.1	0.0
Entire country	13.8	6.0	6.5	21.2	1.0	27.2	2.6	21.2	0.5

Source: Official Statistics of Finland, ser. XXIX, A:29 (Helsinki: Valtion painatuskeskus, 1967), p. 12.

The weakness of Social Democrats in the provinces of Oulu and Lapland is striking: for example, in 1962 the share of votes picked up by the Social Democratic party and the Social Democratic League in those most northern electoral districts was essentially no greater, in total, than the figure for the Coalition party. Lastly, as far as mass support for Communism is concerned, it is proportionately greatest in the provinces of Oulu and Lapland and in Pohjois-Savo (within the electoral district of Kuopio province).

Table 9, which supports these facts, gives the percentage of the vote by electoral district that was received by the various parties in the 1966 parliamentary election. These figures alone, it is true, do not give a clear picture of the situation because Finland's large electoral districts are geographically, as well as economically and even politically, still very heterogeneous territories.

In voting behavior research conducted recently in a number of countries, the primacy of economic-social divisions has been established among factors determining party division. In Finland, too, interview information is available regarding the correlation between social class and political position.

The information in Table 10 is based on a Finnish Gallup poll taken in the fall of 1958. Social class was defined in terms of profession; but it is to be noted that a grouping based on the individuals' own class identification produced essentially the same result. Of the workers who gave their party affiliation, 80 percent supported one or the other of the labor parties; of the farmers, 64 percent the Agrarian party; and of the white-collar workers, 76 percent one of the three

Table 10. Voters grouped by social class and party preference, 1958

Party preference	Farmers (308)	Workers (421)	White-collar (133)
Social Democratic party	3%	34%	14%
SKDL	9	34	5
Agrarian party	54	5	5
Other bourgeois parties	17	11	61
No preference	17	16	15

Source: Eric Allardt, "Structural Cleavages in Finnish Politics," Helsingin yliopiston sosiologian laitoksen tutkimuksia no. 6, 1961 (mimeographed), p. 1.

other bourgeois parties. Looked at in another way, one can say that 85 percent of Agrarian party supporters were farmers and 82 percent of the workers' party supporters were laborers, but only somewhat less than half (45 percent) of supporters of the Coalition and People's parties were white-collar workers. The same sort of results were also obtained in an opinion poll of 1948.[13]

Social class thus turns out to be a very important factor influencing party choice in Finland, but on this basis alone one cannot arrive at a very exact explanation of party division. As Onni Rantala notes, "even in multiparty countries, as in Finland, social classes and parties are a long way from being completely identical; in other words, political and social group boundaries are not the same."[14] There are a number of conspicuous exceptions to this political division based on classes, aside from the fact that all parties naturally receive some support from people living in different circumstances. Small parties on the bourgeois wing, most notably the Coalition party and the Swedish People's party, receive considerable support from farmers and workers. At this level of analysis one cannot explain the division of labor into Communist and Social Democratic supporters any more than one can explain the division of middle-class voters into supporters of the Coalition and Finnish People's parties, or the division of small farmer-lumbermen located in remote areas into supporters of the Center party and the left parties.

It is easiest to find an explanation for these exceptions with respect to the Swedish People's party: its voters are united by a common language and cultural inheritance that overshadows economic and other factors. According to estimates made by the party's central bureau, 80 percent of "Swedish Finland's" Swedish-speaking electorate voted in 1962 for the Swedish People's party, 13 percent for the Social Democrats, and 7 percent for the People's Democrats. From this one also sees, indirectly, the social composition of the party's voters: the party receives support from all social classes on the language basis, although its electorate is not a mirror image of the country's Swedish-speaking population because support given to parties of the left surely comes for the most part from workers.

In a 1966 sample the Coalition party was composed of 20 percent

13. Onni Rantala, *Konservatiivinen puolueyhteisö* (Vammala, 1956), pp. 23–25. In 1966 a new Gallup poll was taken; see *Helsingin Sanomat*, Dec. 9, 12, 15, 21, 30, 1966, and Jan. 6, 1967.

14. Rantala, *Konservatismi*, p. 37.

farmers, 12 percent workers, 28 percent salaried employees, and 40 percent management types. Relatively speaking, the party understandably received most of its support from the upper and middle classes; in any case, it has been able to keep farmers and workers in its ranks, so its electorate is still somewhat heterogeneous. A certain number of more well-to-do farmers evidently vote for the Coalition party in different parts of the country, and in one area, Etelä-Pohjanmaa, farm support for the party seems even broader. One finding which fits this picture is that members of Parliament elected from Pohjanmaa and belonging to the Coalition party, and even the Swedish People's party, are more "rural" in outlook when compared with members of their groups elected from other parts of Finland; in other words, they are inclined to break with their own groups and cast ballots with the Center party on those parliamentary votes in which rural problems are of major concern.[15]

The most significant and perhaps the most interesting exception to a party system that fits the economic-social pattern of class cleavage is, however, the rather even division of workers into Social Democratic and Communist supporters. In this respect Finnish political life is unique, if one takes as a point of comparison the other Scandinavian countries. By analyzing interview material and election statistics, Erik Allardt has attempted to shed light on the support base of the Social Democratic and Communist movements.[16]

The general finding about greater conservativeness in women holds here too. Working-class women support Communism less, and the bourgeois parties more, than men; this phenomenon is particularly true among the urban population. With respect to men, a 1958 poll showed that in urban areas they split rather evenly between Social Democrats and People's Democrats, but that support in the countryside for Communism was clearly greater. The phenomenon of strong support in the countryside, especially among workers, should be

15. Nyholm, *Suomen eduskuntaryhmien koheesio*, pp. 98–107, 117–118.

16. Of Erik Allardt's many research reports the following should be mentioned: "Structural Cleavages in Finnish Politics," Helsingin yliopiston sosiologian laitoksen tutkimuksia no. 6, 1961 (mimeographed); "Facteurs économiques et sociaux du vote à gauche en Finlande," *Cahiers de sociologie economique*, no. 6 (May 1962), 258–266; "Patterns of Class Conflict and Working Class Consciousness in Finnish Politics," in Erik Allardt and Yrjö Littunen, eds., *Cleavages, Ideologies and Party Systems: Contributions to Comparative Political Sociology* (Turku, 1964), pp. 97–131; "Social Sources of Finnish Communism: Traditional and Emerging Radicalism," *International Journal of Comparative Sociology*, 5, no. 1 (March 1964), 49–72; Erik Allardt and Pertti Pesonen, "Cleavages in Finnish Politics," in Seymour M. Lipset and Stein Rokkan, eds., *Party Systems and Voter Alignments* (New York, 1967), pp. 325–366.

considered a special feature of Finnish Communism. If this dichotomy is carried further on a geographic basis, one can show that the Communists gain their staunchest support from workers in the rural areas of eastern and northern Finland. The greatest increase in support for the People's Democrats during the years 1948–1958 occurred, moreover, in the rural communes of northern Finland. Economic backwardness and low incomes are characteristic of the Communist-dominated communes in this part of the country; the population is made up essentially of lumbermen and small farmers who must seek part of their income from forestry work and who are considered workers. Research has shown that these are the population groups subject to seasonal and market-caused unemployment, which is known to be a factor that increases Communist support. Those who vote for the Social Democrats are, above all, the better-paid workers of the urban centers in southern and western Finland who have not experienced unemployment. Especially in northern Finland it is a fact that Social Democracy attracts different population groups than either Communism or the Center party's social agrarianism.

Economic factors alone, however, do not result in a satisfactory map of the support base for either large workers' party. Communists are also numerous in communes with a higher income level located in the country's southern and western areas; in fact, in absolute numbers they are more numerous there than in the north because the vast majority of the population lives in the southern half of the country. On the other hand, a definition of one's social position is still rather crude; more refined classifications, which rest on additional criteria of stratification, suggest that in terms of social position Communists are generally somewhat lower than Social Democrats.

It is interesting that the "backwoods Communism" of eastern and northern Finland has its own special characteristics. In the first place, it does not seem to have much of a connection with earlier socialist traditions. Even though there was a rather strong correlation between the vote received in both the south and the north by the Social Democrats in 1954, broken down by communes—as well as by the People's Democrats in the south—and the Social Democratic vote of 1916 and the number of Reds killed in the Civil War, one does not find any sort of positive correlation in the communes of northern and eastern Finland between the Communist vote and traditions. Communism's mass support in these areas is a much newer phenomenon; voting activity having once been much lower than the average for the country, a large segment of the population suddenly took part in political activity as "new voters" after the Second World War. Social Democrats were not successful when competing for the allegiance of these voters; it is possible that they did not even try very hard. Furthermore, Communism in the eastern and northern areas does not have the same bond to economic-social conditions that Social Democracy does in both areas and that Communism does in the south. There is, however, a positive correlation in the north between Communism and unemployment, whereas a similar correlation for Social Democrats is negative. The organizational activity of the People's Democrats has evidently been of fundamental importance in the activization of voters in a left radical sense. "Backwoods Communism" in the country's eastern and northern parts is now interpreted as an extremism which may emerge as the level of demands suddenly increases in remote areas where the population has only limited possibilities for social and political participation. This activism is considered more expressive than instrumental, an emotional outburst and an end in itself rather than a means to attain certain goals.

But there seems to be an even more general, much older, political difference between these two parts of the country. Eastern and northern Finland are also more radical as far as the bourgeoisie is concerned. The Finnish-speaking representatives elected from this area in the last two elections to the peasant estate (1904–1905) were almost all Young Finns, whereas the representatives from the country's southern and western parts were primarily Old Finns.[17] It is difficult to say to what degree this divergence (for which there is not yet a satisfactory explanation) is a direct reflection of present behavioral patterns, but in any case the two-fold geographic division is apparent; Allardt notes that national research on political behavior which fails to take this division into consideration is doomed to failure and he has, therefore, carried out his ecological analysis separately for these two areas. The results strengthen those general observations which suggest that the Center party in terms of its support base is more conservative in the country's southern and western parts than in the north and east. In the latter area the party has more support

17. See Eino Jutikkala, "Political Parties in the Elections of Deputies to the Estate of Burgesses and the Estate of Farmers in the Finnish Diet of Estates," *Sitzungsberichte der finnischen Akademie der Wissenschaften 1960* (Helsinki, 1960), pp. 167–184.

among the backward communes than among the modernizing industrial communes. The two-fold division is also clearly apparent in the parliamentary activity of elected representatives. According to Nyholm, the Center party's representatives from the provinces of Oulu and Lapland differ from other members of their group in that they are inclined to support the left in those parliamentary votes where the division generally follows a line between the bourgeoisie and the left. During the 1948–1951 Parliament, eight of the ten most "left-leaning" Agrarian representatives were from the electoral districts of Oulu and Lapland; one came from Kymi province and one from the western electoral district of Kuopio province. The most "bourgeois-leaning" representatives were in the electoral districts of western and southwestern Finland. The SKDL representatives elected from nothern Finland are inclined to approach the Center party by evidencing more sensitive "rural" positions than do the party's representatives elected from other parts of the country.[18] One can also assume that the matter of tactics is of concern to both parties, since they are the major competitors in northern Finland. In the countryside of Oulu and Lapland provinces, Finland is not far removed from a two-party system; the Center party and the SKDL receive about four-fifths of the vote in the rural communes of these electoral districts. It is interesting to speculate on the influence that modernization of economic and social conditions will have on voting behavior in this area. In other places the Social Democrats also compete effectively for votes of the many small farmers and forestry laborers. This competition presupposes that the voters do not see much difference between the three largest parties. It would even appear that Social Democracy has remained more radical among the masses than within the leadership, whereas the situation may be just the opposite as far as Communism is concerned. An understanding of the difference between the Social Democratic party and the SKDL is in any case more vague in the countryside than in the cities.

Although party grouping in the Scandinavian multiparty system attempts to coincide with the economic and social divisions of society, available information thus demonstrates the incorrectness of the notion that economic factors and motives are the sole or decisive variables in party choice. Economic factors are intertwined in a

18. Nyholm, *Suomen eduskuntaryhmien koheesio*, pp. 92–97, 114–117.

complex way with many others, historical-social, religious, and so on, whose impact may vary greatly in different circumstances. Emotional factors are an important influence in the formation of political opinions, and so explanations which are too rational easily become one-sided. When analyzing political opinions of small groups and individuals, one discovers that a wide range of factors connected with the interaction of individuals—factors not easily visible to an outside observer—may be the decisive variables. Political behavior may be based on matters of seeming insignificance, on the special conditions and experiences of individuals and of small groups, and on events which taken by themselves are perhaps minor but which become emotionally charged and whose significance consequently looms large and lasting.

For example: the influence of poverty on political attitudes is not so simple as is often imagined. Its influence has been shown to be dependent upon the kinds of economic reference groups selected by the poor—in other words, with what social groups they compare their own position. The support for Communism may be relatively small in backward, predominantly agricultural areas where social class differences are felt to be small and where the relationship between employers and employees has remained patriarchal and contact with the outside world is minimal. But when contact with the outside occurs, and when class differences grow as social relationships change, poor people become conscious of their position, their level of demands rises, and discontent begins to take the form of political radicalism. These sorts of phenomena are found in Finland in the political development of rural parishes and villages. In fact, it has been proven that in the eastern parts of the country, where small farming predominates, the receptivity of small farmers to Communism may be very small in economically homogeneous areas but the proximity of some large farms may, on the other hand, appreciably increase that receptivity. In the latter instance, people living in difficult circumstances have visible points of comparison with which they can easily contrast their own conditions.

Research focusing on different professional groups has shown that the type of work and work surroundings, as well as the certainty of making a living, are perhaps even more important factors in terms of political attitudes than the size of one's income. There is a tendency to support the extreme left among occupational groups whose earnings fluctuate and whose jobs depend on market changes, whose working conditions are unsatisfactory and whose social position is low, and who are isolated and have relatively little contact with other social groups. These features are characteristic, for example, of construction workers, stevedores, miners, and lumbermen. A related factor is unemployment, the influence of which on the formation of political opinion has been found to extend far beyond the actual period of unemployment. When examining the territorial strength of Communism in the country's various communes today, one can still see signs of the unemployment of the 1930's, which weak employment practices in Finland were not able to ward off.

In the above case, economic factors that were once influential have given birth to enduring forms of behavior maintained as an inheritance from one generation to another. These factors have become historical in the sense that they are no longer a direct influence, and as such they often are no longer a conscious part of an individual's motivation. In addition to unemployment, there may be many other factors of such strong impact that they produce far-ranging political traditions.

Traditions based on historical factors produce political climatic areas where factors determining political behavior are frequently quite independent of present economic conditions. One of the most striking findings of ecological research carried out in different countries has been the territorial stabilization of political positions. Researchers have tried to map political climates and isolate the factors influencing their formation and preservation. Many are content merely to speak of regional factors, placing them on an equal footing with economic and social factors as determinants of voting behavior. Mentioning them is not, of course, an explanation; it merely signifies recognition of the existence of climatic areas. One must find from the present or past those primary factors which have brought a territorial form of behavior into being and which maintain it. Thus it seems impossible in an examination of the present to find consistent variables providing a satisfactory explanation for political behavior in all parts of the country. In some areas the constancy of a prevailing pattern of political behavior can be explained through reference to the existence of economic and social conditions which correspond to that pattern. More interesting than this, and requiring a special explanation, is the case in which a certain political "hue" is preserved in spite of a change in external circumstances or in the political situation.

Political traditions can be found in large as well as small areas, in both entire rural communes and in separate rural villages and industrial communities. Looking at the relationship between the parties of the left one can, for example, locate two different climatic areas of eastern Finland: Pohjois-Savo and Northern Karelia. In terms of economic conditions there is no decisive difference, but because of the influence of certain conditions—for the most part already a part of the past—the former area has remained strongly under Communist control, whereas Social Democrats have traditionally been a majority in the latter. Northern Karelia in the 1920's remained almost wholly apart from the struggle within the labor movement; Pohjois-Savo became the strongest center of Communist activity. Another example is the present-day electoral district of Vaasa province, which in general outlook has long been conservative. The Coalition and Center parties are strong in the Finnish-speaking parts of this area, whereas the leftist parties suffer from an inhospitable climate; of the factors which have created this climate one should mention the homogeneous economic and social structure of the population as well as its keen sense of patriotism. Also striking is the relatively little support received by leftwing parties, particularly the People's Democrats, in Kymi province in southeast Finland. A partial explanation of this phenomenon is the area's general economic structure; it is difficult to say whether past experiences have influenced the formation of opinion as one approaches the Russian border.

Membership. Modern parties are large election organizations whose immediate aim is winning for their own candidates the largest possible number of votes. A party's strength and influence depend essentially on how many citizens with the right to vote have given it a mandate to represent them in political life. But success at election time presupposes an extensive, effective, and functioning organizational network, a capable leadership, a sufficiently large and active group of "militants" or field workers, and, of course, rather large sums of money. Expressed in the language of a businessman, a party organization sells to citizens those policies which its leaders produce in Parliament, in the Cabinet, and in communal administrative organs. Successful sales necessitate effective advertising and a broad sales network. In terms of mass support, a party may be looked upon as a collective body consisting of all who declared themselves supporters of the party at election time. The core of a party organization, however, is its membership, which is an organized group in which features peculiar to the whole party as a collective body appear in sharp relief.

The advent of universal suffrage in conjunction with parliamentary reform (1906) was a great impetus for the organizational development of parties; it turned loose bourgeois groups into mass organizations practicing uninterrupted activity. Even in the 1920's and 1930's, however, it was still possible to point to a clear difference between the Social Democratic party on one hand and the bourgeois parties on the other. Even at that time the Social Democratic party was a clear-cut mass party, which tried to enlist its electorate as party members, which kept careful records of its associations and of its dues-paying members, and which practiced systematic political indoctrination. In the Coalition, Progressive, and Swedish People's parties, features could be located that Duverger considers characteristic of those conservative and liberal groups which he calls cadre parties; their members were passive as well as few in number. Because the vast majority of associations seem to have been active only during elections and as internal communication was weak, only rough estimates are available concerning their membership and their active sections. In 1937 the Coalition party had about four hundred and fifty registered associations, but it is estimated that only one-third of them functioned regularly. These parties tried to achieve with moderate numbers what the Social Democrats sought with large masses. In election activity and in the financing of party work they did not rely on masses, but rather on influential individuals and experts, and the recruiting of members did not have the same meaning for them as it did for the Social Democratic party. Akseli Routavaara notes in his history of the Coalition party that "one can say that it was only after the [Winter and Continuation] wars that the organizational activity of the Coalition party gained momentum in the sense and way that real field work of a political party should take place."[19]

In this scheme the Agrarian party was somewhere between the extremes before the Second World War. Its organizational activity was more developed than that of the other bourgeois groups, but it hardly reached the level of the Social Democrats. Not until 1927 did the party have a full-time secretary, and in 1935 only four district

19. Akseli Routavaara, *Kolme vuosikymmentä Kansallisen kokoomuspuolueen vaiheita* (Helsinki: Kansallisen Kokoomuspuolueen Keskusliitto, 1949), p. 57.

organizations had full-time secretaries. Party membership (36,953) is mentioned for the first time in the 1938 party yearbook. Of interest is the fact that in 1939 the Social Democratic party had 32,897 members and the Coalition party about 11,400.

Immediately after the Second World War, the organizational activity of parties developed by leaps and bounds with a speed theretofore unknown. Within a few years party membership figures increased many times over compared with the prewar period, and by the early 1950's membership of many parties had grown almost to their present strength. Only the irretrievably doomed Progressive party was unaffected by this process.

Today all parties have a registered membership core which fluctuates in size. Use of published membership statistics, however, is complicated by the fact that they cannot be considered wholly reliable or appropriate for comparative purposes. The parties may follow different standards for determining who should be considered a member for a given period of time, and it is likely that the statistical process involves many estimates and the rounding off of numbers. It is necessary to fall back on estimates because it is difficult for central bureaus to gather membership notices for all basic units within the prescribed period of time. There is no rush to delete from membership lists those who change parties, those who change residences, and those who fail to pay membership fees. Actual membership figures are also lower than official claims because the same individual may belong to many organizations simultaneously and thus be counted numerous times. An example would be the Satakunta district organization of the National Coalition party, whose "book membership" in 1950 was 9,354 but whose actual membership was only 6,765.[20] These reservations must be kept in mind in perusal of Table 11, which gives membership figures in 1965 for parties represented in Parliament; the figures include individuals belonging to actual party organizations and to women's organizations and some members of youth groups. For many parties one can only make a rough estimate; figures are rounded off in thousands.[21]

Organization of the electorate for party work has been most extensive in the small Rural party. Of the larger parties, the Center party leads, with almost every second voter also a party member;

20. Rantala, *Konservatiivinen*, pp. 8–9.

21. Information concerning party membership is based on party reports or statements made by the central bureaus.

Table 11. Party membership in 1965, votes received in 1966, and party membership as a percentage of votes received

Party	Members (1965)	Votes (1966)	Members as percent of supporters
SKDL	154,000	502,635	31
Social Democratic League	12,000	61,274	20
Social Democratic party	105,000	645,339	16
Rural party	20,000	24,351	82
Center party	283,000	503,047	56
Liberal People's party	10,000	153,259	7
Swedish People's party	50,000	141,688	35
National Coalition party	83,000	326,928	25
	717,000	2,358,521	30

Source: Based on information provided by the parties.

this party's greatest organizational advances appear to have been made since early in the 1950's. The next highest organizational percentages are found in the Swedish People's party and the SKDL, whereas the new Liberal People's party has remained far behind. Internal conflicts among Social Democrats have been the most visible cause of both an absolute and a relative decline in membership. As has been noted, a totally new period in the development of the Coalition party's membership began after the Second World War, when continued politicization of social life and the expansion of parties caused a change in attitudes previously held by the party and its supporters. Approximate membership for the SKDL is divided among various organizations; there are about 70,000 members in the League's own basic units and about 55,000 in the Communist party. Of the members in the SKDL basic units, 10–15 percent also belong to the Communist party.

Party members differ from party supporters in that they are more interested in politics and have more information about their party; they are tied more closely and more permanently to it and they are more active as opinion leaders, election workers, and voters than the electorate remaining outside the organization. Nevertheless, a substantial number of party members remain passive, and because the number of interested members fluctuates it is not possible to determine directly from membership figures the scope and liveliness of organizational activity. Rantala notes: "Only part of the membership attends party functions; some handle practical matters, but the majority of members are satisfied to record their names on membership lists, to pay dues, to follow in the press the activities of their party, and to vote in elections." In this respect he distinguishes between three types of membership in the Coalition party's Satakunta district organization: the passive majority, members who attend party functions (comprising about one-fifth of the collective body), and a much smaller group responsible for practical matters. According to another investigation, carried out in Pohjois-Häme, only one-third of the members indicated an effort to carry on indoctrination work in their neighborhoods; approximately the same number had not even talked about party affairs with outsiders.[22] According to research done in Tampere in 1958, participation in campaign work depended essentially on the degree of party identification; even in this case, however, an average of only one-third of the members of parties tried to advance their opinions in their neighborhoods—and, on the other hand, only one-third of the total number of "active campaigners" in question were party members.[23]

The Communist party is of unique type in Finland, a totalitarian party attempting at the ideological level to give its members a complete "world explanation" and at the practical level to entrust them with many tasks and duties and thus bind them closely to party work. But SKP leadership is also worried about the inclination of its members to remain passive.

It is perhaps easiest to activate members otherwise in a party like the Center party: its members have clear motives and common concrete objectives, its programmatic efforts are closely connected with the daily problems of its supporters, and within it the feeling of solidarity and unanimity is great when compared with the rest of society. In this respect the position of the Coalition and People's parties, for example, is quite different. Postwar development has, it is true, increased the political activity of the middle class and has caused it to understand more clearly than before the significance of

22. Rantala, *Konservatiivinen*, pp. 101–106; Rantala, *Konservatismi*, pp. 150–167. See also Erik Allardt and Pertti Pesonen, "Citizen Participation in Political Life in Finland," *International Social Science Journal*, 12, no. 1 (1960), 10–13.

23. Pesonen, *An Election in Finland*, pp. 175–176.

collective action in defense of its own social position and economic advantages. But many in the middle class still show no interest in, and even an antipathy toward, party work; they are not so eager as farmers and workers to reveal their party preference through membership. In terms of social structure the membership of the Coalition and People's parties is rather heterogeneous; and, though nonmaterial factors obviously are important as a bond uniting the members, that incentive is not obviously present which activates the masses in interest parties pursuing clearly defined material goals. Distressing in terms of party recruitment is the fact that it is difficult to identify supporters because they are spread out among society's groups. One generally does not seek party membership; rather, one accepts an invitation to become a member. Thus these parties must overcome special difficulties even if they should try in some other way to expand their membership activity and to make it more effective.

It would be interesting to examine the social structure of parties' membership and to make comparisons with the structure of the parties' supporters, but unfortunately there is insufficient information for such a study. In the 1950's stratification of the membership of the Coalition party's district organizations in Satakunta and Pohjois-Häme was as follows:

	Satakunta 1950	Pohjois-Häme 1957
Farmers	33.2 percent	22 percent
Middle class	14.6	43
Workers	6.4	5
Leading white-collar	24.0	23
Unclassified	21.8	7
	100.0 percent	100 percent
	(6,485)	(300)

The basis of classification for Satakunta was the entire membership of the district organization, for Pohjois-Häme only a sample of the total membership. One can, in any case, see that the Coalition party's membership differs considerably in social structure from its electorate. The most striking feature is the obvious under-representation of workers in the party organization. Certain social inhibitions probably make it more difficult for workers who support the Coalition party to join it as members.[24]

On the extreme left, the different nature and goals of the SKDL and the SKP are also reflected in membership structure. Of the SKDL's own members in 1960, 74.3 percent were workers, 19.1 percent small farmers, and 6.6 percent small employers and white-collar workers. Of the Communist party members in 1957, 86.0 percent were workers and only 3.4 percent white-collar workers.[25]

PARTY ORGANIZATION

Organization Types. For the most part, postwar development has erased from Finnish political life the old division between cadre and mass parties. The more significant groupings want to be mass parties, and so they are all organized with the same pyramid shape that can be examined either from the bottom or top. At the bottom are the basic units, or local associations, formed by the rank and file and functioning more or less actively; at the top are the party congress, the executive organs, and a central bureau with many salaried employees. Parallel with the actual party organizations are the women's and youth organizations, as well as certain special organizations and front organizations.

Occupying a special position is the SKDL, that unique organizational structure designed as a broad political body for cooperation and having its own organization to which the Finnish Communist party—with *its* own organization, rules, and program—is attached. The League's other member units are the Democratic League of Finnish Women and the Socialist League of Students. When the SKDL was founded, in 1944, the aim was to create a national organ of cooperation, composed of political organizations seeking common goals, without an independent local organization. When cooperation was not realized in practice the League began to build its own organizational network; the hundred or so workers' associations which had withdrawn from the Social Democratic party in 1944–1948 were available for membership in the SKDL. In these years, during the first phase of activity, the cooperative nature of the

24. Rantala, *Konservatiivinen*, p. 48; Rantala, *Konservatismi*, pp. 40–41.

25. *SKDL:n toimintakertomus VI ja VII liittokokouksen väliseltä ajalta* (Tampere, 1964), p. 29; *Suomen kommunistisen puolueen XI edustajakokous, Helsinki 29.5.–2.6.1957* (Kotka: Etelä-Suomen Kirjapaino, 1957), pp. 63, 370.

organization was most evident; during the setbacks of the late 1940's, however, those with the weakest ties to the League dropped away and it became more clearly an organization for radical left workers and small farmers.[26] The Communist party turned out to be the only party desirous of cooperation, and so the SKDL itself began to resemble a unified party grouping.

As an organization the SKDL is not, of course, identical to the SKP; as mentioned above, each has its own organizational network and separate membership. By nature, too, they differ: the SKP is a revolutionary class party striving for Socialism; the SKDL is presented to both its supporters and opponents as an organization with the goal of unifying people with different world outlooks in order to better the means of livelihood for the nation's poorer people, to defend democracy, and to secure peace. The SKDL is a rather open organization directed toward mass action, whereas the SKP is a closed group drawing together for effective action the most active of the radical workers. Overlapping is evident from the composition of the leadership and from what seems to be complete unity of action in communal as well as national politics. Candidates for election to Parliament are not divided into Communist and non-Communist People's Democrats, although in actual fact the SKDL parliamentary group is composed mostly of Communists.[27] At the SKP congress in 1957 it was stated that the leading organs of the SKDL district organizations were "too much under the control of Communists" and that research had revealed that about 30 percent of a sample of executive board members of the SKDL associations belonged to the Communist party.[28] Communists constitute the most active group in the extreme left, so their influence is also great within the SKDL's own organizations. The Communist party appears to be able to use the association effectively for its own purposes, and the strength of the SKDL in parliamentary activity is of course a welcome addition.

26. See Yrjö Enne, *SKDL:n asema, luonne ja tehtävä. Suomen kansan demokraattisen liiton VI liittokokouksen (H: gissä 31.3–3.4.1961) alustukset, maatalous- ja kalastusohjelmat, julkilausumat* (Tampere: SKDL, 1961), pp. 26–27, 38–41.

27. Of the 49 People's Democrats elected to Parliament in 1945, 41 belonged to the Communist party; in 1948 the figure was 33 of 38 (*Katsaus Suomen kommunistisen puolueen toimintaan VII ja VIII puoluekokouksen välisenä aikana* [Helsinki, 1948], p. 13). In the present Parliament (1966–1970) there are only 3 People's Democrats who do not belong to the Communist party.

28. *Suomen kommunistisen puolueen XI edustajakokous*, p. 245. In 1948 it was said that the SKP formed "the skeleton of the People's Democratic movement in our country"; *Katsaus*, p. 13.

In his central committee report to the party congress of 1957, secretary-general Ville Pessi stated:

Recently it has been suggested that perhaps there is no longer any need for both the SKDL and the party . . . But the central committee is of the opinion that the SKDL has an important function as a broad mass organization, and that it has performed, and is performing, valuable work in various fields on behalf of the nation's working population. As far as the party is concerned . . . our country's working class needs the Communist party in order both to complete present tasks and to lead the working masses to Socialism.[29]

The SKDL is, therefore, treated in this book as a party comparable to other parties, even though it has many special features. Even in SKDL circles it is admitted that the League evidences "outward signs of a party."[30]

Basic Units and Communal Organizations. At the base of the party pyramid are basic units with different names; the small parties try to establish at least one for each commune and the large parties one for each precinct or population center. The number of basic units and communal organizations in 1965 follows:

	Basic units	Communal Organizations
SKDL	2,100	300
Social Democratic League	458	47
Social Democratic party	1,357	176
Rural party	1,138	110
Center party	2,796	309
Liberal People's party	300	–
Swedish People's party	97	–
Coalition party	716	–

When comparing these numbers one must take into consideration the factors of imprecision mentioned in connection with membership statistics. The figure for the SKDL does not include the basic units of the League's member organizations.

Local associations are generally formed on a territorial basis, with

29. *Suomen kommunistisen puolueen XI edustajakokous*, p. 67.
30. *SKDL:n VI liittokokouksen alustukset*, pp. 38–39.

a residential pattern; even the Social Democratic parties have professional and factory associations in only a few of the largest cities—attention was directed to founding them only after the Second World War. Communists, however, place great emphasis on activity at the place of work: it is important for them to put sections into operation in factories, in ports, and at labor sites, where daily contact with the membership can easily be achieved and where one can engage in continual propaganda among nonparty members at work. This kind of organization does, however, have certain drawbacks, for example a fear of discrimination and difficulties in maintaining contact with members after work hours; in fact, even the SKP may be leaning toward territorial sections.[31] In the SKDL, in 1964, there were only eighteen professional associations.[32]

Because parties seek great numbers of members and are consequently open, it is easy to become a member; attendance at an association meeting or approval by an executive board is usually all that is required. New members are naturally expected to approve of the party's general principles and efforts and are not permitted to be members of another party. Greatest flexibility occurs when recruiters issue membership cards prior to formal approval from an executive board, as happened, for example, in the Coalition party.[33] In this respect, too, the Communist party differs from other parties; by nature it is a closed organization, and every individual application is considered according to rules at the city or district level. A comparison of the number of members and basic units also shows that this party's primary organizations are on average the smallest. When necessary they are divided into still smaller units, unregistered party groups.

The general task of basic units is to disperse information and propaganda and carry out educational activities of benefit to the party by organizing meetings as well as lectures, discussions, and entertainment, by distributing literature, and by performing educational work on a personal basis. Elections, which constitute a peak period in activity, involve many additional duties: collection of funds, participation in the nomination of candidates, founding of voters associations, election advertisement, procurement of absentee

31. See *Suomen kommunistisen puolueen XII edustajakokous Helsingissä 15.4.–18.4.1960* (Helsinki, 1960), pp. 65–66. In March 1948 only 169 of 830 primary party organizations (basic units) were at the place of work or on the basis of a trade; *Katsaus*, p. 7.

32. *SKDL:n toimintakertomus*, p. 29.

33. Rantala, *Konservatiivinen*, p. 54.

ballots, and arrangement of transportation. Basic units are understandably in a key position within the organization because the effectiveness of the party's activity depends upon the energy they expend. It is at this level that one has contact with the public and that personal propaganda work is most effective. Within many parties new forms of activity have been developed which prevent rigidity and bureaucratization of an organization and which preserve the energetic qualities of its membership.

Associations have their own rules, which are approved on the basis of a model prepared by the central organization and which are therefore consistent within a given party. The highest power reposes in an association's meeting, at which an executive board or government and usually a chairman are chosen. One peculiarity is that leftwing parties due to internal conflicts have made special arrangements whereby control over basic units can be more easily retained. Three members within the Communist and Social Democratic parties can prevent the resignation by or dissolution of a primary organization or association.

Just above the basic units in the Social Democratic parties, the Center party, and the SKDL, are communal organizations. These are founded in communes where many primary organizations exist and where a common organ is necessitated by communal politics.

The city and territorial (regional) organizations of the Communist party can be considered on a par with the communal organizations of the parties mentioned above. In certain parts of the country the Coalition and Swedish People's parties also use a territorial division, which forms a weak intermediary step in organizational structure.[34]

District Organizations. District organizations are the provincial units of parties. A district organization is based on division of the country into electoral districts: it either encompasses an entire electoral district, or else the latter is divided into a number of district organizations. The Center party has the largest number of district organizations, a total of 22. In 1965 the People's Democrats had 17, the Social Democratic party and the Coalition party 16, and the Social Democratic League, the Rural party, and the Liberal People's party 14 each. The Swedish People's party has established a district organization in only four electoral districts. The purpose of

34. *Ibid.*, pp. 68–70; see also *Svenska folkpartiet inför partidagen 1962* (Helsingfors, 1962), pp. 21–42.

district organizations is to bring together the basic units operating in their areas and to act as a link between the party's central leadership and the basic units. They direct and support in various ways the activity of local associations. They, too, organize meetings, educational and ceremonial occasions, discussion days, and organizational courses, and they handle publications. They gather money for the party's treasury through collections, raffles, business activities, and other means, and they maintain relations with the party press. It is an important task of a district organization to direct preparations by the party for parliamentary and presidential elections in its area.

The greatest power is exercised by the district meeting, which takes place once or twice a year, in accordance with party rules, and to which the primary organizations and the communal organizations send a certain number of representatives; it appears that the most common arrangement is to permit each basic unit to send one representative for every 50 members. The ruling body of the district organization is the district executive committee, which is elected at the yearly meeting and which usually consists of 10–20 members. District organizations maintain offices where work is directed by paid district secretaries or directors.

Central Leadership. Above the districts are the various organs of the parties' central leadership. The highest is a party congress—for the Communists a congress of representatives and for the Swedish-speaking Finns a party assembly—which meets every year in accordance with regulations by the Swedish People's party and every other year by the Center, Liberal People's, and Coalition parties, but only every third year by the Social Democrats and the People's Democrats. Representatives to a party congress are elected by district or primary organizations either at meetings of the organizations or by a membership vote similar in procedure to that followed for district meetings. Membership voting is characteristic of parties of the left. Also present at a congress are members of smaller decision-making and administrative organs, the highest party functionaries, the parliamentary group, and representatives of the party press and special organizations. Insofar as the SKDL is concerned, it should be noted that the League's own district organizations send one representative to the League congress for every 300 members, whereas district organizations of the SKP and other member units must have 1,200 members for each representative. A party congress resolves important questions of principle and determines the main lines of action; its task is, among other things, to appraise on the basis of reports the prevailing economic and political situation and the state of the party. It also determines what specific measures are needed, approves changes in the party's program and rules, determines economic guidelines for the party, examines fiscal and action reports, handles proposals from lower party organizations, and elects members of a more restricted body that wields power between party congresses.

This restricted body, which meets several times a year, is for the SKDL a League council (at most 60 members), for the Communist party a central committee (35 full members), for the Social Democratic party a party council (about 50 members), for the TPSL a League council (about 60), for the Center party a party commission (about 100), for the Liberal People's party a party council (66), for the Swedish People's party an expanded central board (68), and for the Coalition party a council (60). The rules of the Center party and the Social Democratic parties state that in electing members to the council or commission seats must be divided among districts on the basis of membership figures, whereas in the Coalition party this division is carried out on the basis of the number of votes received in the last parliamentary election. The latter method is perhaps a heritage of the 1920's and 1930's, when, due to organizational backwardness, it was the only feasible method; in any case, it seems characteristic of a conservative grouping which has originated from a cadre-type party.

Even these organs, which are composed for the most part of members representing district organizations, are too large to be convened more than two or three times a year. Executive tasks and decision-making related to even the most important political questions are thus entrusted to a still smaller group: a party executive committee (the Social Democratic party), a league executive committee (SKDL and TPSL), a central board (the Center party and the Swedish People's party), or a board (the Coalition and Liberal People's parties). To take care of daily problems the smaller group may also elect from its members a working committee. In the Communist party even these tasks are handled by the central committee, whose flexibility and consistency in managing daily problems are overseen by an economic auditing committee. Within the SKP a 9 to 15-member inspection committee acts as a special party tribunal.

Every party has its central bureau in the capital, where, led by the party secretary, work is done by a number of employees like the organizational, information, research, and parliamentary secretaries, as well as bookkeepers.

At different levels, and especially at the top, a number of permanent or temporary secondary or staff organs not mentioned in party rules are joined to the line organization: committees, executive committees, commissions, and discussion committees. Some are merely administrative organs or research and investigatory groups in special areas; others, for example, the agricultural and middle-class committees, represent an interest organization which has gained favor in the postwar period. In question is either a spontaneous organization of occupational and social groups within the party or an activity organized by the leadership with an eye on population groups for whose support the party is competing.[35] Particularly in the action organization of the Communist party, a central role is played by specialized sections and bodies.

Structural Differences. Organizational development in the postwar period, which in a way can be compared with the crucial period of 1905–1908, has greatly narrowed the gap between mass and cadre parties that was still apparent in the 1930's. In the 1930's the former type was represented by the Social Democratic party, the latter by the small bourgeois groups, with the Agrarian party occupying a position somewhere between the two. The rapprochement seems to have been reciprocal: on one hand, the Agrarian-Center party has become a very large and stable organization and, in addition, the Coalition and Swedish People's parties have also become more closely knit and broader bodies resembling a mass party; on the other hand, the Social Democratic party has become more of an election and less of a political indoctrination organization when compared with what it was thirty years ago.

Earlier structural and action differences have not, however, totally disappeared. In general one can say that the left is characterized first by a more centralized party administration, and second by an emphasis on democratic practice. The right is characterized first by territorial, ideological, and social decentralization, and second by the passivity of its members and a delegation of authority

35. See Rantala, *Konservatiivinen*, pp. 64–67.

at various levels. For example, district organizations of the Coalition and People's parties act quite independently of the central leadership. The latter generally cannot give them binding orders; it can only make proposals and recommendations. The Social Democratic party has long sought to achieve far-reaching organizational democracy. The democratic nature of its internal procedures reaches a peak in the party referendum, which the executive committee can initiate in party organizations when a specific question arises. A referendum must be carried out if requested by three district organizations. A referendum was at one time decisive—it could change or overturn a decision of even a party congress—but today it is merely advisory in nature. The rules of the Social Democratic League also contain passages about a party referendum. A different matter is the fact that oligarchy, which is generally characteristic of party activity, and bureaucracy, which is especially characteristic of the activity of mass parties, prevent organizational democracy from functioning as planned.

Different views always exist within parties, and this may lead to the formation of groups, which can result in serious disagreements over the path to be followed. In all parties from the extreme left to the right there is occasional competition between different groupings, as for example between a right and a more leftist direction, and between social classes and geographic areas. The forms taken by this internal group activity are dependent upon social structure of the membership and the type of organization. In reference to the characteristics mentioned above, parties can be classified in terms of two main types. The largest are relatively homogeneous in social structure but inflexible and centralized in organization; the smaller parties are heterogeneous, loose, and decentralized. The Swedish People's party is the clearest manifestation of the second type. In terms of social structure it is the most diffuse grouping imaginable, within which there has been, since the founding of the party, a more or less sharp struggle between the upper and lower classes, the right and the left, as well as between the capital and other Swedish-speaking parts of the country. Every now and then groups are organized within the party either to further the special interests of some population group or to defend positions at variance with the party's general line. But the party is so loose organizationally that there is no demand for a united, firm line—except on certain fundamental questions. It is therefore possible for groups to compete without fear of radical countermeasures. Occasionally, for example in connection with the 1919–1920 Aaland Islands question and again in 1923 when an opposition supported by industry and the business world appeared, internal conflicts have become very serious, but unity has nonetheless prevailed.[36] As an example of ideological decentralization in the party, the 1914 social program evoked so much discontent among party members that it was decided at the 1917 party congress that the program should be abandoned and the matter of social reform left to individual members and blocs operating within the party.[37] Disagreements within inflexible and centralized parties, whose supporters have well-defined concrete goals and are more united, may, on the other hand, turn into bitter struggle if the group which has emerged as a majority demands that the minority adhere and adapt to the general line. The continued growth of oligarchy in party life serves to make these internal discussions even more passionate. Under these circumstances it is no longer solely a question of disagreement over an action program or methods; rather, an outright power struggle between leaders and leadership groups assumes great significance.

The Social Democratic party has, in particular, suffered from internal conflicts and splits. After the Civil War it had to adopt a position with respect to Communism, and in the 1920's the "center" group was critical of the policies followed by the party leadership.[38] The party had barely recovered from the crisis following the Second World War when an open power struggle began in the mid-1950's (between the "Leskinens" and the "Skogs") and resulted in the formation in 1959 of the TPSL. There have also been disagreements within the Agrarian-Center party, although they have not been so intense as in the Social Democratic party. Now and then there have been small groups of farmers who have split off from the party and who have tried to compete with the mother party at election time. The last case was in 1959 when the Farmers' party was formed. In the 1958 election an opposition group had appeared in northern Finland outside of the Agrarian party and with its own candidates, receiving a total of some five thousand votes in the provinces of Oulu and Lapland.

36. See Rafael Colliander, *Svenska folkpartiet i Finland 1906–1926* (Helsingfors, 1926), pp. 66–67, 77–81.

37. *Ibid.*, p. 156.

38. See Juhani Paasivirta, *Suomen poliittisen työväenliikkeen kehitys* (Porvoo, 1949), pp. 65–69.

The Communist party, with its organizational slogan "democratic centralism," is radically different from other parties. United in a special type of organization and under oligarchic direction, the party is a disciplined body led from above and capable of both effective mass agitation and illegal underground activity—having had a quarter-century of experience with the latter. Paragraph 10 of the party rules states: "Democratic centralism is the organizational principle. It means that extensive democracy is secured for party members as part of their inalienable rights, and that the centralization required for the unification, direction, and specialization of party work is carried forward within the framework of party democracy." Democratic centralism seeks first of all to ensure that in the making of decisions the leadership is familiar with the positions and opinions prevailing among the party's membership; secondly, it seeks to ensure faithful adherence to decisions which have been made. The system presupposes that free discussion—in the spirit of the principles of Marxism-Leninism—precedes a decision, but that everyone then submits to the decision. Opposition groups and opinions at variance with the accepted line are not permitted. "For the Communist party, whose task is the realization of gigantic social reform, centralized leadership is a necessity. It is one of the decisive ways in which the forces of the party and its allies can be directed in a single direction in order to achieve the party's most important objectives."[39] Nevertheless, open disputes have affected the activity of this party, too, in the second half of the 1960's.

Special Organizations. Special organizations, by nature more or less political, working on the fringes of party organization and formed either on the initiative of the party leadership or as a result of efforts by member groups to become more independent, are characteristic of modern party life which seeks some sort of "totality." After the Second World War, there was a noticeable increase in activity by women and youth. An attempt has been made to ensure a continued growth in membership by starting political education at an early age; an attempt has also been made to draw women, politically more passive than men, into party activity. All stable parliamentary parties have parallel organizations; it is, however, difficult to say which motive has exerted the greatest influence in the setting up of

39. Erkki Kauppila, "Demokraattinen sentralismi puolueemme johtavana järjestöperiaatteena," *Kommunisti*, 13, no. 9–10 (May, 1957), 315.

special organizations—an attempt to make political activity more effective, or the fact that women and young people want their own organizations in which they can work as they please. The women's organizations are the Democratic League of Finnish Women (SKDL), the Social Democratic Central League of Women (the Social Democratic party), the Social Democratic Women's League of Finland (TPSL), Women of the Center Party, Women of the Liberal People's Party, the Swedish Association of Women, and the League of Coalition Party Women. Corresponding youth organizations are the Democratic Youth League of Finland, the Central League of Social Democratic Youth, the Social Democratic Youth League of Finland, the League of the Young Center, the Liberal Youth League, the Swedish Youth, and the League of Coalition Party Youth. Many parties also have organizations for younger children.

These women's and youth groups have their own separate organizations, with basic units, districts, and so forth. A general practice in communities that do not have independent associations is for women and young people to found unregistered clubs or sections that act in conjunction with primary party organizations. Since there are also many women and youth members in party organizations and, likewise, adults in youth organizations, the membership figures for these separate organizations do not indicate the total size within the party of the groups in question, and the figures are probably not entirely appropriate for cross-party comparisons. It can be said, though, that the youth activity of the Center party is the most developed: in 1965 there were about seventy-five thousand members in the League of the Young Center.

Front organizations form their own groups within the separate organizations; they are ostensibly for nonpolitical activity, although in practice sports, temperance, cultural, trade, and other associations are founded to serve party goals. These sorts of organizations established on party initiative are found more often among leftist than bourgeois parties; a partial explanation is that the large nonparty citizen organizations have been more or less "bourgeois in spirit," or at least they have been considered as such.

Mention should also be made of the Swedish Workers' League of Finland, within the Social Democratic party, and the Christian Democratic Group, within the Swedish People's party, which are more closely affiliated with party organizations.[40]

40. See Rantala, *Konservatiivinen*, pp. 70–75.

Features of Party Activity. Only selected features of present-day multifaceted party activity directed at many levels can, of course, be covered in this section. Party leaders realize that it is not enough to expand their organization, recruit members, and found sections; the established machinery must be capable of utilization in party work. In a report of the Coalition party, following a statement concerning progress in organizational work, it is noted: "The danger exists, however, that our party organization is merely becoming more technical and that it neglects its role of political educator and opinion-maker in those areas of most concern to our political opponents. In organizational activity one must move forward to a new stage, to political activeness, which presupposes further growth and refinement in political education."[41] One of the most obvious efforts of modern parties is to avoid "technicalization" or bureaucratization—an effort to increase party consciousness and activity by members as well as to establish contact, through organizational work, with the party's voters and the electorate's undecided intermediary groups. It has, therefore, been necessary to move away from those rigid, regular organizational meetings so characteristic of stable mass parties where communications from higher authorities are read and answers prepared, lectures heard and reports delivered. In their stead are more free-wheeling gatherings, where timely political questions are discussed and pleasant evenings are spent with friends. In fact, "house get-togethers" have become a central form of activity in the countryside for Center party and SKDL associations; the activity of the Social Democratic party also points in this direction.[42] It can be said that on the right, basic unit meetings greatly resemble old-fashioned gatherings of neighbors and acquaintances. Rounding out the forms of basic unit activity are celebrations, trips, competitions, hobby circles, and the like. Various mass gatherings are especially characteristic of the SKDL; in the winter of 1962–1963 the League's organizations arranged a total of 3,692 public occasions at which there are said to have been over 113,000 people.[43]

The passage quoted above from the Coalition party report stresses the significance of political education in party work. More effective training in party institutes or elsewhere, through organized courses

41. *Kansallinen kokoomus, toimintakertomus 1961* (Helsinki: Kansallinen kokoomus, 1962), p. 16.

42. See, for example, *SKDL:n toimintakertomus*, pp. 34–35.

43. *Ibid.*, p. 35.

and study clubs, and through study, lecture, and discussion days is a second special feature of activity by modern parties. It is hoped that this activity will train organizational cadres—key personnel, party functionaries, and election workers—for practical party work and, at the same time, increase party awareness and social knowledge among rank-and-file members. Educational work in the large parties is conducted on a broad front; it extends from functions organized by basic units to nationwide courses and discussions organized by the central leadership.

Traditionally the parties of the left have paid great attention to study group activity. A common study organization, the Education League of the Workers, was founded in 1919; its activity, however, has been complicated by the fact that it is maintained jointly by organizations (Social Democratic and Communist) which represent very different political and social points of view.[44] In 1959 there were over 140 study clubs in the Social Democratic party—of which, in fact, only 70–80 met regularly—and 27 registered study organizations. The SKDL had 175 study club gatherings in 1963–1964 with a total of 1,850 students. In all, the SKDL's activity included 255 courses, clubs, and other forms of study, with a total number of 3,650 students.[45] Actual organizational schooling is perhaps most effective in the Communist party.

The district, communal, and primary organizations of the Center party and its women's organization arranged a total of 1,399 courses and discussion occasions in 1965 with some 28,000 participants. Within the Coalition party 582 educational occasions, attended by 10,281 party members, were organized at the communal and area level in 1961.[46]

Parties engage in extensive informational and publication activity, including preparation of member reports, pamphlets and flyers for elections, programmatic literature, newspaper and journal articles, and movies. The daily press will be examined in chapter IV. An effort is also made through information and propaganda activity, which is assuming proportions of mass communication, to reach every individual separately. For the internal activity of the parties

44. Sven Lindman, *Studie- och diskussionsgruppens roll i partilivet. Partistudier 2* (Åbo, 1957), pp. 74–77.

45. *Pöytäkirja Suomen sosialidemokraattisen puolueen XXV puoluekokouksesta 1960* (Helsinki, 1961), p. 125; *SKDL:n toimintakertomus*, p. 34.

46. *Keskustapuolue 1965* (Helsinki: Kirja-Mono Oy, 1966), pp. 32–33; *Kansallinen kokoomus, toimintakertomus, 1961*, p. 16.

this means that, in addition to the usual exchange of letters carried on by associations, even more material is mailed to individual members; and at election time it means bulk mailing of material to individual voters. Some party journals are merely organization publications designed to unite party members, whereas others, with a focus on ideological questions as well as on daily political events and internal organizational matters, are directed toward wider circles.

The Financing of Activity. Political organizations rarely give much public information about their financial affairs, and it is therefore difficult for an outsider to form impressions on the subject. It is not a question of funds for party work being obtained through illegal means, or through means otherwise considered inappropriate; secrecy probably stems frcm a general sensitivity about revealing sources of income.

All the tightly organized parties now have membership dues, whose share of the budget varies greatly. Membership fees have more than an economic meaning for party activity in that their payment serves as a basis for membership statistics.

Leftwing parties have traditionally attempted to finance their activity through membership dues collected from the masses, and dues are highest in these parties. In the basic unit, part of the collected dues—the total amount is determined by the organization itself—remains with the unit, while the remainder is divided in specified proportions between the communal organization, the district organization, and the central bureau. In 1963 the annual dues paid by members of the labor parties fluctuated between 5–15 marks. In 1960 a Social Democratic party congress established three classes of membership dues, based on personal income. In the most numerous class, the second class, membership dues amount to 40 Finnish pennies a month (100 pennies equal 1 mark; 4.2 marks equal 1 U.S. dollar). In addition, district and communal organizations may also collect membership fees from basic units. In the Social Democratic league, in 1963, annual district and party dues totaled 4 marks 80 pennies for men, 2 marks 40 pennies for women.

Membership fees in the bourgeois parties have been lower, in some cases merely nominal. Most common is a fee of several marks a year; if the fees are higher, they generally include a subscription to a party paper. Membership dues in the Center party are relatively insignificant; the activity of basic units and of district organizations is financed mainly through milk and grain collections, a part of which is kept as a tax by the party. According to the budget for 1963, almost one-fifth of the central organization's estimated expenditures were covered by these taxes. Primary organizations in the Coalition party pay some taxes to district organizations, but the central bureau receives no share of the membership dues. The arrangement in the Liberal People's party is basically the same. Primary organizations of the Swedish People's party pay membership shares to the central board, but this money covers only a small portion of the party's total expenditures.

For the bourgeoisie, therefore, the significance of membership dues in the financing of party work is relatively small. Expenditures of the central bureaus are fully covered (practically speaking) and district expenditures to a great extent through other means: collections, gifts, raffles, celebrations, business activities, support fees, and aid from auxiliary organizations. Only after the Second World War does there seem to have been a shift, especially in the smaller bourgeois parties, to a fairly regular annual taxation of members.

But even on the left other revenues are probably greater than the income from membership fees. For example, dues as a percentage of Social Democratic expenditures has dropped considerably; in 1933 it was 23.5 percent, in 1939 19.9 percent, and in 1951 only 8.4 percent.[47] Fund-raising efforts which are typical of the left include dances and other entertainment organized in party buildings or in rented space, as well as the collection of a service tax from wages earned in communal and other civil service work.

In general, party organizations are in financial difficulty, since for the most part they have to function on the basis of uncertain "temporary income." The need for money is naturally greatest in election years, when efforts to collect funds and solicit gifts are intensified.[48] Like many other organizations, parties have also sought security through state aid. Since 1967, the state budget has included 10,000,000 marks for this purpose. Parties receive 50,000 marks for each member elected to Parliament.

47. Sosialidemokraattinen puoluetoimikunta, *Alustuksia sosialidemokraattisen puolueen puoluekokoukselle 1952* (Tampere, 1952).

48. Fiscal information comes from party bureaus and action reports. See also Rantala, *Konservatiivinen*, pp. 104–105; Tarja Flemming, Marja Nikkari, and Esko Niskanen, *Turun poliittiset yhdistykset*, Turku: Turun yliopiston valtio-opin laitos, eripainossarja, A, no. 1 (1961), 75–77.

Election Organization. Most parties do not consider the organization as described above sufficient for election campaigns, primarily because of its passiveness and sluggishness. On the eve of elections an effort is made to mobilize the most active cadres under centralized leadership and within the framework of special electoral organizations including the support organizations of the Center and Coalition parties and the field organization of the Social Democratic party. The Swedish People's party has adopted something resembling a support organization, whereas the Liberal People's party relies on its primary organizations for campaign work. The same procedure is followed in the People's Democratic League, which, however, has at its disposal the machinery of the Communist party with its trained cadres.

The pillars of electoral organization in the Center and Coalition parties are the parish support leaders, who direct "support men" in areas generally formed by precinct. The support leaders, in turn, receive orders, instructions, and election material from territorial executive committees, district executive committees, and the party's central bureau. Support leaders of the Coalition party are also tied to primary organizations in their commune; the leaders are elected at autumn meetings of these basic units, and they are dependent on instructions from the executive boards at this local level. The field network of the Social Democratic party also includes communal leaders and liaison men placed in precincts of primary and communal organizations, in city sections, and in places of work. In the Swedish People's party, as an election draws near, electoral districts are divided into special electoral areas each of which has a designated representative. Local agents, selected by the basic units, and other field workers operate under their direction.

The task of this special organization is to handle preparatory work and to get supporters to the polls on election day. The most important pre-election duties include the dissemination of propaganda material, personal enlightenment work, the organization of election forums, and close observation of the activity of other parties. The forging of electoral organizations is probably based in part on an understanding —more evident today than ever and confirmed by research—of the overriding importance of personal contact as a vehicle for propaganda. It is relatively easy to set up such a network, although it languishes and has a tendency to fall apart if it has no function after an election. The Swedish People's party sets up an electoral organization separately for each election, whereas the Social Democrats, the Center party, and the Coalition party try to maintain their organizations and keep them active, give them other tasks, and join them to the party's action organization. Courses and discussions are organized for support men or liaison men; they receive various materials in the mail—summaries of political events, memoranda dealing with organizational work, and so on—and they supervise the work of the organizations in their community, trying to keep them active. But difficulties can arise between two organizations which function on a permanent basis side by side; it is said that within the Finnish People's party there has, consequently, been opposition to the formation of a special election network.

Parliamentary Group and Party Organization. A special question related to party organization is the relationship between a party's leadership and its parliamentary group. Examined in terms of principle, a democratic system presupposes that members of Parliament act independently and are free from tutelage because they receive their "credentials" from the electorate, which as a group is much broader than party memberships and on whose mandate the political exercise of power is constitutionally based. In reality, however, the parliamentary group and party organization are joined to each other by many bonds, and members of Parliament represent their party more than the electorate. As party organizations become broader and more tightly knit, the dependence of members of Parliament upon party leadership is greater. Parliamentary elections in Finland are strictly party elections; parties determine the nomination of candidates and carry out the campaign fight, and only those individuals on party lists have any real chance of being elected. Proportional representation with large electoral districts also serves to bring parties forward at the expense of individuals.

In all parties some effort is made to keep parliamentary groups at least formally separate from party organization; party rules contain only meager references to members of Parliament and to the relationship with party organization. A general conclusion is that members of Parliament have no official decision-making position in the leading organs of any party; only in the Center party has a parliamentary group been given the right to name its representatives to the party's commission and board, three to the former, one to the latter. In some other parties, members of Parliament are permitted to attend and speak at meetings of these organs. The subordinate relationship of parliamentary groups is demonstrated by the fact that a group must present its activity report to a party congress or party commission.

In spite of the party supremacy that appears during elections, parliamentary groups do have some freedom of action; in this respect there are fundamental differences between parties. A general conclusion is that a group's dependence on party organization is weakest on the right and that it increases as one moves to the left. When applying this sort of model one must, of course, consider how many of the group's members also belong to the party's leading organs. If, for example, most members of a party executive committee are members of Parliament, flexible cooperation between party leadership and the group can be achieved, and the question about their relation is redundant; at the other extreme, differences of opinion—even a power struggle—may occur, at which time the features characteristic of each party are best perceived.

The most independent parliamentary groups are those of the Coalition party and both People's parties; they have long emphasized their independence from party organization. This situation has its roots in the prewar period, when organizational activity by these three parties was relatively primitive and when participation in elections and in parliamentary work was the raison d'être for parties. These groups are relatively independent in their determination of policies to be followed in Parliament, negotiating with the party leadership on the most important questions.[49] On matters of Cabinet participation and withdrawal of support, the final power of decision in the Coalition and Swedish People's parties rests with the parliamentary groups, although the opinion of the party boards may weigh heavily as a decision is reached. The Liberal People's party has made a decision stipulating that the parliamentary group and the party board shall resolve jointly the question of Cabinet responsibility.

In the Center party an attempt has been made to achieve both a division of labor and flexible cooperation in the relationship between the parliamentary group and the party, on one hand by granting a certain "autonomous" position to the group in its own sphere of

49. The following provision was included in paragraph 14 of the 1959 rules of the National Coalition party: "joint meetings between the parliamentary group and the party leadership must be organized when discussing Cabinet participation or other political questions of great importance, as well as on the initiative of either in a given matter"; *Kansallinen Kokoomus r.y:n säännöt* (Helsinki: Kansallinen Kokoomus, 1959), p. 15.

activity and, on the other hand, by making it possible for the party leadership to influence decisions. The party commission and the parliamentary group together resolve the question of participation, and a party member who enters a Cabinet without permission places himself outside the party. The parliamentary group of the Social Democratic party has traditionally been more closely attached to party organization than is true for the bourgeois groups. Characteristic of the socialist mass parties is a certain distrust by the active membership toward members of Parliament, whom they fear will, as professional politicians, undergo an *embourgeoisement* and become corrupted; the activists therefore attempt to supervise the activity and preserve the dependent status of members of Parliament. The position of the parliamentary group seems, however, to have become stronger insofar as the Social Democratic party has divorced itself from the theory of class struggle, approached the other parties in terms of parliamentary cooperation, and become one of the leading government parties. The dependent status is also weakened by the fact that many leading individuals in the party are also members of Parliament; the party is therefore led in both organizational and parliamentary work by the same "inner circle," and serious conflicts do not arise. The party executive committee and the parliamentary group resolve the question of Cabinet participation; in the last analysis, the power of decision rests with the party council. The parliamentary group has complained of neglect in negotiations, although as it has gained in general strength it has made advances in that line, too.

In spite of striking differences, all of the aforementioned parties seek a certain balance and division of labor in the relation between party leadership and the parliamentary group. Party leadership takes charge of organizational work, whereas the parliamentary group oversees parliamentary activity. In no party do members of Parliament, by virtue of their position, have unconditional control over party machinery and party activity, but in no party have they been relegated to a position of complete submission; they have, rather, been granted a certain self-determination, which they doggedly defend. Quite different is the situation on the extreme left, where the SKDL parliamentary group works closely with the leadership of the League and the Communist party. This group is not a separate, independent unit of action but, rather, one part of the party organization. The vast majority of members of Parliament who are People's Democrats are members of the Communist party, for whom party discipline also exists in Parliament. It is, therefore, natural that group cohesion in parliamentary votes is greatest in the SKDL parliamentary group.

Party Leaders. Characteristic of Finnish political life is the absence of recognized and dominant party leaders. It is true that the Social Democrats have had Väinö Tanner and the Agrarian party Santeri Alkio and Urho Kekkonen, but these are exceptions. All parties have leading personalities who form, with the party oligarchy, a collective summit, but it is rare that one of them becomes an undisputed party leader such as occurs in the other Nordic countries. This holds true for the center as well as for both extreme groups; it is reflected in the fact that during a Cabinet crisis one party may have many candidates of almost equal standing for prime minister. Chairmanship of the parliamentary group or of the party's ruling organ does not indicate a position of real leadership in the party. It is difficult to provide a satisfactory explanation for this phenomenon, which can be traced back to different historical-political factors. One point to be considered is the fact that the tasks of party chairmen and parliamentary group chairmen in Finland are generally entrusted to different individuals, whereas in Sweden, for example, both are in the hands of one person.

GOALS AND METHODS

At this point it might be wise to clarify briefly the nature of the parties, as well as their ideological and practical goals; this must, of course, be done roughly and on the basis of programmatic statements. In Finland it is considered an absolute necessity for each party to have its own ideology, appearing in a program of principles. As mentioned in a program statement of the Social Democratic party, the purpose of a program of principles is "to reveal the nature of the party, its goals and methods, as well as to bring forward at the same time those nonmaterial values on which they are based."[50] As a further refinement, and with an eye on practical politics, special short-range or long-range programs are prepared for various areas.

50. *SDP, periaateohjelma, Frankfurtin ja Oslon julistukset* (Helsinki: Paasipaino, 1963), pp. 3–4.

The importance of ideologies and programs should, however, not be overestimated: in today's political struggles they appear to be taking more and more of a back seat. They do not always reveal the real goals of parties, nor do they reveal the whole truth. Analysis of the arrangement and length of different parts of a program, the use of words, and other such factors can indeed shed light on the special nature of parties, but when seeking a realistic and detailed explanation of goals and methods it is perhaps more fruitful to examine the parliamentary and Cabinet activity of parties as well as the statements and actions of party leaders and party organs on certain concrete questions.

SKP and SKDL. On the extreme left, the SKDL represents a contemporary "popular front tactic," whereas the Communist party represents the Marxist tradition of class struggle. The SKDL has tried hard to emphasize its character as a mass organization and its separateness from the Communist party, and it has shaped its program accordingly. Major focus in the SKP program is on long-range goals, and the study, application, and development of Marxist-Leninist ideas is considered the central task of party activity. SKDL activity, by way of contrast, is directed along more practical lines in the sense of establishing and achieving immediate goals.

In 1957 the Communist party approved its first uniform program, built around old principles and containing earlier programmatic statements which have been reworked. The SKP stresses that it is the party of the working class and the heir of its half-century tradition of class struggle; it is, therefore, the only party which openly concedes its class nature. In terms of doctrinal structure, there is an international Communist "class ideology of the proletariat," and the party "considers scientific socialism, adapted and developed in accordance with Finnish conditions, as its guide to principled action."[51] Its activity is based on the notion that the state is always an instrument of the ruling class used to oppress groups in a subordinate position. Characteristic of the capitalist state is a constant, relentless class struggle and a dictatorship of the bourgeoisie. The development of capitalism in Finland has led quickly to a strong concentration of capital in the hands of a few large companies and their ruling capitalist circles—in great part, the renowned "twenty families."

51. Olavi Borg, *Suomen puolueet ja puolueohjelmat 1880–1964* (Porvoo: WSOY, 1965), p. 332.

On the other hand, an economic squeeze, uncertainty about being able to make ends meet, and a feeling of insecurity are spreading among even broader segments of the population. The antithesis of interests between society's basic classes makes it impossible to transform the present system by degrees into a socialist system. Social revolution "has become in Finland, too, a historical necessity." The transitional state is a dictatorship of the proletariat. The most important reforms in this phase of development are the nationalization of enterprises controlled by large companies, a thorough land reform, the realization of a planned economy, the promotion of cooperatives in the fields of industry as well as agriculture, and a determination through legislation of the position of trade union organizations. When society is internally harmonious, when there are no longer exploiters or exploited—only one party, the Communist party, will remain; parties are by nature instruments of social struggle between classes. A socialist system, on the other hand, opens the road "to a gradual transition to a Communist society, which will realize the principle: from each according to his ability, to each according to his needs."

Hertta Kuusinen notes in one of her writings: "The Communist party will never attempt a revolution or seizure of power by a minority. That social change, or revolution, which Communists consider their goal presupposes support from an absolute majority of the population."[52] But Communists have their own understanding as to how "the will of an absolute majority of the population" is to be achieved; it does not occur solely within the framework of parliamentary activity as provided in the Finnish constitution: "We do not agree with those who explain that a democratic path is exactly the same as a parliamentary path . . . A democratic course is not limited to parliamentary elections and to discussions and votes taking place within the walls of Parliament's chamber. Democracy must not exclude special activity by the workers, activity by trade union and other mass organizations." This interpretation was advanced by Matti Janhunen in his presentation of the new program to the 1957 party congress.[53] During a discussion in the mid-1960's concerning goals and tactics of the radical left movement, the central committee of the Communist party issued a statement, based on a

52. *Kipinästä tuli syttyi. Muistiinpanoja Suomen kommunistisen puolueen 40-vuotistaipaleelta*, 3rd ed. (Helsinki: Yhteistyö, 1958), p. 223.

53. *Suomen kommunistisen puolueen XI edustajakokous*, pp. 81–82.

Marxist theory of the state, in which emphasis was put on the significance of freedoms and rights in even a bourgeois state, on the influence of national peculiarities in shaping a socialist system, and on the party's desire to achieve revolution through peaceful means. However, "only after a thorough scientific investigation can it be determined in more detail what the conditions are in Finland for a peaceful transition."[54]

Membership in the SKDL is said to be open to every party, organization, and individual accepting the program of principles ratified by the League. Because of this, the 1949 program was loosely constructed and included only "short-range"—to be sure, very radical—demands and aims. The program did not, in fact, demand approval of socialism, or recognition of a socialist world outllook, as conditions for membership. Elsewhere, however, it was clear that the League was similar to the Communist party in point of departure: the conflict between the class that possesses and the class that does not, characteristic of bourgeois society, was seen as extending its influence to all areas of social life, and the state was viewed as "a violent machine in the hands of the ruling class to discipline the subordinate classes."[55] In effect, conclusions derived from practical situations were also alike.

In 1967 a new program was drafted for the League,[56] in which a more liberal note is struck in the observation that contemporary society requires greater tolerance and more intellectual freedom. In SKDL circles it is felt that relatively extensive political democracy has been firmly established in Finland and that its achievements must be held in high esteem. At the same time, however, society must be seen as a whole; political democracy in many respects is merely formal so long as democracy does not extend to other areas, above all to economic, social, and cultural life. It is, moreover, economic life which forms the basis of social policy. An extension of democracy in this area means the adoption of socialist solutions, "which means a gradual transition to a socialist system." The primary means to achieve this goal are: planning and direction of the entire national economy; nationalization of production and commercial enterprises,

54. *Marxilaisesta valtioteoriasta ja Suomen tiestä sosialismiin* (Kuopio: Kustannusosakeyhtiö Savon Sana, 1965).

55. Taisto Johteinen, *Kuntalaisten parhaaksi. Kansandemokraattisen kunnallispolitiikan perusteita*, 2nd ed. (Tampere: SKDL, 1960), pp. 5–6.

56. *Suomen Kansan Demokraattinen Liitto, Periaateohjelma* (Tampere: Kirjapaino Sanan Tie, 1967).

insofar as this is appropriate in terms of the economy and social justice; the setting up of new industries run by the state; participation by workers in the decision-making process at the enterprise level; and the realization of extensive tax reforms. The position of the agricultural population should be improved by enlarging the size of holdings, preventing land from becoming the object of speculation, and fostering cooperative activity among farmers.

The social demands in the program do not differ fundamentally from the usual leftist pattern. But in the cultural section there is reference—which at the same time mentions the significant intellectual freedom of recent years—to "bourgeois consciousness supported by the right," which retards the emergence of a leftist climate favorable to reform. This ideological power of the right must be restricted in schools, church, the army, and mass media as well as science and the arts. "Since our goal is the construction of a more democratic society, it is evident that all changes must be realized democratically."

During the 1960's there has been an important change in both the internal life and external position of the radical leftist movement. Within the movement, among both Communists and People's Democrats, there has been a decided liberalization in ideology and practical activity that is in part a reflection of the natural change in leadership generations. In this process, the new leaders of the SKDL have stressed its democratic nature and its position as a mass organization of the left separate from the SKP. After becoming an opposition force in 1948, the Communists naturally turned to sharp criticism of policy decisions and bourgeois society as their major task. The above liberalization, coupled with external events in parliamentary life, removed obstacles in the 1960's to renewed cooperation among the leftist groups; the formation in 1966 of a Cabinet which included Communists, Social Democrats, and Center party representatives changed, at least temporarily, the position of the movement. The transformation was from a radical force in opposition to society, only partially responsible for policy, to a force seeking reforms sometimes of a radical nature.

In this process of development, the internal cohesion of the movement has broken down. The People's Democrats seem to have remained quite unified behind changing slogans, but slowly emerging differences of opinion within the Communist party have turned into open conflict, with the more dogmatic "old Communist" minority retaining its hold over a number of the party's lower organizations. Internal disputes, along with other factors, have weakened the movement and have caused defeats in the second half of the 1960's.

Social Democrats. A general finding is that party ideologies expressed in programs of principle change more slowly than party activity; they are not "current." Programs and external slogans symbolizing the party are often consciously retained even though they are far removed from practice. In fact, the action goals and methods of the Social Democratic party have shown considerable development over the decades; but the original Forssa program of principles, prepared in 1903, was still in force after the Second World War. In party circles it was admitted that this program no longer revealed the true nature, tactics, and goals of the party, but it was not until 1952 that it was reworked.

Long-range goals are now viewed in practical, not theoretical terms. The dogmatic language of the Forssa program has been dropped and attention given to new conditions and to experiences gained in practical politics over half a century. One of the factors most important in terms of principle is the statement concerning tactics. According to the Forssa program, the party would use "all means appropriate and in keeping with the population's natural feeling of justice"[57] in order to achieve its program. The party could not long continue with such a broad mandate, and in 1952 a practical view was formally adopted: "Since democracy is both the form of life for a free person and a necessary condition of social democracy, the Social Democratic party of Finland demands acceptance of democratic and parliamentary tactics in all political activity."[58]

The program's basic slogans are: socialism and democracy, an independent nation, and a cooperative world. It states that the party's energies are directed along two main lines, on one hand toward protecting the interests of the living—particularly workers and small farmers—through social reforms and, on the other hand, toward creating a more just and more secure society through development of the political, economic, and social systems.

State control over the means of production was considered a self-evident principle in the old program, but it has now become appropriate to question even socialization. The economic part of the

57. Borg, *Suomen puolueet,* p. 32.
58. *SDP, periaateohjelma,* p. 15.

present program is not constructed on the basis of socialization but rather on the basis of a socialist planned economy. These two notions are not identical and not necessarily tied to each other, although it is felt that a planned economy cannot be realized unless certain industries occupying a key position in the life of the economy are transferred to state control and ownership. Enterprises should also be transferred to state control "insofar as it is appropriate in order to do away with the conflict between labor and capital and to destroy injustices arising from private ownership."[59] Due to efforts by the labor movement and to laws of economic development, the capitalist system has already in part been transformed into a system based on social ownership and production; and, further, it is changing into a socialist planned economy. Because state socialism has come under question, and it is impossible to draft blueprints for a model society of the future, one cannot say in advance how long this form of organization will be suitable. As everyone who has followed Finnish politics can affirm, attempts at socialization now play a rather small role in the practical action of the Social Democratic party.

Seeking to achieve a "welfare state," Social Democrats have set three main goals: maintenance of full employment, improvement in the structural relationship between the national economy and the different occupational fields in order to achieve further growth in national income and labor productivity, and creation of a system of social security. The second point leads necessarily to the agricultural and industrial questions, and it presupposes significant structural changes with respect to agriculture and the agricultural population. The party condemns the postwar land settlement policy, which splintered farmland into small, unproductive units, and believes that too large a portion of the population does agricultural work that is of marginal value and contributes weakly to the growth of national income. Agriculture must be made profitable by increasing the size of landholdings and new job opportunities must be created for the superfluous rural population by developing industry—the only way to raise the nation's standard of living. The party has set the development of industry, especially state-run industry, as its immediate economic goal. This calls for a complete industrial program and standardization of national economic planning. The most important aspects of the social program have been the development of housing projects, the achievement of general unemployment insurance and

59. *Ibid.*, p. 14.

health and disability insurance, reforms in the system of health care leading to free hospitalization and institutional care, and free or inexpensive medicines, as well as changes in legislation pertaining to job regulation and job safety.

There have been many phases in the transformation of the Social Democratic party from an opposition group, which early in the century was politically isolated and clung to the principle of a sharp class struggle, into a postwar parliamentary-democratic party very loosely tied to Marxism and advocating center policies. Until the Civil War, the party held to its Marxist doctrine and sought from it a guide to action. As early as the 1920's this line was challenged by a revisionist tactic, which caused contradictions and some wavering until the new Western notion of social democracy's essence and duties took hold among party leaders in the next decade. As the party moved toward the center, cooperation with the Agrarian party was natural. Finland's special conditions, the radicalism of the workers, and competition from the Communists, however, have influenced this policy and have been responsible for dissension within the party.

The Social Democratic League has criticized Social Democratic policies after the Second World War for having concentrated too heavily on solutions to daily problems in neglect of broader-gauged matters that have been relegated, in part by design, to the background. This has resulted in a diminution of interest and activity by workers. The League announces that it is undertaking "to develop and maintain purposively the fundamental goals of Social Democracy in the economic and social spheres."[60] The party feels that a planned economy as well as collective and centralized allocation of capital are required if balanced economic growth is to continue. A longer-range goal is the socialist state, in which natural resources, credit institutions, the major industrial enterprises, power facilities, mines, enterprises engaged in foreign trade or domestic wholesaling, and other large and important enterprises have been shifted to public ownership. The party pays special attention in its programmatic statements to a "democratization of production"—to development of a system in which workers through the mediation of organs elected by them play a decisive role in the making of production decisions that affect their own labor input and its use. As a practical measure, the party supports the formation of production

60. *Polttopisteessä II* (Helsinki: TPSL, 1960), p. 4.

councils organized by industrial branch, constructed on corporate principles, and having a central organ. In general one can say that the goals of the TPSL do not differ much from the goals of the Social Democratic party, although the League attempts to appear more leftist.

The Finnish Rural Party. Movement and spontaneous political action by small farmers have traditions that go back many decades. Although the Rural party is not a direct successor to the small farmers' movement of the 1930's (its birth was tied to differences of opinion prevailing in the Agrarian party in the 1950's and to the person of Veikko Vennamo) it can, nonetheless, be considered a part of that tradition.

The party's 1959 program is directed at "small farmers, independent laborers, and small entrepreneurs"[61] who, it is said, are the country's greatest though diffuse democratic force. The goal is to unite this force and "to prevent destructive and devisive work among the nation's largest population group, an incitement to battle one against the other, that is rooted in the ideology, and led by the propaganda and money, of the old parties."[62] In two respects this program is unique, as Olavi Borg has demonstrated.[63] By nature it is strongly instrumental and designed to attract voters with propagandistic goals. It includes an unusual mixture of both bourgeois and socialist demands and views, making its principles heterogeneous and placing it on the political spectrum between the bourgeois and socialist parties.

In the concluding, index-like section of the program, which covers immediate practical goals, the questions dealt with most often concern the above-mentioned population groups and remote communities. In the beginning section, which is phrased in terms of principles, attention is given to the sharp contradiction between society's "great" and "small," a notion that the groups represented by this party are being squeezed by the forces of an industrialized collective. "The growing might of the state and of money weigh heavily upon and threaten small farmers, independent laborers, and small entrepreneurs. At one time the population was enslaved by landed estates, large property owners, and a foreign-language upper class.

61. Borg, *Suomen puolueet*, p. 340.
62. *Ibid.*, p. 341.
63. Borg, *Suomen puolueideologiat*, pp. 102–107.

As a barter economy develops, these forces are joined by the powerful forces of the rich . . . Along with the rich are the misusers of public and organizational power who seek to oppress the population in abuse of their position."[64] Thus the program has certain "populist" features. There is constant reference to the misuse, and abuse, of public power.

The Center Party. The Agrarian party was an example of that structural duality which is an essential part of even clear-cut interest parties: as a substructure there was the promotion of economic interests on behalf of certain social groups, and as a superstructure there was an ideology rural in spirit and colored by a peasant romanticism through which the party sought to temper, and perhaps conceal, the interest character of its political action. The basic ingredients of the party's ideology concerned the conflict between town and country: growing urban supremacy threatens to destroy pristine rural culture, which must be defended and protected from the negative features of city culture. Johannes Virolainen has crystallized the essence of a rural outlook:

> One must give up urban patterns of thought; questions of importance to the motherland must be seen in a broader context. Momentary success must not be purchased at the price of the nation's future. Surely it is possible for us to link the advantages brought by technical development to an ordering of life which guarantees preservation of the human being. This sort of order is found in rural society . . . The essence of a rural outlook is formed by the belief that for the future of the entire nation the formation of large, densely settled areas must be prevented and a suitable balance worked out between cities and the countryside.[65]

In light of this ideology, it is natural that the Agrarian party devoted most of its attention to agricultural policies in an attempt to improve economically the position of agriculture and the position of the agricultural population. The party directed the postwar land settlement policy, hoping this would strengthen the foundation of agriculture. It waged a constant battle, primarily with consumer groups, over prices for agricultural products and the related questions of state subsidies and wages. The prices and sale of raw wood, affecting the interests of forest owners, also occupied an important position in party policy.

64. Borg, *Suomen puolueet*, p. 342.

65. Johannes Virolainen, *Maaseutuhenkinen elämänkatsomus* (Helsinki: Maaseudun nuorten liitto, 1949), pp. 138–139.

Since the 1950's, however, as a result of changes in social structure, the Agrarian party has made an obvious effort to branch out and attract nonagricultural segments of the population. Because of this effort, and because of the Agrarian party's important political position, the party now represents a more independent line on nonagricultural questions as well.[66] In this respect, approval in 1962 of a new general program and a program of goals for the 1960's was an important step forward. Although a special task in the 1950 program was still "unification of the rural population into a national party for effective direction of the nation's and the countryside's affairs,"[67] this limitation was left out of the 1962 program. An effort was made to treat questions in different areas with equanimity, as well as to determine goals in support of general centrist views. The next logical step was to change the organization's name: in 1965 it became the Center party.

The Center party pledges its support for an economic system built on free enterprise and private property because only this system offers the conditions necessary for the realization of political freedom and economic democracy. The party accepts neither socialism nor a system in which economic power is concentrated in the hands of a few owners and large companies. Small-scale private enterprise in all areas must be promoted, whereas monopolization of the means of production must be opposed and the activity of companies run by big capital effectively supervised. If private enterprise is not capable of producing, or does not want to produce, on the basis of national economic interests, the state must take over. The program clearly reflects the party's traditional antipathy toward socialism on one hand and big capitalism on the other.

The party feels that industrialization of the country is essential. But industrialization should not be limited to the nation's southern and southwestern parts; the state must resolutely pursue a policy of industrialization which leads to new factories and industrial centers in eastern and northern Finland as well as in other undeveloped areas. In order to prevent an expanding industry from becoming a center of dissatisfaction and malpractices, there must also be an expansion of industrial democracy; workers must become share-

66. Ahti Karjalainen, "Maalaisliiton viides vuosikymmen," *Herääva maaseutu* (Porvoo, 1956), VI, 262.

67. *Maalaisliiton puolueohjelma sekä järjestösäännöt* (Helsinki: Maalaiskuntien Liiton Kirjapaino, 1951), p. 5.

holders in their enterprises and they must be given a role to play in factory management.

To ensure healthy social development, agriculture and forestry must be considered equal in all respects to industrial occupations. Agriculture must be based on free ownership and small-scale farming; special attention must therefore be given to the preservation and survival of plots with insufficient land. The central task for agriculture is to satisfy the needs of one's own nation, to achieve and maintain self-sufficiency. Agricultural profitability must be increased through rationalization, but since climatic conditions make it impossible for Finnish agriculture to succeed without society's support, production must be protected through tariffs and other measures. Income for the agricultural population must be guaranteed by law, so that this segment of the population can share in the rising standard of living on an equal footing with others.

The Center party focuses on state planning, through which all productive forces of the nation are to be effectively utilized and through which the difference in educational opportunities and the standard of living between the country's developed and backward areas is to be erased. Production activity and cultural institutions must be located evenly in different parts of the country, by following a state policy of "dispersed-centralization." The party's special concern for backward rural areas is thus patently evident at a programmatic level. Even in social policy the party attempts to act so that the state will guarantee the farming population, and especially small farmers, the same comforts and social security benefits enjoyed by factory workers.

Over the decades certain changes are evident in the generally centrist line of the Agrarian-Center party. In a certain sense, the postwar orientation is more "leftist." Both foreign policy factors and an internal power struggle have been influential in effecting this change. Keen competition with Social Democrats and Communists for the support of the socially diffuse, and politically unstable, population group composed of small farmers and lumberers draws the party leftward and makes it difficult for a rightist orientation of even temporary duration to emerge. It is understandable that this line is not always satisfactory with agricultural producers—which sometimes causes conflicts within the party—but in terms of power it is a necessity, which means that control over the party has for the most part been retained by the group representing a social-agrarian orientation. As has been noted, there have been attempts in recent years to expand the party's base of support in another direction: toward the middle class in the countryside and in population centers.

The Liberal People's Party. The Finnish People's party, founded in 1951, attempted to fill the void in political life created by the discontinuance of Progressive party activity and it also attempted, of course, to increase the influence of the liberal center. The Progressive party had gained a firm position in the period of accommodation following independence and the Civil War when it supported, on principle, the establishment of a parliamentary republic, as well as a policy of amnesty and reconciliation in the squaring of accounts after the war. When conditions became stabilized, the party's position began to weaken and its supporters moved both to the left and to the right, again directing their attention to interest politics. The economic and social program of this ideological center party was not sufficiently concrete to attract large numbers of the electorate, and it had the appearance of being too "intellectual."[68]

The Finnish People's party tried to construct its ideology in the tradition of the Progressive party; it sought through progressive-mindedness to extend its roots all the way to "the oldest Young Finn movement."[69] The party was explicitly founded as a center party taking as its ideological basis a national, social-liberal outlook. The party's founding manifesto was directed at citizens in society's middle groups, whose number had grown rapidly but whose influence in political and economic decisions appeared to be minimal. Among social-liberal circles, the younger leadership of the League of Liberals and the People's party sought even more emphatically, in the mid-1960's, programmatic goals for a new liberal people's party.

The 1965 program of the party begins with these words: "The Liberal People's party is a national party sympathetic to reform with an outlook based on respect for unrestricted growth of the individual as well as on modern liberalism, *social liberalism*, resting on social and human responsibility."[70] The creation of circumstances

68. Sven Lindman, *Studier över parlamentarismens tillämpning i Finland 1919–1926* (Åbo, 1937), pp. 34–36.

69. Suomen kansanpuolue, *Kansanpuolueen 10-vuotisjuhlallisuudet 5.2.1961* (Helsinki, 1961), p. 5.

70. *Liberaalisen kansanpuolueen yleisohjelma* (Liberaalisen kansanpuolueen julkaisu no. 2), p. 3.

advantageous for full development of an individual requires active work that will have an impact on society: rational planning and an effective and long-range social policy designed to carry out plans for development. The party is attempting to crystallize this goal, established in major areas of endeavor, with the following slogans: an educated society and democracy in education; democratic economic enterprise and planned economic policy; social justice and security.

Cultural policy is an important part of the social-liberal view, and the party does, indeed, present clear programmatic goals in this area. The development of teaching and of schooling is, in addition to being a necessity for the major goal of liberalism—the development of a spiritually broad and independent person—also a burning practical necessity in modern society. The fundamental task is to raise the entire nation's level of knowledge. To its ideology of an educated society, the Liberal People's party joins the demand for democracy in education: territorial and social factors which interfere with the most advantageous development and utilization of an individual's talents, and those of the entire nation, must be eliminated.

The cornerstone in a system of democratic economic enterprise is the opportunity for self-employment and the right to ownership. The first duty of public authorities is to create the general conditions necessary for enterprise, competition, and profitability. In those sectors of economic life which have a social (that is, service) character society must, however, intervene by regulating, supporting, and if necessary assuming direct control over production. Concentration of economic power in the hands of a few, whether individuals or the state, is considered contrary to the principle of a democratic economic enterprise. Healthy development of the national economy presupposes total economic planning, which means that special attention is given to market and employment, as well as to social, cultural, and territorial points of view.

The principle of justice and social security requires that those incapable of productive activity, or those participating with insufficient inputs, be supported through adequate and effective transfers of income. These transfers should not, however, become a permanent basis for the standard of living of any population group; they should be part of an effort to bring members of society back into effective production.

It has been noted that the birth of the Finnish People's party was in part tied to the change in the structure of Finnish society which took place after the Second World War. It was necessary that a party be formed which would look after the interests of center groups and stress their importance in society. Without doubt the new Liberal party gets, and expects to get, most of its support from the same circles, but in characteristic fashion, it avoids attaching itself to specific social strata or professional groups. The party conveys the impression that in its programs it is seeking to formulate social policy for the whole of society. It sees conservatism, which it fears, in rightism as well as in agrarianism and even in petrified socialism.

The progressive center has suffered throughout the decades from organizational weakness. Its importance in the political life of the country has, however, been much greater than one would suppose from the pervasiveness of its organization (measured in terms either of party membership or members of Parliament) or from its functional activeness. These parties have assumed Cabinet responsibility many times; on one hand, the Agrarian-Center party has reacted favorably toward them when seeking the formation of centrist governments and, on the other hand, these parties have sought cooperation in the belief that this is the best way to be heard. They have, of course, often had an impact on Cabinet policy and on individual decisions; but as small government parties they have also been involved in decisions which have not pleased their members or their electorate.

The Swedish People's Party. The Swedish People's party is a special feature of the party system in Finland: its foundations are entirely different from those of the other parties. Sven Lindman has even gone so far as to question whether one can call it a party if the term is used in a narrow sense.[71] The cohesive force is nationality; in fact, the party has had a unified, concrete program only on questions concerning the fundamental cultural interests of the country's Swedish-speaking inhabitants. The solidarity of this population group, as a minority and a cultural collectivity on the defensive, is so strong that natural conflicts between different economic-social groups can to a large extent be concealed. The party's nature is clearly apparent from an introductory section in the brief programmatic declaration of 1937: "The purpose of the Swedish People's party is to unite on a patriotic basis Finland's Swedish-speaking

71. Lindman, *Studier*, pp. 31–32.

population in defense of its position and rights in the fatherland."[72] In other respects, too, this program was descriptive and unique: divided into two parts, the second part contained goals sought by the Swedish People's party as a patriotic and democratic party, the first contained goals pursued as a Swedish party. Only in the first part could one find concrete goals, which were restricted to this party in appeal and were consequently used to justify the existence of the party. But in 1964 the party approved a new program—thoroughly modernized, much broader, and more detailed. General political goals overshadow special tasks, although the latter are not, of course, forgotten. The Swedish People's party seeks to demonstrate that it is a national grouping interested in all aspects of social policy. The detailed nature of the program is striking: it first presents the party's general understanding of matters in various policy areas, and then party wishes and demands on separate, concrete questions. The term "bourgeois" has been abandoned, but this has little significance in terms of general programmatic orientation. Program statements reflect compromises between a more conservative and a more liberal orientation. As before, there is firm attachment to the principles of private property and a free market economy. In the section dealing with social policy, the influence of the newer social-liberal orientation is evident.

The party is, thus, a heterogeneous and loose union in which internal group activity has been brisk. As mentioned earlier, pressure from members or supporters has on occasion forced the party to abandon its concrete action program and has permitted individual representatives and internal groupings to do as they see fit. In the 1917 program it was stated explicitly that different factions having their own programs can exist within the party as long as they are not in opposition to the party's general goals.[73] Since the Swedish People's party has not been united on major economic, cultural, and social questions—and sometimes not even on the nationality question—and since competing opinion groups have appeared within the party, special difficulties arise when seeking to locate it on an uninterrupted party continuum from left to right. In general, however, a certain dominant line can be found which makes it possible to fit the party into the system on the basis of broad political factors. The

72. *Program för Svenska Folkpartiet i Finland* (Helsingfors: Lindbergs Tryckeri Aktiebolag, 1954), p. 1.
73. Colliander, *Svenska folkpartiet*, p. 157.

party has always been on the bourgeois side of the front. Crucial in this respect is the fact that the party originally began as a conservative grouping of the upper class and only later became a general people's party. The reconciliation of Finland's Swedish-speaking "toilers" to the party line was evidently helped by the fact that they themselves were relatively conservative—not at all comparable to subject minorities, often politically radical, found in many other countries. As a result of divisions among the bourgeoisie during the controversy over Finland's form of government, the Swedish People's party drew closer to the Coalition party; in the sense of a rightist orientation, these sympathies remained throughout the 1920's. In the early years of independence a reserved attitude toward the system of government that had been adopted, coupled with positions on certain important questions—such as the amnesty and land questions—created a situation in which the Swedish People's party was even more rightwing than the Coalition party.[74] Little by little, however, there was a shift toward the center as the more liberal and radical bourgeois elements gained a foothold. One can probably consider the subsequent party line as representative of a liberal bourgeois world outlook in which a strong emphasis on the principle of justice is an integral part. There is a tinge of old-fashioned liberalism in the new liberalism, and, in any event, the party must consider its conservative wing.

According to its program, the Swedish People's party will cooperate with other parties and opinion groups on questions about which there is agreement concerning goals and means. Flexibility in action and in cooperation with others has served to intensify the absence of a firm position on economic and social questions. But because its support is not based on positions taken with respect to these questions the party has been able to deal realistically with matters under dispute and has been able to promote conciliation and unity. Wanting to avoid identification with opposition on the right and seeking to further the special interests of the group it represents, the party has in the postwar period generally been desirous of Cabinet cooperation with the large center groups; it has become common practice to include one or two Swedish-speaking ministers in most Cabinets.

The National Coalition Party. The Coalition party is a conservative party and as such it has adopted the principles of conservatism in

74. See Lindman, *Studier*, pp. 32–33.

thought and action. Conservatism is not considered a system of ideas, a tightly knit ideology; but rather an attitude toward life, a certain way of approaching social and political phenomena. Conservatism differs greatly from one country to another, and from one time period to another; Finnish conservatism, which was late in arriving, has developed special features and has deviated from existent models. There are, however, some principles common to all conservative movements: emphasis on faith, morality, and the family and solicitude for the nation as a whole; holding to the right of private property and to a free competitive economy; observance of traditions, experiences, and reality as circumstances change; a reserved, cautious attitude toward social reform and the application of a democratic system.[75]

Following international currents, Finnish conservatism made a great effort at reform after the Second World War and especially in the 1950's. Special factors which hastened this effort were the rapid changes in the structure of society, the general radicalization of political life, and research findings that indicated the party was losing to other parties many of its working-class and middle-class voters.[76] This led to the adoption of a new program in 1957 which is built on old principles but which also includes liberal and forward-moving slogans typical of a new conservatism. "Dynamic conservatism," which has been influenced by both liberals and Western socialists, has renounced its earlier timidity and is now seeking to formulate positive proposals; it speaks less about traditions and more about changes in society, about goals which must be pursued and about means which should be utilized.

In the economic sphere, the slogans of the Coalition party are a people's capitalism and a social market economy. The basis of economic life should be the right to private property and a free social market economy, which will create conditions most favorable to improvement in the living standard of both individual citizens and the entire nation. Overt and covert attempts at socialization must be prevented. Enterprise activity is a primary task of neither the state nor the communes; their role should be limited to creating favorable conditions for private enterprise. The Coalition party reacts adversely to a planned economy, since it fears that programs which are detailed and adopted for long periods of time will promote

75. Rantala, *Konservatismi*, p. 20.
76. See Rantala, *Konservatiivinen*, p. 27.

a centralization of power, hinder individual activity, and make difficult the flexibility required by changing conditions. But the party does not come out in support of the other extreme, ownership by just a few, either. The goal is people's capitalism: as many citizens as possible should become owners. Everyone must achieve this goal on his own, but society should create the conditions necessary for work and for saving. In addition to private ownership of an enterprise, people's capitalism also involves ownership of housing, stocks, bank accounts, special consumer goods, farming and forestry land, and summer homes.

In addition to free and profitable enterprise, signs of a social market economy include responsibility by the entrepreneur for his freedom, for the collectivity, and for his workers, as well as a close relationship between employer and employee. The state has the right to intervene in the economic life of the nation only as an exception, in order to keep competition within healthy limits. A social market economy leads to a reduction in tension between capital and labor and to a mutual rapprochement between employers and employees.

From a national point of view, increased industrialization and further development of agriculture are considered vital by the party. The attitude taken on the latter points to reliance by the Coalition party, insofar as agriculture as an occupation is concerned, on the more well-to-do farmers. The party reacts negatively toward the postwar policy of land division, in which it sees political speculation. It demands that the splitting up of profitable farms, and the formation of unprofitable farms, be prevented and that farmers be permitted to run their farms without the constant threat of expropriation. Agriculture should be developed in such a way that it can function as "healthy enterprise activity."

The position with respect to social questions has become more positive. The Coalition party does not, however, support mass subsidies; the present monetary transfer system is viewed as party politics, not social policy. As is generally true of conservative parties, it follows an individualistic line in social policy; social assistance must not be distributed according to some sort of formula—support must be given only to those who through no fault of their own are in need of assistance. On the other hand, assistance rendered by society must be preventive. Those who need aid must be given an opportunity to make it on their own, because a social policy which promotes production and which is preventive decreases the need for outright grants and develops in the individual a feeling of responsibility and a desire to make an effort.

During the first two decades of independence, the leaders of the Coalition party saw many weaknesses in Finland's system of government. They reacted critically toward "pure-bred" parliamentarism and parliamentary predominance, and they attempted to strengthen the position of the Cabinet and of the president. Since the Second World War, the party's trust in parliamentarism has increased; the party did, in fact, during its long period of opposition, seek to strengthen the prestige and influence of Parliament. This effort was apparent in party demands that there be a reduction of exceptional powers granted to the government. In its program the Coalition party strongly opposes state leadership and centralized authority. The state must not be an end in itself but rather a form of cooperation leading to an orderly arrangement of the life of citizens, their ability to get along, and their comfort. The individual—as a citizen and human being—is more clearly than ever before at stage center in the new program, and there is a desire to defend his dignity and freedom against both the state and interest groups.

Throughout the decades the Coalition party has emphasized the importance of the bourgeois front as a counterweight to efforts by the leftist parties to change the existing social system; but because of the hesitant and negative stand of the center groups, above all the Agrarian party, only rarely has there been real cooperation between the bourgeois parties. Before the Second World War the Coalition party remained aloof from the Social Democrats, although in recent times, especially in the 1950's, a significant convergence in relations between these two parties has occurred. The bourgeois center, for its part, wanted to withdraw even further from the right. In fact, it was not until many years after cooperation between the Agrarian party and the Social Democrats had ceased, in the second half of the 1950's, that the first general coalition government of bourgeois parties came into being.

In the years following the Second World War, the position of the Coalition party was not very strong; it had lost many of its propaganda weapons and felt hamstrung in the sensitive political situation. However, as conditions became more stabilized, in the early 1950's, the rightist front began to gain strength and to function more actively. During its long period of opposition, the Coalition party engaged primarily in criticism of the groups holding power.

In the name of economic expertise and the "interests of all" the party directed most of its criticism at economic policy, demanding, among other things, a check on inflation, a revitalization of the national economy, and a freeing and revival of occupational activity in the areas of enterprise production, foreign trade, and housing policy, as well as prices, wages, and credit. A second main theme, colored by ideology, was the demand that politicians, parties, and even pressure groups become more moral politically and that they develop a sense of responsibility based on a total view.

In his comparative analysis of ideologies, Borg shows that programmatic structures clearly depict the interest character and "system needs" of parties.[77] The amount of attention given to different points is conspicuously related to the interest field and social structure of the party's actual or model group of supporters, even though emphasis on some points is also related to the most important aspects of ideology. Indeed, the program of the National Coalition party—which is considered an ideological party—reflects through its emphasis on labor relations the special interest character of the party, a fact confirmed by research at other levels of analysis. In addition, of course, to the linguistic and cultural efforts of the Swedish-speaking part of the population, the old program of the Swedish People's party was also influenced by the strong commercial and industrial interests of the party's parliamentary group. The most descriptive feature of the Agrarian party's 1950 program was the great attention devoted to agricultural and forestry questions. As far as the Social Democrats are concerned, emphasis was placed on the general principles of a national cultural policy. Typical of the program for the Finnish People's party was an emphasis on teaching, education, and enlightenment; this, too, corresponds with the general findings and information about the party's social and interest background. An interest orientation was also detected in the programs of the extreme left, even though some major points in the SKDL program are related to circumstances surrounding the birth of the party; the program of the SKP, in turn, is colored by Marxist-Leninist theory. Looked at as a whole, it was quite easy to differentiate between parties with the variables selected. More refined interpretations could have been achieved only through further research; the primary question is, of course, attitudinal content on points of interest.

77. Borg, *Suomen puolueideologiat*, p. 159.

III Pressure Groups

THE POSITION AND TASKS OF PRESSURE GROUPS

The Conditions for Pressure Politics. The activity and effectiveness of pressure activity is determined by many different factors, such as 1) a group's strategic position in society, 2) a group's internal characteristics, 3) the structure and operation of governmental institutions and parties, and 4) the economic and social conditions of a particular country.[1] The position of pressure groups therefore varies from one political system to another. It is closely related to party conditions and to the prevailing system of party government—already well developed in most democratic countries before the recent ascent of pressure organizations. Pressure politics are most needed, and can best flourish, in a two-party country such as the United States, where both parties appeal to all social groups and thus avoid an attachment to a specific interest group or ideological orientation. If the two-party conditions of the United States increase the need for pressure politics in that country, so, on the other hand, do factors exist in the political systems of Europe's multiparty countries which may cause the activity of pressure groups that are especially large and supported by mass strength to become effective and threaten the parliamentary exercise of power.

The influence of pressure groups and their effectiveness are particularly striking in Finland. As Lolo Krusius-Ahrenberg notes: the stability of party life and the ability of public officials to exercise power, and the extensiveness of state economic activity as well as the strength and centralization of interest organizations, are those quantities to be measured when figuring out the conditions of

1. See Henry W. Ehrmann, "The Comparative Study of Interest Groups," in H. W. Ehrmann, ed., *Interest Groups on Four Continents* (Pittsburgh, 1960), p. 1.

pressure politics in a parliamentary democracy. In order to maintain a balance, the sum of the two latter variables must not exceed the capacity of the two former variables.[2]

A natural basis for the rise of pressure groups has been the broadening of the power of the state and its branching into an ever-increasing number of areas: the more the various activities of society are politicized, the more organizations there are with political interests to be guarded, and this results in the expression of political desires and the formation of pressure groups. Of particular significance in this respect is state intervention in the economic life of the country through different regulatory measures: this brings into the arena of the political power struggle the mighty economic and labor market organizations with mass support. Because of the war effort and the effects of the Second World War, regulation of economic life by public authorities has been much broader in Finland than, for example, in the other Nordic countries. In certain respects, however, the modes of action set forth in the Constitution pose difficulties for the achievement of regulatory action through decisions of public officials. Many matters which in other countries can be resolved through ordinary legislation or even decree necessitate in Finland the observance of procedures required for amending the Constitution. Particularly important in this respect is the strong protection given to the right of private property; since legislative measures in such cases are generally declared urgent, one-sixth of the members of Parliament participating in the vote can prevent a firm decision. To be noted also are the rules regarding postponement, and the necessity of a stipulated majority in the consideration of certain tax bills. A Cabinet can thus face difficulty when seeking to achieve its program, even though it may have simple majority support in Parliament.

The influence of pressure groups is proportional to the kind of parliamentary power exercised as well as to the internal strength and ability of parties to oppose organizational pressure in parliamentary activity. In this respect the situation in Finland is, from the point of view of pressure groups, advantageous. The country's party life is to a great degree unstable. It has been in a strong state of ferment, and it is characterized by keen competition for electors.

2. Lolo Krusius-Ahrenberg, "Synpunkter på intresseorganisationernas politiska frammarsch," *Vår syn* (Helsingfors, 1957), III, 110; Lolo Krusius-Ahrenberg, "The Political Power of Economic and Labor-Market Organizations: A Dilemma of Finnish Democracy," in Ehrmann, ed., *Interest Groups*, p. 37. These two articles have also been used as a basis for the presentation which follows.

In these conditions parties cannot resolutely oppose organizational pressure, because members of the organizations are part of the electorate. A "party line" representing broader and more unifying points of view does not last; it succumbs to more narrow interests. On the other hand, the weakness of Cabinets, Parliament, and parties tempts pressure groups to go it alone and to rely on direct action. From their point of view, activity that takes place through Parliament and parties always has certain disadvantages—but they are particularly great in the small-party conditions of Finland. Organizational representation in Parliament is very strong; but because only about one-fourth of the electorate is behind even the largest party, all parties are too small to be able to satisfy the needs of the large interest organizations and thereby keep them from using external means of pressure. Indeed, the workers' trade union movement does not have a unified group at its disposal in Parliament; the workers' political representation is divided among a number of sharply different parties. The same sorts of difficulties exist for organizations of civil servants and salaried employees acting through Parliament. A diffuse party institution again gives birth to weak Cabinets, which have had great authority to act in the economic sphere on the basis of laws but which have not had sufficient strength to perform these duties.

In contrast to parties, interest organizations in Finland, as in the Scandinavian countries generally, are strong and centralized. It is difficult to find areas in modern society where organization for the pursuit of common interests has not occurred, and it is characteristic of Scandinavian societies that organizations occupy positions which resemble monopolies in their own spheres of activity. In Finland, to be sure, linguistic and political factors have caused a certain diffraction, but in Finland, unlike some other countries, it is not the sort of division along ideological, religious, territorial, and other lines that brings about competition and weakens efficiency. The recent history of the Confederation of Finnish Trade Unions (SAK) demonstrates the importance of this fact. The political influence of the organization seems to have risen continually after the Second World War up until the mid-1950's, at which time a curve showing power increments began to drop, in large part because of internal quarrels which led to a split within the trade union movement.[3] The

3. Väinö Huuska, "SAK: n toiminta painostusryhmänä 1950-luvulla," pt. 2, *Politiikka*, 4, no. 2 (1962), 95–98, 105–106.

importance of interest groups in white-collar areas, however, has evidently grown insofar as the organizing process has been accompanied by a unification—by a merging of organizations into larger collectives.

Experience shows that internal quarrels and tense situations occurring within organizations are apt to give a sharpness to expressions of political desire. Indeed, the competition and pressure of Communists caused Social Democratic leaders of the SAK to take more active and sharper stands in the 1940's than often would have been preferred by the Social Democratic party.[4] The same phenomenon can be found in other organizations. Attempts to raise the low level of organization have also sharpened positions. Competition between two parallel organizations may lead in different situations to different results. For example, the division of public and salaried employees into trade union organizations of the workers on one hand and trade union organizations of salaried employees on the other obviously has made the political action of both more lively. It is, however, possible that an organization competing for negotiations and contracts with another labor market force—whether an organization or public officials—will be satisfied with lesser achievements if it can only gain the status of a recognized body.

The Tasks of Pressure Groups. Activity by pressure groups in democratic politics is a completely natural, even necessary, phenomenon complementing party politics. Pressure groups have a certain representational function which parties and members of Parliament elected from different geographic districts cannot perform. In accordance with their nature, parties are, even in multiparty countries, general organizations which seek support that is as broad as possible. This requires that they avoid a close association with any special group and that in their programs the most important aspirations of many groups be arbitrated and aggregated into a whole which is as influential as possible and which at least to some degree corresponds to the "general interest." Thus they cannot be special organizations of unified groups seeking ideological or material goals, organizations which would have the necessary expertise and which would be able to present effectively their viewpoints, both to governmental authorities and to the public. This is the task of pressure groups. In the modern welfare state, public power has extended to

4. See Carl Erik Knoellinger, *Labor in Finland* (Cambridge, Mass., 1960), pp. 109–111.

areas which used to be part of the nonpolitical field handled by social organizations; it is natural that these organizations seek to influence decisions which affect them and which have now become political.

It is no longer only a question of organizations using the state to their own advantage and of the state attempting to regulate, watch, or even directly oppose their activity; in actual fact the state uses them in many ways for its own purposes; Gunnar Heckscher even asserts that one finds more traces of real corporatism in present-day Sweden than one does in the old Swedish four-estate society or in Fascist Italy.[5] Organizations have been given many specialized tasks to perform at various levels of legislation and administration; this has increased their influence and perhaps also their sense of responsibility. It has become common practice to form temporary or permanent organs of experts at various levels of administration, especially the central administration level. The task of some of these organs is to investigate, explain, and advise, whereas others exercise broad decision-making power. In Finland the most prominent organs have been the economic councils. The councils are composed of politicians, experts on the national economy, and representatives of pressure groups; with their aid the government charts its economic course and attempts to determine the position of different groups on immediate and projected solutions. Labor boards and courts dealing with job accidents illustrate the fact that this arrangement applies even in the selection of officials who exercise judicial power. Organizations are also permitted to represent their membership before a public official, and to an ever-increasing degree public officials seek out the opinions of organizations on current problems even when there is no direct obligation to do so. Today it is generally acknowledged that this sort of cooperation is advantageous to both sides.

PRESSURE GROUPS IN DIFFERENT AREAS

It is, of course, impossible to provide an exhaustive list of the groups which are influential in political life at a given moment in time, and, likewise, positioning them within the framework of a

5. Gunnar Heckscher, *Staten och organisationerna*, 2nd ed. (Stockholm, 1951), pp. 258–262.

unidimensional classification raises many difficulties. Also, it is not always easy to decide where the boundaries should be drawn when dealing with pressure groups. By pressure groups one generally means citizen organizations whose activity is of the aforementioned type, but when special conditions prevail parties that are constantly in opposition may, for example, act as pressure groups with respect to a country's government. In like manner administrative officials and public institutions—ministries and their departments, central offices, state business enterprises, organs of district and local administration—attempt to influence political decisions in their favor through pressure politics. On the other hand, these institutions may act as "second-degree" pressure groups, pursuing the goals of certain interest groups in society; indeed, it is said that in many countries the ministry of agriculture brings pressure to bear on behalf of the interests of the farmers.[6] In this connection it should be noted that high civil servants have a direct line to parliamentary committees, where they often serve as experts on request. Especially in unstable political systems, the army is often a decisive factor in the making of the most important political decisions; when it intervenes directly, with its mass strength, it is often considered a separate political force comparable to parties and pressure groups. In earlier decades the Finnish army showed an occasional desire to participate in political decision-making at the "highest level," and even now it seeks to safeguard its own administrative interests through pressure group tactics. It should be noted nevertheless that since the end of the Second World War certain labor market organizations have demonstrated an obvious interest in the direct exercise of political power, for example by attempting to achieve their own explicit representation in the Cabinet.

In the following section, falling back on a simple, customary division, certain pressure groups in a number of fields are presented. In choosing these organizations an attempt has been made to select those which are considered most important in, or at least typical of, the field.

Industrial and Commercial Organizations. The organizational network of industry and commerce is composed of numerous dissimilar groups that perform different tasks. Some focus on economic policy, others on labor market policy. The task of the former is to protect

6. Jean Meynaud, *Les groupes de pression en France* (Paris, 1958), p. 39.

the production and production-technical interests of their members against other employers and against state power; the latter deal with employer problems. In addition, there are organizations that oversee tasks in both areas.

The most influential, though not the largest, of the central organizations working in the industrial sphere is the Confederation of Finnish Wood Processing Industries (Suomen Puunjalostusteollisuuden Keskusliitto), which was founded in 1919 to protect the common interests of the wood processing industry in the areas of legislation, state and communal administration, and trade and tariffs. Employers in the paper and wood pulp industry are almost one hundred percent organized, whereas in the timber industry field some small production branches and enterprises remain outside the confederation. The confederation is, above all, a central organization of sales associations, and, as it represents the nation's most important export industry, it concentrates its activity as a pressure group predominantly on international trade agreements.

The Federation of Finnish Industries (Suomen Teollisuusliitto), founded in 1921, is the economic policy organization of the large domestic market enterprises that watches over production interests. Its members include associations of different production areas as well as private industrial establishments; in 1965 the number of the former was 21, and there were scores of the latter. The total number of member firms was 380, with about 147,000 wage-earners in their employ.[7] When the total number of industrial establishments is compared with those belonging to the federation, it is clearly seen that organizing is more scattered and weaker here than in the wood processing industry. By far the largest of the associations belonging to the federation is the Association of Finnish Metal Industries. As an organization representing primarily domestic market industries, the federation focuses its attention on trade policy as it relates to imports and tariffs. In terms of internal economic policy, it attempts to influence on behalf of its membership those measures taken by the state which deal with domestic trade and the domestic price level.

A substantial portion of the nation's industries belongs to these two large central organizations. In addition, however, there are a

7. Information presented in this chapter concerning numbers of organizations and of workers comes from activity reports or orally from the central bureaus of the organizations and is, therefore, based on official statements.

number of associations in medium and small industry as well as in certain special fields; mention should be made of the League of Industrial Entrepreneurs, the Confederation of Handicrafts and Small Industry, the Textile Council, and the Chemical Confederation.

The Confederation of Finnish Employers (Suomen Työnantajain Keskusliitto, STK) is the central organization of the employer associations, which are primarily for different areas of industry, and is concerned with questions related to the labor market. In 1964 there were 27 member associations in the confederation, representing almost all areas of industry, and through them about 2,000 enterprises; there were about 288,000 workers in the service of these industrial establishments. The STK is composed primarily of private industrialists. It is significant that of the enterprises which are either run or owned by the state, stock-type enterprises are within the STK framework. The largest employer association is the Employer Association of Finnish Wood Processing Industries; following it are the Employer Association of Finnish Metal Industries and the General Group of Finnish Employers. The latter occupies a special position in that it does not represent a unified area of industry; it acts as a general employer's organization for many narrow areas encompassing a small number of enterprises.

Of the central organizations of employers, the STK is the oldest and largest; it consequently has achieved the most influential position on the free labor market as well as with respect to state offices and institutions. Employers in Finland have not become so tightly organized as, for example, in Sweden—only after the Second World War was there a fundamental increase in activity—and a substantial number of small employers have remained outside this form of cooperation. However, in their own activity small employers must to a great degree accept the policy of the organizations. The common organ of negotiation for employer organizations (the STK, the Confederation of Commerce Employers, and the Employer Association of the Countryside) is the Joint Committee of Finnish Employers.

It is difficult to assess the extent and effectiveness of constant pressure from industry's large organizations because these groups generally do not conduct their political activity in the open. At least occasionally, in connection with certain special questions, one can assume that it is very great because the organizations represent a broad and significant sector of the nation's economic life.

Of the pressure groups working in the area of commerce, one should first mention the chamber of commerce institution, whose activities extend into industry and transportation. The Central Chamber of Commerce of Finland was founded in 1918; twenty chambers of commerce from different parts of the country and several chamber departments, which seek to protect the interests of business life and direct its development, have joined this body. They try to influence public authorities by volunteering suggestions and by providing, on request, opinion on matters related to their fields of specialization.

In addition, there are many significant economic policy groupings in the sphere of commercial activity; the organizational network which they form depicts to a great degree the competition that has reigned for half a century between the cooperative movement and private employers. Finland's first central cooperative organization, the Central Organization of Finnish Cooperatives (SOK), was founded in 1904. Conflicts over direction split the cooperative movement into two parts during the First World War, and in 1916 the workers' consumer cooperatives founded their own central organization, the Confederation of Consumer Cooperatives (KK), to represent progressive-minded cooperatives. The vast majority of the cooperative membership in the former are part of the agricultural population, whereas industrial workers are most heavily represented in the latter. Otherwise the two organizations are almost equal in numbers and sales. Swedish-speaking cooperatives have their own central organization, Finland's Swedish Cooperative Association. The association for wholsesale employers is the Association of Wholesalers, to which some ten wholesale associations in different areas belong; the Confederation of Retailing acts as the central organization for retail trade. Other organizations active in the field of commerce that should be mentioned are the Association of the Self-Employed, founded in 1933 to uphold the principle of private enterprise, and Finland's Foreign Trade Association, which seeks to promote exports.

Persons in other branches of business life such as food and accommodations and credit and insurance institutions, as well as property owners and transportation employers, also watch over their economic interests through organizations acting as pressure groups; it is not possible to treat them here. The Confederation of Commerce Employers (Liiketyönantajain Keskusliitto, LK), founded in 1945, serves as the joint independent central organization of the commerce field broadly conceived, and likewise of production employers in different areas. At the end of 1966 it included four member associations and a general group representing 17 departments. At the same time there were in all about 117,000 salaried employees and workers in the service of the more than 2,000 enterprises belonging to the confederation.

Agricultural Organizations. Organizing a unified professional representation among the agricultural population presents many difficulties and, indeed, the organizational network in this field has remained in certain respects diffuse. This is a result of the fact that the agricultural population is heterogeneous in structure and does not form, either socially or politically, a unified group. The size of farms, the kind of crop, farming technology, natural conditions for the practice of agriculture, and other factors influencing wealth and social position vary greatly. In addition to this, political factors have a disruptive influence; a large number of people earn their living from agriculture and its related occupations, and this means that most parties compete for support of this part of the population. The diffuseness of the social and economic structure of the agricultural population lays a good foundation for this competition. In many pressure groups working in the agricultural area one finds a strong political coloring, and some organizations are even founded directly by political groups. It has already been noted that the extensiveness of pressure politics by interest groups is proportional to the extensiveness of the state's economic activity; it is therefore understandable that agricultural interest groups are politically very active. After the Second World War a structural change in agriculture which was very significant economically and socially, and about whose purpose there has been much discussion, was effected. A disadvantageous feature of the change was the fact that the formation of minuscule small-farming plots has increased the need for economic support from the state and has necessitated measures designed to provide additional income for the holders of these small plots. Agricultural questions consequently have occupied a central position in the state's economic policy.

By far the most important and influential of the agricultural pressure groups is the Confederation of Agricultural Producers (Maataloustuottajain Keskusliitto, MTK), an economic policy organization of agricultural producers which was founded in 1917 and has experienced rapid growth since the end of the Second World War. The confederation's organization extends to all parts of the country, but the center of gravity is understandably located in the more prosperous territories of southern and western Finland. From the confederation's membership statistics it is clear that the degree of organization among land owners invariably increases as the size of the farms increases. In the beginning of 1966 the MTK organization included 17 regional associations and 445 local associations of agricultural producers; in all, its membership included 162,300 farm owners and 230,000 other individual members (mostly family members). Of those owning farmland, 83 percent had less than 15 hectares.

The task of the Confederation of Agricultural Producers is to look after the economic and social rights of agricultural producers and to protect the position of agriculture and forestry with respect to other occupations. In the parliamentary sector, matters of special interest to the confederation are—in addition, of course, to the budget—the tariff law, tax laws, social legislation, and, above all, legislation concerning the price and income level of agriculture. Since the farming population is made up of producers who own plots of various sizes and who live in different economic conditions, it is understandable that the MTK is structurally somewhat diffuse and that there are conflicting views within the membership. The line most strongly represented in the confederation's leadership is probably that of producers located in the more developed and more properous parts of the country; there is, however, a second orientation, representing territories that are more barren with a preponderance of small farms, which is connected to the dominant political line in the Center party. The MTK has, of course, very close parliamentary relations with this group, but their views do not always coincide.

Parallel with the Confederation of Agricultural Producers is a corresponding Swedish-language central organization, the Central Association of Swedish Agricultural Producers, which was founded in 1946 and has about 25,000 members.

Three different confederations, because they are strongly bound to party politics, are active among small farmers. This phenomenon illustrates the competition that exists between the three big parties for support of the small farmers. The largest of the organizations is the bourgeois Confederation of Small Farmers (PVK), controlled by the Center party, which was founded in 1922. Its membership in 1965 was about 78,000. As a counterweight to the League of Small Farmers (PVL), founded in 1906 and later controlled by the

Communists, the Social Democrats established the League of Finland's Small Farmers in 1949. Membership in these organizations in 1965 was about 42,000 and 19,000 respectively.

Of the organizations acting as pressure groups in the agricultural area, mention should also be made of the venerable and broad-based Confederation of Agricultural Societies and the labor market organization (small in membership) called the Employer Association of the Countryside.

Trade Union Movement. It has already been noted that Nordic organizational life is generally characterized by a density of the organizational network, by a high degree of citizen organization, and by strong centralization in every area. But within the Finnish trade union movement, which seeks to protect the economic interests of the workers, features exist that point in another direction. Organizing began late and has progressed rather slowly; the workers have been divided among many central organizations which are in competition with each other and which are sometimes seriously weakened by internal conflict.

Peculiar to Finland, first of all, is the fundamental difference between the trade union movement of workers and that of salaried employees. An attempt to emphasize social position and an aversion to the political ideology of the labor movement caused civil servants and salaried employees, after they had begun to organize, not to rely on the workers' trade union movement but to found their own confederations and general organizations. Even during the interwar years trade union organizations did not have any particular interest in the "petty bourgeois" movement of civil servants and salaried employees. After 1944 a significant rapprochement occurred, and SAK's civil servant membership, which included primarily lower service personnel of the public sector, grew continually until the mid-1950's (14,600 in 1945, 25,300 in 1955). But as a result of a split which began at the end of this decade, the central organization lost most of its civil servant organizations; they either joined a competitive central organization or remained "independent." Significant also is the fact that even the lower-salaried employee groups of the private sector, foremen, for example, have for the most part remained apart from the trade union movement.[8]

8. Knoellinger, *Labor in Finland*, pp. 147–152; Väinö Luoma, *Valtion virkamiesten järjestäytyminen Suomessa* (Turku, 1962), II, 170–188.

Of the top organizations of the workers' trade union movement, first mentioned should be the Confederation of Finnish Trade Unions (Suomen Ammattiyhdistysten Keskusliitto, SAK), whose roots go back to Finland's Trade Union Organization, founded in 1907. After the Civil War the latter came under Communist control, and the Social Democratic trade unions, wracked by political conflicts, began in the late 1920's to withdraw from the Trade Union Organization, which was proscribed by the courts on a charge of revolutionary activity. On the initiative of Social Democrats, the SAK was founded in 1930 as a new trade union central organization. It began to gain recognition as a central labor market organization in the 1930's, but it was only following the Second World War, after its membership had risen substantially and after labor relations had been reworked, that the social significance of SAK increased decisively. In 1937 the membership was 64,000, in 1945 300,000, and in 1947, when a record was achieved, 342,000. Since 1947 the membership has decreased considerably, mostly because of internal political quarrels.

According to its rules, SAK is an organization independent of parties. But because its membership is composed in the main of those who vote for the political left and it has thus maintained close relations with parties of the left, it is understandable that the confederation has been drawn into party politics and the internal disputes of the labor movement. Following the Second World War there has been a constant struggle within the SAK between Social Democrats and the Communists. The quarrels came out into the open after the People's Democrats wound up in parliamentary opposition in 1948; they reached a climax in the following years with the expulsion of seven Communist-led unions, most of which later returned to the central organization. Since then the leadership has remained firmly in the hands of the Social Democrats, but in the mid-1950's internal conflicts within that party became a new factor disrupting the trade union movement.

Individuals belonging to the Social Democratic opposition (the "Skogs") were, indeed, the decisive group within the SAK; but, since the leadership of many member unions supported the party's majority line or a trade union line which was opposed to party politics, the confederation was not able to hold together as the struggle became more intense. Some 20 unions resigned from the SAK, and many individual unions divided so that the minority withdrew and founded a competitive organization. In 1960 the opposition coalesced in final form by establishing its own confederation, Finland's Trade Union Organization (Suomen Ammattijärjestö, SAJ). But certain unions that were part of the workers' trade union movement remained independent and refused to join either central organization. In the beginning of 1969 the situation was as follows:

SAK	24 unions	298,000 members
SAJ	16 unions	90,000 members
Independent unions	5 unions	128,000 members

Negotiations aimed at reconciliation finally achieved results in 1969, although complete harmony was lacking in the absence of endorsement by the SAJ. The Confederation of Finnish Trade Unions (Suomen Ammattiliittojen Keskusjärjestö, SAK) became the new central organization, and at the founding congress, or shortly thereafter, it was joined by 24 SAK unions, 5 independent unions, and 6 SAJ unions (with a membership of approximately 40,000). There were, therefore, a total of some 465,000 in the member unions (in late 1969 there were signs that agreement had been reached concerning a merging of the entire SAJ with the confederation). The next step agreed upon for a strengthening of forces was unification of parallel unions. Based on membership figures for 1968, the largest of the new SAK member organizations are the construction workers' union (68,000), the metalworkers' union (57,000), the union of municipal workers and civil servants (49,000), the paper industry workers' union (32,000), and the united organization of civil servants (36,000).

Internal disputes concerning form of organization have also caused difficulties. At the founding congress of the old SAK, in 1930, an industrial union principle was approved as the basis for the trade union movement's organizational activity: this means that member unions encompass all professional groups of the same industry. Thus workers in repair shops of the wood and paper industry production establishments, for example, belong not to the metal workers' union, but rather to the trade unions in the wood processing sphere. This principle, which has been ratified in many congresses, has nevertheless remained unrealized in practice; activity is still based in part on a craft union foundation. At the moment some unions are pure industrial unions, some are unions of the same craft, and some are mixed. This has resulted in internal disagreements over both union limits and the right to conclude labor contracts, and it has also strengthened, when compared with the past, the notion of unions of the same craft.

Because of the above factors and certain others related to the history of the nation's political life, Finland is considerably behind the other Nordic countries when it comes to the trade union movement. On one hand, organization is relatively low percentage-wise and, on the other, the education of members in trade union principles of the Nordic countries has remained relatively insignificant. It is estimated that only about one-third of the workers who could be organized do in fact belong to trade union organizations. These internal difficulties in the movement, together with the fact that many parties compete for the support of its membership, partially explain the sporadic nature of the SAK's political positions and tactics after the Second World War. In this light one can perhaps understand the fact that the SAK has on numerous occasions threatened to launch a general strike (and once, in 1956, it even declared one) in support of political demands—a form of struggle which in Western trade union circles is considered old-fashioned.

The degree of organization varies greatly. It is highest, ninety to a hundred percent, in certain narrow occupations such as those of seamen, publishing house workers, and locomotive engineers where a high craft skill, traditions, or other factors produce strong group identification. From this the organizing drops off as one moves to the broader industrial areas and to industrial unions; it is lowest outside industry, namely, in agriculture and forestry. Women have much less interest in the trade union movement than men; the large number of women in the labor force helps explain Finland's low percentage in terms of organization.

The lowest echelon in the organizational structure is the trade union section, which brings together workers from the same craft or industrial field in a given locality. Sections can unite to form local trade union organizations, whose tasks, however, are limited to activities such as educational work and the organization of demonstrations. The second echelon is the trade union, made up of sections, and the third is the central organization, formed by the trade unions. The organs of the confederation which handle administration and exercise decision-making power are the congress, the council, and the working committee. Characteristic of the newer Finnish trade union movement has been an effort to centralize the exercise of power whether it be a question of internal organizational life, labor market policy, or pressure activity. Ultimate decision-making power of the trade union sections is rather limited in the SAK. The trade unions constitute the echelon where agreements with employers are made and where labor fights take place, but even in such matters as these the confederation, especially after the Second World War, has increased its influence. Through its general economic policy positions and through general agreements concluded with employer organizations, the confederation has determined the direction of trade union policy and has established a framework within which the unions must fit their activity. On many occasions the SAK leadership has also negotiated and reached agreement with the Cabinet on economic policy decisions affecting the fundamental interests of the trade union population. The demand for speed and effectiveness has led, too, to a concentration of power in the highest executive organs, in the working committee as well as in the hands of the principal salaried employees. Especially in the 1950's, the chairmen of the SAK and of its largest member unions were among the most influential political leaders in Finnish society.

Organizational efforts by civil servants and salaried employees are related to a powerful growth of these groups during the period of Finnish independence and also to a change in their social position. A deterioration in economic position brought about by crisis and inflation during and after the First World War provided the first real impetus to the movement of salaried employees and a new, even more rapid spurt occurred after the Second World War, partially for the same reasons. Other factors prompting this development were the spread of a feeling of insecurity and uncertainty in the civil service as a result of internal political changes, as well as the example of achievements by the workers' trade union movement. The organizing of salaried employees is generally assumed to have really started only after the Second World War—an assumption that does not, however, hold true in all respects. As early as the 1930's the degree of organization was relatively high; in 1939 it was about one-third, many times higher than the figure for the workers. It is nevertheless true that the trade union movement of salaried employees was characterized by a very great diffuseness and a weakness in labor market policy. The latter was in part due to the fact that in Finland the trade union movement of salaried employees has to a great degree involved public employees. Before the Second World War, three-quarters of the organized salaried employees were serving in the public sector; in 1959 the share was two-thirds. According to Luoma's estimate, the total number of members in the movement of salaried employees and civil servants was about 150,000 in 1950 and about 200,000 in 1959; the percent organized is said to have fluctuated between 40 and 50.[9]

After the First World War, in 1922, a central organization, the Association of White-Collar Labor (HTY), was founded to unite the movement of salaried employees; but it was joined by only a small portion of those who were organized, and its prestige and influence on the labor market was rather small. During the Second World War, in 1944, a wholly new top organization was founded in its place, the Confederation of White-Collar Labor (HTK); in 1956 its name was changed to the Confederation of Salaried Employees and Civil Servants (Toimihenkilö- ja Virkamiesjärjestöjen Keskusliitto, TVK), which better describes the composition of membership. In 1956 the organization's membership surpassed the 100,000 mark. At the end of 1965 there were 29 member organizations with a total of 152,000 members in the TVK. The largest of the unions are the Union of Civil Servants (38,000 members), the Union of Finnish Teachers (25,000), the Union of Nurses (14,000), and the Union of Communal Civil Servants (14,000). Thus, within the confederation the employees of the public sector are by far the largest group (about 70 percent of the membership). It should be noted that the Union of Civil Servants is itself a central organization with its own suborganizations.

Over the years the TVK has attempted to dispel those prejudices held by both state and private employers as well as by the workers' trade union movement concerning collective action by civil servants and salaried employees; and it has been able to a great degree to stabilize its position as the top organization of its own organizing sector. Although wage and labor questions are officially within the jurisdiction of member organizations, the TVK has increased its activity in this sphere through direct negotiations and general agreements. At the same time it has renounced its earlier sensitivity about the use of direct action and effective pressure tactics. The membership's heterogeneity is the only factor still hindering adoption of a unified policy.

9. Luoma, *Valtion virkamiesten,* II, 47–48, 188–204.

The trade union movement of salaried employees differs fundamentally from the workers' trade union movement in that integration within the former has been noticeably weaker. Right after the Second World War it appeared that it would be possible for the HTK to become a top organization uniting the vast majority of organized salaried employees. But growth soon ended, and in the early 1950's an outright decline occurred. Some organizations resigned from the HTK or stayed apart from the outset in the belief that their own special interests would not be furthered through membership in the central organization. They either remained independent or founded their own central organizations. At the end of 1950 about half of the organized civil servants and salaried employees were in the TVK (55 percent in 1959).

In 1946 the technical employee organizations founded their own labor market organization, the Confederation of Finnish Technical Salaried Employees, to look out for the interests of technical management, primarily in industry and transportation. In 1965 it had about 16,000 members. In the beginning of the 1950's, people with academic degrees also began to organize separately; the immediate reason was the postwar decline in economic and social position of university-trained persons when compared with other wage-earners, and also the fact that the former did not consider it possible to achieve sufficient protection for their special interests in the central organizations, where they were a small minority. On the basis of preparatory steps taken by the Council of the Academic Professions (AKAVA), set up in the spring of 1950, a Council of Academic Cooperation was founded at the end of the year. In 1954 it became more firmly established as a registered association and took for its name the earlier abbreviation Akava. The membership is composed of 36 associations that are wholly or primarily professional, totalling about 29,000 members in 1965. Close to half the members are in public service, and the activity of Akava is, indeed, designed primarily to bring pressure to bear on state organs and institutions. Unlike the other trade union central organizations, Akava is organized horizontally: all individuals with an academic degree can belong regardless of field and job. Some of the members are also, through other organizations, in the TVK.

The degree of organization for state civil servants is very high; at the end of the 1950's at least four-fifths (about 70,000 employees) of the civil service was organized. The civil servant movement has, however, remained relatively diffuse, reflecting the fact that the civil service consists of individuals from many different social strata. Service personnel have been inclined to find their way into the workers' trade union movement. In 1951, when the SAK share of the civil servant movement was at a peak, about 40 percent of all organized civil servants and about 70 percent of service personnel belonged to this central organization. By 1963 most had withdrawn from the competing trade union organizations. In 1959 about 43 percent of the organized civil service was affiliated with the TVK. A substantial minority is still outside the top organizations of both branches of the trade union movement; of these the most significant and most influential group is Akava. Since each central and cooperative organization represents, to a great degree, its own civil servant stratum—SAK, SAJ, and VY representing those in the lowest wage brackets, TVK (the Union of Civil Servants) the middle groups, and Akava the highest—there is a certain competitive, tense relationship between them and they have not been able to achieve any substantial cooperation.[10]

In addition to the trade union groupings discussed above, mention should be made of organizations of the self-employed, which generally are small in membership but some of which have considerable political influence based on the key position of a professional group in the social structure, on social prestige enjoyed by the membership, and on the group's strong internal solidarity. These organizations are, to mention only two examples, the Union of Finnish Architects and the Union of Finnish Doctors.

Other Pressure Groups. Some of the most visible pressure groups, which defend the economic interests of producers, employers, and workers, have been discussed. It would, of course, be possible to identify many other interests which bring people together in pursuit of political power. Organizations which act as pressure groups are formed not only by individual persons but also by public associations (for example, the Association of Finnish Cities and the Association of Rural Communities). Pressure groups usually result from a "natural" development of society, and their activity is designed to be lasting. But in some instances exceptional conditions have given rise to their foundation; examples would be the organizations of Karelians who lost their native homes (to the Soviet Union, as a

10. *Ibid.*, 170–204.

result of the Winter and Continuation Wars) and the organizations of war invalids.

Spiritual organizations, which, relying on their ideology, seek various nonmaterial goals that they consider of general utility, form a separate category. It is difficult empirically to draw a clear line between interest-political and ideological-political pressure groups because, as has been noted, in the activity of most organizations special interests and ideological goals mesh to some degree. Some of the most influential ideological-political groups in Finland are the temperance organizations, whose activity is not questioned by any political group and whose positions have had an important impact on state and communal decisions concerning the promotion of temperance.

PRESSURE POLITICS

Methods of Pressure. The tactics used by pressure groups can be divided into three main categories: 1) Pressure groups attempt to influence state power through propaganda which will affect public opinion. 2) Pressure groups attempt to influence the composition of leading party and public organs; in other words, they strive to get people who will react favorably toward their own interests and ideals into those positions. 3) With an eye on their own interests, pressure groups seek to influence decisions and measures taken by party leaders and officials. It is this activity to which the term "pressure politics" in its more narrow usage refers.[11]

Propaganda. Long-term shaping of public opinion occupies an important position in the program of all large organizations with economic means at their disposal. In this propaganda work use is made of mass meetings, demonstrations, national celebrations, the press, literature, movies, radio, and television. Pressure groups attempt to make themselves heard not only through their own publications, but also through the pages of daily newspapers and economic and other publications.

An example of an organizational publication with a mass circulation is the organ of the MTK, *Maaseudun Tulevaisuus*, with a circulation in 1965 of about 160,000. Papers with the largest circulation,

11. Jussi Teljo, "Painostusryhmät ja painostuspolitiikka," *Sosialistinen Aikakauslehti*, no. 11–12 (1953), 418.

however, are the consumer newspapers appearing in the field of commerce that are ordered by private merchants and cooperative enterprises for their customers (for example, *Pirkka*, *Yhteisvoimin*, and *Kuluttaja*). In addition to this general educational work, groups seeking political influence also attempt to win the support of public opinion through short-lived propaganda campaigns related to special questions.

Personal Politics. Looked at from a broader perspective, parties and pressure groups seek the same goal: to maximize their power in society so as to achieve their most important ends. The difference is that the pursuit of political power[12] is only one—not always the most important—form of action for pressure groups, and their political activity is of an indirect sort. There are, however, exceptions to the latter dictum; in some cases pressure groups attempt to participate directly in the exercise of public power. Sometimes, when the parliamentary situation is confused, there is discussion concerning the formation of a special "labor market Cabinet." This term generally means a government like a caretaker Cabinet—a government that is based on economic organizations rather than parties and in which the main emphasis is consequently on the representation of opposing labor market interests. In connection with certain Cabinet crises, these organizations have shown obvious interest in Cabinet portfolios. Since 1944 many SAK chairmen, and some chairmen of its member unions, have sat in the State Council—not always, to be sure, with the permission of their organizations. In the spring of 1962 three leftwing ministers, who were named openly as explicit representatives of the SAK, joined the predominantly rightwing Cabinet of Ahti Karjalainen. During negotiations over the new Cabinet, the TVK also voiced a demand for its own representation in the State Council alongside the SAK. Organizational leaders of the industrial producers have also been in Cabinets as "independent ministers."

Normally pressure groups act through parties, trying to see that acceptable individuals are selected as key personnel and representatives within the parties. This effort becomes most evident during general elections, at which time the influence of those groups can be seen from the preparation of election platforms to the nomination of candidates and the election campaign. Organizations try to influence

12. The adjective "political" is used here in its usual narrower sense.

the nomination of candidates in the appropriate parties, and competition between interest groups can arise because of the limited number of positions. For example, in the structurally heterogeneous Coalition party this type of group activity appears frequently. Pressure groups ascertain how candidates feel on specific questions, and they disseminate propaganda on behalf of those candidates who promise to support their demands. Before the 1958 parliamentary election, the Confederation of Taxpayers sent candidates a questionnaire in which it sought their opinions on the desirability and possibility of lightening the tax burden. Later the confederation recommended to the voters in newspaper advertisements the candidates whom it considered suitable. A concrete example of pressure group electoral activity is offered by the conduct of the SAK in the 1958 election, when that organization and its organs openly supported the Social Democratic Skog-line candidates.

How strong is organizational representation in different parliamentary groups? Light is shed on this question by Lolo Krusius-Ahrenberg's research concerning representation by the most important economic organizations in the Parliament elected in 1951.[13] The results are summarized in Table 12, in which, because it was prepared on the basis of a textual presentation and because the degree of support given to organizations varied greatly, the numbers cannot be considered wholly accurate.

In general the table illustrates the fact that pressure groups in Finland's multiparty system approach their own parties and the fact that organizational representation in Parliament is very strong. Since it was possible to interview only about half of the People's Democrats sitting in Parliament, including this group was not feasible. Employer interests in industry and agriculture are understandably represented only in the bourgeois groups, mainly the Coalition and Swedish People's parties. Support for private enterprise in commerce is strongest on the right wing, whereas support for the cooperative movement is strongest on the left. Insofar as the latter group is concerned, the bifurcation of the cooperative movement along major political lines caused the leftist cooperative men to represent, without exception, the Confederation of Consumer Cooperatives, while their bourgeois counterparts represented SOK. Agricultural producers are, as pointed out above, very close to the

13. Lolo Krusius-Ahrenberg, *Kring intresserepresentationen i vår riksdag* (Helsingfors, 1955).

Table 12. Organizational representation in parliamentary groups elected in 1951

Members of Parliament	Coalition party 28	Swedish People's party 15	Finnish People's party 10	Agrarian party 51	Social Democratic party 53
Industrial employers	8	2	1	–	–
Agricultural employers	2	2	–	1	–
Self-employed	11	2	3	1	–
Cooperative activity	5	6	1	43	45
MTK	5	6	–	37	–
Small farmer organizations	–	–	–	5	5
HTK	7	1	6	3	–
SAK	–	–	–	–	20

Source: Based on information in Lolo Krusius-Ahrenberg, *Kring intresserepresentationen i vår riksdag* (Helsingfors: Svenska Handelshögskolan, 1955), pp. 9–24.

Center party, even though there are a substantial number of individuals representing these producers within the Coalition and Swedish People's groups. According to Krusius-Ahrenberg, the small farmer organizations limit their connections to the three largest groups; each of these politically tinged confederations had its supporters and adherents within the corresponding party. White-collar workers were represented in all the bourgeois groups and, relatively speaking, especially within the Finnish People's party group. Representatives of the SAK, and of the trade unions which remained apart from it, were—as might be expected—found only within the groups on the left. In this respect a special feature of the SKDL group was that, with leadership of the SAK in the hands of the Social Democratic majority, many of the members of Parliament who were interviewed felt that they were not direct representatives of the SAK; they represented its mass membership or the Communist-led unions which had been expelled from the SAK. This research called attention to the fact that direct representation of production organizations has remained, quantitatively speaking, small. In itself, however, this does not indicate weak political influence on the part of those organizations; on one hand they operate in other, less visible, ways and, on the other hand, the interests of industrial employers find strong general support in parliamentary groups of the Coalition and Swedish People's parties.

In his investigation of the social background of members of Parliament elected in the years 1907–1939, Martti Noponen noted the significance which participation in the handling of organizational duties had for the preliminary training of the members. It was discovered that before being elected to Parliament, almost 95 percent of the Social Democrats and about 80 percent of the Communists had participated in leading organs of the workers' trade union movement or in other nonpolitical organizational activity; this was particularly characteristic of the trade union and cooperative movements. In bourgeois parties, the fields from which most members of Parliament came were agriculture, cooperative work, production and private enterprise, and youth work.[14]

The substantial concentration of each field's organizational representation within certain party groups does not, however, mean that there is a close alliance in Finland between interest groups and

14. Martti Noponen, *Kansanedustajien sosiaalinen tausta Suomessa* (Porvoo, 1964), pp. 263–273.

parties; neither does it mean that interest groups participate directly in party activity, with their own membership and economic resources. As mentioned earlier, the small size of individual parties prevents them from satisfying the demands of the central organizations. Indeed, those parties upon which the trade union movement of salaried employees, as well as employers in industry and business life, could lean have been able to count on only about one-quarter of the seats in Parliament. The MTK has, of course, maintained very close relations with the Center party, but their interests have not always been in harmony. In the 1950's it became apparent on numerous occasions that the political line of social-agrarianism could not satisfy the interests of the producers.

Traditionally the closest association has been between the political and trade union movements of the workers. Even though the SAK proclaimed at its founding congress that it was an organization independent of parties, and even though it prohibited both its unions and basic units from belonging to parties and the collecting of party dues in conjunction with the collection of fees for trade union organizations, it has cooperated closely with the party whose members have controlled the leading SAK positions. In the second half of the 1940's, the Social Democratic party worked actively on the trade union front in order to preserve its position in the leadership of the SAK and its unions. When the situation had become stabilized and a Social Democratic majority in the confederation was assured, the party began to withdraw from the battlefield. In the 1950's the roles changed, so that the Social Democratic leadership of the SAK is now attempting to increase its influence in the party. In their cooperation the party and the trade union organization sought to support each other, although differences of opinion were not, of course, absent. To resolve these problems a special negotiating body was set up in the late 1940's. After the general strike of 1956 relations began to cool and they soon broke off completely. The SAK began to support the Social Democratic opposition (which, however, has been of relatively little use to the SAK) and the Social Democratic party began to cooperate with the SAJ.[15]

When classifying the tactics used by citizen organizations in their pursuit of political influence into two general categories, external pressure and activity within parties, attention is usually called to the exercise of power at the "parliamentary level," in Parliament

15. Huuska, "SAK:n toiminta," pp. 8–16.

and in the Cabinet, where direct participation of organizations—functional representation—remains, as mentioned, an exceptional phenomenon. In public administration, however, direct participation by organizations has been quite extensive. This linking of organizational representation to administration is carried out, above all, within the framework of secondary organization. It is achieved by establishing in support of public offices, for assistance in the preparation, execution, and supervision of matters and for execution of planning, explanatory, and research tasks, permanent committees, boards, commissions, and negotiating bodies composed essentially of individuals who in their duties are explicit representatives of interest groups and who are often named by the organizations themselves. Generally the activity of these organs is of an advisory and clarifying nature, but some of them also exercise administrative decision-making power. The form of organization under consideration is treated in more detail in Chapter IX.

The question of an even more direct movement toward a corporative system arises when the state entrusts its own administrative duties to private organizations, giving them economic support and the right to exercise public power but reserving to itself the right to supervise the execution of these duties. Taking part in this indirect administration, which over time has developed in irregular fashion and is consequently quite heterogeneous in organization, is a whole group of collective bodies from various spheres: chambers of commerce, forestry associations, agricultural advisory organizations, and organizations in the social area, to mention only a few examples.

Pressure Politics. The tactics of actual external pressure fluctuate according to the situation and the possibilities at hand; they extend from the most refined attempts at influence to the most radical of measures and they may be ethically right or wrong, legal or illegal. The most common means used by pressure groups to promote their goals are informal and propaganda work, carried out with the aid of the mass media; the submission of proposals in the form of memoranda and statements as well as in personal conversations and negotiations; threats and bribes; and direct action, in other words, the imposition of direct sanctions.

Pressure groups attempt to extend their activity to all areas where political decisions affecting them are made. From their perspective the forms of activity which are of primary importance are, of course, parliamentary legislative work and economic administration. In general one can say that large influential organizations direct their pressure toward groups which are as large as possible, toward entire party groups and committees; whereas smaller organizations focus more on individual, select representatives. In the field of legislation the pressure groups utilize an indirect right of initiative by presenting to the Cabinet and to members of Parliament proposals for new legislation. It would be interesting to know how many Cabinet proposals and bills submitted by members of Parliament begin, in fact, with citizen organizations; it seems that their role has grown as legislation has expanded and become more specialized. Pressure groups in the different stages of the legislative process attempt to promote approval of proposals that please them and rejection of those they consider detrimental to their interests. In the area of special legislation, the statements by outside experts invited to committee sessions may have an important impact with respect to the content of a law; it should be remembered that many laws are drawn up in final form at the preparatory committee stage. Interest group representatives are generally called as experts, and the possibility of an organization's giving its opinion on an issue depends in part on its "representation" in the committee.

In the state's annual budget social groups are given economic benefits in various forms, and they are also given certain burdens. The importance of the budget debate for pressure groups can be seen from the fact that when a matter is before Parliament in the fall of the year the flood of memoranda, delegations, and "lobbyists" is at its highest point in Parliament.

Especially in the field of economic policy, however, the Cabinet seems to have become the primary target for pressure from large organizations as, for example, the study by Huuska in the 1950's demonstrates. On one hand the Cabinet has broad decision-making powers in this area; on the other hand primary initiative—the drawing up of plans and the presentation of proposals—is within its jurisdiction, even though the final outcome may be determined in Parliament. According to Huuska, the SAK usually launched its efforts with a memorandum directed to the State Council; the organization aired its views concerning the factors which should be considered, or gave a direct opinion about the content of the decision. If this did not produce results, a new memorandum was prepared that, in more important matters, was delivered by a delegation and with instructions. The next steps, in order, were a sharpening of demands by calling a meeting of the SAK council, threats to use direct action, and, as a last resort, implementation of the threats. The activity was usually open, sometimes emphatically so, since an attempt was also being made to influence public opinion.[16]

Insofar as the classic distinction between decision-making and executive institutions has become blurred and the significance of the administrative machinery as a political factor has increased, organizational pressure directed at this sector has also become more apparent than before. An attempt is being made to shift even more decision-making power to administrative offices; for example, ministries and central offices have already been given far-reaching decision-making powers and have consequently, and understandably, attracted the attention of pressure groups. The initiative in soliciting opinion from organizations often comes from state officials themselves; after having received a committee report or when preparing their own legislative measures, they inquire in advance about the position of organizations in that particular area. In many instances the contact may occur through negotiating bodies and boards which are support organs for the offices.

The extreme form of pressure is a reliance on direct action, which is the beginning of open opposition to public authority. Depending upon the position of the group in question, direct action takes different forms. Sharp political forms of struggle in the areas of industrial production and commerce are so rare that one need hardly mention them. The most recent example of an open struggle by a producer organization was the delivery strike begun by the MTK in March 1956, which amounted to a refusal to sell agricultural products for general consumption. The strike ended within a few days when the organization decided that it had received sufficient guarantees from the Cabinet concerning the position of agriculture vis-à-vis the wage-increase demands of the SAK.

Above all, the interest organizations of wage-earners are those which resort to direct action. The workers' trade union movement on three occasions has launched a political struggle on all fronts using a general strike: in 1905 and 1917 attempts were made through general strikes to support demands for political and social reform, whereas in 1956 a general strike was used to force the Cabinet to accept either a lowering of food prices and of other costs, or, alter-

16. *Ibid.*, pp. 92–94.

natively, an increase in wages. About 420,000 workers took part in the 1956 strike, which lasted 19 days and during which about 6.9 million workdays were lost—more than the total from 1950 to early 1956. For examples of restricted, but very important, struggles which have ended successfully for the organizations of certain occupational fields, one can turn to the strikes of locomotive engineers and seamen. The Seamen's Union in particular has been able to win approval of its demands by repeatedly taking advantage of the fact that shipping during winter is dependent upon the use of ice-breakers.

Since wage questions for civil servants are, in the last analysis, resolved by decisions of public officials, the pressure politics of those organizations which represent civil servants is linked to a general effort aimed at improving the economic position of the membership and the professional body. The organizations of civil servants and salaried employees also resort to strikes as a weapon: for example, in 1947 a civil servant strike included some 50,000 people but lasted only a few days. More common, however, are certain other tactics, above all job boycotts, which affect both state and communal positions and which in many cases have been successful. Mass resignations are also part of the open methods of struggle used by these groups. The question of a civil servant's right to strike seems open to dispute; in jurisprudence one still meets the argument that civil servants have the right neither to strike nor to threaten strikes.

Through a legal negotiating system an attempt has been made to promote peaceful resolution of labor market questions affecting the state and its civil servants. According to a 1943 law and decree on the subject, officials must, before they make decisions on matters related to the work of civil servants, give civil servant organizations which are accepted by the State Council as suitable for negotiation an opportunity to familiarize themselves with the proposals and to influence through negotiation the action that will be taken. In practice the looseness of the regulations has created some confusion, since the right to negotiate has been given to a large number of organizations, even those which represent civil servants only to a very limited degree. In similar fashion, communal office-holders have been given the right to negotiate. The procedure to be followed in the annual review of wages for civil servants, so that changes in the level of earnings will remain in correct proportion to changes in the level of earnings for the general labor market, is determined by special laws.

IV The Press

The first prerequisite for activity by newspapers is freedom of speech, in the Western sense of the term. In Finland it is based on paragraph 10 of the Form of Government Act: "Every Finnish citizen is granted freedom of speech and has the right to publish written or pictorial material without prior approval from anyone . . ." Important supplements to freedom of the press are the decrees concerning the availability of public documents. Freedom of the press during wartime is sharply curtailed for obvious reasons, and even under normal conditions of peace the state regulates press activity to a degree.

The Nature of the Finnish Press. The present situation with respect to Finnish newspapers is the result of developments which have been determined both by conditions peculiar to Finland and by international currents; in the latter sense, the Finnish press has generally followed Scandinavian lines of development. The country's first newspapers appeared in the second half of the eighteenth century, but these were isolated, scattered efforts; real development began only in the 1820's and 1830's, in a spirit of enlightenment and national awakening. Even then growth during the first decades was very slow; in 1850 only about ten insignificant papers were published, once or twice a week. Reactionary policies, including stiff censorship decrees, squeezed the press hard and prevented free dissemination of news or open discussion of national and political questions. In 1850 it was decreed that only religious and economic literature would be permitted in the Finnish language. The liberalization of economic, political, and spiritual life in the 1860's provided new impetus, and the significance of newspapers as a chronicle of daily events and a formulator of public opinion increased substantially.

At the turn of the century there were about eighty papers. By this time almost all cities had papers, but their circulation was so small that only every third family received one paper a week at home.[1] The years of Russification, 1899–1905 and 1908–1917, brought things to a standstill; final liberation occurred as the nation gained its independence in 1917. The Communist press, however, felt the oppressive arm of the authorities in the 1920's and 1930's; it was only after the Second World War that it was permitted to exist freely and openly.

Newspapers have become quite extensive during the period of Finland's independence. The question has not been so much one of increase in the number of papers as of growth in circulation, in frequency of appearance, and in size. Small papers appearing three times a week were characteristic of the 1920's; only after the Second World War has a large daily paper been available for all homes. From a political point of view, the most important aspect of newspapers is the daily press, interpreted here as including papers that appear at least three times a week. In 1965 the total circulation of the daily press thus defined was about two million: given the population of the country, this is a very high figure. In terms of circulation and population, Finland in 1960 ranked about tenth in the world as a newspaper-reading nation.[2]

Characteristic of the Finnish press are a multiplicity of newspaper enterprises and a dependence on parties. In 1965 91 daily papers appeared in Finland, of which 25 appeared seven times a week, 32 six days a week, 3 five days a week, 6 four days a week, and 25 three days a week. In addition to this, there were some 10 small newspapers appearing twice a week, about 100 local papers, and some 10 local sheets financed by advertising and distributed free of charge.[3] The large number of newspapers makes possible, of course, the appearance of many different shades of opinion, but at the same time it prevents the circulation growth of individual papers and keeps a substantial part of the press poor and weak. This phenomenon is in part connected with the political nature of the press

1. For information concerning Finland's communication development, see Paavo Seppänen, "Muuttuva yhteiskunta ja tiedotustoiminta," *Mainostaja*, no. 1 (March 1962), 5–9.

2. United Nations, *Statistical Yearbook 1961*, table 182. A daily newspaper in international statistics collected by UNESCO, however, is considered, unlike the above, a publication that appears four or more days a week and contains general news.

3. According to official statistics, 238 newspapers appeared in Finland in 1965; *Statistical Yearbook of Finland 1966*, table 351.

and the sharpness of party lines; competition forces parties to maintain many organs which are only marginally profitable or which are, even in business terms, clearly unprofitable enterprises. Competition likewise has led to a continued growth in frequency of appearance. Ever since the 1860's the vicissitudes of the daily press have been closely tied to development of the nation's parties and have followed the division of opinions among parties; indeed, the vast majority of newspapers are either clear-cut opinion papers or papers combining news with opinion.

Connected with the growth in total circulation and stiff competition, there has been in the Western press a decrease in the number of papers, a centralization of ownership, and a commercialization of the press. These features can also be seen in the recent history of the Finnish press. National papers which appear in Helsinki and which are well established as disseminators of news are increasing their circulation, as are the large regional papers, whereas small papers are caught in a squeeze even worse than before. Commercial competition leads papers to pay still more attention to their news sections and to break away from close dependence upon parties and their one-sided views. In the latter respect, however, Finland's press has not yet changed its character.

Party Division. When newspapers are examined in conjunction with an analysis of a nation's political system, attention is focused on party alignments with the press. In Finland the daily press is concerned in the main, since local papers are formally nonpartisan and they remain aloof from politics; furthermore, information about their circulation is very difficult to come by. In terms of political dependency, however, there are substantial differences both between various groups and within each group, which makes it difficult to divide the press into opinion groups. It is rather easy to see the political "color" of papers published by the leftwing parties, the Center party, and the Swedish-speaking population, but this color is much more difficult to perceive in papers that support the right and the liberal center. In addition to papers which are clearly organs of the Coalition party there are many others which declare themselves independent and are not viewed by the Coalition party as its direct representatives, but which on political matters adopt—some to a greater, some to a lesser degree—the position of the right. In 1966 the Liberal People's party did not have a single daily newspaper,[4] although there are a number of large independent papers (some of which were once organs of the Progressive party) which in their political positions are close to the center.

Daily papers are divided into opinion groups in Table 13; also noted is the share of the popular vote received by parties in the 1966 parliamentary election. As mentioned, the classification of papers leaves room for interpretation, and the positioning of some is certainly open to debate. It is impossible to acquire exact information about circulation for a given moment in time. Figures based on compilations by the Circulation Examination Company in 1965 have been used as the primary source, but in many cases it has been necessary to rely on information from an earlier year. In the case of small papers which have not been subject to examination and which have not released circulation figures, one can only make estimates.

Table 13. Daily press by party affiliation, 1965

Party affiliation	Number of papers	Circulation in thousands	Percent of total circulation	Percent of vote in 1966 parliamentary election
National Coalition party	11	390.4	18.9	13.8
Independent papers, close to right	9	86.1	4.2	–
Independent papers, close to middle	6	519.7	25.1	–
Swedish People's party	13	155.8	7.5	6.0
Center party	14	327.4	15.8	21.2
Social Democratic party	10	121.0	5.9	27.2
Social Democratic League	1	23.9	1.2	2.6
SKDL	7	130.0	6.3	21.2
Independent and nonpartisan papers	20	312.1	15.1	–
Total	91	2,066.4	100.0	92.0

Source: Based on information released by the Circulation Examination Company (Levikintarkastus Oy).

4. In 1961 the organ of the Finnish People's party, *Turun Sanomat*, declared its independence.

Nevertheless, Table 13 gives a satisfactory picture of total circulation and of its division by party affiliation.

In examining papers that are acknowledged organs of parties, the Coalition party is seen to have a certain over-representation; the party's share of total circulation is close to 20 percent but it is only 14 percent in terms of percent of electorate. For the Swedish People's party the ratios are roughly comparable, whereas the Center party, and especially the Social Democrats and People's Democrats, are badly under-represented in circulation. The Center party, however, has at its disposal many large regional papers, while the press of the labor parties—with the exception of the main organs—is composed entirely of the group's internal organs, which lead a rather tortured existence. With respect to the Swedish People's party, those Swedish-language newspapers which declare themselves formally independent (for example, *Hufvudstadsbladet*) are included in the classification, since they openly support this party.

The above ratios do not give a wholly accurate picture of the situation (for example, with respect to the Coalition party) because there are 10 or so papers which hold fast to their independence of political groups but which nonetheless are rather close to a party line. If these papers are taken into consideration, the Coalition party's share of total circulation is about 23 percent. The Liberal People's party, as noted, does not have a single public organ; in 1965 it had its own columns in only 2 Center party papers (*Kymen Sanomat* and *Karjalan Maa*). The 6 liberal papers referred to in column 2 of Table 13, which account for a substantial portion of the daily press circulation, generally adopt a position on political matters which is bourgeois or centrist but which cannot be called a "People's party" line. In any case, aggregate data show that close to 72 percent of Finland's daily press circulation is bourgeois and that the left newspapers account for only 13 percent. The independent and nonpartisan papers mentioned at the bottom of the table constitute a third group, but even these papers can perhaps be considered primarily bourgeois in general orientation.[5]

The weakness of the labor parties with respect to the press is characteristic not only of Finland; it is found in many other countries, too. The daily press in Sweden, in 1966, could be broken down in

5. Two papers which are independent but close to the Center party are also included in this group.

terms of political orientation as follows: right newspapers accounted for 24.4 percent of total circulation, Center party newspapers 3.4 percent, People's party 48.1, Social Democratic party 19.7, and Communist party newspapers 0.1 percent.[6] The disparity becomes even greater in Finland if one also examines frequency of appearance because bourgeois oriented papers generally appear more frequently than do organs of the left.

The question of press dependency on parties is tied to ownership relations, about which detailed information is not available. As a common characteristic one can say that newspaper enterprises normally take the form of joint stock companies and that ownership has remained in the hands of many people. In Finland one does not find to any appreciable degree an attempt to concentrate ownership in the hands of a smaller group, a development that has already gone far in the United Kingdom and the United States. However, party ownership, which is very strong on the left, is to a degree comparable to this centralization. Publishing companies on the left are generally controlled by labor's political and other organizations, and because of this the papers are by nature definitely political and can all be considered official party organs. The picture is less clear insofar as the bourgeoisie is concerned, because only in a few exceptional cases are the bourgeois parties and other political organizations, formally speaking, in a commanding position with respect to their papers. Although the Swedish People's party does not own a single newspaper, the Swedish-language daily press openly supports the party. The Center and Coalition parties have their own permanent organs—the latter has direct ownership of one paper—although there are different shades of dependency; in addition, many independent papers are very close to the right. The independent Center papers do, on occasion, support the People's party (for example, by supporting its candidates at election time), but these papers nonetheless have no desire to tie their hands and at times are sharply critical of the activity of the People's party.

Table 13 shows that the disparity between parties with respect to the press concerns not so much the number of papers as their circulation. The labor parties have many organs, but in general no more than 10,000 copies are printed. Likewise, the circulation figure for the Swedish-language press is low when compared with the number of papers, but there is a natural explanation for this: the growth

6. Nils Andrén, *Svensk statskunskap* (Stockholm, 1968), p. 128.

potential of Swedish-language papers is, of course, exhausted when the newspaper needs of the Swedish-speaking population in a given circulation area are satisfied. The explanation with respect to the Finnish-language press is more complicated. Attention is often given to the differing financial status of citizens, and without doubt this factor has some significance. But one should perhaps start from the fact that bourgeois, especially right and liberal, papers are generally older than Socialist and many Center party papers; the former had an established position and reading public when the latter began to compete with them for readers. In this respect the workers' press is also hurt by the fact that it is definitely political. As such, paying less attention to the development of news and to other sections which lie outside the realm of party politics, it is not able to arouse sufficient interest among readers and to satisfy their demands. In fact, it has been proven that the reading public's interest in political material found in newspapers is not very great and that a reader and newspaper may represent quite divergent political viewpoints. A large rightist paper can reign in an area predominantly leftist in orientation, as, for example, *Aamulehti* reigns in the city and environs of Tampere.[7] Finally, it should be noted that firms publishing labor papers have generally been ideological-economic enterprises, which have not always sought as large a profit as strictly commercial principles would dictate.

The Most Important Daily Papers. The chief organ of the Coalition party, which appears in the capital, is *Uusi Suomi* (circulation 87,800). It was founded in 1919 as a successor to *Suometar* and *Uusi Suometar*. There are many shareholders in the company which publishes the paper, and much is made of the fact that no private group on the right has achieved a commanding position from which it can dictate the paper's editorial principles. In recent years Tampere's *Aamulehti* (95,800) has risen to a position which equals, and in circulation even surpasses, *Uusi Suomi*. Of the other Coalition party papers mention should be made of *Satakunnan Kansa* (47,000) in Pori, *Karjalainen* (41,200) in Joensuu, and *Vaasa* (53,800) in Vaasa. These are the largest, constantly growing, newspapers in the areas, but the Coalition party has other papers which are less widely distributed but appear 6 or 7 times a week.

Of the papers formerly tied to the Progressive party that are close

7. See Pertti Pesonen, *An Election in Finland* (New Haven, 1968), pp. 48–51.

to the political center, mention should first be made of *Helsingin Sanomat* (256,100); a majority of the shares in the company which publishes this paper are owned by the Erkko family. Led by that family, the paper has become a modern commercial news and advertisement paper which seeks more to depict opinions than to influence them openly. Even in campaign discussions the paper has sought a certain balance and attempted to remain an unbiased observer, although research shows that it has supported candidates of the People's party.[8] The same company also publishes the evening paper *Ilta-Sanomat* (63,800). Other liberal centrist papers, medium-sized in Finnish circumstances, are *Etelä-Suomen Sanomat* (40,200) in Lahti, *Turun Sanomat* (98,500) in Turku, *Kaleva* (53,200) in Oulu, and *Länsi-Savo* (16,700) in Mikkeli.

The organ of the Center party's leadership in the capital is *Suomenmaa* (formerly *Maakansa*, 34,400). Since the paper does not have much chance to sell well where it is published, increasing its circulation is difficult; it has, in fact, had financial difficulties, which have forced it to suspend publication intermittently. More significant is the fact that the party has a number of organs in different parts of the country, some of which are the dominant papers in their areas: *Savon Sanomat* (53,200) in Kuopio, *Keskisuomalainen* (50,400) in Jyväskylä, *Ilkka* (23,900) in Seinäjoki, *Etelä-Saimaa* (29,600) in Lappeenranta, and *Pohjolan Sanomat* (24,100) in Kemi. Papers of the Center party appear 6 or 7 times a week.

The nation's largest Swedish-language paper, *Hufvudstadsbladet* (68,200), is formally independent; but in fact it is close to the Swedish People's party, as are the other Swedish-language daily papers. The majority of its stock has been transferred to a Swedish-language foundation. An evening paper, *Nya Pressen* (9,000), is published along with *Hufvudstadsbladet*. Other papers reflecting the political interests of the Swedish-speaking part of the population are small and in many instances appear only 3 days per week. Swedish papers with a wider circulation are *Vasabladet* (19,900) in Vaasa, *Västra Nyland* (11,500) in Tammisaari, *Jacobstads Tidning* (8,200) in Pietarsaari, *Borgåbladet* (8,500) in Porvoo, and *Åbo Underrättelser* (6,800) in Turku. The *Åland*-paper (7,400) appears in Maarianhamina.

The Social Democratic and People's Democratic press is composed

8. Jaakko Nousiainen, *Tutkimus eräiden sanomalehtien vaalipropagandasta vuoden 1956 presidentinvaaleissa* (Vammala, 1958), pp. 17–24; Pesonen, *An Election in Finland*, pp. 130–133.

of small local organs whose position is inferior to that of the corresponding bourgeois papers and whose main significance, therefore, is as media for internal party communication and propaganda. Their activity is made still more difficult by the fact that Social Democratic and People's Democratic papers often compete in the same community for the support of workers. The chief organ of the Social Democratic party is *Suomen Sosialidemokraatti* (38,500); other organs, ranked according to circulation, are *Kansan Lehti* (16,200) in Tampere, *Pohjanmaan Kansa* (10,000) in Vaasa, *Saimaan Sanomat* (9,600) in Lappeenranta, *Pohjolan Työ* (8,800) in Oulu, and *Uusi Aika* (8,600) in Pori.

Since the beginning of 1958 the SAK has published a paper in the capital which appears 7 days a week: *Päivän Sanomat*. Purportedly an organ of the union-organized wage laborers, in reality its founding was strongly influenced by the Social Democratic opposition group's need for a newspaper; in this spirit the paper has not eschewed political stands. In the election campaign of 1958 it moved to strictly party-political lines. In the fall of that year the Social Democratic opposition recognized the paper as its organ, and in the beginning of the following year it became the exclusive possession of this group —later of the TPSL. In 1965 the circulation was 23,900.

Early in 1957 the organ of the Communist party, *Työkansan Sanomat*, and the organ of the Finnish People's Democratic League, *Vapaa Sana*, merged to form *Kansan Uutiset* (57,400), now published jointly by these organizations and the largest of the workers' daily papers. In general the daily papers which espouse the political line of the extreme left are organs of the SKDL; obviously they are more tightly tied to a party than are the papers of other groups. Of the SKDL papers published outside the capital, mention should be made of *Hämeen Yhteistyö* (10,300) in Tampere, *Satakunnan Työ* (10,300) in Pori, *Kansan Sana* (about 10,000) in Kuopio, and *Kansan Tahto* (21,700) in Oulu.

Activity and Significance of the Press. To phrase the question concretely, how does the press participate in political activity and in what forms does its "party color" appear? In general terms the party press feels duty-bound to inform the public of political events, plans, decisions, and actions, to interpret and criticize positions taken by the various groups, to make the public aware of its own party's demands and viewpoints through well-reasoned arguments, and to enlist citizens in active work on behalf of the group supported by the paper. Political material, and material that is politically colored, can be included in all sections of a paper, in articles as well as in news items and, of course, in paid advertisements. The presentation of political views is a special task of the feature section, particularly in editorials and political polemics; characteristic of the latter is an emphasis on current problems, a choice of words appropriate for sharp comparisons and assertions, and a light style that is popular and emotional in its appeal in contrast to the rather serious, matter-of-fact style of editorials. In its news sections the Finnish press, unlike the press of some other countries, reports extensively on matters discussed in Parliament and by other political organs. One can also detect the shade of a paper's political attitude in its presentation of news, especially through an examination of headlines as well as the form and selection of published material. Little space is given to the speeches and statements of opponents, while much attention is given to the publication of material favorable to one's own party.

Political discussion in the press is generally very lively, although it really becomes active just before general elections; then papers provide their parties with text and advertisement space and thus become, for a short while, media for intense party propaganda. Open campaign propaganda colors all sections of a paper and gives a sharp polemical, one-sided tone to the discussion. My study of Helsinki's largest daily papers, mentioned earlier, demonstrated that the vast majority of campaign articles appearing in party papers just before the 1956 presidential election were strictly propaganda; nonpartisan material accounted for 33 percent of the total in *Helsingin Sanomat*, but in the other five papers examined it fell from a high of 17 percent to a low of 5 percent for *Vapaa Sana*. Most space was devoted to support for a party's own candidate; this was followed by attacks on competing candidates and parties. With the exception of *Helsingin Sanomat*, no space was devoted to an objective presentation of opposing points of view; practically speaking, nothing positive could be found about the presidential candidates of other parties.[9]

In certain respects a newspaper is a very useful instrument of communication and propaganda by parties. It reaches every home on a daily basis, and its content is sufficiently diverse that everyone finds something of interest in each issue. Propaganda can be slipped

9. Nousiainen, *Tutkimus*; see also Pesonen, *An Election in Finland*, pp. 211–226.

into the columns in many different forms: it can be joined to daily questions of interest to readers, and it can be hidden in other texts to assure that it will be read but that its presence will not be so striking. One prerequisite for influence, of course, is that a newspaper reach the reading public. As far as Finland is concerned, there is not much information available on how many papers are read and what articles are selected. Research conducted by Martti Qvist in Helsinki in 1953 indicates that newspapers are evenly divided within society; newspaper reading seems to be independent of, for example, educational level and economic situation. Here, too, it was demonstrated that the political structure of the reading public is not reflected in the choice of paper. In the 1953 municipal election in Helsinki, parties of the left received 45.4 percent of the vote although the newspapers of these parties accounted for only 9 percent of the regular reading public and 13.5 percent of subscriptions.[10]

The political influence of newspapers is a very difficult phenomenon to measure. Indeed, there are conflicting views on the matter. On one hand, mass communication media—one of which is the press—are considered, in terms of their significance, a major political force; this is apparent from the fact that one of the first moves a new party makes is to seek its own organ, as well as from outcries that the growth of propaganda through mass communication media is leading to mass processes in opinion formation and to a further weakening of individuality. On the other hand, the press is viewed as having very little direct influence on political activity. This view is based on the finding that the reading public's interest in editorials and other "more serious" political material in papers is not particularly great, on the rather common phenomenon that most of the press at election time represents a position quite different from that of the parties which emerge victorious, and on interview research concerning the voting preferences of individuals.

Empirical findings demonstrate the two-stage flow of information: first is the dissemination of information, beliefs, and ideas to key individuals in small groups (opinion-transmitters) through papers, movies, and radio; second stage consists of small-group discussion that criticizes, interprets, and weighs information. Each small group has its own opinion-transmitters who, with the aid of personal contacts, carry the dissemination and interpretation of information further along and who are generally of the same social status as the

10. Martti Qvist, *Lukemisharrastus* (Hämeenlinna, 1960), pp. 103–118, 187–188.

individuals they influence. Pesonen in his 1958 study concludes that although the residents of Tampere considered newspapers and radio by far the most important sources of information, small group discussions rather than direct mass communication were more effective in bringing about a change in voting intention.[11]

News Bureaus. In this connection one should mention the politically oriented news bureaus, tied to parties, which pass on political and economic material as well as general news and article material to papers of the same persuasion. *Lehdistön Sanomapalvelu* (LSP) serves the Coalition press; *Uutiskeskus* (UK) and *Keskustapuolueen Sanomakeskus* the Center party; *Työväen Sanomalehtien Tietotoimisto* (TST) the Social Democratic press; and *Demokraattinen Lehtipalvelu* (DPL) the People's Democratic press. The papers also receive material directly from the central bureaus of the parties.

The Finnish News Agency (STT) is a news bureau owned by newspaper enterprises and managed basically as a cooperative company; it supplies both domestic and foreign news to all party and nonparty newspapers and it is responsible for some news broadcasts of the Finnish Broadcasting Corporation. Most of the nation's daily papers avail themselves of this service. For the reporting of foreign news, STT has made reciprocal service agreements with leading news bureaus of different countries. It receives political material by telegraph from Reuters, Agence France Presse, and Deutsche Presse-Agentur. As far as Finland is concerned, it should be noted that STT has exclusive rights, in accordance with a 1920 agreement, to the dissemination of official State Council news. Even though STT has, to a certain extent, a semi-official position, it is in economic and other respects an enterprise independent of public authorities that strives for strict impartiality in its handling of domestic political events. Its activity is, therefore, based on principles of news bureau policy which are generally accepted in Western countries; news service, which considers exactness and objectivity its goal, must be independent of financial support and supervision by governmental authority or by parties and other special interest groups.

11. Pesonen, *An Election in Finland*, pp. 283–345.

Part Two Governmental Institutions

V Finland's Constitution

UNDERPINNINGS OF THE POLITY

Origins of the Constitution. The political forces examined in Part One can be considered, in Duverger's terminology, the substructure—the basic ingredients—of a political system; governmental institutions, whose composition and mode of action will be treated in Part Two, constitute the superstructure. The fundamental provisions concerning governmental organization, which is the totality formed by those institutions, make up the constitution.

The Constitution of Finland is contained for the most part in a number of laws, legal statutes which have come into force with the cooperation of Parliament. They are divided into two groups, fundamental laws and ordinary laws. The most important provisions of the Constitution are found in fundamental laws, which have been given a certain sanctity and inviolability so that difficult procedures must be followed before they can be enacted, changed, or rescinded. An ordinary law can never violate a fundamental law.

First among the fundamental laws is the Form of Government Act (Hallitusmuoto, HM), which forms the foundation for activity by the state. During the period of Russian rule (1809–1917), Sweden's 1772 Form of Government Act, with appropriate changes, was in force in Finland. The preparatory work for Finland's present act was begun in 1917, although more than two years had elapsed before the matter was finally resolved. In accordance with a manifesto issued by the Russian Provisional Government, the Finnish Senate on March 31, 1917, established a constitutional committee, which, led by K. J. Ståhlberg, was charged with the drafting of proposals for the new act and for temporary changes in the existing constitution.

Having prepared many other drafts, the committee finally, in early October, completed its proposal; on December 4, 1917, the Senate presented to Parliament a proposal based on the committee's recommendations. In the committee proposal Finland was to become a republic, loosely tied to Russia; the committee wanted a provision in the Form of Government Act in support of parliamentary government, but at the same time it proposed a separation of powers consistent with the preservation of a balance between social forces. The constitutional committee in Parliament began considering the proposal but, with the outbreak of the Civil War, was not able to complete its work. After the war had ended, in the spring of 1918, it became clear that supporters of a monarchy had increased their strength considerably; two proposals for a monarchy were made during the year to a badly truncated Parliament, but they were not accepted as urgent matters (necessitating a five-sixths majority). Nonetheless, on October 9, 1918, turning to the 1772 Form of Government Act, the German Prince Friedrich Karl of Hesse was proclaimed King of Finland. Later, when plans for a monarchy in Finland were dropped after Germany's surrender and the Finnish parliamentary election of 1919, a republican form of government was approved by Parliament as normal legislation, after a number of intermediary stages. On July 17, 1919, it was ratified by Finland's regent, Gustaf Mannerheim. This superceded the old Form of Government Act, the Act of Union and Security of 1789, and all provisions in other laws and decrees which were in conflict with it. In all essential respects the new Form of Government Act resembled the proposal of Ståhlberg's constitutional committee; it is still in force today, very few alterations having been made.

The Form of Government Act contains an introduction and eleven sections. In the first section general provisions concerning matters of principle are set forth about the Finnish state as a full-fledged republic, sovereign power belonging to the Finnish people, legislative, executive, and judicial power, and citizenship and state territory. In the second section the general rights of citizens are listed, and the third section deals with the fundamentals of legislation. General provisions about the position and activity of the president and State Council are in the fourth and longest section; the fifth concerns the courts, the sixth public finance, the seventh the defense establishment, the eighth education, the ninth religious communities, and the tenth public offices. The final section deals with the first presidential election, the constitutional sanctity of the Form of Government Act, and an annulment of previous laws.

The second significant fundamental law is the Diet Act (Valtiopäiväjärjestys, VJ) of January 13, 1928, which sets forth rules regarding the organization and duties of Parliament. Its core is the earlier Diet Act of 1906; in spite of later changes, the central principles of the new Act remain in effect. Other fundamental laws are the law regarding Parliament's right to examine the legality of actions taken by members of the State Council and the Chancellor of Justice (Attorney General), November 25, 1922; the law regarding the High Court of Impeachment, November 25, 1922; and the law concerning self-government for the Aaland Islands, December 28, 1951. In terms of the Constitution, important ordinary laws are those concerned with the election of members of Parliament (June 30, 1955), the election of a presidential electoral college (June 30, 1955), and the election of a president of the Republic (February 22, 1924); and laws relating to the Supreme Court and the Supreme Administrative Court (July 22, 1918) and the law concerning the number of State Council ministries and their fields of competence (March 30, 1922). Perhaps some less important regulations, such as Parliament's rules of procedure (December 19, 1927) and rules of the State Council (December 17, 1943), can also be included as part of the Constitution.

The Basic Character of the Polity. Finland's form of political organization is based on the country's old political order dating back to the period of Swedish rule, on foreign models, and on the constructs of political philosophers; it is, therefore, made up of many different and to a certain extent contradictory parts. As Fredrik Lagerroth notes,[1] Finland's form of government is a peculiar mixture of doctrinaire and empirical, foreign and domestic. The principle of popular sovereignty and the primacy of Parliament are clearly expressed in paragraph two of the Form of Government Act: "Sovereign power in Finland belongs to the people, who are represented by their delegates assembled in Parliament." In other respects there is in the political order a convergence of features from two different types of government: the European parliamentary system and the American presidential system. Without doubt the former,

1. Fredrik Lagerroth, *Moderna författningar mot historisk bakgrund* (Stockholm, 1955), p. 202.

monistic principle was meant to be primary: an attempt was made to achieve democracy in Finland through radical means, and the Form of Government Act clearly favored the modern parliamentary type of government. Most important in this respect is the fact that as far back as 1917 Parliament added a provision to the Diet Act that followed the model of France's 1875 Constitution, concerning political responsibility of members of the government. The principle of parliamentarism was then included in the 1919 Form of Government Act by establishing that members of the State Council must enjoy the confidence of Parliament.

Along with the monistic principle, however, the principle of separation of powers was included in the Constitution. In paragraph 2 of the Form of Government Act there is a clear differentiation, following the three-fold division advanced by Montesquieu in the mid-eighteenth century, between legislative, executive, and judicial power. The constitutional committee of Ståhlberg had pointed out in arguments on behalf of its proposal that in modern constitutional states a separation of powers has been realized more or less consistently, which "unquestionably provides the guarantee necessary for individual freedom and regular activity of social forces." It was felt that centralization of power—even in the hands of Parliament—would easily lead to oppression and would interfere with the normal course of national life. There was no desire to give Parliament exclusive power, and so the presidency was given powers which are unusually great for a parliamentary-type state; at the same time conditions were established which permit him to exercise these powers in independent fashion. His independence from other state organs and his exercise of power, based on a direct mandate from the people, were emphasized by providing that he should be indirectly elected by the people by a method formally the same as that of the United States. Supreme executive power is entrusted to the president; in addition, for general governance of the state, there is a State Council composed of a prime minister and the necessary ministers.

The notion of a separation of powers, realized in the Constitution, is, however, based more on the national past than on political theories. Even the 1772 Form of Government Act, in force during the period of Russian rule, called for a dualism: a sharing of supreme power by the sovereign and the Diet. In connection with events occurring at the time of Finland's independence, Social Democrats advocated a system in which Parliament would hold sway, but other parties considered the preservation of the dualistic principle appropriate, and many powers formerly exercised by the sovereign were thus given to the president. Like the Grand Duke, the Russian emperor, he can dissolve Parliament and appeal to the people by calling for new elections. He participates with Parliament in legislative work, and he has the power to veto and thereby postpone the enactment of laws passed by Parliament. History has shown that, in matters under his jurisdiction, the president's exclusive right of decision-making has not remained an empty formality.

In other respects, Finland's political order adopted much that was old and tried. One should mention that the position and duties of the State Council still reflect to a great degree that duality of governmental power which arose during the period of Russian rule, for national and geographic reasons, between the Grand Duke and the Senate. Insofar as judicial power is concerned, the principle of the separation of powers has been consistently applied in the spirit of Montesquieu. Judicial power is exercised by the courts (the highest are the Supreme Court and the Supreme Administrative Court), which are independent of the government.

It is often emphasized that of the constitutions established in conjunction with arrangements made following the First World War, Finland's Form of Government Act is the only one still in existence. This can probably be considered a sign that fundamental organizational questions were resolved in satisfactory fashion during the drafting stage and that the Act is flexible enough to adapt to changing circumstances. Historical factors—such as firm commitment to the nation's own fundamental laws during Russification—probably explain the fact that constitutional laws in Finland enjoy unusually great respect. Indeed, the Finnish people prefer not to change them without weighty reasons; when necessary, they are temporarily bypassed by laws which are approved following constitutional procedures but which are not in themselves fundamental laws.

There is reason to emphasize here, too, that the character and forms of political activity are not solely dependent upon legal norms which have come into force through proper decisions; these norms form only a frame, large or small, within which customs and practice shape the political system and give it special features of its own. One knows the primary importance of parties in political life, yet no mention is made of them in constitutional laws. The situation is similar for parliamentarism—the Form of Government Act merely refers to the principle of political responsibility for members of the State Council; the special features of Finnish parliamentarism have been constructed around this principle since independence, dictated mainly by the party system and general political situations. As a third example, one can refer to the relationship between the president, the State Council, and Parliament, which in different situations is subject to fluctuations—sometimes great—and which over time, remaining within the framework of the Constitution, can move far from those principles which formerly guided lawmakers.

FUNDAMENTAL RIGHTS OF CITIZENS

Looked at as a whole and conceived of in broad terms, "human rights" can be divided into three groups. The first is active political rights, of which the most important unquestionably is the right to vote. In the second group there are general rights, most of which are freedom rights, which ensure citizens of a preserve beyond the power of state intervention. The third consists of social rights, for example, the right to a summer vacation, to an old age pension, and to a free elementary education. Of most interest here are the rights in the second category, which are also called fundamental rights of citizens. They are listed in the second section of the Form of Government Act, "General Rights and Legal Protection of Finnish Citizens." The rights in question are equal for all Finnish citizens, but they do not extend to foreign residents in the country. In actual fact, however, foreigners occupy a position which in most respects is comparable to that of a Finnish citizen when it comes to fundamental rights, although they cannot demand for themselves through reference to the Constitution the legal protection envisaged by the fundamental rights.

Of the fundamental rights, mention should first be made of the equality principle, in paragraph 5 of the Form of Government Act: "Finnish citizens are equal before the law." This provision is binding for lawmakers as well as administrators, and it means that all citizens in similar circumstances must be treated alike and no one placed in a privileged position on the basis of such factors as birth, wealth, or social position. Every Finnish citizen "according to law" —within a framework determined more precisely by legislation—is protected in terms of life, honor, personal freedom, and property.

In practice, the rather general constitutional provision concerning the protection of property has probably caused the most problems. Within Parliament there has been frequent discussion of the legislative procedure to be followed when considering laws which restrict in various ways the right to private property. The question of expropriation of property in the name of public need, and of full compensation, is determined separately; the Form of Government Act permits this to be regulated by an ordinary law. The only stipulation with regard to social rights is the very imprecise statement that citizen labor enjoys special state protection. Most commonly this is seen as meaning that the state should concern itself with preservation of tranquil working conditions for laborers, prevention of unnatural exploitation of labor, and protection of workers from dangers to life and health threatening them on the job and that it should undertake positive measures to make a worker who is injured or ill fit once again for work. Especially after the Second World War, there has been great emphasis on legislation seeking to protect the labor force; it thus attempts to make more effective the abovementioned social rights of citizens.

In the Form of Government Act the right of residence and freedom of movement within the country are secured for citizens—meaning that a Finnish citizen cannot be deported from the country, extradited to a foreign country for a crime, or prevented from returning to Finland even though he may not have been issued a passport. He can freely choose his place of residence and move unimpeded from one community to another unless this right is restricted by law. In certain special cases freedom of movement is also restricted under normal conditions, for example, in cases of vagrants, individuals under observation for drinking and on parole, and people residing or traveling in the border zone. The right of a citizen to leave the country is dealt with as a separate matter.

A Finnish citizen has the right to practice religion publicly and privately, insofar as this does not conflict with the law and with good taste, and to refrain from accepting any particular faith. He can freely leave one religious organization and join another; the only condition for leaving is that he be at least eighteen years of age. Freedom of religion in Finland means freedom of conscience and freedom to worship, as well as freedom of religious association. The 1922 law regarding religious freedom contains more precise statements about the right of worship and religious congregations.

Paragraph 10 of the Form of Government Act guarantees citizens free speech, freedom of assembly, and freedom of association. The framework for these rights is worked out in more detail by special laws. Free speech, which includes freedom of the press, means here the right of citizens to state their opinions publicly on all matters without hindrance from the authorities. Accordingly, the 1919 law regarding freedom of the press adopts a system whereby there are no advance obstacles for the preparation and dissemination of published material; all that is required is observance of certain regulations, and individuals accused of misusing the right of free speech can be brought before the courts. The same principle is followed with respect to plays presented to the public, whereas movies, based on a 1945 law, are subject to censorship before they are released. A movie board and a movie inspection section are the organs that carry out this examination. In accordance with a 1907 law on public meetings, every Finnish citizen is permitted to organize a public meeting without having to seek permission in advance; if a meeting is held outdoors in a public place, however, the police must be notified beforehand. Detailed provisions concerning freedom of association are contained in the 1919 law of association—which has nevertheless become obsolete in many respects, due to the brisk development of associational activity. The law deals only with ideological associations, and it distinguishes between registered and unregistered associations. An association does not have to be registered, but only through registration does an association become a juristic person that can own property, conclude agreements, and appear in court as a plaintiff or defendant. If an association acts contrary to law or good taste, administrative officials can forbid its activity until further notice, and an association can be dissolved completely through a court ruling. In terms of the political activity of a democratic nation, the above-mentioned rights are highly respected and very important. The central methods of action in a democratic system, such as elections, parliamentary debates, voting, party activity, and press activity, are possible only on the basis of liberal freedom of speech, freedom of association, and freedom of assembly.

Closely related to these freedoms is the principle of publicity, which is directed at officials of the state and of self-governed communities and which includes, on one hand, publicity concerning the handling of certain matters and, on the other hand, the obligation to release information (a major point with respect to administrative officials).

A 1951 law concerning the availability of public documents stipulates that they are public and at the disposal of all Finnish citizens. There are restrictions on the availability of some documents, and it is possible to declare by law, or under certain circumstances by decree, that matters or documents are to be kept secret. In 1951 a decree was issued which included a number of exceptions to this principle of publicity. The president of the Republic and the State Council may, in certain instances, also declare that a matter or document under consideration shall be kept secret.

Inviolability of the home is also a fundamental right under special protection in the Constitution, as is the secrecy of postal, telegraph, and telephone communications. If a Finnish citizen comes before a court, he can be tried only in that court which by law has jurisdiction over his case. And, further, it is forbidden to bestow noble or other hereditary titles in Finland.

Because of the country's two languages, the language question is also touched upon in the fundamental rights of the Form of Government Act. Finnish and Swedish are established as national languages of the Republic, and the right is secured for citizens to use whichever of the two is their mother language in court and before administrative officials; they are also secured the right to receive official documents in their mother language. The intellectual and economic needs of both segments of the population are to be satisfied by the state on the same basis. The primary purpose of these provisions in contemporary circumstances is to protect the interests of the Swedish-speaking minority.

This list of fundamental rights, contained in the second section of the Form of Government Act, is not in itself exceptional; in the spirit of liberal ideology inspired by the French revolution, the limits of a citizen's personal "autonomy" are contained in broad statements of principle that do not touch to any great extent the social rights which have become so important in modern times. However, the application of these provisions in Finland is distinctive, as Paavo Kastari has demonstrated in his many studies: although these provisions do not play a direct role in court action, it is thought that established practice secures fundamental rights in Finland perhaps better than in any other country. The significance of the system of fundamental rights is especially evident in the way in which it restricts the freedom of action of lawmakers in areas protected by rights.

During the period of autonomy, an accepted practice permitted interference with rights secured by the Constitution through adoption of a law—following procedures for a fundamental law—which made *exceptions* to the provisions in question, but which left the fundamental law itself intact. Because there was a desire at that time to avoid changes in fundamental law, this method made it possible with changing circumstances to increase flexibility of the Constitution and preserve legal forms in political activity. This unusual arrangement was adopted in independent Finland: the last paragraphs of the Form of Government Act and the Diet Act permit exceptions to the provisions of these laws on the basis of a law approved in accordance with the procedure followed when passing a fundamental law. Traditional respect for fundamental law has led to great caution in legislative work pertaining to interference with fundamental rights. Many provisions which in other countries can be enacted through ordinary laws must be approved in Finland by observing the difficult procedure set forth for adoption of a fundamental law. The protection of property by fundamental law has occupied a central position in this respect. An example from the regulation of economic life is the extraordinary law, a law dealing with the regulation of economic life under exceptional circumstances, which was first approved in 1941, and remained in force until 1956 and which gave extensive powers of decision-making to the State Council in order to protect the livelihood of the population and the economic life of the nation. This course of action is made possible on a broad scale by reference in paragraph 67, clause 2, of the Diet Act to an urgent procedure for the adoption of a fundamental law—designed to be used as an exception—which, it is true, requires agreement in Parliament. An indication of the importance of fundamental rights and their practical application is found, for example, in the fact that attempts at socialization following the Second World War clashed with them to a certain extent and were rebuffed.

With an ordinary law one can, in accordance with paragraph 16 of the Form of Government Act, impose restrictions necessary during times of war or insurrection and regarding individuals in military service. This provision is the basis for the law passed in 1930 regarding a state of war, which empowers the president to declare the nation or any part of it in a state of war for reasons of defense or the maintenance of legal order. When a state of war exists, private property can be deeply affected; other public rights, such as freedom of speech, assembly, and association, can also be restricted. It is the president who declares an end to the state of war, though there are no precise provisions about this in the law; indeed, the state of war declared in November, 1939, remained in effect until September, 1947. These two laws, regarding a state of war and regulation of economic life, are part of the enabling acts, which mean a temporary transferral of Parliament's legislative power to the government—to the president and the State Council.

Citizenship. For the vast majority of the population the attainment of Finnish citizenship has been no problem because one is usually a citizen through birth. In accordance with a 1941 law about attainment and loss of Finnish citizenship, persons in the following circumstances gain citizenship by birth: 1) a child born in wedlock whose father is a Finnish citizen; 2) a child born in wedlock whose mother is a Finnish citizen and whose father is not, and who is not, on the basis of birth, a citizen of another country; 3) a child born out of wedlock whose mother is a Finnish citizen.

A foreigner may by decision of the president become a citizen if he so requests. Assumption of citizenship requires, however, that 1) he be at least twenty-one years of age, 2) he have made his actual residence and home in Finland for the past five years, 3) his way of life be known as irreproachable, 4) he be able (and, presumably, able in the future) to provide for himself and his family, and 5) he renounce citizenship of a foreign country. In some cases exceptions can be made to these requirements. Minors generally become citizens with their parents.

An individual who applies for and is granted citizenship in a foreign country immediately loses his Finnish citizenship. When a Finnish citizen becomes a citizen of a foreign country in some other way, he loses his Finnish citizenship if his actual residence and home is outside Finland; if he lives in Finland, he loses citizenship when he moves from the country. A Finnish citizen who has citizenship in a foreign country or who seeks foreign citizenship may through petition be released from Finnish citizenship. In this case the petitioner living in Finland may be forced to leave the country within a specified period.

INTERPRETATION OF THE CONSTITUTION

It is appropriate in connection with discussion of the Constitution and public rights to deal with one more special question: interpretation of the Constitution, a very important problem—particularly insofar as it concerns the constitutionality of laws—in all democratic systems. In some countries special courts of constitutionality have been established, whereas in others the public courts, for example the Supreme Court in the United States, have the power to determine whether a particular law is in consonance with the constitution. In Finland, as in the Nordic countries generally, there is no systematized procedure to deal with this problem; rather, the matter has been dependent upon practice.

In paragraph 92 of the Form of Government Act it is stated that "if a provision in a decree is contrary to a fundamental or other law, it is not to be applied by a judge or any other official." Two conclusions can be drawn: on one hand, examination of the constitutionality of decrees can almost always be made in the courts; on the other hand, courts do not have the right to determine whether or not a certain law is constitutional. On a number of occasions it has been suggested that this power of interpretation be given to the Supreme Court, but the proposals have failed because of opposition from Parliament. In a proposal made by the government in the summer of 1918 for a new form of government, it was suggested that there be a provision stating that "if a law not passed in accordance with the procedure for a fundamental law contains a provision contrary to a fundamental law, the Supreme Court is not to apply it; the Supreme Court should demand that the error be rectified."[2] Parliament's constitutional committee, however, threw out this point, stating that it is unwise to give so much power to the Supreme Court. In subsequent proposals concerning the form of government, the view of the parliamentary committee prevailed. The negative arguments presented in Parliament were based on the notion that judicial review of constitutionality would not be necessary because Parliament would be able to perform this duty satisfactorily in connection with legislation. However, a background factor seems to have been a fear that if the Supreme Court were to receive these powers, it could encroach upon the powers of Parliament and could become in this respect a "second chamber" with Parliament.

In practice the matter has been settled along different lines. Questions concerning interpretation of a fundamental law are

2. *Toiset valtiopäivät 1917, hallituksen esitys no. 62, asiakirjat III* (Helsinki: Suomen Senaatin kirjapaino, 1918), p. 30.

generally resolved in Parliament, in actuality by its constitutional committee, whose interpretation is sought in unclear cases and whose judgment is binding on Parliament. In difficult judicial questions, the committee turns to experts, often professors of law, giving great weight to their opinions. Frequent use, treated above, of legislation which departs from the usual pattern of fundamental laws has had an important impact in fixing this practice. When the committee is dealing with laws which in one way or another concern fundamental laws, especially general rights of citizens, it must often interpret the content of fundamental laws and must decide what procedure should be followed in discussion of a given matter. If there is some uncertainty about interpretation, a preference is shown for fundamental law procedure in order to avoid violation of the Constitution. A general duty of the speaker of Parliament, moreover, is to review in Parliament the constitutionality of the lawmaking procedure.

There are several other means of review. The chancellor of justice, who is regularly present at sessions of the State Council, makes sure that proposals by the government are prepared in correct form; he also has the opportunity to express an opinion when a law approved by Parliament goes to the president for his signature. The president, too, plays a role as guardian of the Constitution. It is significant that before a proposal by the government is presented to Parliament, and before ratification, the president can request an opinion from the Supreme Court or the Supreme Administrative Court or both. An event which occurred in 1923 illustrates the importance of this practice. When a law approved by Parliament—the lex Pulkkinen, a law concerning expropriation by the state of land purchased illegally—came before the State Council for ratification and execution, the Council went on record in favor of ratification; but two members who were present, the Chancellor of Justice and the Solicitor General (Ombudsman) of Parliament protested and argued that the matter should be dealt with in the manner prescribed for fundamental laws. President Ståhlberg requested an opinion from the Supreme Court, to whose negative stand the State Council yielded, and the law was not ratified. Several years later Parliament passed a new law, following procedure for a fundamental law, and it came into force.

In general, the problem of interpretation of a fundamental law, left open when the Form of Government Act was drafted, has not in the opinion of all jurists been satisfactorily resolved. Present guarantees concerning the constitutionality of laws are influential only in conjunction with the legislative process; effective postlegislative control is absent. It is therefore obviously possible to pass a law which conflicts with a fundamental law and which must be applied by officials. Parliament's constitutional committee hardly can be considered an appropriate "constitutional court"; neither is the president's right to request opinions a foolproof means of review. But because political forces feel that the present system satisfies practical needs, reforms have not been deemed necessary.

VI Parliament

Representative Democracy. Citizen participation in governmental activity takes different forms in different systems. In the large and complex societies of today the only practical form of popular government is, generally speaking, indirect or representative democracy, where the task of citizens forming the electorate is to choose organs and individuals that exercise public power and make binding decisions. The central institution of such a system is the national legislature. Since the First World War there have, however, been efforts to increase the population's own influence by turning to methods of direct democracy—to the referendum and initiative. Indeed, provisions concerning popular referenda are included in the constitutions of many countries, both people's democracies and Western democracies. Of Finland's closest neighbours one can cite Denmark, whose 1953 Constitution considerably broadened the 1915 system of popular referenda.[1]

Finland's political system is based on the principle of a purely representative democracy. In paragraph 2 of the Form of Government Act it is stated: "Sovereign power in Finland belongs to the people, who are represented by their delegates assembled in Parliament." There is, therefore, no provision in the constitutional laws for a popular referendum, although it would, of course, be possible on the basis of a special law. Thus in 1931 an advisory popular referendum repealed the prohibition law by an overwhelming majority. In 1917 a popular referendum became permissible in communal affairs, but these provisions were overturned two years later.[2] In Finland, unlike Sweden, the question of adopting a popular referendum has not evoked much discussion.

1. See Poul Meyer, *Politik, statskundskab i grundtraek* (Copenhagen, 1959), pp. 80–84.
2. As far as is known, the separation and independence of Huopalahti from the

The Finnish Parliament (eduskunta). The question of reforming Parliament so that it would meet the needs of political activity in an independent democratic nation was no longer timely when Finland broke away from Russia; in most important respects it had been resolved some ten years previously, in 1906, when there was a radical shift from a four-estate Diet to a unicameral Parliament elected on the basis of universal and equal suffrage. The change seemed even more radical since popular representative institutions in even the most democratic nations were at that time bicameral in form. It was, however, necessitated by an atmosphere of crisis; it was born of the pressure of forces that had pushed through to the surface from below, and it was accepted as a necessity even in quarters where the reform was considered too far-reaching. Socialists, who gathered their forces and became conscious of their full strength during the 1905 general strike, would not settle for less, and other parties eventually gave in to these demands. The parliamentary reform committee, chaired by Robert Hermanson, did, it is true, defend in principle a bicameral system; but the committee felt, in view of the country's special conditions, that a unicameral parliament "provides greater guarantees with respect both to unity and to a consideration of the interests of the broad masses."[3] The arguments in favor of a unicameral legislature went no deeper than this. During discussion of the reform by the Diet a vote was taken only in the estate of the nobility; even here only a small minority opposed a unicameral system. As the nation became independent, a few necessary changes were made in the Diet Act, but it was not entirely reworked until 1928.

Compared with other political institutions, the position of Parliament is primary; this is shown by the declaration in the Form of Government Act that Parliament is the representative of the Finnish people. But it is not the sole organ of popular representation, because the president of the Republic can also be considered a direct representative of the people. Parliament's right to exercise public power is, it is true, restricted by provisions entrusting certain powers to other organs, such as highest executive power and general governing of the state to the president and the State Council and judicial power

---

Helsinki commune in 1919 is the only instance of a popular referendum held on the basis of the 1917 communal law. See John E. Roos, *Haagan kauppalan historia* (Helsinki, 1950), p. 51.

3. *Eduskunnanuudistamiskomitean mietintö* (Helsinki: Otava, 1906), p. 58.

to independent courts. In the end, however, it is Parliament which has the power to change the Constitution; it can independently reorganize the relationship between the state's highest organs.

PARLIAMENTARY ELECTIONS

Political activity in representative democracy reaches a peak with elections, carried out at regular intervals short or long, by means of which the population selects a number of its most trusted citizens. In Finland, as in most other countries, parliamentary elections are politically the most important, though in the 1950's and 1960's presidential elections have become equally important. For many years the two hundred members of Parliament were elected every third year, but a change in fundamental law made in 1954 provides for elections every fourth year—the general practice abroad. Parliamentary elections are held on two days early in the spring, on the third Sunday in March and the following Monday. If the president dissolves Parliament and calls for a new election, voters cast their ballots on the first Sunday and following Monday of that month which begins closest to sixty days from the official notification regarding a new election.

The Right to Vote and Eligibility. "Every Finnish citizen, man or woman, who is twenty years of age before an election year has the right to vote." This first point of paragraph 6 in the Diet Act affirms the democratic principle that suffrage is universal for all citizens who are of age. A second principle is equality: every individual entitled to cast a ballot has one vote. In certain cases, special circumstances lead to a loss of the right to vote: this right is not given to wards, nor to individuals who have not been registered in the country as Finnish citizens for the last three years or who have been sentenced to a work camp or to compulsory labor for vagrancy. Also deprived of suffrage is an individual who has lost his rights by a decision of the courts and an individual who during a previous election was responsible for irregularities or interference with election freedom.

For an enfranchised person to cast his ballot, his name must be on the voting register, which is prepared by election boards on the basis of voting precincts and which includes the names of all enfranchised residents in a precinct. The basis of the voting register is a

Regis.

list, prepared by a provincial official for this purpose on the basis of the previous year's census, of Finnish citizens residing in a precinct who meet the minimum age requirement. The election board makes the necessary corrections and additions to this register. Since it is important that the register be complete, it must be made public for a week beginning on January 15 (assuming that the election is held in March). If one feels unjustly disenfranchised or finds that he has been left off the register, or if one feels that another individual has been unjustly enfranchised, a complaint can be lodged with the election board. Dissatisfied with the decision, an individual may seek rectification from a provincial government.

Everyone who has the right to vote, with the exception of regular soldiers, is "eligible"—in other words, can be elected a member of Parliament. The chancellor of justice, members of the Supreme Court or the Supreme Administrative Court, and the ombudsman are, likewise, not permitted to be representatives. No one can be forced to become a candidate for election to Parliament but, if elected, one is not allowed to step down without legal cause or some other reason that wins approval in Parliament. It is to be noted that eligibility is not tied to place of residence. For example, a resident of Helsinki can become a candidate in any electoral district, even in a number of electoral districts at the same time. Generally, however, the principle of "localism" prevails: in other words, a large majority of representatives live in the electoral districts from which they are elected. In 1962 23 of the 1,252 candidates ran in two or more electoral districts, and one candidate stood for election in a total of 14 districts; these candidates are usually party leaders or otherwise well-known individuals whose candidacy is seen as bringing votes to a party and thus securing the election of other candidates.

The Electoral System. Electoral systems can be divided into two main groups: plurality systems and proportional systems, both of which in practice have taken many different forms. Proportional representation is based on the notion that a parliament should be a miniature replica of its nation; in other words, different groups in the electorate must be represented in accordance with their varying strength. For practical reasons, however, the principle of proportionality cannot be applied with complete accuracy: using different methods, one also arrives, to a certain degree, at different results.

Members of the Finnish Parliament are chosen by direct, proportional, and secret election. Elections are conducted by electoral districts, which, in accordance with paragraph 4 of the Diet Act, must number at least twelve and no more than eighteen. Presently the number of districts is fifteen. The division of seats among electoral districts is done by the State Council before each election on the basis of district census figures. In practice this method favors areas with an abundance of people who cannot vote, such as children. Candidates from these districts are consequently elected with a vote which is smaller than average. To avoid this disparity, it would be natural to use the size of the electorate as the basis for division. Only one representative is elected from the Aaland Islands, and so elections in this district follow the plurality principle. Otherwise, as Table 14 shows, the number of seats by electoral district fluctuates from nine to twenty-one.[4]

The formal nomination of candidates takes place through voters associations. A voters association can be formed by at least thirty enfranchised citizens of the same electoral district. A candidate can be nominated by leaving with the central election board of a district, no later than the fortieth day before election day, a document certifying the formation of an association, a candidate list, and a petition for inclusion of the list in the aggregate of candidate lists for the district. An association is permitted to place in nomination only one individual, but an alternate candidate may also be mentioned in the list to provide for situations in which a candidate must withdraw before an election. Before the election of 1954 it was possible to nominate two candidates, though single lists prevailed; but since this arrangement made a voter's personal choice difficult and permitted parties to maneuver in their placing of candidates, it was abandoned by a change in law late in 1953.[5] The same person may, however, be the candidate of many voters associations within a single electoral district.

An individual is chosen by each association to manage its affairs. Voters associations in an electoral district may also join together in

4. It was not until just before the 1948 election that the Aaland Islands were detached from Turku province, South, and made into a separate electoral district. Until 1939 Finland's northernmost electoral district, Lapland, sent only one representative to Parliament.

5. According to the 1906 election law, it was possible to have three names on each list and the names could be rearranged by the voter. In 1935 the number of candidates was limited to two; the right to rearrange the order of candidates, a right which had been exercised to only a very limited degree by the electorate, was also done away with.

an election bloc; in this case the candidate lists of voters associations belonging to the same election bloc are placed under the same heading in numerical order in final form. A public statement by the voters associations in question is required for the formation of an election bloc; a common name for the bloc may also be proposed. The same voters association can belong to only one bloc, which may nominate only as many candidates as there are seats allocated to its electoral district. Formation of election blocs is strictly a matter of choice, although it is common practice because through it significant advantages are gained in the division of seats. In reality the nomination of candidates is determined by parties, which stand behind the voters associations. In fact, Parliament received a proposal in February 1969 calling for a change in the electoral law that would shift the nomination of candidates wholly to registered party organizations. The proposal has been passed, and the formal method of nomination described above will be used for the last time in the 1970 election.

Table 14. Electoral districts, 1966 parliamentary election

District	Number of enfranchised voters	Number of seats	Number of enfranchised voters per seat
Helsinki	341,086	21	16,242
Uusimaa province	261,979	18	14,554
Turku, South	238,143	16	14,884
Turku, North	188,114	13	14,470
Aaland Islands	14,129	1	14,129
Häme, South	204,192	14	14,585
Häme, North	175,406	12	14,617
Kymi province	217,313	15	14,487
Mikkeli province	137,882	10	13,788
Northern Karelia province	111,658	9	12,406
Kuopio province	155,258	12	12,938
Keski-Suomi province	144,859	11	13,169
Vaasa province	268,911	20	13,446
Oulu province	226,378	18	12,577
Lapland province	115,153	10	11,515
Entire country	2,800,461	200	14,002

Source: Official Statistics of Finland, Ser. XXIX, A:29 (Helsinki: Valtion painatuskeskus, 1967), pp. 11, 18–21.

The determination of election results in Finland is done according to the d'Hondt method, which takes its name from its creator, a nineteenth-century Belgian jurist. First, the number of votes for each list is counted; then, by adding together the votes cast for the lists of an election bloc, the number of votes for each election bloc is determined. Ballots cast for a single list form a simple voting group, whereas the ballots cast for lists of the same election bloc are called a unified voting group. The ranking of candidates belonging to the same election bloc is determined by the number of personal votes each candidate receives. The candidates of a unified voting group are then assigned "comparison numbers" in such a way that candidate number one receives the total vote of the election bloc, candidate number two half the vote, number three one-third, and so forth. This method is followed for all election blocs; finally, all candidates are ranked on the basis of these figures. Beginning with the highest figure, as many candidates are selected as there are seats to be filled from the electoral district.

The following example sheds further light on this procedure. In 1962 a total of 14 representatives were elected from the district of Turku Province, North, and there were 6 competing election blocs: the Agrarian party plus the Finnish People's party (48,375 votes), the People's Democrats (40,361), the Social Democratic party (33,968), the National Coalition party (29,835), the Social Democratic League (6,114), and the Small Farmers (3,241). The figures assigned to the candidates of the 4 largest election blocs follow:

Agrarian party plus People's party	SKDL
1. 48,375/1 = 48,375.0	1. 40,361/1 = 40,361.0
2. 48,375/2 = 24,187.5	2. 40,361/2 = 20,180.5
3. 48,375/3 = 16,125.0	3. 40,361/3 = 13,453.7
4. 48,375/4 = 12,093.8	4. 40,361/4 = 10,090.3
5. 48,375/5 = 9,675.0	5. 40,361/5 = 8,072.2

Social Democratic party	Coalition party
1. 33,968/1 = 33,968.0	1. 29,835/1 = 29,835.0
2. 33,968/2 = 16,984.0	2. 29,835/2 = 14,917.5
3. 33,968/3 = 11,322.7	3. 29,835/3 = 9,945.0
4. 33,968/4 = 8,492.0	4. 29,835/4 = 7,458.8

These figures show that the first bloc received 4 seats (all went to the Agrarian party), the People's Democrats received 4, the Social Democrats 3, and the Coalition party 3. Votes for the Social Democratic League and the Small Farmers were not sufficient to win a single seat. In this connection it is appropriate to mention that the placing of candidates in an election bloc consisting of many parties necessitates a certain skill. If the votes received by one party are concentrated around only a few candidates and the votes for a second party are spread out among many candidates, it may turn out that the party with the most votes nonetheless receives fewer seats.

The greatest possible "mathematical equity" in the division of seats occurs when an entire country is one electoral district; division of seats in this case would be determined by a comparison of the total strength of parties. For practical reasons, however, Finland is divided into many electoral districts, which leads in election results to deviations from exact proportionality. When determining the outcome in small districts, figures must be roughly rounded off, which means victories and defeats for different parties as deviations from a completely proportional division. Furthermore, the d'Hondt method is unjust for smaller groups. A party receiving 5 percent of the vote would win 10 seats if the country were a single electoral district, but in most districts today this vote is not sufficient to win a single seat. Illustrative in this respect is the outcome of the 1962 election as it affected the Social Democratic League. That party received a total of 100,396 votes (4.4 percent of the valid votes), but these votes brought only two seats.

Statistics clearly show that the electoral system favors large parties by giving them a disproportionately large representation, whereas small parties suffer from it to a corresponding degree. A concentration of mass support in unified geographic areas regularly wins for the Agrarian party a significant over-representation which during the years 1919–1958 averaged 5.4 seats in Parliament. The Social Democratic party also benefited from the electoral system before the Second World War, but the appearance of the People's Democrats after the war as a competitor for the same electoral groups has meant that the party's number of representatives corresponds rather well to proportionality on a national basis. It should be noted that in 1962 the Social Democratic groups received some 20,000 votes more than the Agrarian party but 13 seats less. The People's Democrats sometimes win a few seats, sometimes lose a few, due to election technicalities. The other parties have been under-represented, the Coalition party generally by 1 or 2 seats, the Progressive and Finnish People's parties by more. Defeats for the Swedish People's party are reduced by a concentration of support in only a few electoral districts. In Helsinki, Uusimaa, and the Province of Vaasa, not to mention the Aaland Islands, it is one of the large parties. In 1966 the Social Democratic League received 8,753 votes for each seat, the Center party 10,266, the Social Democratic party 11,733, the Swedish People's party 11,807, the SKDL 12,259, the Coalition party 12,574, the Liberal People's party 17,029, and the Small Farmers' party as many as 24,351. This is not a permanent ranking because there can be great fluctuations from one election to the next.

Since independence there have been many proposals for changing the electoral system to allow more exact proportionality in the division of seats, but opposition from the large parties has doomed these efforts to failure. In public the parties argue that greater fairness in this respect would also lead to greater political dispersion. Small parties attempt to cope with the problems of proportional representation by forming election blocs, but even the conclusion of these blocs is made difficult by the sharpness of party lines and stiff competition, as well as by the possibility of unwelcome surprises when seats are divided up among parties in a single election bloc.

Characteristic of proportional representation, unlike a plurality system, is the fact that it is not sensitive to changes which occur in positions of the electorate. Very substantial changes in voter opinions are necessary for a decisive effect on the relative strength of parties in Parliament. A gain or loss of ten seats by a single party is exceptional. Many adaptations of this system bring parties foward at the expense of individuals. This is especially true in "list elections," when the voter simply gives his support to a candidate list prepared by some party without being able to change the order of the names in the list. The system used in Finland avoids both extremes. The voter casts his ballot for an individual candidate, but his vote also benefits the entire party. Studies show, however, that most voters first select a party and only then an individual from that party.[6] The ordering of candidates within an election bloc is determined by the number of votes they personally receive, whereas the division of seats between election blocs—usually parties—is based on the total number of

6. Pertti Pesonen, *An Election in Finland* (New Haven, 1968), pp. 324–325.

votes received by the blocs. Shifting in the 1954 election to single-name candidate lists was an attempt to give the voter more opportunity to show which individual candidate he favors within the framework of a certain election bloc.

Campaign Preparations. A five-member central board in each electoral district directs campaign preparations and the election; members of the board are chosen in part by the State Council and in part by the communal council, where meetings of the board are held. An election board serves as the local authority in each voting precinct. In rural communes the council selects this election board in such a way that different parties are represented on it. In cities the bench of magistrates and in towns the disciplinary court act as an election board; if necessary, they are divided by voting precinct into sections and are strengthened with additional members. Within the central administration, the ministry of justice takes care of election matters; it directs and supervises the work of the boards.

The central election board undertakes certain preparatory work for the election, determines its outcome, and provides each elected representative with credentials. The most important preparatory tasks are examination and approval of the petitions which have come from voters associations and preparation and publication of the final combination of candidate lists. The ordering of election blocs is determined by lot, whereas the ordering of candidates within an election bloc is determined by the date on which the lists are left with a board; the latter condition allows parties the chance to place their candidates in preferred order. Some parties arrange their candidates alphabetically, others place them in an order they would like to see followed by the voters. Candidate lists are given consecutive numbers, so that the first candidate of the first election bloc is number two. The central election board also determines names for election blocs. A printed sheet of the final combination is sent to voters associations, election boards, and communal authorities; it is also available to the public. It is the task of a central election board to print ballots for the electoral district. The preparatory work of election boards is concerned mainly with drawing up voting registers and the practical arrangements for voting.

Campaign Activity of Parties. In Chapter II it was mentioned that the nomination of candidates for positions of public trust and the maintenance of political activity by citizens (as well as an increase in that activity as elections draw near) are among the most important tasks of parties. Parliamentary elections in Finland are party elections; parties manage the nomination of candidates, organize a propaganda campaign to support them, and completely dominate the election field. Practically speaking, individuals not belonging to party organizations are powerless at election time; the position of small political groups outside the established parliamentary parties is not much better.

Nomination of candidates is by party district organizations either in general meetings or in meetings of the district executive committees. Preparatory measures necessary for final decision-making vary, however, from one party to another, depicting the nature of an organization's structure and activity as well as the different degrees of organizational democracy. The nomination of candidates is strictly a private, internal, party matter; in Finland it does not have the public character it has in the United States, where primaries are a fundamental part of an election. Social Democrats seek a more democratic method; party rules provide for a referendum concerning nominations. On the basis of proposals by party sections and communal organizations, district executive committees of the Social Democratic party print a ballot with the names of candidates in alphabetical order. The referendum is held on specified days and in specified places; every party member who has paid his dues is permitted to cast a ballot. After this, the district meeting, or the district executive committee empowered by the meeting, decides on the organization of candidate lists and voters associations as well as on the question of election blocs. In a way this method resembles the primary system in the United States. The result of the party referendum, however, is not necessarily binding; the party executive committee, acting in cooperation with the district meeting or district executive committee, has the right to place other people in nomination who were candidates in the electoral district party referendum, although the figure may not exceed one-quarter of the total number of candidates. The same arrangement is set forth in the rules of the Social Democratic League.

The methods followed by other parties are more free-wheeling and ill-defined. They all recognize the right of their basic units to make proposals, but there are differences in subsequent steps. The People's Democrats seek the opinion of all members by conducting referenda, generally held in basic unit meetings, but the results are not binding on the district executive committees and on the special election discussion committees, which decide upon candidates. In the Center party it is the district meeting which nominates candidates; the party's central board (executive committee) has recommended as the basis for discussion at this level an advisory party referendum, but in the absence of such a referendum the district meeting takes under discussion in unchanged form the proposals made by the party's basic units and territorial meetings.

In small parties it appears that the influence of members in the nomination process is smaller, the power of decision resting with party leaders as well as with the district meeting and district executive committee. Nevertheless, solicited or unsolicited proposals by local associations also form the basis for discussion in these circles. Indeed, the district executive committees of the Coalition party solicit proposals from basic units and then prepare candidate lists for consideration by the district meetings. And before this there may be straw votes in the basic units. According to the study published by Rantala in 1956, the procedure in the district organization of Satakunta was roughly as follows: the district committee determined the wishes of local associations and then prepared a candidate list which was discussed in the district meeting. The district meeting made the final decision with respect to candidates, their number, and the form of the list. Advisory straw votes were not general; they were held in only a few local associations. The number of participants in meetings where there was discussion of candidates, and where decisions were made, was nonetheless appreciably greater than in the usual member and yearly meetings. The central leadership of the party did not have the right to interfere with the district nominations.[7]

The importance of parties in the nomination process is, therefore, great. Initiative comes from the party; a candidate does not choose a party; rather, the party chooses a candidate, and only party "blessing" makes a candidate really eligible. District organizations function rather independently under normal circumstances, but a party's central leadership occasionally intervenes in order to ward off efforts which represent narrow localism and which depart from the party line, or in order to give sufficient weight to campaign tactics. The degree to which a party's internal local and group

7. Onni Rantala, *Konservatiivinen puolueyhteisö* (Vammala: Vammalan Kirjapaino Oy, 1956), pp. 160–161.

interests come to the surface in nominations is otherwise dependent upon the structure of a party's membership. These interests are strongest within parties which are structurally the most diffuse, within the Coalition and Swedish People's parties. If all the candidates nominated do not fit in the election bloc, it is necessary to eliminate some through very awkward arbitration.

The nomination of candidates is an extremely important part of the election process in democratic as well as authoritarian systems. Since it is not regulated by decisions of public authority, nomination has been left completely in the hands of party organizations. Speaking frankly, this means that three-quarters of the electorate have no chance to influence directly the execution of this early screening. Participation by party masses in the nomination process varies from one party, and electoral district, to another. Participation occurs primarily in the form of "advance nominations"—proposals made in local associations—and in the form of party referenda and straw votes that follow. It seems that in most parties, however, a substantial number of members are bypassed; the real power of decision is exercised by regional leaders of the parties and by persons with a mandate to participate in party congresses.[8]

Every party naturally sets up at least its own election bloc, but, in addition, a number of election blocs composed of two or more parties are regularly formed before elections. They are negotiated in good time, while nominations are being made. These alliances generally have been concluded only by bourgeois parties because cooperation between Social Democrats and People's Democrats in parliamentary elections has not become a reality—nor has contact across class lines between leftists and the bourgeoisie. The Coalition party, desirous of forming a "bourgeois front," has perhaps been most eager to join election blocs, but in general it has been able to gain the support of only small bourgeois groups; the Agrarian-Center party has sought to remain aloof from the right. In the 1962 election ninety-one election blocs were concluded, of which some twenty cut across party lines among the bourgeoisie. People's Democrats, as well as the Social Democratic party and the Social Democratic League, went into the election with their own election blocs.

Parties throw all their strength into the campaign struggle. The

8. Information concerning the nomination of candidates comes from party bureaus. See also *ibid.*, pp. 160–179; "Paikallisista puolue-elimistä presidentin valitsijamieheksi," *Helsingin Sanomat*, Nov. 1, 1955; Pesonen, *An Election in Finland*, pp. 170–174.

core of an election network, which handles practical campaign preparations, is a party's permanent organization; it can be supplemented by special election committees and support organizations (see Chapter II). Propaganda work on behalf of candidates is divided up among a party's central organs, the district organization, and the voters associations; to a great extent this is done in different ways by the various parties. In long-range terms a general feature of development has been a swelling, at the expense of private electioneering by a candidate and his voters association, of party influence and of centralized, uniform party propaganda. Duverger appropriately notes: "A modern electoral campaign might be likened to a concerto for solo instrument and orchestra: the candidate corresponds to the solo instrument, the sound of which tends to be more and more lost in the general din of the orchestra."[9] The large mass parties particularly—the Social Democratic party, the People's Democratic League, and the Center party—exercise centralized control over their propaganda. The significance of voters associations in the election campaign is limited; often they are formed only to satisfy formal requirements connected with nominations, and, in addition, not all of them have sufficient wealth to conduct a private campaign. An effort is made to ensure that candidates appear in the election campaign under common slogans and that they all are presented strictly as representatives of a party and of interest and ideological goals sought by the party. Since the 1950's, however, there has been a new direction within the three largest parties: a significant growth in separate electioneering by individual candidates and voters associations. One can assume that the shift to single-name candidate lists played a great role in this respect.

Election campaigns in smaller bourgeois groups, which approach the cadre-type party, have long been conducted in more diffuse forms and on a more individual basis. The significance of separate member groups is seen in nominations, and, during the propaganda work which follows, leading organs of these parties give voters associations relatively great freedom of action, which leads to far-reaching separate electioneering and sometimes even to direct competition between candidates of the same party. The Liberal People's party, which represents in purest form a cadre party in economic

9. Maurice Duverger, *Les partis politiques*, 4th ed. (Paris: Librairie Armand Colin, 1961), p. 403. The English translation is from Maurice Duverger, *Political Parties*, trans. Barbara and Robert North (London: Methuen & Co., 1961), p. 366.

difficulties, would be delighted to see candidates and their voters associations finance their campaign propaganda independently. Territorial and group interests have a disruptive effect on campaign activity by the Coalition and Swedish People's parties. In his discussion of Coalition party activity in Satakunta, Rantala states: "In practical campaign preparations by the district organization, groups and group interests have an important position and substantial power. Some of the members have preferred to work and donate their talents to an individual person, a group, and a voters association, rather than to the district organization or an election bloc; the latter, consequently, have lost considerable resources and good labor."[10] In its resolutions on the subject of campaign propaganda released prior to an election, the central board (executive committee) of the Swedish People's party has considered it necessary to note that candidates who have been included in the party's election blocs must show unconditional loyalty to the party and the election bloc and must refrain from attacking other candidates in the election bloc. The origin of campaign propaganda—notices, printed material, posters—must be clearly identified so that there will be no confusion between a party's official propaganda and the campaign literature of individual voters associations.

The most multifarious means of propaganda are utilized during an election campaign. Campaign platforms and party candidates are made known through speeches, campaign meetings and celebrations, newspapers and journals, campaign literature distributed by mail and in person, posters, movies, and personal indoctrination. The forms and extent of propaganda depend decisively, of course, upon the nature of the campaign organization and upon the size of available funds. In some countries an effort has been launched by public authorities to watch over and restrict the use of funds in an election campaign, but in Finland the parties' hands are free in this respect.[11]

The Election. Parliamentary elections are conducted by commune or, if a commune is divided into voting precincts, by precinct. Residents of a commune must be formally advised of an election in the same manner that communal notices are published in the commune. All rural communes with more than 1,500 residents and cities

10. Rantala, *Konservatiivinen*, p. 183.

11. Detailed coverage of the 1958 election compaign in Tampere is contained in Pesonen, *An Election in Finland*.

and towns with more than 3,000 residents must be divided into voting precincts. In the countryside the division generally coincides with primary school districts. Everyone must vote in the precinct of residence, in other words, where one is included on the voting register. An individual temporarily absent from his home community has been able to vote elsewhere by obtaining an absentee ballot for his precinct. Beginning in 1970, such individuals may cast a ballot through the mail in advance of an election. The election laws of 1955 made it permissible to vote in hospitals, as well as in Finnish legations abroad, in certain other places of representation, and on Finnish ships.

The casting of a ballot is directed and supervised by the precinct election board. The ballot in use, the short ballot, does not include a list of the candidates; rather, the voter must make a mark in a circle provided on the ballot. When it has been affirmed that an individual is a registered voter, he is given a ballot on which he records, in the privacy of a booth, the number of his electoral district's candidate list that he desires to support. He then folds the ballot, gives it to the election board to be stamped, and drops it into a closed ballot box. But an elector may also vote for someone who is not on the combination of candidate lists: he writes the selected name, his profession or work, and his place of residence in space provided on the ballot for this purpose. (In 1966 only 161 voters took advantage of this opportunity.) In the election hall there is a voting assistant who, on request from a voter, helps record his choice and is bound to keep secret any information gathered in the course of casting a ballot.

The counting of ballots is begun in the evening of the second day of the election, immediately after the polls have closed; preliminary results, which naturally do not include absentee ballots, are available soon after midnight. The final results are announced by the central election board of each electoral district; the board also issues credentials for those elected and it determines alternate members of Parliament.

Election Participation. Table 15 shows, for parliamentary elections held during the period of a unicameral legislature, the number of votes cast as a percentage of all enfranchised citizens. Statistics demonstrate that during the period of independence voter turnout has continually risen; each decade shows an increase by ten in the

Table 15. Voter turnout in parliamentary elections, 1907–1970

Year	Enfranchised	Voters in percentages: Of all enfranchised citizens	Men	Women
1907	1,272,873	70.7	–	–
1908	1,269,177	64.4	68.9	60.3
1909	1,305,305	65.3	70.5	60.6
1910	1,324,931	60.1	64.9	55.8
1911	1,350,058	59.8	65.3	54.8
1913	1,430,135	51.1	55.9	46.7
1916	1,442,091	55.5	60.1	51.4
1917	1,441,075	69.2	73.1	65.7
1919	1,438,709	67.1	69.5	65.1
1922	1,489,022	58.5	63.0	54.5
1924	1,539,393	57.4	61.7	53.7
1927	1,638,864	55.8	59.7	52.4
1929	1,719,567	55.6	59.6	52.1
1930	1,722,588	65.9	68.6	63.6
1933	1,789,331	62.2	66.4	58.5
1936	1,872,908	62.9	67.3	59.1
1939	1,956,807	66.6	71.3	62.4
1945	2,284,249	74.9	77.5	72.7
1948	2,420,287	78.2	81.0	75.9
1951	2,448,239	74.6	78.4	71.4
1954	2,526,969	79.9	82.9	77.4
1958	2,606,258	75.0	78.3	72.1
1962	2,714,838	85.1	86.1	84.2
1966	2,800,461	84.9	86.1	83.9
1970	3,095,000	82.2	83.2	81.4

Source: Statistical Yearbook of Finland 1967, table 376 (Helsinki: Tilastollinen päätoimisto, 1967), p. 346.

percentage figure. In the 1920's voter turnout was very low, which to a great extent may reflect the political situation of the period. Turnout after the Second World War has remained very high, and in 1962 a new record was achieved. The absolute number of voters has also risen because of a growth in turnout, a growth in population, and a lowering of voting age (from 24 to 21 in 1944, from 21 to 20 in 1969). The number of participants in the 1922 election was 870,825; in 1939 the figure was up to 1,302,348; and in 1966 it climbed to 2,370,046.

When electoral districts are examined geographically, it is clear that participation is weakest in the Aaland Islands region. In 1966 voter turnout was as low as 50.7 percent. There is no real election campaign or party competition in this district, since election of the candidate belonging to the Swedish People's party is from the outset beyond question. Otherwise voter turnout in 1966 fluctuated in electoral districts from 83.1 to 86.9 percent. The highest percentages were recorded in the provinces of Oulu and Lapland. One of the most important phenomena in the development of political life has been the significant rise in voting activity in Finland's isolated northern parts after the Second World War. There are also differences in participation between rural and urban areas, but they are relatively small. Starting from a cross-pressure hypothesis, on the basis of election statistics, Allardt has explained the differences in communes and has shown that turnout, with some exceptions, is generally high in areas which are socially and politically homogeneous —in other words, in those areas where cross-pressures on individuals are relatively weak. Turnout consequently tends to be high where one party is dominant, where political traditions are strong, where the structure of economic life and the social structure of the population are similar, and where the values of the dominant political and religious movements are in harmony with each other. The finding that Swedish-speaking citizens vote more frequently than the Finnish-speaking population also fits the cross-pressure hypothesis. And, turnout is above average in those areas where there is much support for the SKDL. This is a result either of greater activity on the part of Communist voters or of the fact that the party is somehow able to draw even passive individuals to the polls.[12]

From Table 15 it is apparent that men have always been more diligent voters than women. Insofar as Helsinki is concerned, there is also information from the 1951 election about the connection of other social variables to voting frequency. Age is an important factor affecting participation. Weakest among voters were the youngest age groups, followed by the oldest age groups; middle-aged people were the most active. Although turnout among men aged 21–25 was 70.1 percent, it rose to 85.2 percent in the 56–60 age group.

12. Erik Allardt, *Social struktur och politisk aktivitet* (Borgå, 1956).

Among women the differences were even greater. There were clear differences in all age categories between married and unmarried persons. Turnout for married men was 84.1 percent, whereas for unmarried men it was only 67.1 percent (corresponding figures for women were 81.1 and 69.8 percent). Significant is the fact that, except for the younger and oldest age groups, unmarried men were less inclined to vote than unmarried women; it was hypothesized that this stemmed from the great mobility of many unmarried men. It was also possible to conclude that individuals at a high economic and social level voted more frequently than members of lower social groups. Among businessmen, industrial managers, and white-collar workers with academic degrees, voting turnout by men was 86.0 percent and by women 83.5 percent, whereas corresponding percentages for physical laborers were 76.3 and 72.6.[13]

Research in Finland and abroad has demonstrated that political participation is by nature cumulative. This is related to the finding that individuals interested in politics and individuals with strong party identification are especially active voters; in Finland, for example, they try to cast their ballots on the first day of an election. In addition, it has been shown that the strength of an individual's desire to vote is a relatively permanent characteristic, although special campaign situations may cause variations in the general level of voting desire.[14] Information on election participation does not by itself, however, say much about the political activity of individuals, which is a more involved phenomenon; one can even speak of "passive voters"—individuals who, in other respects, are not at all interested in politics and elections.[15]

COMPOSITION AND ORGANIZATION

In Finland, unlike many other countries, the number of members of Parliament is firmly established in fundamental law, in paragraph 2 of the Diet Act; since 1907 the number has been two hundred. Considering the nation's population, this figure is large; years ago the parliamentary committee on reform began with the notion that

13. Erik Allardt and Kettil Bruun, "Characteristics of the Finnish Non-Voter," *Transactions of the Westermarck Society* (Åbo, 1956), III, 55–76.

14. Pesonen, *An Election in Finland*, chap. ix.

15. See Pertti Pesonen, *Valitsijamiesvaalien ylioppilasäänestäjät* (Vammala, 1958), pp. 136–147; Erik Allardt and Pertti Pesonen, "Citizen Participation in Political Life in Finland," *International Social Science Journal*, 12, no. 1 (1960), 27–39.

in a sparsely settled country such as Finland the number of members of Parliament should be large rather than small so it would be easy for different opinions to gain representation. Statistics for 1966 show that there was one member of Parliament for every fourteen thousand citizens entitled to vote. Today the duration of Parliament is four years. By lengthening the period as the workload of Parliament constantly increased, it was hoped that working conditions, which are disturbed considerably by campaign preparations during the entire session preceding an election, would be more tranquil for members of Parliament and that there would be greater continuity in Parliament's activity.

Members of Parliament. The formal eligibility requirements for members of Parliament have been mentioned in an earlier connection. In addition to these, other qualities are demanded of citizens if they are to become real candidates and if they are to have a chance of being elected. What sort of people are elected members of Parliament? From a political viewpoint, party affiliation (shown in Table 16) is, of course, most important. In this respect the composition of the electorate is reflected, though not exactly, in its chosen representatives, since the system of proportional representation used in Finland "oppresses" small groupings to a certain degree. In terms of numbers of members of Parliament, the loss or gain by a party of a few seats is possible in an election even though there may not be significant changes in the relative number of votes received. This is a result of election alliances, as well as how the "last" seats, in other words, those with the lowest assigned figures, happen to be divided. In the 1962 election the Agrarian party picked up five additional seats, even though the party's share of the total vote was almost exactly the same as it had been four years earlier.

In Table 17, members of Parliament for the years 1945–1958 are grouped according to the occupational branch in which they worked when elected to Parliament for the first time. The Social Democratic parties and the Progressive and Finnish People's parties are treated as single groups. Individuals in agriculture and forestry have always been the largest single occupational group in Parliament. Most of the members of Parliament in this category are, naturally, in the Agrarian party group. Close to half of the members, or five times the percentage for the population as a whole in 1950, were public servants and self-employed. The number of public servants elected—

the number of state, communal, and church officials—has decreased substantially since the four-estate Diet and the beginning of a unicameral legislature. The self-employed, primarily lawyers, editors, and organization functionaries, have rather consistently held a quarter of the seats. Relatively few individuals from industrial occupations have been elected if, as a point of comparison, the share of the total population working in industry, commerce, and transportation and communications is considered.

The importance of social classes in political life has already been discussed. In preparing Table 18, members of Parliament have been divided into social strata on the basis of objective criteria—on the basis of profession and professional position. If, however, subjective criteria had been used (class identification as seen by the individuals themselves) the results would differ in many respects.

Because this classification is similar to the grouping of the entire population mentioned on pages 15–18, some comparisons are possible. The greatest disparity exists for the two extreme classes. It was estimated that 3 percent of the working population in 1950 belonged to the upper class and 55 percent to the working class, whereas over 40 percent of the members of Parliament elected after the Second World War were upper class and only 6 percent working class. Parliament cannot, therefore, be considered a miniature replica of the population. Generally speaking, voters are quite willing to select as their candidates individuals of a higher social position. And this is very natural; parties seek to elect individuals to Parliament who are best educated for political activity, but such people, especially in the labor parties, break with their original social background as this education process proceeds. Indeed, professional politicians in the labor parties—party functionaries and editors—have traditionally been the largest single group. Most members of Parliament from the working class are found in the People's Democratic group. The vast majority of representatives from the National Coalition and People's parties belong to the upper class, whereas about half of the Agrarian party representatives are farmers.

If one examines the origin of members of Parliament, a much greater correspondence is found between the support base for parties and the social position of representatives. Noponen's research shows that about three-fifths of the labor party representatives were born in worker families and that about three-quarters of the fathers of Agrarian party representatives were farmers.

Table 16. Parliamentary seats by party, 1907–1970

	Party						
Election year	Finnish party; National Coalition party	Young Finnish party; Progressive party; Finnish People's party; Liberal People's party	Swedish People's party	Agrarian party; Center party	Social Democratic party	Socialist Workers' party; SKDL	Others[a]
1907	59	26	24	9	80	–	2
1908	54	27	25	9	83	–	2
1909	48	29	25	13	84	–	1
1910	42	28	26	17	86	–	1
1911	43	28	26	16	86	–	1
1913	38	29	25	18	90	–	–
1916	33	23	21	19	103	–	1
1917	32	24	21	26	92	–	5
1919	28	26	22	42	80	–	2
1922	35	15	25	45	53	27	–

1924	38	17	23	44	60	18	–
1927	34	10	24	52	60	20	–
1929	28	7	23	60	59	23	–
1930	42	11	20	59	66	–	2
1933	18	11	21	53	78	–	19
1936	20	7	21	53	83	–	16
1939	25	6	18	56	85	–	10
1945	28	9	14	49	50	49	1
1948	33	5	14	56	54	38	–
1951	28	10	15	51	53	43	–
1954	24	13	13	53	54	43	–
1958	29	8	14	48	48	50	3
1962	32	13	14	53	38	47	3
1966	26	9	12	49	55	41	8
1970	37	8	12	36	52	36	19

Source: Official Statistics of Finland, ser. XXIX 1–14, A:15–29 (Helsinki: Keisarillisen Senaatin kirjapaino, Valtioneuvoston kirjapaino, Valtion painatuskeskus, 1909–1967).

[a] This category includes the IKL seats (14 in 1933, 14 in 1936, and 8 in 1939), the 3 seats won by the Social Democratic opposition in 1958 on its own lists, 2 seats for the Social Democratic League in 1962 and 7 in 1966, and seats won by other small parties.

Table 17. Occupational groupings of members of Parliament elected 1945–1958

Occupation	Coalition party	Swedish People's party	Progressive party; Finnish People's party	Agrarian party	Social Demo-cratic party	SKDL	Total		Entire population, 1950, percent
							Number	Percent	
Public service	32	10	15	12	21	6	96	22.2	9.2
Self-employed	2	7	4	16	47	38	114	26.3	
Agriculture and forestry	16	8	–	77	14	23	138	31.9	41.5
Industry and handicrafts	2	–	4	2	7	20	35	8.1	29.2
Commerce	11	3	2	3	15	5	39	9.0	6.9
Transportation and communications	–	–	–	–	1	–	1	0.2	6.0
Others, or without occupation	–	1	1	–	3	4	9	2.1	7.2
Unknown	–	–	–	1	–	–	1	0.2	–
Total	63	29	26	111	108	96	433	100.0	100.0

Source: Based on information from Martti Noponen.

Table 18. Social stratification of members of Parliament elected 1945–1958

Class	Coalition party	Swedish People's party	Progressive; Finnish People's party	Agrarian party	Social Democratic party	SKDL	Total		Working population, 1950, percent
							Number	Percent	
Upper class	59	21	22	51	31	18	202	46.7	3
Middle class	1	3	4	13	63	36	120	27.7	22
Farmers	3	5	–	46	12	19	85	19.6	20
Workers	–	–	–	1	2	23	26	6.0	55
Total	63	29	26	111	108	96	433	100.0	100

Source: Based on information from Martti Noponen.

Looked at as a whole, Parliament is composed of the educated and the skilled. Of the individuals elected to Parliament in 1958, about a third had academic degrees and about half at least a junior high school education. Over two-thirds had a vocational education. The average age of members in the early years of the unicameral legislature was only a little over 40, but it has now risen to almost 50 (49.3 in 1958). There were 28 women elected in 1958, 27 in 1962, and 33 in 1966. The renewal of Parliament is important both in terms of principle and practice. The number of new representatives, elected for the first time, varies somewhat: it averaged 46 for the years 1948–1962. Participation in communal work has been an important preparatory step for members of Parliament. Of those elected in the period 1907–1939, about two-thirds had previously served as chairmen of a communal meeting and as chairmen or members of a communal board or council. Almost the same number were serving when first elected to Parliament, or had served previously in positions of trust for the party on whose lists they were elected; for Social Democratic members of Parliament the figure was over 90 percent.[16]

The Position of Members of Parliament. The legal position of members of Parliament is covered by special provisions granting representatives greater independence from public officials and more effective security in criminal law than is granted other citizens. This parliamentary immunity means that a member of Parliament may not be prosecuted or deprived of his liberty for opinions expressed in Parliament or for some other behavior in the consideration of parliamentary business unless Parliament with at least a five-sixths majority gives its consent. A representative may not be arrested for a crime when Parliament is in session without the consent of Parliament, unless a court has ordered that he be arrested or unless he is caught in the act of a crime for which a sentence of at least six months is mandatory. In terms of his duties, a member must observe right and truth in his actions. He is obliged to obey fundamental laws, but he is not bound by any other instructions. Paragraph 11 of the Diet Act forbids an imperative mandate, the legal validity of instructions given by the electorate or by political groups. In practice, however, there has been a development toward a certain imperative mandate: members of Parliament are to a great extent bound to the

16. See Martti Noponen, *Kansanedustajien sosiaalinen tausta Suomessa* (Porvoo, 1964).

political line of their parties. In principle each member of Parliament represents the entire Finnish nation, but in fact he represents his party primarily; more and more he is significant only as a member of a parliamentary group. Rules about a representative's behavior state that he must act with dignity and avoid words which are offensive, derisive, or otherwise inappropriate.

A representative must consent before assuming the duties of a member of Parliament; once officially elected, he cannot resign unless he can show a legal obstacle or some other reason acceptable to Parliament. In 1951 Parliament refused to accept a resignation based on reasons of health; the representative's arguments were not considered sufficient. It was asserted in heated discussion at a plenary session that pressure from his own party was the real reason the representative had submitted his resignation.

Members of Parliament receive an annual salary which Parliament fixes by special law. In 1968 the salary was approximately three thousand marks per month. Representatives who live more than thirty kilometers from Helsinki receive a per diem allowance for the period that Parliament is in session. Members of Parliament are permitted a first-class ticket on the state railways for free trips during the term of office. A fixed, relatively high salary has become even more important now that members of Parliament are becoming professional politicians as the sessions lengthen; since Parliament is in session most of the year, it is very difficult for representatives living far from the capital to manage another job or profession. A member of Parliament is also entitled to a state pension, which begins when he reaches the age of sixty or, if he is still a member of Parliament then, when his parliamentary activity ends. Parliament's Committee of the Secretariat can also grant special pensions.

Parliamentary Groups. Parliament's political units are party groups, which are not mentioned directly in laws dealing with Parliament but which in many ways enjoy de facto recognition; in any case, they have held a central position in activity of the institution since 1907. Parliamentary groups do not function apart from party organizations but are tightly tied to them (see Chapter II). A large number of party leaders are usually members of Parliament, which gives them the chance to direct and supervise the group's work and to fit it easily into other party activity. Representatives are elected through parties, so that it is understandable that when Parliament convenes after an election all the new members attach themselves to their own groups. Party organizations have, moreover, begun to require of candidates a commitment to join the party's parliamentary group after election to Parliament. The Coalition party, for example, has since 1954 made a written agreement with its candidates.[17] "Independent" representatives may exist when members of a group resign or are expelled during a term in office. In the fall of 1957 the Social Democratic group expelled four representatives of the party opposition when they joined, against party wishes, the Cabinet of V. J. Sukselainen. A member of Parliament who resigns from his group usually joins some other group, however.

All parliamentary groups are tightly organized. They elect a chairman, vice-chairman, a secretary, and a treasurer; Social Democrats and People's Democrats also have a working committee, and the Center and Coalition parties have a commission. Activity by party groups is now supported in part by the budget. Groups regularly hold meetings in their own rooms in Parliament (usually once a week); a group's policies and positions are discussed and, in the case of very important political matters, decisions are made binding on all representatives. If a decision is taken in favor of group unanimity, the chairman frequently brings his group's position to the attention of Parliament—in connection, for example, with discussion of an interpellation.

An individual representative's freedom to discuss and resolve matters is, therefore, limited. Above all he belongs to a party group, where there is not much room for personal views. There are, however, certain differences between groups in terms of party dependence. Discipline is exceptionally tight on the extreme left, in the People's Democrats group, which is generally very united. The other extreme is perhaps the Swedish People's party, whose internal heterogeneity makes unanimity difficult and forces the party leadership to grant members great freedom of action. It should be noted that party discipline is unconditional only with respect to the most important political matters; a substantial number of matters that make up the daily work of Parliament are not considered by the groups, the only external factor which must be considered by a representative participating in these matters being the probable reaction of his electorate. Local political viewpoints often have a strong impact on the adoption of positions, even though a representative's depen-

17. Onni Rantala, *Konservatismi ja sen kannattajat* (Tampere, 1960), p. 116.

dency on his home area and his electorate is not so great in Finland as it is in countries where there are single-member election districts and a plurality system.

Pekka Nyholm has conducted detailed research on the cohesion of parliamentary groups and the position of members of Parliament during the period 1948–1951. He used a special cohesion index to measure group unity in open votes. An index figure of 100.0 was assigned if a group voted unanimously; if the group divided into two parts roughly equal in size, the index number was 0.0. By taking an arithmetic average, group cohesion for a longer period of time was possible—from 397 open votes during the period 1948–1951. The index for the various groups was:

SKDL	95.1
Agrarian party	87.3
Social Democratic party	86.6
Coalition party	84.0
Progressive party	82.0
Swedish People's party	74.5

The index has a rather narrow spread, but clear differences emerge and are consistent with earlier findings about party structure and the position of parliamentary groups. Group unity is strongest in the People's Democratic League and, generally, stronger in centrally led mass parties than in the loose and diffuse offspring of cadre parties. The SKDL and the Swedish People's party are in a category by themselves, whereas differences between the other four groups are relatively small. Examining the relations between unanimous and scattered votes, it was found that the SKDL group voted unanimously in 83.6 percent of all votes, the Progressive party in 70.5 percent, the Agrarian party in 56.9 percent, the Coalition party in 55.2 percent, Social Democrats in 48.1 percent, and the Swedish People's party group in 49.7 percent. The share of unanimous votes is thus very great in all parliamentary groups. The method used did not directly answer the question of whether or not the high degree of cohesion was predominantly a result of a natural, spontaneous unanimity, of mediation, or of unanimity brought about by external force and group discipline. But Nyholm concluded that conflict between a party's interest requirements and personal conviction on the part of a member of Parliament was generally resolved in favor of freedom of action for the representative. A strong reliance on group discipline is hardly feasible in groups other than the SKDL.

Examining votes as a whole, only a relatively small number of matters voted upon have an important meaning for party groups. Finland's parliamentary system, based on multiparty conditions, does not require the almost total group cohesion that exists in the United Kingdom, where most parliamentary votes can be considered votes of confidence. In this respect the right has traditionally emphasized individual freedom as opposed to group dependency. After they have been elected, Coalition party candidates are obliged to join the party's parliamentary group. In parliamentary work, however, they are bound, on the basis of a written agreement, only by paragraph 11 of the Diet Act.[18] The advanced specialization of parties is understandably responsible to a great degree for the fact that voting divisions usually follow party lines—even though there may be no attempt to achieve formal unity through group discipline. In most parliamentary groups, however, a regular dispersion of forces was also found; some representatives are inclined to differ from the majority's position on the basis of certain permanent factors.

Group cohesion is not, of course, stable; it varies with the subject at hand and with the parliamentary situation. Nyholm shows that group cohesion tends to grow as the political side of a subject becomes more significant. Cohesion in votes of confidence is almost always complete.[19]

A Diet. The annual period that Parliament is in session is called a diet (valtiopäivät). Diets begin on the first day of February unless determined otherwise in the previous diet. A regular diet is one hundred twenty days, although Parliament can decide to shorten or lengthen it. The number of matters to be discussed has increased substantially since the 1920's, and this has led to a lengthening of the diets. Parliament today is in session almost throughout the year. Diets are divided into a spring session and a fall session; an attempt is made in the spring to complete work by late May or early June, and after summer vacation, sometime in early September, the diet is reconvened. Diets often continue into January of the following year. In years when a new Parliament is elected that will meet in the fall

18. Rantala, *Konservatismi*, p. 116.

19. Pekka Nyholm, *Suomen eduskuntaryhmien koheesio vuosien 1948–1951 vaalikaudella ja vuoden 1954 valtiopäivillä* (Helsinki, 1961).

there are "long diets" lasting until spring or summer. The President is empowered to call Parliament into extraordinary session to deal with certain important questions: because Parliament is in session almost the entire year, this provision no longer has any practical significance—on one hand extraordinary sessions are unnecessary and, on the other hand, there is hardly any time for them.

Functionaries and Organs. Before beginning its ordinary work, Parliament in session must perform certain basic tasks. First, there is the election, chaired by the eldest member of Parliament, of a speaker and two deputy speakers. Within five days of a session's opening, committees defined by law must be formed; this is done indirectly, by at least forty-five electors chosen by Parliament for the entire period between elections. But Parliament itself elects a grand committee in plenary session; and, as provided in the Diet Act, a committee of the Secretariat and examiners are appointed. Parliament selects a general secretary after the post is declared open; its agreement with the secretary can be broken when a new Parliament is elected.

It is the duty of the speaker to call Parliament into plenary session, present matters and lead discussion, present proposals for final adoption, maintain order, and close the session. He also sees to it that nothing contrary to fundamental law is considered. A general custom after the Second World War has been to elect as speaker either a Social Democratic or Agrarian member of Parliament; often the prime minister is from one of these two parties and the speaker from the other. Although the speaker is a politician and a member of a party group, he must observe strict nonpartisanship in his actions and seek through his position and prestige to play a mediating role in the parliamentary struggle. It is established custom that the speaker does not propose bills or participate in votes and discussions at a plenary session and is not a committee member, though he can be present at committee meetings. The speaker, the deputy speakers, and committee chairmen form the Speakers' Council, which plans the agenda for Parliament and makes related proposals.

Plenary Sessions. Consideration of a matter takes place in a plenary session of Parliament; preparatory work is done by committees. The hundred ninety-nine representatives sitting opposite the speaker in the round chamber of Parliament are arranged so that representatives of the Swedish People's party are to his extreme right, SKDL representatives to the extreme left, and other representatives between the groups in the usual left-right order. Members of the State Council, the chancellor of justice, and the ombudsman may be present at sessions and they may take part in discussions but not in decision-making unless they are members of Parliament.

Compared with many foreign countries plenary sessions of the Finnish Parliament are held relatively infrequently—once or twice a week. Matters are discussed in an order previously determined by the agenda. The Diet Act provides that government proposals must be discussed first. Since representatives generally have received printed or mimeographed documents concerning matters to be discussed, presentation may be limited to mention of an agenda number.

Before a decision is reached, members of Parliament have an opportunity to express opinions and make their own proposals. Every representative is permitted to speak as often and as long as he wants, provided that he does not stray from the matter at hand and does not use the inappropriate language mentioned above. The government has on two occasions proposed a change in the Diet Act which would permit Parliament to limit the number of times a representative may speak, but both proposals were rejected. Members of the State Council, the chancellor of justice, and the ombudsman are permitted to speak first, as is the representative chosen by a committee for some special matter. Normal procedure may also be interrupted to permit a representative to reply briefly to remarks made by another member of Parliament. Everything spoken in a plenary session is recorded in the minutes, even the interjections.

When discussion is declared ended, the speaker of Parliament presents a resume of proposals made and brings the matter to a vote. If there are a number of proposals, one is pitted against another until all have been voted on. The quickest and simplest method of voting is to stand. If in the opinion of the speaker there is some doubt as to the outcome, or if a representative requests it, a machine-recorded vote is held. A third possibility is open vote by ballot.

If the speaker considers a matter contrary to fundamental or some other law or contrary to a previous decision made by Parliament, he must refuse to bring the matter before Parliament or to bring it to a vote. If Parliament is not satisfied with the speaker's ruling, the matter is sent to the constitutional committee, whose opinion is binding.

Every representative is permitted to use his native language, Finnish or Swedish, in discussion. Committee reports and statements are in both languages, although the Finnish text is used as the basis for discussion. Statements in Swedish are translated into Finnish, and, correspondingly, a Swedish-language representative who does not know Finnish is able to get an individual translation of Finnish statements, of proposals by the speaker calling for a vote, and of communications delivered only in Finnish. The speaker's resumes of parliamentary discussions are in both languages.

Committees. The committee system, in its present form a product of long development dating back to the period of Swedish rule, occupies a central position in the work of Parliament. Committees do not have independent decision-making power; their task lies in preparatory work and the presentation of proposals to Parliament. All important matters must be prepared in committee before final consideration by Parliament, and some matters must be dealt with by a number of committees. Government proposals and legislative bills, reports to Parliament provided for in fundamental law, and fiscal bills and petitionary bills must be considered in committee unless they are rejected out of hand, whether tabled or not. Committee consideration is obligatory when changing parliamentary rules, when considering questions that result from Parliament's right to examine the legality of action taken by members of the State Council and by the chancellor of justice, and when deciding between Parliament and the speaker on rulings by the latter. A committee may also receive a proposal, made after discussion of an interpellation or after a State Council communiqué or notice, concerning Parliament's decision on a particular matter. Parliament can, if it so wishes, entrust committees with the preparation of matters which, according to the Diet Act, need not be considered in committee; such matters include decrees and decisions of the State Council that must be examined in Parliament. With the growth and specialization of legislation, the center of gravity in discussions has shifted more and more to committees, where representatives are able to examine in detail—more so than in plenary sessions—questions in narrow, special fields; representatives in committee can also turn to outside expertise. When a legislative proposal returns from committee, it very often passes through the other stages of consideration quickly and without significant changes.

Committees are divided into two groups, standing and extraordinary committees. There are five of the former, set up at each diet: constitutional committee, legislative committee, foreign affairs committee, finance committee, and bank committee. The finance committee must have at least twenty-one members, the bank committee at least eleven, and other standing committees at least seventeen. The jurisdiction of each committee is defined by the Diet Act. When necessary, Parliament can also establish extraordinary committees; they are proposed at the beginning of a diet by the speakers and, as the session continues, they can also be established after a proposal by the Speakers' Council or a single representative. In practice, many extraordinary committees have become permanent because they are regularly re-established: they include the economic committee, the legislative and economic committee, the education committee, the agriculture and forestry committee, the social affairs committee, the defense committee, and the transportation committee. As examples of more temporary extraordinary committees, there are the pension and tax committees of the late 1950's. A matter which, one might think, should be discussed by a standing committee may be given to an extraordinary committee for preparation, with the exception of matters which must by law be prepared in a standing committee.

Committee members, as mentioned, are selected by electors; if the electors cannot agree, a proportional rate is applied. Party groups stress their parliamentary experience in nominating candidates, as well as their abilities and skills in a given field. At their first meetings the committees select a chairman and a vice-chairman from among the members, as well as a secretary who is an outside salaried civil servant. In addition to their duties as leaders of discussion, chairmen have one special task, namely, presentation of committee views on important matters before a plenary session of Parliament. The rapporteurs mentioned in the Diet Act are not used. It is customary, in fact, for the chairman of the finance committee to present the budget report to Parliament. Committee chairmen are respected, so that groups seek to place their leading politicians in those posts.

A committee has a quorum if two-thirds of its members are present. Unlike plenary sessions of Parliament, committee meetings are closed. Certain outsiders are permitted to attend, however: members of the State Council, for example, who cannot be elected members, are permitted to participate in meetings and discussions unless forbidden to do so by the committee. The speaker and deputy speakers may be present but do not have the right to participate in discussions (unless, in the case of deputy speakers, they are members of that committee). A third group is composed of outside experts, who generally leave after making a statement and before actual consideration of a matter begins. The Diet Act permits a committee to establish subcommittees, which report independently in the name of the committee. In practice this is a rather rare phenomenon. It is, however, quite usual for committees to set up sections, which prepare matters for final consideration by the entire committee.

Determination of the committee to which a matter is sent is made by Parliament upon a proposal by the Speakers' Council, usually approved with no opposition. The order in which matters are considered is set forth in the work plan prepared by the Speakers' Council for plenary sessions and committees. First priority is given to statements made to other committees, second priority to legislative proposals which have been postponed until after a new election; then come government proposals, reports to Parliament, and decrees and decisions of the State Council which must be communicated to Parliament. Last in order of consideration are bills submitted by private members of Parliament. The result of a committee's labor is a report, to be made to Parliament, that is composed of both the committee's reasoning and its proposals. Minority members may append a written dissent to the report. In addition to reports, committees make statements to other committees. A committee may be obliged by Parliament to seek statements, but it may on its own initiative request a statement. A committee is bound by the rules of Parliament to give a single report on bills dealing with the same matter, unless special considerations require a different procedure. Following usual procedure, one often ends up with "cluster reports," including many proposals made by the government and by private members of Parliament.

A forty-five member grand committee, established explicitly for the consideration of legislative matters, is an institution peculiar to the Finnish Parliament. Its establishment represented an attempt to ensure sufficiently careful preparation and consideration of matters and to preserve in the unicameral legislature some of the advantages of a two-chamber system. The grand committee's work style is to a degree different from the style of special committees. Grand committee meetings are not public, but they may be attended by all members of Parliament and some civil servants of Parliament. Committee reports usually do not include supporting arguments, nor are dissenting opinions appended.

The Principle of Continuity. Until 1918 each diet of an election period formed a complete unit; matters not resolved by the end of one diet had to be reintroduced at the beginning of the next and discussed all over again. A law approved in 1918, however, established the principle of continuity, according to which a matter which has not been wholly resolved in one diet may be picked up by the next one at the point where consideration broke off—except in cases where a parliamentary election has intervened. Consideration of government communiqués and announcements, as well as questions and interpellations, may not be continued in the next diet. There have been proposals to extend the principle of continuity to the establishment of committees, but Parliament has considered it best to select committee members at the beginning of each diet.

DUTIES AND ACTIVITIES

In the old doctrine of separation of powers, it is customary to view legislation as a parliament's most important duty; indeed, a parliament often is established as a state institution for the express purpose of passing legislation. Activities related to the preparation of laws are readily apparent in the work of members of the Finnish Parliament, but the old doctrine is not wholly successful in describing its position and powers. They could perhaps be best characterized through speaking about the making of major policy decisions affecting the nation and about the supervision of their realization in practice. The execution of this general duty includes not only participation in the making of legislation, but many other activities prescribed by the Constitution; listing them would not, however, give an exhaustive picture of the situation, since legislatures also have other, more general, functions which in Finnish political culture are tied to the realization of democratic values. Above all, the latter include the representation and promotion of society's changing ideological views and special interests; acting as an open discussion forum for the nation (a task which has retained its importance in spite of the increasing effectiveness of mass communication and the tightening of party groups); political education and the maintenance of a high level of citizen participation; and training of the top political leadership. One of the most important tasks of a legislature and its party groups in a parliamentary state, unmentioned in constitutions, is the maintenance of a viable government.

The powers at Parliament's disposal to achieve the general goals mentioned above can be divided into six categories: 1) legislation, 2) economic management of the state, 3) supervision of the government and overseeing of the administration, 4) independent administrative activity, 5) participation in the conduct of foreign affairs, and 6) tasks connected with the exercise of administrative law. The second and fifth categories (and, to a degree, the third) are treated in later chapters and will not be covered here.

Legislation. The president and Parliament are given the right to initiate legislation. The president exercises this right by passing on to Parliament proposals that have been prepared by the State Council, which are called government proposals and upon which no time limit is placed. Paragraph 28 of the Diet Act states that "the president of the Republic indicates at the opening of a diet what government proposals will be submitted to Parliament. Proposals which cannot be made at this time may be presented at a later date for consideration by Parliament." In practice the procedure is somewhat different. The president can, to be sure, present the government's legislative program in his opening speech to the diet, but there is no formal notification; proposals reach Parliament as they are prepared by the government and at such time as is considered auspicious. The preparation of legislative proposals involves a number of bodies: the legislative department of the ministry of justice, other ministries, permanent and ad hoc commissions, and other administrative offices. Many legislative bills get started outside Parliament and the government on the basis of proposals made by pressure groups and individual citizens. Until 1928 it was customary for ministers to present governmental proposals at plenary sessions of Parliament, but these proposals are now sent to Parliament with a presidential memo. Provisions exist for the withdrawal, with cause, of a government proposal no matter what the stage of consideration.

The right of parliamentary initiative is exercised when members of Parliament propose a bill in one of three forms. Paragraph 31 of the Diet Act defines initiative by Parliament as 1) a legislative bill, a proposal in the form of a law concerning the passage of a new law, or the amendment, explanation, or annulment of an existing law; 2) a fiscal bill, a proposal concerning appropriations in the state budget for the following year; 3) a petitionary bill, a proposal that Parliament urge the government to take steps in a matter under the government's jurisdiction. To set legislative matters in motion, members of Parliament frequently use petitionary as well as legislative bills, but the former are less effective in the sense that the bill remains dependent upon action by the government even though it may have been approved by Parliament.

It is characteristic of parliamentary procedure in Finland and Sweden that private bills normally must be introduced by members of Parliament at the beginning of a diet, during a short period of general initiative, after which time exceptional circumstances are required for submission of a bill. A member of Parliament must propose his legislative bill, fiscal bill, or petitionary bill before noon on the fourteenth day of a diet following an election or, in other cases, within ten days of the opening of a diet. A bill may not be submitted later unless cause is given by: 1) a decision already made by Parliament, 2) the presentation or withdrawal of a government proposal, or 3) some other occurrence during the course of the diet. In these cases a bill must be left with the secretary of Parliament no later than seven days from the time when its initiator is considered apprised of the situation. The transmission of a government proposal to Parliament generally (today almost exclusively) leads to use of this special legislative initiative. Parliamentary bills seek either to broaden the scope of the proposal or to resolve some aspect of the matter in a different way. It is primarily the speaker who decides in each case whether or not the right to propose a bill exists. In these situations rules are interpreted as strictly as possible. A legislative bill submitted during a diet must be directly related to the proposal in question; in fact, the bill may include only those changes which could, during regular consideration of the matter, be proposed without a bill. It is customary during a diet to have a score or so of these legislative bills.

Parliament's right to legislative initiative is also exercised within strict limits by the finance committee and the bank committee; the former may make proposals concerning some taxes to be collected during the following year in order to balance the budget; the latter may exercise its right of initiative in matters concerning changes in the bylaws of the Bank of Finland. There are several exceptions to the general provision that legislative initiative is a prerogative of the president and Parliament. Initiative in matters concerning church law can be exercised only by a synod, which makes proposals to the State Council and the president for consideration as government proposals. Likewise, through the government, the Regional Assembly of the Aaland Islands exercises legislative initiative in matters that are of concern only to the region but that are under national legislative authority.

In legislation, the government occupies the leading position. Its proposals, unlike those initiated in Parliament, are not restricted by time or other considerations, and the government has a much better chance than do members of Parliament to prepare its proposals thoroughly. Government proposals are high priority matters in consideration by Parliament, and they are usually adopted. This arrangement is natural and common in parliamentary states, where it is considered the task of a government to provide Parliament with proposals and incentives and to direct its work. Even formally, Parliament's right of legislative initiative can be considered secondary in importance. In considering Parliament's effective work, leading to positive results, it must be said that the government is the most important employer for members of Parliament. Of the 230 government proposals in the 1950 diet, 191 were adopted and 13 were rejected. The figures for 1955 were 179 in total, 131 adopted, 1 rejected; for 1957 they were 223, 169, 10. Private member legislative bills have been numerous, especially since the early 1950's, but a substantial number are not considered during the period between elections; most of the others are rejected. Table 19 shows the fate of legislative bills submitted to diets of Parliament in the period 1954–1957. Taken as a whole, only 7 percent of the private member legislative bills submitted during the period in question were approved in one form or another. Moreover, most of the bills which were approved meant only minor changes in already existing laws. Although there is support for proposed changes and reforms, bills are usually rejected on the grounds that the matter should be thoroughly gone over by the government in order to achieve the best results. The political situation causes certain fluctuations in the

Table 19. Private member legislative bills before Parliament, 1954–1957

Diet	Number of bills	Adopted	Rejected	No final resolution
1954	189	20	91	78
1955	106	8	67	31
1956	79	3	46	30
1957	123	3	56	64
Total	497	34	260	203

Source: Jaakko Nousiainen, *Eduskunta aloitevallan käyttäjänä* (Porvoo: WSOY, 1961), p. 118.

importance of Parliament's legislative initiative; it ebbs when stable majority coalitions rule and flows with the formation of narrow-based minority or caretaker governments.

Once a government proposal has reached Parliament and is announced in plenary session and distributed in printed form to the representatives, it is presented for referral to committee. Even at this early stage, in the referral discussion, members of Parliament may express opinions on the matter. If one wants to become more familiar with the matter, he may request that it be tabled, postponing committee referral until a later session. There is no separate announcement about legislative bills; they are presented for direct referral to the appropriate committees.

A committee may consider a matter promptly and release its report quickly or it may pigeonhole the matter for a lengthy period, which is often the fate awaiting private and less important bills submitted by members of Parliament. Committees, as mentioned above, are often divided into sections, make frequent use of outside experts, and request statements from other committees when advisable. Matters in special committee are considered three times. In the first consideration, a proposal or bill is read, there is general discussion, and a decision is made as to the necessity of hearing experts. Parliament's committees are guaranteed by paragraph 53 of the Diet Act the right to receive from officials and public institutions, with the assistance of the prime minister or some other appropriate minister, all necessary documents and information. Experts include ministers, civil servants from the ministries and central offices, outside experts in different fields, and representatives of interest organizations. Statements are generally oral, although they may be supplemented by written memoranda. As far as the committee is concerned, its decision comes in the second reading on the basis of a government proposal, a bill submitted by representatives, or a proposal advanced by a section of the committee. In the third reading a proposal drafted by the secretary as the committee's report is examined, insofar as this task is not entrusted to the chairman and the secretary. A committee may, however, act otherwise by unanimous decision. If, with respect to a legislative proposal, a committee reacts negatively to a point included in the report, the committee may suggest in a special clause that the government make a new proposal taking into consideration Parliament's objections. This clause of desire is debated in plenary session during the third reading of the legislative proposal; it is, of course, dropped if the proposal is approved. Individual members of Parliament also have the right to propose clauses of desire.

A committee report is first presented in plenary session for tabling; the first reading occurs in a later (usually the following) session. A report may be tabled again by two representatives. In this case, and, generally, the purpose of regulations on tabling is to provide representatives with sufficient time for familiarization with and consideration of a matter. In the first reading no decisions as to the content of a legislative proposal or its approval or rejection are made; after discussion, which reveals opinions of the government, party groups, and individual members of Parliament and the position of the special committee, a matter is sent to the grand committee. Consideration by this committee is also by nature preparatory. All legislative matters prepared by special committees pass through the grand committee, whose task is, in addition to examining the proposals for content, to watch for consistency in form. Matters are usually considered only once in the grand committee; sections may be set up, experts called upon, and statements sought.

In the second reading the legislative proposal is gone over point by point on the basis of the grand committee's report or some other proposal. In this instance there is no compulsory tabling, but a seconded motion is sufficient the first time and a majority decision of Parliament at other times to postpone consideration. If a grand committee proposal is approved with no changes, the second reading is declared completed and the content of the legislative proposal is confirmed. In other cases the matter is returned to the grand committee with changes made by Parliament. Parliament then decides in the continued second reading whether to approve changes made by the committee or to stick with its earlier decisions. Consideration in plenary session is divided into general and detailed discussion. In the latter, each member of Parliament may suggest amendments to the point under consideration. The proposals must stick closely to the business at hand; proposals which go beyond the matter must be made in the form of a bill. To speed the process of consideration, representatives are requested to distribute mimeographed copies of their amendments. In the second reading no decision or proposal may be made concerning rejection of the entire legislative proposal. Only if the grand committee in its report favors rejection may Parliament in the second consideration adopt this position.

The third reading of a legislative proposal may begin no earlier than three days after conclusion of the second reading. This provision attempts in Finland's unicameral legislature to ensure a thorough consideration of matters by giving members of Parliament time for thought before a final decision is reached. Because there are no time limits imposed for the other stages of consideration and because it is possible to get through these stages in one day (on occasion this has been done), the minimum time for consideration by Parliament of a legislative proposal is four days. Parliament in the third reading either approves or rejects a proposal in the form emerging from the second; no substantive changes are permitted. In addition to approval and rejection, there is a third possibility: an adopted legislative proposal can be made to lie dormant until a new election has been held if one-third of the members of Parliament (sixty-seven) support a proposal to this effect made during the third reading. In this case consideration of a matter continues in the first diet following an election, at which time a proposal is considered only once, after a committee report, and is either approved or rejected by a simple majority vote. This provision for postponing a legislative proposal can be considered a far-reaching guarantee of minority rights. A tax proposal, however, cannot be postponed; neither can a proposal concerning the approval of legislative provisions in a treaty between Finland and some foreign power. In practice it often happens that a legislative proposal which has been postponed until a new election is considered to have been dropped as reconsideration begins, because in the interim a law concerning the same matter has been passed on the basis of another proposal.

As mentioned, the most important laws of the Constitution are given a special permanence and inviolability by provision that their passage, amendment, or annulment may take place only in accordance with a special and difficult procedure. Passage of a fundamental law follows the procedure described above during the first and second readings. In the third reading such a proposal can by a majority vote either be rejected or laid to rest until the first diet of a newly elected Parliament, when, after a committee report, it may be approved in a single reading with no changes by at least a two-thirds majority of votes cast. A majority is counted on the basis of "yes" and "no" votes of representatives present. A fundamental law proposal may, however, be resolved in the same diet, or at least during the period between elections when it was put forth, by following an exceptional procedure. In such cases a proposal must be declared urgent, before final resolution, by at least a five-sixths majority of votes cast; it must then be approved by a two-thirds majority of votes cast. A proposal to declare a matter urgent may be made in discussion during the third reading by a committee, the grand committee, or an individual representative. Rather frequent use is made in Finland of the procedure set forth in paragraph 67 of the Diet Act concerning the legislation of fundamental law. But very few laws passed in this fashion have meant the passage, amendment, explanation, or annulment of a fundamental law; most have contained temporary exceptions to fundamental law provisions. Of the 332 laws passed in 1939–1950 following the procedure for legislation of fundamental law, only six really changed fundamental law.[20]

Jan-Magnus Jansson classifies exceptional laws considered by Parliament's constitutional committee during the years 1939–1952 into three categories: 1) laws which contain direct exceptions to fundamental law provisions concerning the highest state organs, 2) emergency laws extending the government's administrative and legislative powers, and 3) exceptional laws which are mixed and difficult to classify more exactly. The first category includes laws on the basis of which parliamentary elections during the Second World War were postponed and a president was elected through an exceptional procedure. The second category of laws generally concerns a partial and temporary transferral of legislative power normally

20. Jan-Magnus Jansson, *Grundlagsutskottets funktioner vid riksdagarna 1939–1952* (Helsingfors, 1954), p. 105.

exercised by Parliament and the president to the president alone or to the State Council. Parliament, however, reserves the right to examine at a later date the decrees issued on the basis of this authority.[21] In this sort of exceptional legislation, urgent procedure—resolution without postponement until a new election—has become the rule. Paavo Kastari points out that of the 550 laws approved following fundamental law procedure from adoption of the Form of Government Act until 1960, about 95 percent were approved as urgent matters; only 31 proposals were approved following normal procedure.[22] The fact that exceptional laws, which are not in themselves fundamental laws, can be changed by following normal legislative procedure (insofar as the changes do not result in further exceptions) is unusual.

A special and difficult procedure must also be followed when a legislative proposal is made for a new or increased state tax lasting longer than a year. At the final reading such a proposal must be approved by a two-thirds majority. Since consideration must also be given to a continued inflow of state tax revenues, such a proposal, insofar as it does not receive the required support on the third reading, must go back to the finance committee, which may propose a tax for one year. This proposal is decided upon by a simple majority vote in a continuation of the plenary session's third reading. Similarly, a law concerning salaries for members of Parliament must receive a two-thirds majority for approval.

When a legislative proposal is approved by Parliament, its form is examined—this is the task of Parliament's examiners—and it is sent to the president for ratification and promulgation. If a law is not ratified, the matter is sent back to Parliament, which may bring the law into force without ratification by approving it unchanged after a new election by a simple majority. But that has occurred only five times, the first dating back to 1933, when Parliament again approved, unchanged, a law concerning primary school expenditures which President Svinhufvud the previous year had refused to ratify. The other four cases have occurred under President Urho Kekkonen. After the 1958 election Parliament again approved in original form changes in an insanity law and a hunting law; in 1962 a change in a primary school law; and in 1966 a change in a law concerning the

21. *Ibid.*, pp. 114–119.

22. Paavo Kastari, "Constitutional Protection of Civil Rights in Finland," *Democracy in Finland* (Helsinki, 1960), p. 62.

Academy of Finland and fellowship funds, designed to promote the highest cultural development. The State Council publishes a promulgated law in a statute book.

The different stages, proposals, bills, reports, debates, and decisions of a reading by Parliament are contained in published minutes, documents, and appendices.

Supervision of the Government and Inspection of the Administration. Parliament has the right and duty to oversee governmental activities in terms of their legality and political expediency. Parliament can hold a member of the State Council and the chancellor of justice legally responsible for their actions; Parliament decides whether a charge will be made in a special high court of impeachment. A minister may be brought to court by a statement from the chancellor of justice or the ombudsman or by a formal reproach from five members of Parliament or a committee (usually the constitutional committee). After a statement from the constitutional committee and an explanation from the minister or chancellor of justice, Parliament decides whether a charge should be brought or whether the matter should be dropped. It is the explicit task of the constitutional committee to oversee continually the observance of legality in the preparation of matters for consideration.

The political or parliamentary responsibility of a Cabinet and its individual members, which includes responsibility for the appropriateness of measures, may be achieved in many ways and with different results. Weapons which are particularly suitable for this purpose are questions and interpellations. According to paragraph 37 of the Diet Act, every member of Parliament may make a simple question about a matter that must be answered by the appropriate member of the State Council. There are two types of questions, written and oral. A written question, exact in content, is passed on to a minister by the speaker. The minister must give a written or oral response within 30 days; if "because of the nature of the matter" he feels he cannot respond, he must notify Parliament of his reasons within the same period. The time limit was adopted in 1948 in the hope that it would prevent delays in or a total absence of responses. Ministers usually give a written response. The procedure is that the speaker of Parliament in plenary session notes the arrival of a reply not on the agenda, calls attention to its distribution in printed form to members of Parliament, and states that it is being recorded in the minutes. An oral question is also passed on in written form by the speaker to a minister, who is obliged to respond at the following Tuesday or Friday session (unless the nature of the matter is an obstacle), but not earlier than three weekdays from the time information about the question is received. After the answer, a questioner may immediately present no more than two additional short questions on the subject, to which a minister must respond at once. This comprises the final resolution of the matter; no discussion is permitted and no decision is made. The confidence enjoyed by a Cabinet cannot be put directly to a test through questions, but questions may be preparatory moves preceding sterner measures. In exercising their right to ask questions, members of Parliament seek information on one hand and, on the other hand, focus the attention of the government on purported defects in society.

Interpellations in continental Europe have become a fundamental part of the political machinery of multiparty systems. In France, particularly, they have become since the beginning of the nineteenth century a primary means by which the plans and measures of the government have been subjected to discussion and criticism in the national legislature and by which it has been possible to determine how much support a cabinet enjoys. In Finland, in connection with the reform of Parliament, a provision (paragraph 32) was included in the 1906 Diet Act establishing a system including a mixed form of questions and interpellations. Interpellations were frequent before independence but, in view of the monarchical system and political oppression which then prevailed, it was impossible to exercise effective political control over the government. Many decisions of Parliament which were similar to votes of no confidence did not shake the Senate; the only exception was Mechelin's request in 1908, an outgrowth of a debate on Finnish-Russian relations, to be permitted to resign. On December 31, 1917, a change in the Diet Act drew a distinction between questions and interpellations. The legal and political significance of the right to interpellate received special emphasis when it was incorporated into a fundamental law provision concerning parliamentary government.

An interpellation is made "to a member of the State Council concerning a matter under his jurisdiction." In parliamentary practice, however, interpellations are generally much broader in scope; although the point of departure may be a matter within the sphere of a single minister, questions are in fact directed at the entire

Cabinet. There are two stages in the interpellation process. First, an interpellation dealing with a precisely defined matter is left in writing with the speaker by one or more representatives—in practice, with the Secretariat of Parliament. Then it is presented in plenary session and tabled for a following session. If during this period at least twenty members of Parliament, including representatives who originally began the interpellation, support it by appending their names to it (or if there are from the outset the correct number of signatures), the speaker announces that he is passing it on to the appropriate member of the State Council. Otherwise it is dropped. The government must reply within fifteen days from the time it receives information about the interpellation. The nature of the matter may mean that there is no reply, but Parliament must be given reasons for the absence of a response. A response, always oral, is given by the prime minister or the minister concerned. Following a response or notification that there will be no response there is discussion, which is ended by the speaker's proposal that there be a "simple passage" to the orders of the day. Parliament may also approve during the discussion a proposal concerning an "amended passage," or it may send the matter to committee. A committee, in turn, proposes amended passage to the orders of the day; Parliament makes the final decision with respect to the content of this proposal. Simple passage means that Parliament accepts the reply and does not, therefore, adopt a particular position. Amended passage includes a position either approving or criticizing the government's policy; at the extreme this may be a vote of no confidence and a demand that the government resign. In many cases, however, the government itself decides whether or not it has received a vote of no confidence.

Interpellations consequently are, above all, weapons in the arsenal of the opposition with which it harasses the Cabinet and criticizes the government's general policy and individual measures, attempting to oust it from power. Significantly, though, from independence until 1968 only four Cabinets (Kallio II 1926, Sunila I 1928, Sukselainen I 1957, and von Fieandt 1958) have fallen due to a vote of no confidence resulting from an interpellation. An interpellation does not necessarily seek to criticize or overthrow a government; members of Parliament may resort to an interpellation in order to receive a thorough explanation of a matter or to present their wishes as to future policy or, in some cases, to show that they are behind the government and are seeking to strengthen its activity.

The following number of questions and interpellations were made in diets toward the end of the 1950's:

Year	Questions	Interpellations
1957	174	5
1958	35	1
1959	89	–
1960	152	1

Clearly, ministers are often burdened with questions. Frequently they are propaganda gestures, which is evident from the striking increase in their number just before an election. Interpellations are by comparison rare; they are important political events, and both the government parties and the opposition prepare carefully for them.

Votes of confidence or no confidence can also be made, and a Cabinet can be criticized, in many other connections: in consideration, for example, of government reports, communiqués and announcements, or matters whose resolution the government wishes to make a "Cabinet question."

Parliament exercises direct supervision over administration in many different ways. Every four years it selects an ombudsman, "a person distinguished in law," to oversee adherence to law in the action of the courts and of officials. Like the chancellor of justice, the ombudsman reports annually to Parliament concerning his activities. As protector of an individual's rights, he occupies basically the same position as the chancellor; the power of both extends to all public officials, from those at the top of the administrative machine[23] to those in organs in charge of communal matters. To avoid overlapping and duplication in their work, a certain division of labor has been established between the chancellor of justice and the ombudsman. Duties which have been specifically assigned to the ombudsman are observance of the law in matters which concern civil servants in the military, protests and petitions of individuals who have been imprisoned or arrested or are in compulsory labor institutions, and the maintenance of order in places of detention. Inspection trips to these penal and work institutions are an important part of the ombudsman's work. A general difference between his and

23. Duties of the ombudsman do not, however, extend to overseeing the legality of actions taken by the president.

the chancellor of justice's work is that the latter observes the execution of laws from above, from the government, whereas the former attempts to protect the rights of individuals in their dealings with public authorities by examining complaints from below and by personal inspection. Matters are generally put in motion on the basis of complaints and petitions; investigation may result in admonitions, the initiation of disciplinary measures, impeachment charges against an official, and an annulment of decisions made by officials. The post of ombudsman was established in the 1919 Form of Government Act, but its importance was not great in the interwar period; in recent times it has become almost equal to that of chancellor of justice as the guardian of legality.[24]

At the opening of every diet or within a month from that time, the government is obliged to deliver a report on measures taken as a result of decisions by Parliament as well as on the most important developments in administrative and foreign relations.[25] Parliament also receives an annual report on the "fiscal situation and its management." State auditors, appointed by Parliament, report on adherence to the budget and on the condition and administration of "state funds." Following the reports, Parliament communicates with the government. Paragraph 36 of the Diet Act provides that the State Council has the right to pass on to Parliament a communiqué or announcement concerning the state's relations with foreign powers or public administration. Consideration of some such matter ends, as does consideration of an interpellation, with a simple or amended passage to the orders of the day. These special communiqués or announcements have not gained much favor in Finland; they are relatively rare under normal circumstances. Their main purpose is to maintain Parliament's right of inspection and supervision. But they are also significant in the sense that Parliament receives information about national conditions which is essential for its work.

Separate mention should be made of after-the-fact control of decrees issued on the basis of emergency laws extending the government's administrative and legislative powers. Parliament has kept this control for itself. Such administrative decrees, issued by the president or the State Council, must be announced to Parliament,

24. Paavo Kastari, "The Parliamentary Ombudsman: His Functions, Position, and Relations to the Chancellor of Justice in Finland," *International Review of Administrative Sciences*, 28, no. 4 (1962), 391–398.

25. In his own report, the ombudsman lists those decisions of Parliament which resulted in government action of an incomplete nature at the end of the year.

which then examines their legality and expediency and can overturn them. During the Second World War and in the late 1940's there were many such matters, but later, as exceptional legislation was reduced, the number decreased.

Administrative Activity. Parliament also has some duties of a more directly administrative nature. First, it should be mentioned that in 1867 the Bank of Finland came under parliamentary scrutiny. Paragraph 73 of the Form of Government Act states that "the Bank of Finland functions under the guarantee and in the care of Parliament, and is subject to supervision by Trustees elected by Parliament." Nine trustees, of whom three form a smaller banking council, are selected for an entire period between elections; in addition to their supervisory role, they also have decision-making power in certain important monetary questions and in matters affecting administration of the bank. Highest supervision is exercised by the Bank Committee, which investigates the state and administration of the bank and provides Parliament with an annual report. Parliament also elects annually five auditors to present a report on the management of the bank and on the funds under the guarantee of Parliament.

In 1937, Parliament was also charged with direct supervision of the National Pensions Institute. Supervision is carried out by twelve trustees elected by Parliament and acting on the basis of their own rules. In 1948 Parliament's administrative power was extended to the Finnish Broadcasting Corporation; the administrative council of this institution is now elected by Parliament. It was hoped that by bringing party representation into the administrative council it would be possible to achieve nonpartisanship in the policies of the broadcasting corporation.

The Exercise of Administrative Law. Parliament's duties touch upon the administration of law in that Parliament can through legislation proclaim a general amnesty and can initiate legal proceedings against the chancellor of justice, the president, or a member of the State Council. In certain exceptional cases Parliament can also directly resolve legal questions by correcting election errors. It has the power to investigate complaints that some representative was not or is not eligible to sit in Parliament, and to change an election result if it turns out that an error occurred because of some crime or mistake; one condition, however, is that a change can no longer be effected by lodging a court protest. It is natural that, otherwise, the more important legal questions not be given to a political organ such as Parliament for resolution.

SPECIAL FEATURES

Party Hegemony. Activity by the Finnish Parliament is formally based on individualism; the Diet Act and Parliament's rules take as their point of departure the fact that there are two hundred members of Parliament, each one of whom represents the entire nation and acts independently in the best interests of the country. Party groupings are not recognized in the Diet Act and Parliament's rules, even though their actual influence in all phases of consideration given to matters, from preparation to final decision-making, has become a factor of major importance. In realistic terms, there is good reason to say that Parliament is composed above all of party groups. A member of Parliament is primarily a member of a parliamentary group, not an individual representative, for whom there does not always seem to be room for personal thought and opinion. Personal characteristics and abilities have lost some of their earlier meaning.

This phenomenon is an integral part of the general features of social development mentioned in an earlier connection, but the electoral system is also partially responsible for the strength and permanence of party groups in parliamentary activity. Proportional representation is based on the notion that Parliament should represent as accurately as possible different opinions in the nation, whereas the main emphasis in a plurality electoral system is on the realization of a viable majority. When the question of parliamentary reform in Finland was being discussed, at a time when supreme power did not rest with Parliament, not much attention was paid to the realization of a viable majority. The institution's representativeness was considered more important. Nevertheless, the principle of proportionality contains, in a certain sense, the notion that representatives sit in Parliament not as individuals but as spokesmen for political groups. In practice, proportional representation requires well-organized party groups for an election campaign, and at election time it definitely brings parties foward at the expense of individuals. Because a member of Parliament owes his election to his own party, it is difficult for him to disregard its decisions—especially since he must think of future elections.

The demand for party discipline is strong on important political questions, particularly those which are central to a party's practical action program. Sometimes, however, representatives have acted in accordance with their own opinions, against a group's explicit position that is supposed to be binding. In these cases a group must decide on a possible punishment for the "insurgent." A member of Parliament who ends up outside his group is not, however, obliged to resign; it is here that one sees most clearly the practical significance of the free mandate principle. In 1912 Parliament refused to endorse the resignation petition of a Social Democratic representative, Kotonen, which he justified on the grounds that the party organization in his electoral district was demanding his resignation.

Ability to Act. The argument used most frequently in support of a plurality electoral system is that the task of a national assembly is not only to represent, but also to rule. This system seeks to divide the votes between two large parties, whereas proportional representation favors small parties and thus promotes the division of Parliament into many minority groups. But party conditions are connected with many historical and social factors; one cannot claim that the electoral system has had a decisive influence on their formation, although it has, without doubt, had a certain significance. Proportional representation unquestionably has contributed, along with other factors, to the fact that in the Finnish Parliament there are six to eight groups, none of which constitutes a majority by itself and none of which is so much stronger than the other groups that it can provide effective leadership. Social Democrats in the 1916 election gained a short-lived majority of parliamentary seats. Lasting, viable majorities cannot be formed through multiparty cooperation because party lines are too sharp and party goals too different. Two or three parties may agree on the resolution of one problem, but their positions on a second question may seriously conflict. Indeed, in Finnish political life there prevails "a war of all against all"; firm political alliances even in Parliament occur only in exceptional situations and for short periods of time. An example of attempted cooperation is the 1945 agreement of the "big three"—the Agrarian party, the Social Democrats, and the People's Democrats—which went much further than the usual Cabinet agreement. There was, however, no precise concrete content to programmatic points in the agreement, and its practical significance in parliamentary work did not become great. The two extreme groups, the Coalition party and the SKDL, have been isolated from other groups in postwar politics, and the main forces of parliamentary life have been the large center groups: the Agrarian-Center party and the Social Democratic party. But they represent different social groups and support different interests, the former the interests of producers and the latter the interests of consumers; consequently, their policy efforts clash more often than they coincide. There must be backroom negotiations, accommodations, and compromises in order to resolve questions that both parties consider important. The result may be logrolling, in which many questions are joined together and resolved by mutual concessions. A real impasse is reached when relations between the large parties are strained to the point that it is difficult to hold discussions and reach compromises.

Effective parliamentary work is hampered by the absence of adequate leadership. In statements made even in Parliament, there is often recognition of the parliamentary-system principle that, in legislation particularly, initiative and leadership should be in the hands of the government acting with the support of Parliament. But in practice the principle is easily given up. Adequate political leadership capable of ensuring work that is systematic and long-term in nature is not found in Parliament; reasons for this are Parliament's heterogeneity, mentioned earlier, and the absence of recognized parliamentary leaders in the groups.

Amount of Work. The growth in recent times of Parliament's workload has become a real problem and has given rise to the question of rationalizing this work. In the 1937 diet there were 515 matters to be considered by Parliament; in 1954 the number was 1,566 and in 1965 3,917. Even though Parliament has lengthened its sessions so that it meets almost throughout the year, it does not have time to consider all matters before it; a substantial number are postponed until the next diet. In 1937 about 8 percent of the matters before Parliament were not resolved; but in 1965 this figure was 52 percent (ever increasing private member bills constitute the bulk). Since government proposals have a high priority in consideration, there is very little time left for consideration of parliamentary bills. At times the right to propose a bill is more apparent than real;

Table 20. Matters before Parliament and their resolution, 1962–1965

Matter	1962		1963		1964		1965	
	A[a]	B[b]	A	B	A	B	A	B
Legislative proposals not ratified, or postponed until new election	20	20	–	–	–	–	–	–
Government proposals	149	126	198	157	235	186	256	239
Bills from Aaland Islands regional assembly	–	–	–	–	–	–	3	2
Decrees	3	1	5	4	2	1	6	6
State Council decisions	5	5	8	6	11	10	10	10
Reports	14	10	18	15	15	12	20	18
Legislative bills	336	62	456	114	540	90	692	207
Petitionary bills	1,010	164	1,322	366	1,480	247	1,917	379
Fiscal bills	643	643	726	726	583	583	729	729
Other bills	5	5	3	3	3	3	6	6
State Council communiqués	–	–	1	1	–	–	–	–
Questions	129	121	146	143	196	191	276	260
Interpellations	1	–	4	4	3	3	2	2
Total	2,315	1,157	2,887	1,539	3,068	1,326	3,917	1,858

Source: Table prepared on the basis of information received from Parliament's secretariat (eduskunnan kanslia).
[a] Total number of matters before a diet.
[b] Matters given final consideration by a diet.

more than half of these bills are not considered, and most that are meet rejection in short order. During the period 1954–1957, 7 percent of the legislative bills were approved in one form or another, 17 percent of the petitionary bills, and 6 percent of the fiscal bills. Depending on the political situation, the significance of Parliament's power to initiate legislation fluctuates within certain limits.

Table 20 shows how many different matters came before Parliament in the period 1962–1965 according to unofficial statistics and how many were fully considered in diets comprising one election period.

In terms of measures designed to rationalize Parliament's work, it has been noted that the effective working time of the Finnish Parliament is relatively short; plenary sessions are normally held only twice a week, on Tuesdays and Fridays, and their length is ill-defined, depending a good deal on how quickly matters have been considered in committee. It has been suggested that committees should assume responsibility for preparatory work in order to speed up the process of consideration; it has also been proposed, following the example provided by popular assemblies in some other countries, that restrictions be imposed upon a representative's right to speak and initiate bills. But Parliament resolutely rejected proposals to this effect made by the government in 1951.

VII The President of the Republic and the State Council

PRESIDENTIAL ELECTIONS

Electoral System. The question of how to elect a president of the Republic was the subject of disagreements difficult to reconcile and a continued exchange of opinion during the debates over the Form of Government Act; even in later years it has repeatedly been the subject of discussion. It has received special significance, perhaps an exaggerated significance, because the method of selection was viewed as an essential part of that system of weights and counterweights by which it was hoped to achieve some sort of balance in the relationship of strength between Parliament and the president. In the report of Ståhlberg's constitutional committee in 1917, and in the form of government proposal, based on the report, submitted to Parliament in December 1917 by the Svinhufvud Senate, it was proposed that the president be selected by direct election to be carried out in two stages if no candidate should get a majority on the first ballot. This idea was later dropped, leaving two alternatives: the election could either be indirect, using electors, or it could be carried out by Parliament. The latter method was adopted in the form of government proposal submitted to Parliament by the Castrén government in May 1919. But the grand committee came out in favor of indirect election, and this was approved by Parliament in its final decision. The result was a victory for the right, which thus hoped to emphasize the president's independent position and freedom from Parliament, as well as his direct mandate from the people.

The president is elected every six years. The people first elect three hundred electors, and they, in turn, carry out the final election. Electors are chosen on January 15–16, following the same system of proportional representation used in parliamentary elections. The division of electoral districts is the same in both elections; the State Council determines the number of electors for each electoral district. Provisions concerning choice of electors are otherwise roughly the same as for parliamentary elections, and preparations for an election are generally similar to those described earlier for a parliamentary election. The nomination of presidential candidates is not set forth in election laws, so parties are permitted to act in whatever way they feel is most appropriate. The matter is usually dealt with by party congresses or party councils, but occasionally a decision is made in a group as restricted as the party executive committee.

The electors gather in Helsinki on the following February 15 and, under the chairmanship of the prime minister, elect a president. No formal discussion of the candidates is permitted and balloting is secret. A candidate is elected if he receives more than half the votes cast on the first ballot. Otherwise a second ballot is held, and if no one receives a majority then the electors vote a third time between the two candidates who received the most votes on the second ballot. If the vote is equal, the outcome is decided by lot. As yet there has been no need to resort to this last procedure, although twice, in 1931 and in 1956, the candidate elected received the smallest majority possible. The ban on formal discussion does not preclude tough and lengthy negotiations between ballots among elector groups or among negotiators appointed by them, concerning tactics on the next round. The large number of presidential candidates and the equal strength of elector groups make this procedure obligatory, unless the election outcome is to be left to chance. The election of 1956, for example, lasted over six hours. In his study based on hundreds of individual interviews, Paavo Hirvikallio describes these backroom negotiations, the most dramatic of which took place during the 1931 election. On the third ballot, Svinhufvud faced Ståhlberg, and when other groups had taken a stand the outcome rested in the hands of the divided and hesitant Agrarian party group; this led to severe pressure, eventually successful, on behalf of Svinhufvud's candidacy.[1]

In the Form of Government Act only one qualification for the presidency is mentioned: the candidate must be a native-born Finnish citizen. If a member of Parliament is elected president he gives

1. Paavo Hirvikallio, *Tasavallan presidentin vaalit Suomessa 1919–1950* (Porvoo, 1958), pp. 46–65.

up his duties as a representative; an individual in state employ who is elected president is likewise released from his position. There are no limitations concerning re-election. The president assumes his duties on March 1 following the election, at which time he delivers a ceremonial affirmation in a session of Parliament.

The procedure set forth in fundamental law is very complicated and time-consuming, and on numerous occasions, under exceptional circumstances, it has been necessary to abandon it. A president has been elected following normal procedure only seven times: in 1925, 1931, 1937, 1950, 1956, 1962, and 1968. In 1919, 1944, and 1946 Parliament elected the president. In 1940 and 1943, during the Second World War, presidential elections were carried out by electors who had been chosen in 1937. In all of these cases it was, of course, necessary for Parliament, following the procedure for fundamental law, to pass a law making exceptions to fundamental law permissible. The procedure followed in 1944, when Risto Ryti resigned, was special in that Marshal Mannerheim was appointed president by law.

Electoral Participation. The statistics in Table 21 illustrate voter turnout in the selection of electors. Participation in presidential elections is noticeably weaker than in parliamentary elections. Over the years, however, interest in presidential elections has grown continually, and the difference vis-à-vis parliamentary elections is being erased. The difference in voting activity which has long

Table 21. Voter turnout in presidential elections, 1925–1968[a]

Year	Cities	Countryside	Entire country
1925	46.2	38.3	39.7
1931	57.8	44.7	47.3
1937	65.6	55.5	57.8
1950	70.8	61.1	63.8
1956	74.2	72.8	73.4
1962	82.5	80.7	81.5
1968	69.3	70.9	70.2

Source: Official Statistics of Finland, ser. XXIX 12, A:16, 19, 22, 25, 27, 30 (Helsinki: Valtioneuvoston kirjapaino, 1926, 1931, 1937, 1951, 1956, 1963, 1968).

[a] Since 1956, towns have been grouped with cities; earlier they were grouped with countryside.

reigned between the city and countryside, and which is appreciably greater in presidential than in parliamentary elections, is an important phenomenon. Until 1956 voter turnout in the countryside was to a surprising degree lower than in cities. This provides a partial explanation for findings concerning the relative strength of parties.

Parties in Presidential Elections. A presidential election is also a party election in the sense that parties nominate presidential candidates as well as electors and organize the election campaign, although party slogans are not quite so open in presidential as in parliamentary elections. Candidate lists have generally been rather clear party lists, however, so the electorate can be grouped, when examining election returns, by party. It is interesting to note the degree to which the electorate considers the presidential election a party election and to which it is ready to break with party dependency by putting personal questions in the forefront. Some light is shed on this problem by comparing parliamentary and presidential elections.

Table 22 shows that the Coalition and Progressive parties have emerged victorious in presidential elections in that their share of the popular vote has been considerably greater than in parliamentary elections. The weakness of leftist parties deserves special attention; only in the 1950 presidential election were the People's Democrats able to win a greater share of the vote than in the previous parliamentary election. The share of the vote won by the Agrarian party was, until 1956, also lower than the vote it received in the closest parliamentary election. There are no important oscillations in the support received by the Swedish People's party in these two different elections. The reason for the unusual division of votes in presidential elections is found, on one hand, in the varying activeness of different population and party groups, and, on the other, in the influence wielded by the personalities of individual candidates on positions taken by the electorate. Especially during the two decades preceding the Second World War, the Socialist parties considered parliamentary elections much more important and showed relatively little interest in presidential elections. These groups have not been able to present candidates who are well known and widely respected; and before 1956, practically speaking, candidates of the left had no chance of being elected president by a meeting of electors with a bourgeois majority. Furthermore, it appears that voters on the left, especially

Table 22. Percentage by party of votes cast in presidential elections and votes cast in previous parliamentary elections[a]

Party	1924 Parl.	1925 Pres.	1930 Parl.	1931 Pres.	1936 Parl.	1937 Pres.	1948 Parl.	1950 Pres.	1954 Parl.	1956 Pres.	1962 Parl.	1962 Pres.	1966 Parl.	1968 Pres.
National Coalition party[b]	19.0	22.7	18.1	21.6	10.4	21.6	17.1	22.9	12.8	18.0	15.0	13.1	13.8	21.2
IKL	–	–	–	–	8.3	8.1	–	–	–	–	–	–	–	–
Progressive party; other liberal parties	9.1	11.5	5.8	17.7	6.3	11.1	3.9	5.4	7.9	4.5	6.3	8.0	6.5	5.0
Swedish People's party[c]	12.0	12.6	10.8	9.0	11.2	10.2	7.7	8.8	7.0	6.9	6.4	6.7	6.0	5.7
Agrarian party; Center party	20.3	19.9	27.3	20.0	22.4	16.6	24.2	19.6	24.1	26.9	23.0	31.7	21.2	20.7
Social Democratic party	29.0	26.6	34.2	30.2	38.6	30.7	26.3	21.8	26.2	23.3	19.5	13.1	27.2	15.5
Social Democratic League	–	–	–	–	–	–	–	–	–	–	4.4	3.0	2.6	2.3
Communist; SKDL	10.4	6.6	1.0	–	–	–	20.0	21.4	21.6	18.7	22.0	20.5	21.2	17.0
Others	0.2	0.1	2.8	1.5	2.8	1.7	0.8	0.1	0.4	1.7	3.4	3.9	1.5	12.7

Source: Official Statistics of Finland, ser. XXIX 11–14, A:15–30 (Helsinki: Valtioneuvoston kirjapaino, 1925–1968).

[a] In 1962 the parliamentary election was held right after the presidential election.

[b] The 1962 presidential percentage, 13.1, does not include votes given to Coalition elector-candidates who were in the Kekkonen election bloc.

[c] Includes the Swedish left.

in the countryside, did not go to the polls in full strength. This is suggested by the aforementioned fact that there is a great difference between numbers of voters in the countryside and in the cities. This is probably also a partial explanation for the earlier relative weakness of the Agrarian party, but one must also consider the shifting of votes to candidates of the small bourgeois parties. The Coalition and Progressive parties were able to nominate well-known, respected men who usually eclipsed candidates of the Agrarian party and on several occasions won the votes of many Agrarian party supporters. The chief candidates in 1925 were Svinhufvud and Ryti, in both 1931 and 1937 Svinhufvud and Ståhlberg. In 1950 Paasikivi was clearly ahead of all other candidates.

After this, however, the situation changed. In 1956 the Agrarian party for the first time surpassed its percentage of the total vote in the previous parliamentary election. Its candidate, Urho Kekkonen, gathered votes outside his party, particularly in the northern part of the country, from voters apparently belonging to both groups of the left. The election seemed to indicate the growing party dependency of candidates and voters. The chief candidates in the election, Kekkonen and Fagerholm, were clear-cut party leaders, who, like the other candidates, participated actively in the campaign. The chances that Social Democrats might elect their own man had increased substantially, whereas the opposite was true for parties of the right.

In 1962 the situation was altogether different. Preparations and the election itself took place, to a degree hitherto unseen in Finland, around groupings which were broader than individual parties, so that it is difficult to fit the results of the selection of electors into the usual party classification. Elector candidates for the SKDL, the Social Democratic party, and the Social Democratic League were all, to be sure, in their own election blocs, and the Agrarian candidates were in the large Kekkonen election bloc. But the Finnish People's party and the Swedish People's party, particularly, were in a state of disarray. Elector candidates of the former were to be found in the Kekkonen election bloc, the party's own bloc, and a joint bloc of the Coalition and Finnish People's parties. Likewise, part of the Swedish People's party directly supported Kekkonen, while another part formed its own blocs. The share of the popular vote received by the different parties, based on a differentiation drawn from official statistics, is given in Table 22. Most striking is the large vote for the

Agrarian elector candidates supporting Kekkonen, compared with the results of the parliamentary election held three weeks later. The Finnish People's party also received substantially more votes in the presidential election than in the parliamentary election, mainly because its candidates belonged to the Kekkonen bloc. It should be noted that the percentage given for the Coalition party in the table is somewhat low because there were Coalition candidates in the Kekkonen bloc who, in the official statistics, were included in the category "others." Social Democrats suffered the greatest defeat in the presidential election.

The 1962 presidential election was perhaps to a greater degree than any that preceded it a personal election. But experience shows that party affiliation generally is not decisive in presidential elections; cross-party grouping centered on personal questions takes place. In his research on the voting behavior of university students in the 1956 presidential election, Pesonen points out that 69 percent of university students expressing a party affiliation voted for the presidential candidate of their own parties and 22 percent for a candidate nominated by some other party. From this it was possible to conclude that party affiliation had a great influence on the selection of a presidential candidate but was not the only factor of importance in determining how one voted. The stronger the party affiliation, the less likely it was that university students were inclined to vote for a candidate nominated by a party other than their own.[2] The same phenomenon was found in broader interview projects. Table 23 reveals the results of a Finnish Gallup poll of December 1955 which focused on voting intentions with respect to the approaching January presidential election.

Opinion of the Electorate. In paragraph 23 of the Form of Government Act it is emphasized that the president of the Republic is elected by the Finnish people. This raises the question of to what extent presidential candidates are discussed in the first stage of an election and to what extent direct public opinion, as expressed in the selection of electors, influences the final outcome of the election. Electors are not bound by any sort of imperative mandate; formally they are free to act and think as they see fit.

2. Pertti Pesonen, *Valitsijamiesvaalien ylioppilasäänestäjät* (Vammala, 1958), p. 156; Pertti Pesonen, "The Voting Behaviour of Finnish Students," *Democracy in Finland* (Helsinki, 1960), pp. 93–104.

Table 23. Voting intentions of individuals by party preference and social class, 1956 presidential election

Presidential candidate	Social Democratic			SKDL			Agrarian party			Other bourgeois		
	A[a]	B[b]	C[c]	A	B	C	A	B	C	A	B	C
	(54)	(348)	(53)	(18)	(112)	(1)	(310)	(82)	(29)	(67)	(113)	(153)
	%	%	%	%	%	%	%	%	%	%	%	%
Fagerholm (Social Democratic)	22	49	53	11	4	–	1	4	–	9	5	4
Kilpi (SKDL)	–	1	–	22	40	100	1	–	–	–	–	–
Kekkonen (Agrarian)	22	12	6	22	27	–	76	77	62	12	10	5
Tuomioja, Törngren, or Rydman (bourgeois)	30	14	28	–	4	–	4	7	28	65	69	83
No preference	26	24	13	45	24	–	18	12	10	14	16	8

Source: Erik Allardt, "Structural Cleavages in Finnish Politics," Helsingin yliopiston sosiologian laitoksen tutkimuksia no. 6, 1961, mimeographed, p. 19.

[a] Farmers.

[b] Workers.

[c] White-collar workers.

In most cases an election campaign revolves around declared presidential candidates. A candidate is not always officially nominated, even though his name may be part of the election campaign. In 1925 the Social Democrats nominated Väinö Tanner and the Communists Matti Väisänen. Risto Ryti was the Progressive party candidate. The Agrarian and Swedish People's parties had no official candidate; neither did the Coalition party, which, however, proposed P. E. Svinhufvud in campaign discussion (he was dropped on the first ballot). Six years later Svinhufvud was the official candidate of the Coalition party; the Progressive party nominated the nation's first president (1919–1925), K. J. Ståhlberg, and the Agrarian party Kyösti Kallio, who, nonetheless, did not receive unanimous support from the party. Social Democrats again nominated Tanner, and many Swedish-speaking Finns supported Svinhufvud or Ståhlberg. In 1937 the Swedish People's party continued its cautious tactics, but other parties nominated official candidates prior to the election. The candidates this time, too, were Svinhufvud, Ståhlberg, Kallio, and Tanner. Ståhlberg was supported by the Small Farmers' party, the Swedish left, and the small People's party, in addition to the Progressive party. In the first normal presidential election of the postwar period, in 1950, the Coalition, Progressive, and Swedish People's parties announced their support for J. K. Paasikivi, whereas the Agrarian party nominated their leader Urho Kekkonen and the SKDL Mauno Pekkala. A great number of Social Democrats evidently wanted to re-elect Paasikivi, but, largely because of campaign tactics, he did not become the party's official candidate. The presidential election of 1956 meant a further tightening of party lines and an elevation of the candidate question to an even more prominent position in the election campaign. All parties had their own official candidates, around whom election activities centered: Kekkonen for the Agrarian party, K. A. Fagerholm for the Social Democrats, Sakari Tuomioja for the Coalition party, Eino Kilpi for the People's Democrats, Eero Rydman for the Finnish People's party, and Ralf Törngren for the Swedish People's party.

But this development was not permanent. Prior to the 1962 election, in order to defeat Kekkonen, the Honka-league was founded. Its initiators were the Coalition and Social Democratic parties, but it was also joined by the Farmers' party, the Finnish People's party (although within the party there was a strong wing supporting Kekkonen), the League of Liberals, and parts of the Swedish People's party. As a counterweight, a broad grouping which cut across party lines formed around President Kekkonen, the candidate of the Agrarian party. The People's Democrats nominated Paavo Aitio, and the left Social Democrats Emil Skog. Due to a dramatic series of foreign policy events, the former chancellor of justice, Olavi Honka, withdrew his candidacy, at which time the Social Democrats nominated a party candidate, Rafael Paasio, and the Coalition party decided to participate in the election with "extinguished lights," that is, without a formally nominated candidate. Parts of the People's parties not in the Kekkonen election bloc followed suit.

In 1968 the line of demarcation between the candidates was much more evident. The People's Democrats, Social Democrats, and Agrarians jointly supported the re-election of Urho Kekkonen, as did the Liberals, who participated with their own slogans as a separate group in the election. Matti Virkkunen, a bank director, was the candidate of the Coalition party, and the Rural party nominated its leader Veikko Vennamo. The behavior of the Swedish People's party was, in this election, too, distinctive: since agreement could not be reached on a common candidate, the party participated in the election as a separate group but did not demand a commitment from its elector-nominees, who supported either Kekkonen or Virkkunen.

As the position of the head of state has become more central in the political life of the nation, the question of procedure for electing a president has become more important. The major problem is how to ensure that the wishes of the electorate, as expressed in the first stage of the election, will have an influence in the final outcome. Opponents of the present electoral system argue, first, that the method now used is too complicated and slow and that it increases unreasonably the number of general elections; and second, that the outcome is dependent upon happenstance and is not always in accord with opinions held by the electorate, since electors do not always keep their election promises and do not consider themselves bound by them. One cannot deny that the criticism is in part justified. With at least five parties competing, the final election has usually been a question of which candidate most party groups of electors feel they can accept; the extent of popular support for each candidate remains a secondary matter. A party system developed to perform other tasks is not easily adapted to electing a president, which causes conflict as well as party maneuvering with a resultant arbitrariness of outcome.

There is always the possibility of a dark horse emerging on the last ballots. Once, in 1925, an individual was elected president who had not officially been a candidate and about whom relatively little was said during the election campaign. Kyösti Kallio was elected in 1937 in spite of the fact that the support received by his election bloc had diminished substantially when compared with the previous presidential election. In elections since the 1950's, however, the connection between an election outcome and opinions held by the electorate is clearer. The total relative vote of groups openly supporting Paasikivi's candidacy in 1950 was almost 30 percent higher than the figure for the parliamentary election held two years earlier. Six years later, the Agrarian party vote rose considerably in comparison with the previous presidential election, and somewhat with respect to the previous parliamentary election. In 1962 over two-fifths of the voters directly supported the elector candidates of the Kekkonen election bloc, in addition to which a large number of bourgeois candidates outside this bloc had announced that they, too, would support re-election of the president. And finally, it was evident in the first phase of the 1968 election that Kekkonen could not be beaten.

How large a percentage of voters in each presidential election supported the winner by giving their votes to election blocs of groups which had placed him in nomination is shown below:

Year	Percentage of voters
1925	19.9
1931	21.6
1937	16.6
1950	37.1
1956	26.9
1962	44.3
1968	61.6

In the first three elections only a relatively small minority was behind the candidates elected president. And it is questionable whether or not the votes given to the Agrarian party in 1925 should be included in the vote for Lauri Relander. In the last four elections the connection has been clearer. One cannot, however, draw far-reaching conclusions from these percentages; they hardly show real support among the electorate for presidents at their time of election.

For decades there has been a demand for reform by most groups, particularly by those parties (the left and the Agrarian party) which have suffered defeats in presidential elections. In this connection there has also been discussion of whether the president's position would be weakened and whether he would become dependent upon Parliament if that body should perform the election. Tuttu Tarkiainen and Sven Lindman have argued that a change in the electoral system would not necessarily have importance in this respect. The decisive factors in an election are parties and their groupings, be the formal election in Parliament or in a meeting of electors. And experience thus far shows that a method of election does not influence the position of the president. Parliament has, as mentioned, elected a president three times: 1919 (Ståhlberg), 1944 (Mannerheim), and 1946 (Paasikivi).[3] It would appear, however, that attempts to have Parliament elect the president are dying out; this arrangement is really out of the question, so important have these elections become in an accentuation of the role of the president. There has, instead, been an effort to make the direct influence of citizens more effective in the decision. There is much more criticism than earlier of a procedure by which a party makes no nomination before a presidential election, or by which there is an attempt in the meeting of electors to advance the name of an individual about whom the electorate has not been able to express an opinion. In the election campaign presidential candidates seek direct contact with the population through propaganda meetings, a custom initiated in 1950 by Urho Kekkonen and adopted six years later by other candidates, although on a somewhat more modest scale. In 1962 Kekkonen set a precedent by being the first incumbent president to participate actively in a campaign on his own behalf.

The following list is of the presidents of the independent Finnish Republic, their periods in office, and their party affiliations:

K. J. Ståhlberg	1919–1925	Progressive party
Lauri Kr. Relander	1925–1931	Agrarian party
P. E. Svinhufvud	1931–1937	Coalition party
Kyösti Kallio	1937–1940	Agrarian party

3. Tuttu Tarkiainen, *Tasavallan presidentin asema Suomen parlamenttaarisessa hallitusjärjestelmässä* (Jyväskylä: Gummerus, 1938), pp. 83–91; Sven Lindman, *Notes on the Presidential Elections in Finland* (Åbo, 1951), pp. 14–17.

Risto Ryti	1940–1943	Progressive party
Risto Ryti	1943–1944	Progressive party
C. G. Mannerheim	1944–1946	No party
J. K. Paasikivi	1946–1950	Closest to Coalition party
J. K. Paasikivi	1950–1956	Closest to Coalition party
Urho Kekkonen	1956–1962	Agrarian party
Urho Kekkonen	1962–1968	Agrarian-Center party
Urho Kekkonen	1968——	Center party

All presidents to date have been bourgeois in political outlook. Agrarians and rightists have served as heads of state most of the time. All presidents before election had occupied leading positions in the nation's political life; a total of five resigned from the post of prime minister in order to assume the duties of president.

If the president is not able to carry out his duties because of sickness or a trip abroad, the prime minister acts as his replacement; if the latter is unable to assume the duties, they are carried out in turn by his replacement (a specially designated member of the State Council). The prime minister retained his former duties while acting as replacement for the president at one time, remaining head of the Cabinet and perhaps also a member of Parliament, but this inconsistency was abolished by a 1956 change to paragraph 25 of the Form of Government Act. If the obstacle is permanent, a new president is elected as soon as possible; he begins his duties immediately after the election.

The president receives an annual salary of 120,000 marks, which cannot be changed while he is in office. In addition, he receives an annual sum of 100,000 marks to meet representational needs. He lives in a state building the maintenance, heating and lighting, interior decoration, and necessary domestic help of which are financed from public funds. Salary and fringe benefits are tax-free. A president in retirement is entitled to an annual pension.

POSITION AND DUTIES OF THE PRESIDENT

In an earlier chapter, in describing special features of the Constitution, the uniqueness of Finland's system of government was mentioned: it brings together parts of two opposing systems, parliamentarism and a separation of powers. These principles are joined in such a way that members of the State Council, who assist the president in the decision-making process, must, in accordance with a provision of the Form of Government Act, enjoy the confidence of Parliament—which means they are dependent on Parliament; but, on the other hand, some important rights concerning highest executive power have been entrusted to an independent president of the Republic. The purpose when constructing the Constitution was not to make the president a mere figurehead for the nation; he was to be a real head of state, in whose hands firm governmental power would be concentrated, and who would represent, along with Parliament and a Cabinet dependent on Parliament, continuity. In this respect Finland's Constitution differed from the constitutions of many other states born after the First World War such as Czechoslovakia, Austria, Poland, Estonia, Latvia, and Lithuania, all of which sought a system of government in which parliament would predominate.

The President's Legislative Power. The president participates actively with Parliament in legislation, mainly by presenting government proposals to Parliament for its consideration. But his cooperation is also necessary in the final phase of the legislative process, since a law approved by Parliament needs the ratification and signature of the president before it is effected. The president may request a statement from the Supreme Court and the Supreme Administrative Court before consenting; he may also refuse to ratify a law, in which case it is returned to Parliament for consideration. If a law is not ratified within three months from the time the president receives it, it is considered rejected; a general custom today, however, is to make a decision concerning rejection in advance of the deadline. Since a law may come into effect without ratification through a procedure mentioned earlier, the president has only a delaying (suspensive) veto; but this veto is effective, and Parliament has overridden it only five times. Moreover, when legislating a law Parliament must take into consideration the possibility of a presidential veto. By the end of the 1965 diet (that is, by April 1966), the president had refused to ratify a total of fifty-three laws which had been approved by Parliament. All presidents except Ryti and Mannerheim have exercised the veto. It has affected rather evenly legislative proposals initiated both by the government and by Parliament and the decision generally, perhaps even in all cases, has been made in official concord with the State Council. An assertion based on a majority opinion in the State Council or, possibly, on a statement by the Supreme Court that a law contains in legal terms errors of form or substance or is not expedient for one reason or another has led to a veto. Such extensive use of the veto can hardly be seen as a sign of presidential or governmental power; it is, rather, a sign of Cabinet inability to direct Parliament's legislative work: almost half the cases mentioned were wholly, or primarily, concerned with laws approved on the basis of government proposals. For its part, Parliament has respected this power of the head of state and has refrained from reacting strongly to its use. Generally the statement is made that it is impossible to approve the law in original form or that the law is no longer appropriate. Occasionally a proposal is considered to have been dropped because of interim legislation.

The president also exercises independent legislative power, free from Parliament, on the basis of a general mandate provided in paragraph 28 of the Form of Government Act. He has the right to issue decrees 1) about matters which have previously been arranged by administrative provisions, 2) concerning more exact provisions for the execution of laws, 3) concerning the management of state property, and 4) concerning the organization and activity of administrative offices and public institutions. The first-mentioned category is a remnant of bygone centuries, when the head of state had extensive power to determine by decree matters dealing with general order and security, occupations, and so on. The president's power of decree has been reduced insofar as these spheres have come under the legislative power of Parliament. A decree may not include provisions which contain a change in law; the president's power of decree under exceptional circumstances, however, goes far beyond paragraph 28 of the Form of Government Act through special powers incorporated in law. Parliament approved a great many such emergency laws in the 1940's when it transferred its legislative power to the president and the State Council; it has sought to control these relinquished powers by retaining the possibility of overturning decrees issued on the basis of these laws. Furthermore, the special powers are granted for only a short period, usually a year at a time. Parliament must be informed, with no delay, of a decree or State Council decision made on the basis of an emergency law, and such a decree or decision must be rescinded by the president or the State Council if Parliament so decides.

Dissolution of Parliament and New Elections. Parliament itself decides about meetings in a regular diet. The president, however, may call a special session of Parliament; he may dissolve Parliament and set a new election to be held during the period between normal elections. This power is quite important because it is not given to heads of state in all republics. Parliament has been dissolved five times since the Form of Government Act was adopted, four times as a result of concerted action by the president and the State Council and once against a unanimous Cabinet supported by Parliament.[4]

The most exceptional and interesting of these occurrences was the dissolution of Parliament in 1924. In August of the preceding year a government led by Kallio imprisoned the Communist members of Parliament, twenty-seven in all, and although the government received a clear vote of confidence from Parliament at the end of the year, President Ståhlberg felt that the situation called for the dissolution of the rump Parliament and a new election. The State Council refused to cooperate and submitted its resignation, after which the President appointed a caretaker Cabinet, led by Cajander, and with its cooperation was able to dissolve Parliament in January. This action by the President evoked sharp criticism from the political right, but it soon subsided. The motive for dissolution, a desire to restore normalcy to political life, was certainly understandable.

The next dissolution occurred five years later (1929). Due to the votes of the opposition parties—the left and the Agrarian party—Parliament rejected in April a proposal by the Mantere government, composed of Coalition and Progressive party representatives, concerning a salary increase for civil servants; the result was that President Relander, at the wish of the Cabinet, dissolved Parliament and called for a new election. It should be noted that the election was a clear defeat for the government parties, and the Prime Minister submitted his government's resignation request to the President immediately after Parliament met. In this case dissolution did not bring about the desired result.

The dissolution of 1930 was caused by the government's attempt to hasten action by Parliament on certain laws—the Communist laws. These proposals, submitted by the Svinhufvud government, were, it is true, approved; but they were not declared urgent—procedure for the legislation of fundamental law was involved—and, consequently, final consideration was postponed until after a new

4. Parliament was dissolved six times, for various reasons, during the years 1907–1919.

election. Communists no longer were able to participate in elections with their own candidates, so the dissolution achieved its goal; the new Parliament approved the laws by a two-thirds majority.

The fourth dissolution was an attempt to assist in formation of a parliamentary Cabinet. After Kekkonen's fourth Cabinet fell in November 1953, political groups were not able to agree on the formation of a government, which resulted in the caretaker-type Cabinet of Tuomioja. To resolve the problem, the President dissolved Parliament in December; a new election was held in March 1954.

Finally, foreign policy events led to an early election in 1962. After the Soviet Union in its note of October 30, 1961, had proposed consultations concerning measures for the defense of the borders of both countries, the Finnish Foreign Minister was sent to Moscow to ascertain in more detail what concrete measures the Soviet leaders had in mind. When it became clear that the Soviet Union wanted assurances of no change in Finland's future foreign policy line, an attempt was made to provide guarantees by dissolving Parliament and calling for a new election, held early in the month of February. The President's role in this dissolution was decisive.

Dissolution of Parliament has, therefore, been relied upon rather infrequently during the period of Finnish independence, although the measure is often mentioned during crises in the political life of the nation and although Parliament and some of its groups have been threatened with dissolution on many occasions. Now and then there are proposals calling for dissolution, especially in connection with troublesome government crises. Generally, however, it is felt that it is "worthwhile" to resort to dissolution only in exceptional situations, when really important questions require an appeal to the nation. A new election under regular conditions does not help much in resolving a problem, since shifts in votes and changes in relative strength are rather small because of rigid formation of political opinion.

It should also be mentioned that, after the Second World War, an election was held at an unusual period of time—in March 1945—which was not, however, a result of dissolution. The term of the Parliament elected in 1939 had been extended twice by exceptional law as the war continued, but with the return of peace it was felt that a new election, as soon as possible, was a necessity; exceptional procedure in this case was made possible by special law.

Foreign Policy Leadership. According to paragraph 33 of the Form of Government Act, the president determines Finland's relations with foreign states: this means that he is entrusted with supreme leadership in foreign policy. The conduct of foreign policy is in actuality one of the president's most central duties and one of his most important and most visible powers. The significance of the head of state in the field of foreign policy has grown considerably, especially during and after the Second World War, that is, since President Ryti's tenure in office, and this has meant a pronounced accentuation of his position. The president's powers are nonetheless restricted in that certain measures require the consent of Parliament. Furthermore, foreign policy matters enjoy no special position with respect to order of consideration: actual decisions must be made in a session of the State Council following a proposal by the minister concerned. And, all communiqués to foreign states or to representatives in those countries must go through the foreign minister.

Foreign affairs, formally speaking, are thus not meant to be the personal prerogative of the president; decisions in these matters, too, must be made in accordance with parliamentary procedures. But, in this field, overemphasis of the importance of legal norms must be avoided. In fact, presidents have exercised a firm hand in the conduct of foreign policy; it would appear that among both political leaders and the general public the notion is gaining strength that the conduct of foreign affairs—especially its political aspects—is the prerogative of the president, who bears great personal responsibility in this area. In many cases the State Council acts more as an adviser to the president and the executor of his will than as a parliamentary Cabinet making actual decisions. It should, moreover, be pointed out that diplomacy—the management of international relations—is anything but the making of official decisions in a session of the State Council. Various official and unofficial appearances by the president—speeches, statements, and personal negotiations—are an important part of the process. The president's personal role in postwar relations with the Soviet Union has been especially influential.

Supreme Command of the Armed Forces. The president is entrusted with supreme command of the armed forces, but he may, in time of war, relinquish this post to someone else; and this has, indeed, happened. When the Winter War began (1939), President Kallio relinquished supreme command to Marshal Mannerheim, who retained it during the period of peace following the Winter War and during the Continuation War. In August 1944, when Mannerheim became president, the positions of president and commander-in-chief were joined in the hands of a single individual. The Defense Council acts as an advisory and planning body, as well as a presidential discussion group, in matters affecting the nation's defense.

Pardons, Immunity, and Naturalization. The president received the right of granting pardons as an inheritance from the monarchs who reigned during the periods of Swedish and Russian rule. In individual cases the president may grant a pardon, after he has received a statement from the Supreme Court, by overturning or lightening a sentence. A general amnesty, however, may be granted only by a special clemency law passed by Parliament. Parliament has approved such laws in the wake of internal political crises resulting in violence, such as the Civil War of 1918, the Mäntsälä Revolt of 1932, the Kemi riots of 1948, and the general strike of 1956.

The president also has the power of immunity, a right to grant in individual cases exceptions to provisions in existing law. But the right to grant immunity must be mentioned separately in a law; these cases are very rare.

As one of his powers, the president may grant Finnish citizenship to a citizen of a foreign country, and he may relieve a Finnish citizen of his citizenship.

Civil Service Appointments. The president makes appointments to the most important public positions. He appoints members of the State Council; the chancellor of justice; the deputy chancellor of justice; presidents and members of the Supreme Court, the Supreme Administrative Court, and the courts of appeal; the archbishop and bishops; chiefs and members of central offices; senior civil servants of the State Council; governors of the provinces; professors at state universities; ambassadors, envoys, and consuls; and a large number of other civil servants. He also appoints officers in the military establishment. In some cases he makes an appointment on the basis of a recommendation by the State Council, the Supreme Court, or the Supreme Administrative Court, but he is not bound by this recommendation. Other positions are filled following the nomination of three individuals, one of whom is appointed by the president. In some cases the president makes a direct appointment with neither a recommendation nor a nomination.

The president appoints by open letter a number of the senior civil servants (civil servants of high trust, as they are called), as well as military officers. A civil servant so appointed may be forced by presidential decision to resign his post if public interest requires it; but objective cause, not mere reasons of party policy, must be demonstrated. As the Second World War came to an end, many such dismissals were caused by change in the domestic and foreign policy situation. The right of appointment is an important power, and some presidents, like Paasikivi, have exercised this right very independently.

Supervision of the Administration. The Form of Government Act permits and obliges the president to exercise general supervision over administration of the state. For this purpose he may request necessary information from chiefs of public institutions and offices or from governments; he may also start an investigation. Continual surveillance includes many different sorts of tasks—which, however, are executed almost exclusively by the State Council, since the president does not have the necessary machinery. The president's office is small: in addition to an office head, it includes only the necessary office personnel.

Decision-making Procedures. Just as important as the type and scope of powers given to the head of state is the way in which exercise of these rights, in other words, the making of decisions, is organized. In this respect an attempt has been made to bind the president to parliamentary forms restricting his independence of action, to bind him to cooperation with a Cabinet linked to Parliament through the question of confidence. The basic rule is that the president makes his decisions in the State Council, in a Cabinet meeting attended by at least five ministers and chaired by the president. In the form of government proposals presented to Parliament in the years 1917–1919, the point of departure concerning the forms of decision-making power by the president was that only the most important matters had to be resolved by him in the State Council; other matters could be resolved by him in the presence of the minister most concerned and one or two other members of the State Council. Parliament, however, felt that a better principle would be to have the president make all decisions in the State Council.

This session, normally held once a week, on Fridays, is called the presidential presentation or the presidential session. Preparatory work on matters to be discussed is carried out in ministries, and most subjects have been under preliminary discussion at a plenary session of the State Council—at a Cabinet meeting directed by the prime minister. In some matters, such as questions about submitting a government proposal to Parliament and about many civil service appointments, this collegial preparation by the Cabinet has received accentuated significance in that the State Council must make an official report to the president. But in other matters, too, where the nature of the preparation has varied somewhat over the decades, the State Council affirms its collegial position and brings it to the attention of the president. There are also matters which are presented directly to the president after preparation in a ministry, bypassing the plenary session of the State Council, such as pardons and petitions for naturalization.

The report is made by the minister in whose area the matter rests. Usually he first presents the opinion of the State Council majority about resolution of a subject; later he presents his own opinion, which may be a dissent. Other members of the State Council are also given an opportunity to express a position, but these statements are only advisory; there is no vote in case of disagreement. Final decision is the president's alone; legally he is not bound to the opinion of the reporting minister any more than he is to a majority or unanimous opinion of the State Council. An open, public conflict between the president and the State Council is most unusual. An attempt is made to mediate these differences of opinion in unofficial negotiations; in most matters the principle of parliamentarism is applied so that the position of the State Council determines the content of a decision. Thus, the president often acts as an adviser to the Cabinet and as a mediator in its internal disagreements.

A decision comes into effect when the president has signed and the reporting minister countersigned it. The countersigner is responsible for the accuracy of the document and, in accordance with the Constitution as interpreted in practice, he is obliged—insofar as he does not wish to give up his portfolio—to countersign the decision even though he may be in complete disagreement with the president over its political expediency. If a decision is found to be contrary to law, the State Council must ask the president to change or revoke it; if the president remains adamant in his decision, the State Council must announce that it is unable to execute the decision. A decision in conflict with an ordinary law must be countersigned by the appropriate minister, but at the same time he must communicate with the State Council. If, however, a presidential decision is in conflict with a fundamental law, the minister must refuse to countersign it.

Every member of the State Council who has taken part in the consideration of a matter is both legally and politically responsible for a decision made in Council by the president. A minister can avoid legal responsibility by expressing a different opinion for the record. A minister who remains silent is considered to be of the same opinion as the reporting minister. This step is not, of course, sufficient to absolve a minister and Cabinet of political responsibility before Parliament. If the State Council—or some of its members—does not want to accept the president's decision and refuses to execute it, the only alternative is resignation. Especially if the question is of an important decision that badly damages the relationship of trust between Parliament and the government, a president's adamancy means resignation of the entire Cabinet. The mere threat of resignation is, understandably, an effective weapon against the president. In this situation—of disagreements reaching the point of open conflict—the president must also consider whether or not it would be possible for him to assemble a new Cabinet that would agree to cooperate in the matter at hand without conflicting seriously with Parliament. In any case, over time, a president's personal and irresponsible exercise of power against the wishes of a Cabinet, and a Parliament behind it, is impossible, even though the president may dissolve Parliament and call for a new election in an effort to cling stubbornly to his own policies. On two occasions an open conflict between the president and the State Council led to Cabinet resignations. In 1924 the Kallio government resigned in a conflict arising over the question of dissolving Parliament, and in 1932 the Sunila government submitted its resignation when President Svinhufvud refused to pass on a proposal supported by a majority of the State Council concerning regulation of interest rates.

Some presidential decisions are reached through a procedure different from the one just described. Matters concerning military command and appointments are resolved by the president outside the State Council, in his office, usually on the basis of a report from the defense minister or the commander of the armed forces. Military matters that can be resolved by the president in his capacity as commander-in-chief are, nonetheless, few in number; it is natural that the commander of the armed forces is the one who usually issues orders. All appointments of officers are no longer considered "office" matters. Today the highest officers, beginning with major general, are appointed by the president in the State Council. It should be noted that a decision concerning the entire State Council (for example, naming a Cabinet and granting it permission to resign) is countersigned by a civil servant from the State Council office, not by a minister. Measures concerning supervision of the administration, and decisions with respect to bringing charges against a minister in the high court of impeachment, do not require the countersignature of a minister in order to take effect.

Beginning with the notion of preparliamentary constitutionalism that the Cabinet, not the president, bears responsibility, the head of state in countries which have adopted a parliamentary system is bound in his decisions to the position of the Cabinet. Countersigning a decision means assumption of political responsibility, and a minister has the right to refuse to countersign a decision if he and the Cabinet do not wish to bear responsibility for it. In this respect, relations in Finland between the president and the State Council are at a half-way point of development. By entrusting to the State Council the preparation and execution of matters to be resolved by the president and by declaring that decisions are to be made in a session of the State Council, presidential cooperation with the Cabinet has been forced, though the president is not tied to Cabinet opinion. Countersigning in Finland has a more restricted meaning than is generally the case; countersigning is viewed as an explicit duty of a minister. Thus Finland may be the only parliamentary state in which the head of state can and does make decisions which run counter to the wishes of the Cabinet or its majority. Written provisions of the Constitution need not prevent the relations between the Finnish president and Cabinet from developing in accordance with normal parliamentary practice; an explanation for preservation of the original mold can be found in factors that will be dealt with in later sections. Paavo Kastari has suggested a contrary interpretation, "a parliamentary interpretation of the constitution," which is based on a provision in the Form of Government Act concerning parliamentarism. In Kastari's interpretation the president should not make a decision if a majority of the State Council is in such sharp opposition that it refuses to assume responsibility. In the event that such a decision is made, it should be considered contrary to fundamental law and not countersigned. But politicians have not acted on this basis, and the interpretation has not received support in legal circles.

Responsibility. The Finnish president is not politically responsible, that is, he cannot be dismissed during his tenure in office for reasons of expediency, and he can be held legally responsible only in extreme situations. He may be held accountable for illegal procedure in his actions only if he is considered guilty of treason. If such is the case, Parliament must be so notified; Parliament by a three-quarters majority of votes may press charges in the Supreme Court, and the chancellor of justice acts as prosecutor. To date, no such charge has been made. Otherwise, the president in his private life is subject to criminal law like other citizens.

Position of the President. During the debates over the form the state should take, and after the new Form of Government Act had been adopted, both left and right expressed dissatisfaction concerning the ability of the adopted system to function. The left considered powers granted to the president too great and unsuitable for a parliamentary form of government. Many rightists, however, felt that the country lacked sufficiently strong government and that in time the center of power would shift entirely to Parliament. Among the latter was Robert Hermanson, who, in a statement concerning the form of government proposal prepared by the constitutional committee in 1917, expressed the view that the president's influence actually would be rather weak and that he would not constitute a real counterweight to a parliamentary majority. Experience, however, showing that it was possible to combine features of a presidential system with European parliamentarism, soon calmed people. Social Democrats were mollified by the fact that Ståhlberg, supported by the left, was elected the first president; some of his actions served to favor these circles in particular. The right, for its part, saw that the president was indeed able to preserve his freedom of action and to exercise the power entrusted to him.

Consequently, it has been possible to maintain in the Finnish system of government that seemingly contradictory duality which was given it at the start. As Tarkiainen notes, "one cannot say that a single power entrusted to the head of state has been completely 'parliamentarized' or has shifted to the hands of responsible advisers."[5] The Finnish head of state has been able to preserve his freedom of action much better than his counterparts in most other countries under parliamentary rule. It is significant that the first occupant of the position, K. J. Ståhlberg, set precedents and established a foundation for the prestige and strong position of the president. On one hand, he sought to rise above parties, to be non-partisan and just; on the other hand, refusing to be a national figurehead as is customary in parliamentary nations, he made independent decisions and exercised great impact, through his prestige, on political development. The dissolution of Parliament in 1924 is considered a real demonstration of strength by a parliamentary head of state; and even during his first year in office Ståhlberg established a foundation for that practice by which it is possible for a president to make independent decisions in the State Council with acquiescence of an opposing Cabinet majority. Two such cases occurred in December 1919, when the President approved in a form at variance with the position of the State Council majority a decree concerning the college entrance examination and a decree concerning certain matters to be reserved for presidential resolution. Most of his successors have at some time refused to pass on to Parliament a legislative proposal urged by the State Council or have included in such a proposal provisions running contrary to the opinion of the Cabinet majority, have issued decrees independently, or have made civil servant appointments with no regard for recommendations and nominations. The president often acts independently in connection with government crises; when Ståhlberg named the first Cajander Cabinet, in summer 1922, Ståhlberg personally selected the ministers and "appointed" one of them prime minister. In this instance one can speak of a real "presidential government." In autumn 1936 Svinhufvud's opposition prevented the entrance of Social Democrats into a proposed majority government. President Kekkonen's personal stand, and independent action based on it, was very clearly felt in 1957–1959, especially when a solution was sought to the government problem which arose during the foreign policy crisis in late 1958 and early 1959.

These examples are extreme cases and as such are of course exceptions. Under normal conditions, the president's independent action in matters calling for concrete decisions is not so great and is less

5. Tarkiainen, *Tasavallan presidentin asema*, p. 336.

conspicuous; the usual features of modern European parliamentarism are then in the forefront of political life. The opportunity for a head of state to exercise power, however, is always present: the president can, if the situation so demands, exercise his rights. Rules of convention restricting his freedom of action are relatively few.

It should be noted that the real position of the president is not revealed merely by his actions in government discussions or sessions of the State Council. Public appearances outside the confines of the State Council, covered only to a degree by ministerial responsibility, are an important part of presidential activity. And it seems that the number and significance of politically important appearances—speeches, trips, and other contacts—has grown since the Second World War, and that they have assumed a much more emphatic personal tone. The role of this sort of personal politics has been considerable in the conduct of foreign relations with countries having authoritarian systems.

"Indeed, there can hardly be any doubt that the role of the president—totally divorced from individuals and situations—has as an institution grown in importance over the years," writes Kastari.[6] Development has thus led not toward a pure parliamentarism; rather, it has brought to the Finnish political system features of a system characterized by presidential dominance. The president has become more clearly a central political force and a symbol of the entire nation. This strengthening of a monocratic institution is a general development of recent years which can be found in different kinds of governmental systems.

Many factors have worked to preserve and increase the personal influence of the president. Juridical factors have their own significance in this respect. The Form of Government Act contains only a brief provision about parliamentarism, whereas the ways in which presidential power is exercised are regulated in detail and with a stress characteristic of the old constitutional type of government. It is customary when examining the head of state's position, and the possibilities of his exercising power, to point to those paragraphs in the Form of Government Act whose interpretation by political scientists and jurists, as well as by practical politicians, remains fixed: those emphasizing the power and independence of the president. Purely "parliamentary interpretations" have not gained support.

6. Paavo Kastari, *La présidence de la République en Finlande* (Neuchâtel, Editions de la Baconnière, 1962), p. 87.

Party conditions in Finland constitute a second important factor. The multiparty system does not permit the formation of unified groups representing cooperation and opposition, and so the president is able to participate with independent measures in the formation of cabinets. On occasion the viability of the parliamentary system has necessitated this sort of intervention. In his relations with the State Council, the president has been supported by the fact that governments are generally heterogeneous and are not able to pursue a policy that is steadfast and consistent. It is understandable that the freedom of action for a president faced by a State Council divided into many groups with different views is greater than would be the case if he were confronted by a unanimous Cabinet.

Lastly, more fluid "background factors" (political situations, as well as the personal ability and strength of presidents) have been significant in shaping the position of the head of state. As mentioned, presidents in peacetime have for the most part remained in the background—as parliamentary heads of state not intervening in daily politics. But there have been times in the history of independent Finland when presidents have considered it their duty, relying on formal position and personal strength, to intervene in the course of events and in the resolution of certain problems. There have been the "normal" difficulties of parliamentary life with party conflicts and government crises; and, there have been dramatic periods of domestic and foreign policy crisis. Most presidents—Ståhlberg, Svinhufvud, Ryti, Paasikivi, and Kekkonen—have been strong and determined political leaders who have sought to control those exceptional situations and who have not been eclipsed by stronger domestic factors.

The president enjoys great prestige. It is as if he had assumed in independent Finland the position occupied by the monarch during the period of autonomy; the notion rooted in a hundred-year monarchy about position and duties of the head of state is not easily dispelled. One illustration of this is the unique convention that the president is above all criticism; in other words it is inappropriate to criticize him openly for measures which he undertakes unilaterally. In this respect, however, the situation is changing: to an increasing degree, democratic criticism also extends to the activities of the president, and he, in turn, avails himself of opportunities to defend his actions and to advance counter-criticism.

THE STATE COUNCIL

Paragraph 2 of the Form of Government Act stipulates that in addition to the president, who exercises supreme executive power, there is also a State Council, set up for "general government of the state," including a prime minister and the necessary number of ministers. There is, therefore, a dualistic type of government in Finland in which a collective body, the Cabinet, only partially dependent on the independent head of state, works with him. In political terms, the Cabinet has on occasion been very closely linked to the president, whereas legally the separation of decision-making power into two parts is more pronounced.

First, a few words must be said about terminology. The terms State Council (valtioneuvosto), government (hallitus), and Cabinet (ministeristö) are often used—as in this book—as synonyms meaning the unit formed by prime minister and ministers. But the first two terms also have a somewhat broader meaning in common parlance. In the broader sense, the State Council includes, in addition to the prime minister and ministers, the ministries directed by them, the State Council office, subordinate to the prime minister, and the chancellor of justice and his staff. The word government is often used to indicate the president and the State Council together, for example, in speaking of government proposals. Furthermore, "government" in the Finnish language also means (as in the previous section), in addition to specific functional organs, a certain activity. But the multiplicity of meanings should not cause confusion: it is usually clear from the context what one is talking about.

The structure and activity of the State Council is regulated mainly by a 1922 law concerning the number and general spheres of activity of State Council ministries, by a 1922 law concerning the resolution of matters in the State Council and its ministries, and by a 1943 decree setting forth rules of procedure for the State Council. The chancellor of justice has his own rules of procedure.

Composition of the State Council. The State Council includes the prime minister and not more than 15 ministers. Members of the State Council, who must be "native-born Finnish citizens known for their honesty and ability," assume their duties and relinquish them at the will of the president of the Republic. The minister of justice and at least one other minister must have passed the bar examination, but there are no demands concerning education and examinations of other ministers. In the Form of Government Act it is stated that members of the State Council must enjoy the confidence of Parliament—a principle of parliamentarism.

The leading person in the State Council is the prime minister, even though not much is said about his special position in laws relating to the Constitution. The principle of collegiality, which has been adopted in Finland, is based on the equality of all ministers, but this does not prevent certain special tasks from being entrusted to the prime minister. In addition to leading the discussion and consideration of matters in plenary session, at a Cabinet meeting which handles matters within State Council jurisdiction, the prime minister must also assume the duties of the president if the latter is temporarily unable to perform them, make appointments to ministerial committees, and act as chairman of the presidential electoral college. Legally, however, he does not have the power to command his ministers, and his vote in sessions of the State Council carries no special weight. The central position of the president limits the growth of the Finnish prime minister's influence and prevents him from becoming such a visible figure in political life as is the case in countries ruled by more genuine parliamentarism.

Within the State Council, the prime minister has his own leadership duties, which over time have become more and more important. His role is significant in the formation of the Cabinet and in the preparation of its program; as leader of government policy, he represents the outward unity of his Cabinet. When participating in debates in Parliament, he always appears as the government's representative and responds to speeches, questions, and interpellations related to general activity of the Cabinet. A defeat for the prime minister means a defeat for the whole government; with his resignation the Cabinet collapses. It is primarily the duty of the prime minister to maintain contact with the president, although in Finland, unlike the United Kingdom, the prime minister is not the only channel between the Cabinet and the head of state. The position created by a prime minister for himself in the State Council depends essentially on his abilities and energy. Important in this respect is the Cabinet's political composition. In a broad-based coalition government the prime minister, seeking to preserve unity in his Cabinet through compromise and defending its policies to the outside world, ends up more like a mediator than a leader and commander.

If the prime minister is unable to carry out his duties, a member of the State Council designated when a Cabinet is formed takes over as his replacement. This procedure was adopted in 1956; previously, the replacement for the prime minister had been the member with the longest record of service, that is, the individual who had become a minister at the earliest date. Since the replacement is usually a chief of some ministry, who assumes the duties of prime minister only temporarily until the latter can resume them, a real deputy prime minister cannot yet be spoken of.

Only an upper limit has been set for the number of ministers; since 1958 it has been fifteen. In Cabinets since that date there have been at least thirteen ministers. Ten ministers function as chiefs of central administrative offices, or ministries, joined to the State Council. The ministries are of foreign affairs, justice, the interior, defense, finance, education, agriculture, communications and public works, commerce and industry, and social affairs.

On a par with the ministries is the State Council office, directed by the prime minister, which in Finland, however, has not developed into a supporting staff for the prime minister; the office takes care of the relatively few administrative matters under its jurisdiction. Ministers have names corresponding to their ministries: foreign minister, minister of justice, and so forth. Under exceptional circumstances a ministry of supply can be formed to deal with economic security for the nation's population, as well as matters related to the regulation of economic life and the use of labor. Such a ministry was set up at the beginning of the Second World War, in 1939, and abolished in 1949. There is nothing to prevent a member of the State Council from being the chief of two ministries, and on occasion this has happened.

Those ministers for whom there is no spot as chief of a ministry are designated either as supplementary ministers or as ministers without portfolio. When there is a full complement of ministers, a supplementary minister has usually (since the 1950's) been appointed to the ministries of finance, agriculture, communications and public works, and social affairs. The State Council confirms the division of labor in a ministry between the chief and the supplementary minister; both work independently in their own areas, without subordination of one to the other. A minister without portfolio is a member of the State Council who is not appointed to any ministry; he acts either as an expert and adviser on general policy questions or he handles preparatory tasks entrusted to him by various ministries. Ministers without portfolio are rare occurrences, and, since the beginning of the 1950's, they have in practice been dropped altogether.

Duties. The State Council is a parliamentary Cabinet that, on a political level and in addition to Parliament and the president, functions as a major planning and directing force; on an administrative level it functions just below the top of the pyramid—just below the head of state—as a central institution where the strings of a multi-branched administrative network meet. Its duties can be divided into two general categories. First, the president in most cases needs the cooperation of the State Council when making decisions; matters to be resolved by the president are prepared in ministries and the State Council, then presented by the minister concerned, and, after the president has made his decision in the presence of the ministers, put back into the hands of the State Council for implementation. But this is not the only, let alone the major, duty of the State Council. It, too, exercises independent decision-making power; it resolves matters which are under its jurisdiction by law, as well as other governmental and administrative matters which have not been reserved for the president or entrusted to some other official. Executive power is, therefore, divided between the president and the State Council in such a way that each in its own area is an independent decision-maker. This duality is a unique feature of the Finnish political system, since only in a relatively few countries could the equivalent, especially in earlier times, be found. Executive power, particularly in constitutional monarchies, is often formally concentrated in the hands of the head of state: a Cabinet formed by ministers acting as chiefs of offices in different administrative areas does not have independent power; its only task is to function as an adviser, even though, in accordance with the principle of parliamentary government, it may in fact exercise those powers given to the head of state.

This dualism in governmental power, legislated in fundamental law, is based on Finland's political history, on the system which was created in 1809 when Finland was detached from Sweden and became part of Russia. In part, political institutions had to be formed anew; there came into being a general governmental organ called the Senate, which was to be the equivalent of Sweden's supreme court and central offices (so-called colleges). Soon this developed into another "domestic government," alongside the Grand Duke, which shared governmental duties with the monarch. The latter, who lived beyond the Finnish border, was not able to manage and supervise all the details of governmental tasks; he reserved direct decision-making power for himself only on questions of the utmost importance. Other matters were entrusted to the Senate, composed of Finns and functioning in the Finnish capital; the Senate was also to ensure execution of decisions made by the emperor. Because the 1772 Form of Government Act stipulated that the king ("he and no one else") was to govern the country, the power given the Senate was delegated, transferred through administrative measures with an eye on expediency; and so the Senate made its decisions in the name of the emperor. This duality then came to be the foundation for determining the relationship between the president and the State Council after Finland had gained independence.[7]

The authority of the State Council is general in that it covers all those governmental and administrative matters which have not been explicitly excluded from its jurisdiction. In unclear cases, the president determines whether or not the State Council is empowered to make a final decision. This general power of action is limited to actual administrative matters, but it is also possible for decrees to be issued through decisions of the State Council. The difference between the president's power to issue decrees and that of the State Council is that the president is permitted by the Form of Government Act to issue decrees concerning certain matters, whereas the State Council must be given explicit powers to do so. Under normal circumstances these sorts of decrees are often issued. Indeed, it can be stipulated in a law passed by Parliament that more exact provisions concerning the execution of a new law rest with the State Council. To differentiate these decrees from presidential decrees they are called State Council decisions. During wartime, and when economic difficulties prevail, the power of the State Council to issue decrees is greatly expanded by special emergency laws. The State Council participates in the legislative work of Parliament by preparing government proposals and publishing a ratified law in a statute book. In actual fact the role of the State Council in even these matters is greater than the president's role.

7. See, for example, K. R. Brotherus, *Suomen valtiollisen järjestysmuodon kehitys*, 3rd ed. (Porvoo, 1963), pp. 51–54.

Division of Decision-making Power. Decisions are made in the State Council at many levels. The Senate was from the very beginning collegial; decisions were made in joint or separate sessions of the departments, and senators had no independent decision-making power. A backlog of matters in the departments, however, led to a decision in the 1840's that matters could be resolved by senators in the departments. The primacy of collegial consideration was retained in the 1919 Form of Government Act; paragraph 40 stipulates that matters under the jurisdiction of the State Council are to be considered in a plenary session, insofar as certain matters are not entrusted by decree to a minister acting as chief of a ministry, for resolution. Thus, collegial consideration in a plenary session should be considered the rule and decision-making in a ministry the exception. In the procedural rules of the State Council, however, the division of decision-making power follows the opposite principle: paragraph 12 of the rules lists those matters which must be considered in general session, and all other matters under the jurisdiction of the State Council are to be resolved in ministries. Reasons of expediency have dictated the principle set forth in this procedural rule. It would be difficult to prepare a complete list of the many trivial matters to be resolved in ministries.

Decision-making power has over the years shifted more and more from the plenary session to ministries, and in actual fact the State Council handles central administration by following, for the most part, the principles of ministerial administration—in such a way, that is, that the proper minister himself resolves, on the basis of a right belonging to the State Council, matters which are in his sphere. But in spite of this development the burden of the plenary session does not seem to have been sufficiently lightened, and so in the 1950's two radical plans concerning reorganization of decision-making power in the State Council and its ministries were presented in committee reports.[8]

In 1922 it became possible to shift decision-making power from ministers to civil servants in the ministries. Law stipulates that such a transferral requires, first of all, a decree specifying those matters that can be entrusted to an office or departmental chief of a ministry or to some other civil servant for resolution on his own responsibility;

8. "Valtioneuvoston rationalisoimiskomitea, komiteanmietintö" (mimeographed, 1953: report no. 37); "Valtionhallinnon organisaation uudistamiskomitea, komiteanmietintö" (mimeographed, 1959: report no. 1).

then there must be a personal order (mandate) from the president to the civil servant in question. In practice, however, it has become customary to delegate this power with only a decree, and this procedure was finally legalized by a change in law approved in 1965. The fact that the decision-making authority of civil servants has remained relatively limited is primarily a reflection of the rigidity of the procedure for transferring decision-making power and of the tradition of reporting established during the period of autonomy. In many ministries the minister is the one who at least formally resolves most matters under the authority of his office.

Decision-making in matters under the jurisdiction of the State Council is, therefore, found at three levels: 1) in plenary session of the State Council, 2) with an individual minister, or 3) with a civil servant in a ministry.

Plenary Session. The State Council gathers in plenary session regularly on Thursdays, but sessions can of course be arranged at other times when necessary. Ministers sit around a long curved table in the meeting room, with the prime minister in the center, the minister appointed as the replacement for the prime minister on his right, the minister with the longest service on his left, and so forth. The presence of at least five members constitutes a quorum. The chancellor of justice attends these sessions regularly; he is obliged to attend unless other official duties prevent him from doing so.

The general procedure for the resolution of various matters is as follows: matters which have come to the State Council from divergent sources or which have been advanced from within are prepared in the proper ministry and, if necessary, also in ministerial committees and the "evening school" (to be discussed below); either the civil servant bearing primary responsibility for the preparatory work or his superior makes a report to the ministerial college; after discussion by the ministers, a decision is reached—by vote if disagreements arise; the minister in whose field the matter lies signs the document or announcement concerning a decision, which is then countersigned by the rapporteur, after which the ministry involved moves forward with practical measures of implementation. In voting, the same procedure is used as in collegially organized courts. Proposals are not paired off against each other as in parliamentary votes; ministers present arguments individually, and a decision follows "in accordance with majority opinion." If there is a tie vote, the position of the chairman is decisive except in matters of discipline, when the most lenient view prevails.

Matters under consideration appear on presentation lists which have been prepared and distributed in advance and which with their appendices contain explanations forming the basis for a decision. An oral report is usually confined to a brief mention of a matter and to a reference regarding the distributed documents. The character of the sessions has, in general, undergone fundamental change. In the 1920's and 1930's matters were thoroughly discussed in the sessions, which meant that meetings had to be held often; beginning after the noon hour, they frequently lasted late into the evening. Now, however, it is possible in one or two hours to get through a very large number of matters. Consideration by a plenary session is to an increasing degree merely a formality. On minor matters there is confidence in the preparatory work done by ministries, and major matters may already have received preparatory consideration by the Cabinet on numerous occasions. The center of gravity in the work of the State Council has thus shifted from the plenary session to ministries and also to the evening school and ministerial committees.

The Government's Evening School. Something new has been established in the State Council over the last quarter-century: an unofficial meeting by ministers once a week to discuss and prepare the most important questions before they are resolved in plenary session or in a presidential session. This evening school of the government, as the meeting is jokingly called, came into existence before the Winter War, in 1937–1939, when Prime Minister Cajander adopted the habit of calling his Cabinet members together on Wednesday evenings to discuss matters on the Thursday session agenda. In this way he sought to speed up and make more flexible the process of official consideration. The new institution was so appropriate that it has been retained, regardless of the political composition of Cabinets. Since the end of the Second World War, either the chancellor of justice or the deputy chancellor has been present for these discussions. Increasingly, experts have also been invited to the evening school: rapporteurs for the State Council, civil servants from the central offices, and interest group representatives.

In the evening school consideration is given both to matters on the agenda of the official session of the State Council and to matters to be resolved in ministries; likewise, important questions of principle, relations with Parliament, and so forth, are considered. An effort is made to reach actual decisions on important matters such as legislation and appointments, and these decisions then receive formal ratification in a plenary session or in a ministry. During negotiations which are confidential and not restricted in form, one can more effectively accommodate opinions and seek the necessary compromise solutions, as well as increase the Cabinet's capacity for action. In this respect, the evening school has had fundamental importance during coalition governments, when a public vote threatens to dissolve the coalition at any time and when consideration by a plenary session runs the risk of turning into a lengthy, stormy debate. The evening school has, therefore, definitely decreased the significance of the official plenary session and can be considered to have gained a semi-official position in the nation's governmental machinery.

Ministerial Committees. In the State Council there are two permanent standing committees for preparatory work, the foreign affairs committee and the finance committee; the prime minister is chairman of both. The foreign affairs committee includes, in addition to the prime minister, three ministers designated by him plus the foreign minister; and the finance committee includes the finance minister, the minister in whose area a particular matter under question rests, and a member designated by the prime minister. If necessary, one additional member can be appointed to each committee. Preparatory consideration in the foreign affairs committee is given to those foreign policy matters "which require it by virtue of their importance." It is customary for the committee to consider high civil service appointments in the administration of foreign affairs, commercial matters, foreign policy speeches and statements, matters connected with state visits, and questions concerning international organizations and conferences. During exceptional periods in foreign policy, during a world war, for example, the committee becomes an influential "inner circle."

The duties of the finance committee can be said to include preparatory consideration of matters of considerable economic importance. The committee has a particularly critical role to play in those matters under ministerial jurisdiction whose consideration thus precedes final consideration in a ministry. On such questions the committee has a certain veto; a ministry may not make a decision that would entail greater expenditure than the proposal approved by the committee. If the committee does not agree with a ministry's intended solution, and if the ministry refuses to reconsider its decision, the matter is given to the State Council for resolution. This arrangement permits the finance committee to exercise very effective advance fiscal control, which can be expanded at the discretion of the State Council by designating matters to be considered in the committee. In order to lighten the burden of the committee, control over less important matters under ministerial jurisdiction was transferred in 1958 to what is called fiscal consideration by the ministry of finance. The finance committee meets regularly once a week, usually on Wednesdays.

Other ministerial committees, whose membership is determined by the prime minister, may be set up when necessary for the preparation of matters to be considered in plenary session. These committees, each of which normally prepares only one specific matter, are set up relatively often, some in an official plenary session and some in the evening school and other unofficial meetings.

Appeals. Decisions by the president are final; no appeal is possible. Resting on the principle that the State Council is not subordinate to anyone in its management of general government, there was at one time little possibility of complaining about decisions of the State Council. Only in 1950, with passage of a law concerning appeals in administrative matters, did a legal complaint about decisions of the State Council and a ministry become possible. Any party who feels that a decision infringes his rights may lodge a complaint with the Supreme Administrative Court, if there are no conflicting regulations in a law or decree; this general right is restricted in certain respects by decrees.

The Chancellor of Justice. The State Council's chancellor of justice, appointed by the president of the Republic, is not a Cabinet member; he is a permanent civil servant whose position is independent of changes in government. According to the Form of Government Act, the chancellor of justice should have "outstanding knowledge of law" and his general duty is "to ensure that authorities and civil servants obey the law and fulfill their obligations, so that no one is deprived of his legal rights." He is also the chief prosecutor, and he supervises the action of other prosecutors as their superior. The chancellor has the right to be present at sessions of the State Council and all courts and offices and to receive information concerning their minutes. He delivers an annual report to the president and Parliament about his activities and about his findings with regard to observance of the law, and at other times, if necessary, he must provide the president and the State Council with information and statements. He is assisted in his duties by a deputy chancellor of justice.

The chancellor is in direct contact with the State Council; legal supervision of the consideration given to matters in the Council is one of his most important duties. He ensures that in consideration of matters there is observance of the legal order and existing regulations. He is obliged to be present (if not prevented from doing so by official duties) at plenary sessions of the State Council and at presidential sessions, and the minutes of these meetings are sent to him for examination. If the chancellor feels that some legal fact in a matter under consideration by the State Council gives cause, he may record his opinion in the minutes of the State Council.

In practice, the chancellor of justice often provides the president and the State Council with written statements concerning legislative matters, general administrative matters, and questions of legal interpretation. The center of gravity in legal supervision by the Council has shifted still more from post-factum observations to prior negotiations; it has become customary for ministers and State Council rapporteurs to turn to the chancellor at an early stage for advice on questions of legal interpretation which are not clear-cut. The chancellor thus has more opportunity to look into a matter thoroughly than he would have in speedy official consideration. Nevertheless, there is a certain conflict in the position of the chancellor; his activity as adviser to the government is not fully in accord with his duty of nonpartisan supervision of the law. Partly for this reason the State Council office in 1963 was assigned a legally trained chief, one of whose duties is to assist the prime minister in legal questions.

Responsibility. Members of the State Council are both legally and politically accountable: the former means responsibility for illegal procedure, the latter for inappropriate procedure. (Political responsibility by ministers, which is part of a parliamentary system of government, is treated in the next chapter.)

A minister and the chancellor of justice may be charged with illegal procedure before the high court of impeachment. Proceedings can be instituted on the basis of a 1922 law concerning Parliament's right to examine the legality of actions taken by members of the State Council and by the chancellor of justice; the individual in question is considered guilty if in his official activities he has been an accessory to obvious illegality or has promoted it, if he has consciously misused his position to the obvious detriment of the nation (viewed as a crime in office), or if he has otherwise clearly acted contrary to law in some official action. Either the president or Parliament may issue an order for indictment. The chancellor of justice prosecutes a case brought by the president and the ombudsman a case brought by Parliament. If the president orders charges brought against the chancellor of justice, an individual appointed by the president acts as prosecutor.

The high court of impeachment has met three times to consider charges brought against members of the State Council. In the first incident, in 1933, the President ordered that a former minister be charged with having consciously entered a false statement in the minutes of the State Council concerning his voting record. But the court concluded that there was insufficient evidence for a conviction. The second occurrence, in 1953, involved charges brought by Parliament against four former ministers for incorrect behavior in giving state aid to private enterprise. Two ministers were acquitted by the court, but the other two were convicted and paid fines as well as compensation to the state. Finally, in the School of Midwifery case of 1961, charges were brought against three former ministers—in this instance by a decision of Parliament—for illegalities alleged to have taken place in a matter concerning a state construction contract.

VIII Parliamentarism

DEVELOPMENT OF FINNISH PARLIAMENTARISM

The Birth of Parliamentarism. During the period of autonomy, senators were personal and trusted appointees of the Grand Duke (the Russian emperor); under those conditions there was no possibility of realizing parliamentarism by making them responsible to the four-estate Diet. But early in the second half of the nineteenth century there were attempts to achieve a parliamentary form of government; one could discern certain primitive features of parliamentarism toward the end of Russian rule. Suitable conditions for the realization of parliamentarism did not, however, appear until after the 1917 March Revolution, and the reform was achieved as a provision of fundamental law with no significant opposition; important in this respect was the belief that the step would diminish the influence of the Russian government on decisions related to Finland's internal affairs. As recommended in the proposal of K. J. Ståhlberg's constitutional committee, an explicit provision about a parliamentary form of government was added on December 31, 1917, to the Diet Act, and it was incorporated into the new Form of Government Act upon its adoption. The principle of parliamentarism is contained in paragraph 36 of the Form of Government Act, which specifies that members of the State Council must enjoy the confidence of Parliament. This principle is, therefore, very clearly expressed in Finland's Constitution. It has already been emphasized that parliamentarism in Finland does not function with optimum efficiency, since the president's strong position brings to it features of the American-type system of dualistic power. Experience shows that it is not impossible to join the independent position of power enjoyed by the head of state to a parliamentary form of government. On the contrary, Ståhlberg was of the opinion that it was the adoption of a parliamentary form of government which permitted the granting of considerable rights to the president.

Development During the Period of Independence. The first decade of independence demonstrated how difficult the achievement and maintenance of majority parliamentarism are in Finland's multi-party conditions. The 1920's were clearly years of minority governments. There were, of course, efforts to form Cabinets with majority support in Parliament, but only on two occasions (the Erich and Ingman Cabinets) was there success. Possible combinations during the first half of the decade were particularly limited, since the Communists were excluded from all cooperation and the Social Democrats remained in voluntary opposition, desiring to assume governmental responsibility only on an emergency basis—in addition to which the center groups drew away from the Coalition party as partners in a government. The period 1919–1924 is called the period of center policies because centrist minority coalitions, formed primarily by the Agrarian and Progressive parties, prevailed during these years. In 1922 there was for the first time experimentation with a caretaker government, led by Cajander. The majority government formed by Ingman in 1924, and the Tulenheimo and Kallio Cabinets which followed, constitute the period of bourgeois coalition governments (1924–1926) characterized by rightist majority or minority coalitions relying on cooperation with the Coalition party. The year 1926 was a turning point in Finnish parliamentary life in the sense that Social Democrats agreed to enter a government and, in fact, to assume sole responsibility under the leadership of Väinö Tanner. The three governments that followed, Sunila I (Agrarian), Mantere (Progressive), and Kallio III (Agrarian), were also single-party governments, though the second was only formally so.

After this, at the start of the 1930's, there was finally a shift to majority parliamentarism and more stable governmental conditions. The first two Cabinets, led by Svinhufvud and Sunila, were bourgeois majority coalitions struggling with the difficulties of political and economic crisis. They were followed by the Kivimäki Cabinet (1932–1936), which remained in office a record number of days, 1,393. The achievement was unique in the history of Finnish parliamentarism, but it was not the result of a firm majority behind it in Parliament. Formed for "the want of something better," the

Kivimäki Cabinet was a bourgeois coalition very ill-defined in parliamentary terms: individuals from four bourgeois parties represented in Parliament were ministers, but only the Progressive and Swedish People's parties assumed governmental responsibility as parties. The Cabinet relied sometimes on the support of bourgeois groups, sometimes on Social Democratic support. The formation in 1937 of a center and left majority coalition led by Cajander—after Kallio's primarily Agrarian Cabinet—meant a new stage in development: cooperation between bourgeois groups had been characteristic, but now there began a period of cooperation between the Agrarian party and the Social Democrats. These two groups became the leading government parties. During the war an attempt was made to achieve a relationship of complete confidence between Parliament and the government, so all parliamentary parties were represented in Cabinets (the IKL only in the years 1941–1943, however).

In 1945 a parliamentary election was held after a six-year pause. "New forces" captured a significant number of the seats; and, after the election, a period of cooperation between "the big three"—Agrarian party, Social Democrats, and People's Democrats—began in the name of a new direction to the left and on the basis of an explicit cooperative agreement. People's Democrats had, to be sure, been in the Paasikivi government preceding the election. Paasikivi's two Cabinets and the Pekkala Cabinet, holding power in the years 1944–1948, were broad coalitions in which there were representatives of, in addition to the big three, small center groups and some independent ministers. This government cooperation, which began to show signs of serious stress toward the end, came to a halt after the 1948 election, which was a defeat for the People's Democrats. In 1951, after a period of transition consisting of two minority governments (Fagerholm's Social Democratic Cabinet and Kekkonen's primarily Agrarian Cabinet), a period of centrist majority coalitions built on cooperation between these two parties began; the period was interrupted for a year, 1953–1954, by Kekkonen's Agrarian-Swedish minority coalition and Tuomioja's semipolitical caretaker Cabinet. Leaving the Communists in opposition in 1948 was not, however, the result of a deliberate decision intended to be permanent. They were present during negotiations which preceded the formation of Fagerholm's Cabinet, but the attempt to continue cooperation failed due to demands by the People's Democrats that were considered excessive. In the government crisis of 1950 the

President recommended a Cabinet built primarily around the three largest parties.

Characteristic of parliamentary life in the years 1951–1957 was the ruling position of the Agrarian party and Social Democrats. Together they had only a slim majority in Parliament, but they sought to strengthen their position by bringing members of some of the small center groups—usually the Swedish People's party—into governments. However, whether it was a question of program or government base, negotiations were almost exclusively between the two large parties; they determined the content of government policy and it was because of disagreements between them that most Cabinets fell during this period.

After the crisis of parliamentarism which broke out in 1957, ruling power was for a decade unquestionably held by the Agrarian party. Factors influencing the termination of cooperation were the split within the Social Democratic party and mutual irritation and disgust; the break in relations was made permanent by foreign policy factors: as long as the Soviet Union distrusted the top leaders of the Social Democratic party, the Agrarian party did not want to sit with Social Democrats in a government.

After Fagerholm's "red earth government" had resigned due to the conflict within the Social Democratic party and disintegration within the Cabinet, V. J. Sukselainen in the spring of 1957 formed a minority government supported by the Agrarian party and the People's parties; it was the task of this government to begin speedy measures to cope with the critical situation in the state's economy. But in the summer the Cabinet partially broke up when the Swedish-speaking ministers, dissatisfied with the government's policies, resigned. Sukselainen filled these vacancies with representatives of the parties remaining in the government. In September the Cabinet was reshuffled so that some ministers resigned in order to make way for the entrance of representatives of the Social Democratic opposition. The leadership of the Social Democratic party opposed this cooperation, and so the "adopted ministers" were soon expelled from their parliamentary group. When Sukselainen's government fell in the fall of 1957, there was no practicable chance of forming a parliamentary government; it was necessary to form a caretaker Cabinet, which was headed by Rainer von Fieandt, director of the Bank of Finland. When this government fell early in the spring after an interpellation, the chances of forming a parliamentary government were no greater than they had been before. A caretaker Cabinet was again formed, this time headed by Reino Kuuskoski. The position of these governments was from the very beginning difficult. They had no real parliamentary base, but they were not able to confine their actions, as would have been the case with temporary civil servant governments, to "routine matters"; they had to make important political decisions and prepare broad legislative bills, which made firm support by a majority in Parliament a necessity.

After the election held in the summer of 1958, negotiations for the formation of a majority government began in earnest; after nearly a month of effort, a five-party Cabinet led by Fagerholm was set up. Excluded were the People's Democrats and the Social Democratic minority, which had formed its own separate group. Fagerholm's Cabinet meant a return to parliamentary conditions and, at the same time, it brought to an end the fourteen-year period of opposition for the Coalition party. The experiment with this broad-based coalition was short-lived, since the government dissolved before Christmas due to foreign policy factors. With great difficulty, an Agrarian single-party Cabinet led by Sukselainen was then formed; when, two and a half years later, this government submitted its resignation for personal reasons expressed by the prime minister, Martti Miettunen became head of a new Agrarian Cabinet. After the 1962 parliamentary and presidential elections an attempt was again made to achieve majority parliamentarism. Success resulted from difficult negotiations; a broad bourgeois coalition headed by Karjalainen was formed, a distinctive feature of which was direct representation (three Cabinet members) for the SAK. It was primarily the Agrarian party that wished to dilute in this way the bourgeois nature of the government. Cooperation between the non-socialist parties continued, interrupted only by the Lehto civil servant government in 1964, during the entire period between elections. The 1966 parliamentary election thoroughly changed the parliamentary setting: a big election victory and, partly connected with this, a resolution of foreign policy difficulties, lifted the Social Democratic party to a position of indisputable leadership and in general made it possible for the socialist groupings to attain a dominant position. The most significant feature of the government solution reached by party leaders was that the People's Democrats finally emerged from their isolation and the weak opposition consisted only of the right and small center groups.

The Nature of Cabinets. In a systematic examination, one can distinguish between five major types of Cabinets during the period of independence. There have been general coalitions, majority coalitions, minority coalitions, one-party Cabinets, and caretaker Cabinets, either politically neutral or partially tinged with party representation. In terms of numbers, beginning with the Svinhufvud Senate, Cabinets during the years 1917–1968 can be divided thus:

General coalitions	8
Majority coalitions	18
Minority coalitions	12
One-party Cabinets	7
Caretaker Cabinets	6
Total	51

This listing shows that majority coalitions have been most numerous, followed by minority coalitions. In some cases classification is difficult: the Ingman Cabinet in 1924–1925 was both a majority and minority coalition, and the base for the Kivimäki Cabinet, considered a minority coalition in the listing, was, as mentioned, somewhat ill-defined. Formally the Tuomioja government was a caretaker Cabinet, but it was clearly constructed along party lines.

General coalitions arose during the exceptional conditions of wartime, when all the nation's forces had to be gathered in support of the war policy and in support of the policy of accommodation during the period of armistice. Although a single party, such as the IKL or the Coalition party, remained outside the government, the Cabinet was not faced by a strong, effective opposition. In the above classification there are eight broad-based Cabinets defined as general coalitions for the years 1939–1946.[1]

Taken as a whole, the number of majority and of minority governments has been equal. A significant phenomenon stemming from the Finnish party system is the fact that the latter have been almost as stable as the former. Since no party alone has a majority, majority governments are the result of compromises between conflicting efforts and different principles; these governments consequently lack a clear line of political action. But the opposition may be strong and united in such cases. In its efforts to struggle against the opposition and to satisfy the conflicting interests of all government parties, a

1. See Göran von Bonsdorff, *Suomen poliittiset puolueet* (Helsinki, 1957), pp. 48–49.

Cabinet easily falls prey to internal squabbles that soon rend asunder the entire coalition. Minority governments, whether one-party Cabinets or minority coalitions, show their political colors more clearly, and they have been favored by their tactically advantageous position in the center of the party continuum; a minority government in Finland has not clearly represented any extreme group. Thus the opposition is divided into two parts, the right and the left, which rarely find themselves in agreement. A Cabinet is able to remain in power for a relatively long time in the midst of even heated political activity by relying now on the right, now on the left.

If one leaves aside the general coalitions, one can say that most governments during the period of independence have been centrist in political outlook. Typical examples are the postwar majority coalitions of the Agrarian party, Social Democrats, and People's parties, as well as many minority coalitions and one-party governments. In the 1920's and 1930's a number of right-center coalitions and general bourgeois coalitions were also formed; but after the Second World War, until 1962, this was not possible mostly because the Agrarian party refused to cooperate with the right.

Caretaker Cabinets deserve special attention. Set up to manage governmental tasks only temporarily, they are a product of exceptional situations and do not fit the normal parliamentary form of government. An attempt is made to avoid them, but it is nonetheless necessary to rely on them when parliamentary cooperation among parties is impossible. Caretaker Cabinets have been set up four times when parties, with an election approaching, have not agreed on the parliamentary base for a new government; once, in 1924, the President established such a government in order to perform a special task set by him. Because individuals have their own political views, it is hardly possible to achieve a completely neutral "caretaker Cabinet." In the 1920's there was a certain rightist hue to the Cajander Cabinets. In addition to six independent ministers in Tuomioja's government, there were four representatives of the Coalition party, three of the Finnish People's party, and two of the Swedish People's party; with good reason this, too, can therefore be considered a bourgeois minority coalition. Furthermore, a political hue cannot be denied in the Cabinets of von Fieandt and Kuuskoski. Kuuskoski's original purpose was to form a clearly semipolitical caretaker Cabinet composed of members from parliamentary groups, but this plan was not realized due to a negative stand taken by the groups.

The government did, however, include a number of individuals belonging to the Social Democratic opposition; further, there were four Agrarians in von Fieandt's Cabinet and five in Kuuskoski's.[2] Because there is no open party representation in caretaker Cabinets and members are often civil servants for the state, it has become customary to use the general phrase "civil servant government" with respect to these Cabinets. Referring to what has been said above, it is perhaps better to consider "civil servancy" a variable which helps in the description of caretaker Cabinets. The Lehto Cabinet, quickly formed at the end of 1963 of civil servants directing different areas of the central administration, probably represents a rather pure type of civil servant government.

These "presidential governments" are born of cooperation between the head of state and the candidate for the post of prime minister; it is mostly presidential confidence that they enjoy. Parliament demonstrates its "confidence" by not passing a vote of no confidence; but ministers in a semipolitical caretaker Cabinet may cooperate with some parliamentary groups. In some situations it is advantageous for parties to preserve their freedom of action and criticism by formally remaining outside of governmental responsibility but at the same time retaining an ability to influence government policy through ministers of the same persuasion.

Parties in Cabinets. Table 24 shows Cabinets for the years 1917–1970 and their members grouped by party. There have often been changes in composition during office, not all of which have been taken into account. The structure of a Cabinet when it began to function or what sort of Cabinet it was for most of the time in office is the point of departure. The table does not, therefore, show the total number of ministers belonging to different parties. In some cases independent ministers who were "political" have been taken from the group of independent ministers and put in the proper party column if they clearly belonged to some party but joined a Cabinet as individuals. It is difficult to make decisions in these cases, since the dividing line between "political" and "nonpolitical" individuals is very fuzzy.

The table shows graphically how the center of party representation has shifted in four decades to the center and left. The Agrarian-

2. V. J. Sukselainen, "Maalaisliiton asema suomalaisessa yhteiskunnassa," *Herääyä maaseutu* (Lappeenranta, 1962), VII, 15.

Center party has most often assumed governmental responsibility and it has also had the greatest number of ministers. In this respect the party has been favored by its tactically advantageous position as the largest center party; as both extreme groups have often been excluded from the Cabinet, and as the government base is thus structured around the center groups, the formation of a viable coalition has necessitated the cooperation of the Agrarian party. The Agrarians used to assume, for the most part, less important ministerial duties; but as more academically trained individuals have entered the ranks of the party, it has also been able to fill the major ministerial positions with its representatives.

The Social Democratic party has had the second greatest number of ministers. Natural explanations for the Agrarian party's big lead are that the Social Democratic party decided only in 1926, following the example of the Scandinavian countries and the United Kingdom, to travel the path of "ministerial socialism" and accept governmental responsibility even under normal conditions; that it was ten years before the Social Democratic party became a government party comparable to the Agrarian party; and that toward the end of the 1950's the Social Democratic party was again in the opposition. From 1937 until 1957 these parties were almost equal in terms of governmental representation.

Of the three small bourgeois groups, the Progressive party formerly was the most important in government policy. The party had capable and experienced men for Cabinets, and in time the center of its influence shifted from Parliament to the State Council. During the period of centrist policies, until 1924, it was in fact the leading government party, but then its significance began to diminish. The Finnish People's party, the successor to the Progressive party, was in many Cabinets but only as a "filler" through which the larger parties sought to widen the base of the government. The Coalition party, as the rightist group, has had to be satisfied in government policy with a position less important than that enjoyed by the Progressive party. Only for short periods of time has this party been more conspicuous in carrying the burden of governmental responsibility; following the Second World War, it was not until 1958 that it became fully "eligible" for Cabinet participation. But political figures from the Coalition party have on numerous occasions been in governments as independent ministers; they have not had parliamentary support from their party, but in any event they have been

Table 24. Cabinets and their political composition, 1917–1970

Prime minister	Period in office	IKL	Old Finnish party; Coalition party	Young Finnish party; Progressive party; Finnish People's party; Liberal People's party	Swedish People's party	Agrarian party; Center party	Social Democratic party	TPSL	SKDL	Independent
		Party								
1. Svinhufvud I	11.27.17–5.27.18	–	2	6	1	2	–	–	–	–
2. Paasikivi I	5.27.18–11.27.18	–	5	6	1	2	–	–	–	1
3. Ingman I	11.27.18–4.17.19	–	3	6	2	–	–	–	–	2
4. K. Castrén	4.17.19–8.15.19	–	–	6	3	4	–	–	–	2
5. Vennola I	8.15.19–3.15.20	–	–	8	–	4	–	–	–	2
6. Erich	3.15.20–4.9.21	–	3	4	2	3	–	–	–	1
7. Vennola II	4.9.21–6.2.22	–	–	8	–	4	–	–	–	–
8. Cajander I	6.2.22–11.14.22	–	–	–	–	–	–	–	–	11
9. Kallio I	11.14.22–1.18.24	–	–	4	–	6	–	–	–	2
10. Cajander II	1.18.24–5.31.24	–	–	–	–	–	–	–	–	11
11. Ingman II	5.31.24–3.31.25	–	3	2	2	4	–	–	–	1
	after 11.22.24	–	5	3	3	–	–	–	–	1

12. Tulenheimo	3.31.25–12.31.25	–	4	–	–	5	–	–	–	4
13. Kallio II	12.31.25–12.13.26	–	6	–	–	6	–	–	–	–
14. Tanner	12.13.26–12.17.27	–	–	–	–	–	13	–	–	–
15. Sunila I	12.17.27–12.22.28	–	–	–	–	10	–	–	–	3
16. Mantere	12.22.28–8.16.29	–	3[a]	6	–	–	–	–	–	3
17. Kallio III	8.16.29–7.4.30	–	–	2[a]	–	10	–	–	–	1
18. Svinhufvud II	7.4.30–3.21.31	–	3	1	2	4	–	–	–	3
19. Sunila II	3.21.31–12.14.32	–	4	1	2	6	–	–	–	–
20. Kivimäki	12.14.32–10.7.36	–	4[a]	4	2	2[a]	–	–	–	1
21. Kallio IV	10.7.36–3.12.37	–	2[a]	2	–	9	–	–	–	–
22. Cajander III	3.12.37–12.1.39	–	–	2	–	5	5	–	–	1
23. Ryti I	12.1.39–3.27.40	–	2[a]	1	2	4	4	–	–	1
24. Ryti II	3.27.40–1.3.41	–	1	1	3	3	4	–	–	2
25. Rangell	1.3.41–3.5.43	1	1	1	2	4	4	–	–	2
26. Linkomies	3.5.43–8.8.44	–	2	1	2	4	5	–	–	2
27. Hackzell	8.8.44–9.21.44	–	2	1	1	4	5	–	–	2
28. U. Castrén	9.21.44–11.17.44	–	1[a]	1	1	4	6	–	–	3
29. Paasikivi II	11.17.44–4.17.45	–	–	1	2	4	4	–	4	3
30. Paasikivi III	4.17.45–3.26.46	–	–	1	1	4	4	–	5	2
31. Pekkala	3.26.46–7.29.48	–	–	–	1	5	5	–	6	1
32. Fagerholm I	7.29.48–3.17.50	–	–	–	–	–	15	–	–	1
33. Kekkonen I	3.17.50–1.17.51	–	–	2	3	10	–	–	–	–
34. Kekkonen II	1.17.51–9.20.51	–	–	1	2	7	7	–	–	–
35. Kekkonen III	9.20.51–7.9.53	–	–	–	2	7	7	–	–	1
36. Kekkonen IV	7.9.53–11.17.53	–	–	–	3	8	–	–	–	3

Prime minister	Period in office	Party								
		IKL	Old Finnish party; Coalition party	Young Finnish party; Progressive party; Finnish People's party; Liberal People's party	Swedish People's party	Agrarian party; Center party	Social Democratic party	TPSL	SKDL	Independent
37. Tuomioja	11.17.53–5.5.54	–	4[a]	3[a]	2[a]	–	–	–	–	6
38. Törngren	5.5.54–10.20.54	–	–	–	1	6	6	–	–	1
39. Kekkonen V	10.20.54–3.3.56	–	–	–	–	6	7	–	–	1
40. Fagerholm II	3.3.56–5.27.57	–	–	1	1	6	6	–	–	1
41. Sukselainen I	5.27.57–11.29.57	–	–	3	3	6	–	–	–	1
	after 7.2.57	–	–	4	–	9	–	–	–	1
	after 9.2.57	–	–	2	–	6	5[b]	–	–	2
42. von Fieandt	11.29.57–4.26.58	–	–	–	–	4[a]	–	–	–	10
43. Kuuskoski	4.26.58–8.29.58	–	–	1[a]	–	5[a]	4[b]	–	–	4
44. Fagerholm III	8.29.58–1.13.59	–	3	1	1	5	5	–	–	–
45. Sukselainen II	1.13.59–7.14.61	–	–	–	1[a]	14	–	–	–	–
46. Miettunen	7.14.61–4.13.62	–	–	–	–	12	–	–	–	3
47. Karjalainen	4.13.62–12.18.63	–	3	2	2	5	–	–	–	3[c]

48. Lehto	12.18.63–9.12.64	–	–	–	–	–	1[a]	–	–	14
49. Virolainen	9.12.64–5.27.66	–	3	3	2	7	–	–	–	–
50. Paasio	5.27.66–3.22.68	–	–	–	–	5	6	1	3	–
51. Koivisto	3.22.68–5.14.70	–	–	–	1	5	6	1	3	–
52. Aura	5.14.70–	–	1[a]	1[a]	–	3[a]	4[a]	–	–	4

[a] In the Cabinet as independent ministers.
[b] Members of the Social Democratic opposition, in the Kuuskoski government as independent ministers.
[c] Representatives of the SAK.

influential in the formulation of government policy. As far as the Swedish People's party is concerned, it has become more or less a rule (especially in the 1940's and 1950's) that from one to three Swedish ministers will be taken into the government. On one hand, the Swedish-speaking part of the population has generally been pleased to have its representatives in the government, and, on the other hand, the party can offer capable individuals to handle demanding ministerial tasks.

The extreme left was accepted as a government party in the postwar situation, in 1944–1948. Parliamentary cooperation with the Communists had previously been unthinkable; in 1948 the extreme left once again became, and for almost twenty years, part of the opposition. Indeed, the number of People's Democratic ministers has remained very small.

Since the 1920's there has been rather frequent use in Finland of independent ministers; there are usually one to three such ministers in the State Council. Some are considered nonpolitical experts, whereas others have been party members and even members of Parliament. The former serve to increase a Cabinet's competence and expertise and the latter, additionally, strengthen the parliamentary base of many weak minority governments. As already mentioned, it is difficult to draw a clear line of demarcation between these two groups. Particularly during the first two decades of independence, independent ministers were close to the small bourgeois groups and thus stressed the bourgeois and rightwing nature of Cabinets. It was only in the 1950's that Socialists became "civil servant ministers." Independent ministers have led all ministries, especially the foreign ministry.

CABINET FORMATION AND RESIGNATION

Cabinet Formation. Formation of a government in British parliamentarism is generally a simple and effortless task. But the procedure is more complicated in countries where the party system is diffuse and where majority parliamentarism presupposes cooperation by many parties. In Finland, too, it has sometimes been suggested that it is the duty of the group or groups that caused the fall of the old Cabinet to form a new one. But Finnish parliamentarism is not British parliamentarism. In certain cases one can indeed feel that the groups responsible for the collapse of a government have a political duty to cooperate in the formation of a new Cabinet, but in reality fulfillment of this duty often proves impossible. It is unthinkable, for example, that the right and the extreme left should form a common government after an election victory or after jointly causing the demise of a Cabinet. Circumstances dictate practice such that the former government parties are not in any way pushed off to the side; they, like other parties, participate in feelers and negotiations. The center of gravity in Finnish parliamentary life is in the political center; therefore Cabinet changes are rarely radical; a new coalition usually includes the same groups, even the same individuals, who suffered a parliamentary defeat. The adaptation of parliamentarism to multiparty conditions in Finland leads, as Sven Lindman has noted, to a subconscious tug of war between traditional British parliamentarism and special political conditions prevailing in the nation.

There have, of course, been Cabinet solutions in which the classical parliamentary doctrine of transferring governmental responsibility to the opposition (which has overthrown the Cabinet or won an election victory) has to a certain degree been followed; but in general it must be said that conditions in Finland are not propitious for such a solution.

In paragraph 36 of the Form of Government Act it is simply stated that the president chooses as members of the State Council native-born Finnish citizens who are known to be honest and talented and who must as ministers enjoy the confidence of Parliament. In practice the matter is much more complicated. Modern parliamentarism is based on parties which, in the formation of a government, come between the president and ministerial nominees and reduce the head of state's freedom of action. Cabinet members in their official duties represent parties, not personal views or their own political positions. Party dependency has grown and has created a situation in which members may not enter a government without the permission of the related party organs. This has always been the position of the Social Democrats, as demonstrated by the case of Senator J. K. Kari in 1906. Leo Mechelin asked Kari, the Social Democratic party secretary, to become a member of his Senate; Kari agreed, although he had not received explicit permission from his party. Kari was expelled from the party, and it was ten years before he was taken back into its ranks. Similar cases have occurred in later years: the expulsion of four "adopted ministers" from the

Social Democratic parliamentary group in the fall of 1957 has already been mentioned. When the Fagerholm government decided in the summer of 1956 to expropriate land for use by the defense establishment in Porkkala, the area formerly leased to the Soviet Union, the Swedish People's party, which had opposed this measure, demanded that its representative (Ralf Törngren) resign. However, at the President's request he remained as an independent minister, causing irritation in the party and even resulting in demands that Törngren be expelled. It is said that Pekkala in 1946 was the last prime minister who independently selected, without consultation with the party leadership, some Agrarian members of his government.[3]

In any case, the initiative to form a new Cabinet belongs with the president of the Republic, who, in accordance with what has already been said, must first establish contact with Parliament's party groups. After a Cabinet has submitted its resignation request, it has become established practice to carry out a presidential round: the president first summons the speaker of Parliament and then the chairmen of the parliamentary groups (beginning with the largest one) and discusses with them the political situation and various possibilities, in order to determine the basis for resolving the crisis. He requests that the parliamentary groups submit statements concerning the government base they favor and he attempts, in accordance with the principles of parliamentarism, to cooperate in the formation of a government which is supported by a parliamentary majority and which is capable, in his opinion, of handling the tasks at hand. In some cases—and this was especially true during the early years of independence—the president may then decide relatively freely who has the best chance of forming a broad-based and strong government, and he may appoint a prime ministerial candidate with instructions concerning the government base. But the course of developments emphasizing party hegemony has meant that parliamentary groups and leading party organs often discuss in advance the prime minister question, making recommendations to the president and informing him of whether or not the individual he is considering will receive their support. The designated candidate continues negotiations with those parties and parliamentary groups whose cooperation is anticipated in the formation of a new govern-

3. V. J. Sukselainen, "Maalaisliiton järjestötoiminta vuosina 1906–1955," *Heräävä maaseutu* (Porvoo, 1956), VI, 159.

ment. If the effort progresses well, agreement is first reached on the outlines of a program and the division of ministerial portfolios among the parties; agreement is later reached concerning details of the Cabinet list. The appointment of individuals for specific posts is done by parties, often as an internal party matter. This was the procedure followed especially during the 1951–1957 period of co-operation between the Agrarian party and the Social Democrats. If the architect of a government, or the individual making inquiries, should fail in his quest, the president turns to another individual and considers other alternatives for the realization of a majority government. At this point the matter may also come to rest entirely in the hands of parties and the parliamentary groups. If the formation of a majority government is impossible, it is necessary to settle for a minority coalition and sometimes even a one-party government; a caretaker Cabinet can be resorted to as an extreme measure.

Party conditions in Finland, depending on the situation, determine a president's room for maneuver when a Cabinet is formed. His influence may be decisive in forming a civil servant government, and the chance for independent action in the formation of parliamentary governments, too, is often increased by a murky political situation, by many different alternatives, and by hesitancy on the part of party groups. Speculation about the president's influence is made difficult by the fact that it is hard to know what goes on behind the scenes and how active a role he has played in a given instance. But, in general, presidents to date have sought to retain their power; even though they have recognized the primary and in some respects increased importance of the party institution, and have let groups reach agreement in peaceful and clear situations concerning a resolution of the government question, presidents have nonetheless acted energetically in difficult cases and have demonstrated that the head of state has not irretrievably lost his position of leadership. A head of state has often exercised personal power during government crises in a way that has not been considered consistent with genuine "monistic" parliamentarism. He has determined which parties are "eligible" for entrance into a government, put pressure on parliamentary groups and hesitant ministerial candidates, and expressed a clear opinion concerning the government base and the individuals entering a Cabinet—and concerning even the government program, as Relander did in the spring of 1925. This activity has on occasion evoked sharp public criticism.

The role of factors with greatest impact in shaping the final outcome of a government solution—the role of the president, of the "creator of the government" (the prime minister candidate), and of party leaders—fluctuates with the situation. An extreme case occurred in 1922, when President Ståhlberg personally chose the ministers in Finland's first caretaker Cabinet and appointed Cajander, his own selection as deputy minister for agriculture, to handle the duties of prime minister. Especially in the 1950's, however, when forming joint Agrarian-Social Democratic governments, the decision rested with party leaders. After Törngren had submitted his resignation request in the fall of 1954, President Paasikivi, immediately following the presidential round and without having appointed anyone to form a government, urged the Agrarian party and the Social Democrats to negotiate the program and composition of a new Cabinet. Committees established by these parties came up with a proposal in the course of negotiations led by the Speaker of Parliament; the sections of the proposal concerned with the composition of a Cabinet, having been approved by the parliamentary groups and the party organizations, were presented to the President, who then made his appointment. The view that portfolios received by a party are at the disposal of that party gave rise during these years to forms at variance with the usual practice in ministerial changes. A case in point occurred in the fall of 1955, when the Social Democratic parliamentary group considered the resignation intentions of two ministers. Väinö Leskinen, wrapped up in his duties as party secretary, was one; he was permitted to resign and a successor was immediately selected. The group's decision, which had already been made public, was then communicated to the President, the Prime Minister remaining merely a bystander.

Parliamentary Confidence. In an earlier connection it has been noted that the concept of confidence must in parliamentary practice be given a meaning which is not customary; this is especially true in multiparty nations where an advance statement of approval is not demanded of the popular assembly and where a cabinet does not immediately request a statement of confidence as it begins its duties. In Finland it is assumed that a Cabinet enjoys the confidence of Parliament until the converse is explicitly revealed. The negative political definition of confidence as the absence of an expression of no confidence, which does seem a little artificial, makes it possible for narrow-based minority governments to remain in power. In 1926, Tanner's Cabinet followed the practice which is more common abroad: it presented its program to Parliament and made realization of the program a matter of immediate confidence. Usually the prime minister merely presents his government's program for the minutes of the State Council, after which it is published. This government program is a brief declarative document from which it is not possible for the opposition or the public at large to gain a clear picture of the Cabinet's plans. Much more significant in respect to the latter are government agreements, which have been the basis for cooperative action in many broad-based coalitions. Agreements between parties in the government, spelling out a Cabinet's concrete action program, were concluded during the 1950's in negotiations between the Agrarian party and the Social Democratic party. These agreements are not always made public, at least not in toto. But when Fagerholm's Cabinet began its work in the fall of 1958, the government agreement was recorded in the minutes of the State Council as a programmatic manifesto.

Resignation of a Cabinet. Many different factors may lead to the resignation of a Cabinet. First, it is clear that a Cabinet must resign when it has received from Parliament a clear vote of no confidence. The interpellation procedure is a handy way for members of Parliament to initiate such action; interpellations are frequently (not always) designed to oust a Cabinet. The formal reason for conflict may in itself be a trivial measure taken by the government; the real reason may be found in general discontent with the Cabinet and in an attempt to replace it with another Cabinet. The existence of conflict leading to a change of government is expressed in many other ways. Resignation often comes about as the result of a decision made by Parliament, unfavorable to the government, on a matter that the government feels must be resolved in a certain way in order for it to continue in office and of which, perhaps, the government has made a direct question of confidence. The government can inform Parliament that one of its proposals or communiqués must be approved as is and that failure on Parliament's part to act will be considered by the government a vote of no confidence; in this case the initiative comes from the Cabinet itself.

In general a decision of no confidence is not tied to any specific form, and it is not necessarily the result of rejection by Parliament of action taken by the State Council or a minister; the main point is that a vote of no confidence should be expressed with sufficient clarity in one form or another. Parliament may seek to achieve this through a decision running contrary to the position of the government, but this is not necessarily the purpose of such a decision; it is then up to the Cabinet to decide whether or not the conflict is so deep that further activity is impossible. Experience has shown that in Finnish conditions governments do not have to be overly sensitive when drawing their conclusions.

The demand for stipulated majorities, a part of parliamentary procedure, sometimes presents difficulties for the application of "orthodox" parliamentarism. When a matter under discussion requires a two-thirds or five-sixths majority, it is possible for a Cabinet to have majority support in Parliament and to be defeated by a minority. If the government has made the matter a question of confidence and resigns, a peculiar situation results. A case in point occurred in December 1954, when Kekkonen's fifth government submitted its resignation request after small bourgeois groups had defeated its proposal to extend for the following year a law regarding regulation of economic life. That crisis was, however, resolved through negotiation.

Causes other than conflict with a parliamentary majority have led most frequently to a resignation request. Factors resulting in the resignation of governments during the period 1918–1968 can be grouped as follows:

Vote of no confidence resulting from interpellation	4
Decision of Parliament contrary to government position	8
Weak support and authority	3
Conflict with president	2
Presidential elections	9
Parliamentary elections	10
Internal conflicts within Cabinet	5
Reasons of foreign policy	5
Other reasons	4
Total	50

Many different factors may combine to influence a change in government, so that a certain subjectiveness in this grouping is unavoidable.

It is customary for a Cabinet to resign following a presidential election even when the incumbent is re-elected. President Ståhlberg, who did not want to follow this custom, expressly requested the Castrén government to remain in office when he assumed the presidential duties. The next president, Relander, did likewise when the Ingman Cabinet offered to resign; but it did resign because of a defeat suffered in Parliament concerning a question of electoral law. Resignation in the years 1931, 1937, 1941, and 1946 was a necessity because the prime minister was elected president. In 1956 the Kekkonen Cabinet actually disintegrated before the presidential election.

Resignation by a Cabinet has, on many occasions, been the result of a parliamentary election. In the above classification, the four cases in which a temporary caretaker Cabinet resigned in favor of a party-based government following an election are included in this group. Perhaps the clearest example of the impact of an unfavorable election outcome was the defeat and resignation in 1929 of the Mantere government. Also, in 1919, 1945, 1948, and 1966 the composition of Parliament changed to such an extent that there was cause for renovating the Cabinet.

In a small country such as Finland, changes in a foreign policy situation easily cause Cabinet changes. Foreign policy factors which became determinants during the Second World War were also influential in 1918, when the Paasikivi government, representing a German orientation, resigned following Germany's defeat. A concrete example of the importance of foreign policy factors was provided in autumn 1958, when the Fagerholm Cabinet was forced to submit its resignation request in view of the badly shaken relations between Finland and the Soviet Union (the Soviet leadership being dissatisfied with the composition of the Cabinet), and in view of internal dissension which had begun to appear within the government. Sometimes a government has broken up solely because of internal conflicts; even when a resignation results from a parliamentary decision running contrary to the position of the government, the basic determinant may be collapse of the government front.

Individual ministers often resign from Cabinets still in office. Usually a resignation is accepted if a minister or his party so desires; but there are also several clear examples of resignations that are the result of a vote of no confidence given to a member of the State Council by Parliament. In 1922 Foreign Minister Rudolf Holsti, who favored a border state policy, had signed an agreement in

Warsaw concerning political cooperation between the new states of Finland, Poland, Latvia, and Estonia on Russia's western border. Two interpellations were made in Parliament and they resulted in a vote of no confidence for the Foreign Minister. Soon, however, the entire Vennola Cabinet submitted its resignation request because of the same matter. When Parliament, in 1948, examined the government's report for 1945, Communist Minister of the Interior Yrjö Leino received an explicit vote of no confidence; the constitutional committee had affirmed that he had exceeded his authority in turning Finnish citizens over to the Soviet Union. Since Leino did not himself submit his resignation, President Paasikivi relieved him of membership in the State Council.

PARLIAMENTARISM AND A SEPARATION OF POWERS

It has been suggested in recent years that a parliamentary system based on a separation of powers has come to the end of the road and is not suitable for modern political action. Duverger considers a head of state merely a remnant from the beginnings of parliamentarism, developed within the framework of monarchy, and feels that an emphasis on the position of the president of a republic causes a division of governmental power and consequently a weakening of this power. Such a system in his opinion is not viable; either a president is weak and does not exercise the great powers given to him in the constitution or he is an energetic man who wants to rule alone, in which case the prime minister, who has parliamentary responsibility, bears the consequences and is placed in an untenable position. From this viewpoint, Duverger even recommends a strengthening of the prime minister's position in an attempt to increase executive power.[4]

In Finland, the system showed its viability soon after independence. And, in Finland (for the most part), it is a "historical remnant" from the period of monarchy that has been preserved rather well in its original form. As mentioned earlier, it cannot be said that a single presidential power has to date been permanently "parliamentarized"; in other words, the president has not surrendered his position to the prime minister, but has retained his position as the holder of highest executive power and has remained the central figure in the nation's public life.

4. Maurice Duverger in *l'Express*, June 12, 1958, pp. 10–11.

The position of power enjoyed by the president causes difficulties in attempts to fit the Finnish political system into the usual typologies. Those who start from a broad conception of parliamentarism, who consider parliamentarism merely a general principle regulating ties between a popular assembly and a cabinet, do not question the parliamentary nature of the system; those who also call attention to the other side, to the relation between a head of state and a cabinet, discover its anomalous and special character. The position of the head of state should without doubt be considered a relative factor in this sort of assessment. When the problem is examined empirically, when the features characteristic of states called parliamentary are considered, it must be acknowledged that Finland's system of government forms its own type—located, as mentioned earlier, somewhere between genuine parliamentarism and the American presidential system.

The President and the Cabinet. Without doubt the Finnish system permits conflicts which are difficult to mediate and even leads to tumultuous clashes between president, Cabinet, and Parliament. A Cabinet in parliamentarism with a separation of powers leans partly on Parliament and partly on the head of state and consequently finds itself in a no-man's-land between opposing political forces. The demand for parliamentary confidence continues to be primary, and, in accommodating himself to party agreements, the president occasionally—as in autumn 1958—has appointed a Cabinet the composition of which has clearly been contrary to his wishes. But for smooth management of governmental policy, under conditions emphasizing the leadership position of the head of state, the relation between the president and the Cabinet obviously cannot be one of indifference.

Specific external conditions and certain approved "rules of the game" have made this system viable. It is essential that a president not under normal conditions attempt to rule by himself; he must, in the consideration of daily governmental matters, refrain from conducting personal policy that is contrary to a clear stand taken by the State Council, and he must make his decisions in accordance with the opinions of the ministers. He must always be flexible in order to avoid clashes. A chance observer may see in Finnish political life during periods of peace, in both foreign and domestic policy terms, only the usual features of multiparty European parliamentarism.

But, as has been mentioned in connection with the position of the president, he is still able in special situations to exercise strong personal power. Even in normal conditions his influence is increasing, due to his great prestige and, primarily, to actual political factors: that it is not possible to achieve close cooperation in Parliament between groups that would effectively direct and supervise government policy; that opinions in a Cabinet composed of representatives from many parties sometimes sharply conflict; that because of this the State Council does not always have a clear line of action to which it steadfastly adheres. If only two parties were competing for power, and if there were to be a truly positive relationship of trust between Parliament and the Cabinet, the president's position would hardly be as strong as it is today—unless, of course, a strong leader of a majority were elected president. Development of presidential power has perhaps gone furthest in the field of foreign policy; after the Second World War, in the most important questions concerning the conduct of foreign affairs, it has become customary for the president to lead while the State Council, recognizing that position of leadership, merely advises and assists.

If the president declines to exercise personal power, he nonetheless must act as a mediating and conciliatory factor in internal Cabinet disagreements. Successful mediation depends a great deal on how well the president, after assuming his duties, has been able to withdraw from party politics and become a "mediator" enjoying the respect of all groups. When an intense party struggle is raging he can, of course, find himself in difficult situations even though he attempts to preserve his nonpartisan stance.

Because personal factors, as well as changing political situations, are the fundamental determinants of the relationship in question, a general presentation easily becomes sketchy and only weakly reflective of reality. The president's relations with the State Council have varied greatly even within short periods of time. Sometimes the president has had little influence on the composition and activity of Cabinets, but sometimes a Cabinet has turned primarily to the president. The duality of political power in the years 1959–1962 received special emphasis because a relation of almost complete positive confidence prevailed between the President, who had come from the Agrarian party, and his Agrarian Cabinets. But since there was very little contact between the government and Parliament, one could speak of parliamentary confidence only in the juridic sense.

The Government and Parliament. The other side of the question at hand is the relation between the government and Parliament. In Finland's multiparty parliamentarism there is no merging of the Cabinet and Parliament; the two institutions remain separate, competing power factors. Cabinets have been inclined to draw away from Parliament due to the fact that in Finland a relatively large number of ministers have not been members; even the prime minister has on many occasions come from outside Parliament. Furthermore, members of the State Council cannot be elected members of parliamentary committees.

The president can to some degree play a balancing role, due to his firm position; but, since Parliament's powers are overwhelming, it can be said that in general Finnish parliamentarism is characterized by government weakness vis-à-vis Parliament. Cabinets have not been identical in this respect, but as a rule the center of power, except in wartime, has been in Parliament. Earlier it was noted how difficult it is to establish and preserve viable majorities in Parliament; under these conditions not even a government structured around a majority is secure or able to effectively direct Parliament's work. It is a common phenomenon that government coalitions based on inflexible parties are weak. Cabinet members feel a closer affinity to their parties than to their colleagues in the Cabinet, so that policy easily becomes contradictory and inconsistent. It is not unusual for a government to refrain from expressing a clear position in Parliament on even important questions, for lack of agreement. In order to avoid a hopeless impasse party groups in the government can agree to compromise solutions, but when a matter gets to the "public arena," to Parliament, they may also "betray" the government and adopt a position in line with the narrower goals of party policy. A minister may even speak against a government proposal in Parliament.

For its part, Parliament has shown relatively little respect for the government, for example, when considering its legislative proposals and the budget. The form of legislative and budget proposals may undergo fundamental change in consideration by Parliament, even to such a degree that the government has had to request that the president not ratify a law approved by Parliament but originally proposed by the government. As was apparent earlier, the suspensive veto regarding legislative decisions by Parliament has been in constant use except during the war years and, together with the budget veto (which can be applied to appropriations included in a parliamentary bill concerned with projected expenditures), it is one of the most important means by which the government seeks to defend itself against Parliament.

The short life of governments is connected with their weakness. Finland has had fifty-one governments from her declaration of independence until the end of 1968, which means that average life span has been about a year. Longest in power (almost four years) was the Kivimäki government of 1932–1936; Hackzell's government in 1944 had the shortest life span, only a month and a half. The average life of Cabinets has remained almost the same over the decades; in this respect a clear development in one direction or the other cannot be determined.

Frequent changes in government are, of course, disturbing in terms of continuity of political development. It is as if every Cabinet must start from the beginning; it must become familiar with its predecessor's plans and must prepare its own, but, when it has had a chance to get acquainted with matters and to begin realizing its plans, it must again resign. Clearly, the realization of efforts which are broad in scope and long-ranged suffers; but there is no reason to exaggerate the significance of these views. In general, political continuity has been preserved fairly well in spite of frequent and protracted government crises; in connection with changes in the base of a government, one cannot speak of radical changes in direction. At the most there are small shifts to the right or left, resulting from the fact that there have rarely been changes in the composition of Parliament that are sudden and great, as well as from the fact that parliamentary changes do not extend to the president or to the civil service. Of the factors that cause a party to accept parliamentary responsibility, an election victory, a decisive role in bringing about the demise of the former government, and the holding of a key parliamentary position should be mentioned. In Finland this last factor has been primary; since the right and the extreme left have been excluded from government cooperation for long periods of time, the center groups have formed the core of a Cabinet time after time.

The fact that one or more of the resigning ministers usually enters a new government also serves to increase continuity—possible because of the aforementioned fact that the government base remains wholly or partially the same. The familiar phrase used to describe

French conditions, "governments change but ministers remain," is also appropriate when characterizing the development of Finnish parliamentarism. This indicates that, at least in some parties, an oligarchy of individuals "eligible to become ministers" has arisen that controls the party's ministerial positions, going no further than perhaps to exchange portfolios within the group. Furthermore, a certain ministerial portfolio may remain in the hands of the same individual in many governments over a number of years. Hjalmar J. Procopé was the "independent" foreign minister in four consecutive governments, 1927–1931, as was Carl Enckell in six governments of 1944–1950. Later, too, after the Second World War, an attempt was made to avoid frequent changes in the post of foreign minister. In the 1950's, these men were foreign minister in two or more governments: independent ministers Åke Gartz and P. J. Hynninen, Ralf Törngren (Swedish People's party), and Johannes Virolainen (Agrarian party). When the Agrarian-Center party enters a government, it always wants the minister of agriculture to be one of its own men. One should not forget that Urho Kekkonen was prime minister in four consecutive governments, 1950–1953, and in a fifth government (1954–1956) after a year's pause.

Summary. In general, parliamentary life in Finland has been more unstable and has been characterized more by a concern for the short run than is true for neighboring Western countries. Divided, weak, and short-lived governments, as well as long government crises whose resolution is difficult and crisis periods of parliamentarism with civil servant governments and other phenomena foreign to "healthy" parliamentarism, are facts which distinguish Finland from the Scandinavian countries—with their relatively stable parliamentary conditions—and which have caused some foreign observers to see outright primitive features in Finnish parliamentary practice. When searching for the causes of these weaknesses, reference is often made merely to Finland's rigid multiparty system; but comparison with foreign countries soon shows that number of parties is not the decisive factor. The causes for the most part are to be found in those special features of parties and the party system discussed in Chapter II; and, perhaps even deeper than these, there are certain general factors outside party formation. In the history of Finland's representative institutions there have been several crisis periods during which peaceful parliamentary development was interrupted and during which violence was used in seeking to change political direction; on this basis there is a certain validity to the assertion that among the Finnish population, regardless of social class, parliamentarism has never enjoyed the respect it has evoked in other Nordic countries.

Two developments of significance to modern parliamentarism, found in many diverse political systems as an integral part of modern society's growth, are the broadening of state leadership and governmental duties and the strengthening of corporate features in the political structure of society. The government's role in Finland, too, has without doubt been accentuated over time. In wartime conditions, and in the postwar period of adjustment following in the 1940's, an understandable effort was made to concentrate power in the hands of the government and Parliament was content with its secondary position. Through exceptional legislation (for example, through a law declaring a state of war and laws concerned with the regulation of economic life) the government determined in detail the course of social life and, as the war dragged on, the center of political power in general rested with the president, the State Council, and the commander-in-chief, Parliament remaining a bystander to a great degree. But as the sphere of state activity has expanded, the government's task under normal conditions, too, has become more important. In this respect, satisfactory results also necessitate an increase in the ability of the government to act. The president's position seems to have been strengthened, but the same cannot be said of the State Council. Finland's party institution cannot produce Cabinets any more stable or stronger than they were in earlier times; but today the effects are more far-reaching.

An increase in the power of organizations is also closely related to the problems of parliamentarism. Great economic interest organizations, acting as pressure groups, have risen to a position alongside Parliament and parties and, in a certain sense, are competitors with them. A government can no longer limit itself to relations with Parliament, but must also consider the mass organizations. This means that the circle whose division into groups supporting and opposing the government determines the nature of a Cabinet and its possibilities for action has in fact gone beyond Parliament and parties; it means that the confidence of parliamentary parties, taken by itself, is no longer an influential factor. Even though a Cabinet has majority support behind it in Parliament, it may be powerless on many questions if pressure groups, supported by mass strength, are "in opposition." These groups are well aware of their influence; they openly present their positions when a government is being formed, and in extreme cases they even demand direct representation in the Cabinet. On the other hand, there is negotiation and mediation concerning important economic decisions, sometimes primarily between the government and organizations, with Parliament having to settle for post-factum formal ratification of decisions which have already been made and which are, in practice, irreversible.

IX The Bureaucracy and Administration of Law

ORGANIZATION OF STATE ADMINISTRATION

Literature on public administration in Finland is sparse, and what has been published deals mostly with the formal, administrative law aspects. Consequently there is no material on political and social questions related to state administration, and the examination that follows must perforce focus mainly on the formal side.

Administrative Hierarchy. At the top of the pyramid of state administration is the president of the Republic. He directs, as holder of highest executive power, the administrative machinery formed by the State Council and its ministries, the central offices, many separate institutions and offices, and generalists and specialists at various subordinate levels. According to paragraph 32 of the Form of Government Act, it is the duty of the president to exercise general supervision over the state administration; but in the absence of his own office machinery, as mentioned previously, direct supervision is not possible and this duty rests mainly with the State Council. The administrative machinery below the State Council is divided horizontally into generalists and specialists (the terms convey the essential difference: specialists handle restricted, special tasks in professional fields, whereas generalists are responsible for all tasks not explicitly delegated to the specialists). As public administration has expanded, it is natural that there has been more and more specialization, with one group of matters after another shifting from generalists to new specialists.

The administration is vertically divided into officials at different levels, higher and lower officials, with the lower official group further divided on the basis of territorial jurisdiction. The organization of generalists in Finland is relatively simple; it is really formed only of the provincial governments, which are subordinate to the State Council (mainly the ministry of the interior), and of law enforcement officers in the rural areas, who are subordinate to their provincial governments. The number of levels among specialists varies. Authorities in charge of special tasks include the central offices and, subordinate to them or directly to ministries, the district offices, post offices, customs offices and examining points, railroad stations, various educational institutions, district engineers, and district doctors.

Organization of the Central Administration. Examination of the administrative systems of different countries shows two main types of central administration: a system of ministerial administration, or a ministry system, and a central office system. In the former, originally a part of the French system and the more common of the two in parliamentary countries, management of the central administration is concentrated to an overwhelming degree in ministries, which have at their disposal the best personnel in the central administration. A cabinet, or ministerial council, composed of their chiefs (ministers) functions as a force which unifies the various ministries. Of the Scandinavian countries, Norway and Denmark have organized their central administration in this way. In Sweden, however, there is a central office system—characterized by the fact that the tasks of ministries are restricted, from a legal point of view and with few exceptions, to the preparation of matters to be resolved by the king and to implementation of decisions. Offices and boards, whose chiefs are career civil servants and which have been established under the ministries for each branch of administration, take charge of the central administration. Ministries and their chiefs consequently do not have much independent decision-making power in matters under their jurisdiction; at the highest level, the king exercises the power of administrative decision-making, and at the lower levels it is exercised by those central offices with independent administrative power.

In Finland a mixed system has been adopted that is a result of historical development; traces of it can be found in both Swedish and Russian rule. The two systems have merged in the nation's highest administrative organization. "General governing" of the nation is a function of the State Council, whose ministries, as units exercising some independent decision-making power, each direct their own administrative branch. But central offices, which occupy a rather independent position with respect to the ministries, also exist for many administrative branches. They are located in Helsinki and their activity extends throughout the entire country. Central offices are very unevenly divided among different administrative branches, so that significant differences exist between them in the entire administrative system. Thus far no clear decision has been made in Finland as to whether administration should be developed according to the central office or the ministry system. Over time, as new offices have been created, each case has been considered on an individual basis in light of expedient factors; consequently decisions have been made in different directions. Examples of separate offices, with dates of establishment, are the state's center of supply and the sales tax office (1941), its technical research institute and its board of patents and registration (1942), its housing board (Arava, 1949), land settlement board (1959), and board of vocational education and housing board (1966); then, there have been the police department in the ministry of the interior (1926) and the veterinary department within the ministry of agriculture (1930), as well as the vocational education department within the ministry of commerce and industry (1942). In the 1920's an effort was made to turn the central administration over to ministries; in 1922 the board for social affairs was joined to the ministry for social affairs and the board of prison administration to the ministry of justice, and in 1925 the board of commerce and industry was joined to the ministry of commerce and industry. But the reforms went no further; today development seems to be in the opposite direction, toward a central office system.

A committee set up in 1955 to discuss organizational reforms of the state administration concluded—in agreement with the results of a similar inquiry in Sweden—that a central office system has faults which must be corrected. It considered the most serious weaknesses to be the absence of necessary expertise in ministries and, stemming from the system, a duplication in consideration of administrative matters that naturally slows down administrative activity and increases its cost. As a proposal for immediate improvement, the committee suggested that matters be reported directly from central offices to ministers and the State Council; but at the same time it proposed more sweeping measures, recommending that thought should be given on an individual basis to the feasibility of joining the administrative central offices to ministries and of merging central offices working in related areas.

Jurisdiction of Ministries. The division among ministries of matters entrusted to the State Council is set forth in a 1922 law concerning the number and general jurisdiction of ministries, in a 1943 State Council regulation, and in decrees concerning ministries and their departments. Since the number of ministries has not changed since 1918 and there have been no fundamental changes in the division of labor between them, the present arrangement is in some respects inappropriate for effective management. In various connections measures have been put forward to achieve greater unity in the administrative areas of general economic policy, labor affairs, and education. The following list includes the general areas of jurisdiction for ministries, as well as the most important central administrative offices subordinate to them.

The Ministry of Foreign Affairs considers matters concerning Finland's relations with foreign states.

The Ministry of Justice considers matters regarding the administration of justice, legislation in matters not under the jurisdiction of some other ministry, and prison administration and state elections.

The Ministry of the Interior considers matters concerning general order and security, as well as internal administration. Border guards are subordinate to this ministry.

The Ministry of Defense considers matters which concern the nation's defense and defense forces. The General Staff of the Defense Forces serves as staff for the commander of these Forces and at the same time as an administrative central office subordinate to the ministry.

The Ministry of Finance considers matters regarding the state budget, money and banking, taxation, development of the nation's economic life in accord with requirements of the national economy, and general statistics. Subordinate to the ministry are the state treasury office, the national board of customs, the excise office, the sales tax office, the main bureau for statistics, the mint, the inspection office for state finances, the state publishing center, an official publication, the postal savings bank, and an office for bank inspection.

The Ministry of Education considers matters of concern to general education, to the Lutheran and Greek Orthodox churches and other religious congregations, to science, art, and sports. Subordinate are the Finnish academy, the national board of schools, the archeological commission, and the national archives.

The Ministry of Agriculture considers matters which concern agriculture, forestry, surveying, land settlement, and veterinary medicine, as well as hunting and fishing. Subordinate are the national board of agriculture, state board of forestry, national land settlement board, forest research institute, agricultural research center, general survey office, central office of meteorology, geodetic institute, state granary, and veterinary college.

The Ministry of Communications and Public Works handles matters related to transportation, the postal and telegraph establishment, state-owned rapids and water works, and state construction activity, as well as other general works. Subordinate to the ministry are the national boards of administration of the state railways, public roads and waterways, post and telegraph, construction, and the state water power commission.

The Ministry of Commerce and Industry considers matters which concern trade, mining, industry, and shipping. Subordinate to the ministry are the national board of navigation, board of patents and registration, institute of technology, institute for geological research, institute of oceanography, office for export and import permits, state supply center, state institute for technical research, and the economic defense planning commission.

The Ministry for Social Affairs handles matters concerning working conditions and related questions, insurance, social welfare, protection of children, national health, social statistics, emigration and immigration, temperance work, and the production, distribution, and usage of spirits. Subordinate central administrative bodies are, for example, the board for social affairs, the medical board, the state office for accident compensation, and the labor council.

The State Council office, directed by the prime minister, handles matters related to formal measures arising from a diet, which concern the State Council and the order in which matters before it will be considered, state publication activity, and other matters to be considered in the State Council that are not under the jurisdiction of a specific ministry. Subordinate to this office is the state's planning commission.

The Structure and Activity of Ministries. During the period of autonomy, ministries were small offices whose primary duty was the preparation and presentation of reports. As such, they remained very undeveloped organizationally. A division in the modern sense between departments and bureaus was not realized; no fixed relations between superiors and subordinates existed. Activity was based on sectors, with duties given to civil servants; the only real superior among parallel rapporteurs was the head of a ministry, a senator. It was not until the 1920's that the organizational development of ministries got under way, partially in response to a reduction in the central office system (which had ballooned in size).

The parallelism of the ministry system and the central office system causes great variation in the organization of ministries. In certain fields the central administration is gathered in a ministry, which is large in numbers of personnel and well developed with departments and bureaus. In other cases, however, administration is overwhelmingly in the hands of independent central offices, and a ministry remains more or less what it was during the period of autonomy. Representative of the former type are the ministry for social affairs, which in 1962 had about three hundred employees, the ministry of foreign affairs, and, to a degree, the ministry of commerce and industry. But the administration of education, agriculture, and communications are most clearly organized on the basis of a central office system. The two systems can exist alongside each other, even within the same ministry. One department of a ministry may be many times more comprehensive than the rest of the ministry put together; such was the case, for example, in the ministry of agriculture before the re-establishment of the land settlement board in 1959. As the form of organization of public administration offices has developed, the most common model is considered to be direct organization, a pyramid system, in which the office is divided into subunits at one or more levels so that each superior directs and is responsible for all work under his jurisdiction. The subunits of ministries are at the first level departments and at the second bureaus (which in several cases have been further divided into sections). In some ministries there are also separate bureaus outside the departments; on the other hand, the division of some departments into bureaus has been incomplete, so that one can find in those departments, parallel to each other, a bureau system and the old system of reporting.

The number of departments within ministries varied in 1962 from two to six. Only the ministry of education lacked any sort of division into departments and bureaus, but in the mid-1960's its organization was thoroughly revamped. In most ministries the total number of personnel was one hundred to a hundred fifty, and about half of the forty-two departments had at most twenty employees.

In addition to their size, departments also differ greatly in terms of general position and procedure. One group is formed by small departments staffed primarily by rapporteurs; beneath them are central offices where, for the most part, preparatory work takes place and a minister or the State Council makes most of the decisions. The power relation within an office—the real center of consideration and decision-making often lying outside the department—does not, therefore, receive much attention; each rapporteur manages rather independently the matters under his jurisdiction. A second group consists of small departments in special fields, such as the civil defense and fire departments of the ministry of the interior, which function somewhat independently in their own narrow areas of specialization and where matters are for the most part considered by people professionally trained in each particular field. Finally, there are a number of large central office departments in which supreme leadership of some broad area of administration is concentrated. They are comparable to the central offices, from which some originated. These departments are characterized by a detachment and independence from a ministry and the entire State Council, a well developed pyramidical organization that includes the key position of the department head, and extensive decision-making power. This group includes, for example, the prison administration department of the ministry of justice, the department for labor affairs within the ministry of communications and public works, and the police department within the ministry of the interior.

In order to preserve continuity and unity in the activities of the State Council, ministries in 1920 were given office heads (permanent secretaries) as the closest assistants to ministers. They handle the internal activity and organization of a ministry, make sure work is completed, bring personnel matters to the attention of a minister and the State Council, hire the more junior office personnel in a ministry, and prepare and present matters concerning the budget. They do not, however, have centralized leadership and responsibility for the consideration and resolution of matters under a ministry's jurisdiction; consequently, they do not occupy the same position as a state secretary in many other countries. Only in the State Council office and four ministries is there a full-time office head; in other ministries one of the department heads performs tasks related to this position.

Thus, with respect to centralization of leadership and responsibility, heads of departments and of independent bureaus occupy a key position under the present system. Some departments are directed by high-ranking civil servants (hallitusneuvos), with legal and administrative training, whereas others are directed by department heads with proper professional training, many of whom have the title of director. Other employees in ministries include government secretaries, bureau chiefs, department and bureau secretaries, and notaries.

Some matters come from outside the State Council for consideration, while others are initiated from within a ministry. The handling of the former by an office begins with the opening and registering of mail and the distribution of documents to civil servants charged with preparation and reporting. This is followed by preparatory work, which includes locating additional information, discussion among civil servants, obtaining oral or written statements from other officials, and authorized travel; and the last are reporting, decision-making, and implementation.

Ministries are monocratic offices, which means that matters entrusted to them are resolved by a ministry head or by a supplementary minister on the basis of a report by a civil servant; or, they are resolved by a properly empowered civil servant on his own responsibility, handled on his own or based on a report by a second civil servant. Of all the ministries, only in that for social affairs and in the ministry of foreign affairs has there been an extensive effort to delegate decision-making power to rapporteurs; the large number of matters to be resolved in the former has made this an outright necessity. In most other ministries, however, effective transferral of decision-making power has been realized only within the framework of a few individual departments. Since more and more decisions are put before ministers, it is impossible for them to make full use of what is, formally, extensive decision-making power. Indeed, "hidden" delegation can frequently be seen in ministries (a minister merely signs a document quickly without familiarizing himself with the matter at hand); responsibility for the decision rests with the civil servant handling the preparation.

In practice, decision-making and reporting within ministries are not so bound to form as they are in a plenary session of the State Council or in a presidential session. A complete oral report should include explication of the matter under consideration, as well as a decision proposed by the rapporteur. In most matters, however, there is no report; after preparing a matter, a civil servant draws up a document and sends it to his minister or to some other superior for signing. Important matters require, of course, personal contact with the decision-maker, but even in this case a formal report is not a regular step; or, at least, it is impossible to distinguish the report from other discussion related to the matter. This flexibility is a necessity, due to perpetual congestion.

A document or written announcement within a ministry concerning a matter which has been resolved is signed by a minister or civil servant, depending on who made the decision, in accordance with procedural regulations, and the matter is countersigned by the rapporteur. If the rapporteur disagrees with the decision he can register a dissenting opinion on the draft of the document or on the list of decisions kept in the ministry.

Central Offices. By "central office" an administrative authority subordinate to the State Council (usually to one of its ministries) is meant—whose task is to oversee a specific branch of administration and whose area of activity encompasses the entire country. Thus each central office functions under the leadership and supervision of a ministry, even though in practice it may be relatively independent. Characteristic of Finnish state administration is a rigidity of the lines delineating spheres of jurisdiction, which means that a higher official cannot resolve a matter covered by the decision-making power of a lower official. Moreover, a tradition stressing the independence of central offices that was established during the period of Russian rule still exerts strong influence.

Central offices can be divided roughly, and somewhat imprecisely, into three groups: 1) central offices engaged in administrative activity, 2) central offices engaged in commercial as well as administrative activity, and 3) scientific central offices, which carry out restricted and special tasks. Most central offices belong to the first group, for example, the national boards of schools, medicine, agriculture, customs, and construction; the second group includes the boards of administration of the state railways, forestry, and post and telegraph; the third includes the main bureau for statistics, the oceanography institute, the central office of meteorology, the geological research institute, and the national archives. There has been discussion in Finland, as well as abroad, about the position of commercial institutions in state administration. Certain weaknesses which impede commercial activity can be seen in the office form; in particular, since the organization of these commercial institutions is tied to laws and decrees, and since their finances are tied to the budget, their leadership does not have the same opportunity to make rapid and independent decisions as that enjoyed by the leadership of private enterprise.

Most central offices are collegial or multimember. The highest decision-making power in this type of office is a college, which includes the office chief (chiefs of large central offices generally have the title of director general) and other civil servants of the highest ranks. The state railway administration board, for example, includes a director general and a general manager serving as his assistant and replacement, as well as eight managers, each of whom heads his own department. Along with the collegial form of decision-making, however, there is also the principle of monocratic offices, which means that office heads and department heads and even lower civil servants resolve matters on their own. Developments seem to have led to a relative decline in collegial consideration and to an increase in decision-making power exercised by individual civil servants. Indeed, it was stated by the committee on reform of the state administrative apparatus in its 1958 report that the collegial method of consideration is applied in Finland more than is necessary. The committee recommended that collegial consideration be given only to matters concerned with the administration of law, to disciplinary matters, to the most important appointments, and to other important administrative matters of broad scope. Collegial consideration has also been restricted in that only the most important and broadest matters are resolved by a meeting composed of all members of an office. In the national board of schools, for example, there are three types of sessions: department sessions, joint sessions of departments, and plenary sessions of an office. The reporting of matters is handled either by the chairman of the session or by that member or civil servant whose duty it was to prepare the matter in question. Consideration follows the same principles observed in a plenary session of the State Council. For management of different sectors within a given area of jurisdiction, central offices are generally divided into subunits like the State Council's ministries. For example, in the railway board in 1966 there were eight departments, which by decree were divided into a total of twenty-one bureaus; if necessary, these could be further divided into sections or offices. The medical board in the same year had nine departments and one separate bureau; the heads of most departments have the title of medical counsellor and they, like the director and director general, must be accredited doctors. Other employees of an office are examiners, assistant secretaries, bookkeepers, notaries, general office personnel, and registrars.

Provincial Government. In accordance with paragraph 50 of the Form of Government Act, Finland is divided for general administration into provinces (lääni), counties (kihlakunta), and communes (kunta). From the standpoint of contemporary state administration, only the provinces are of much importance. A commune is a self-governing territory and not really a unit in the administrative division of the state; a county today is nothing more than a territorial unit for a census official, who keeps the population register and performs a few other duties.

The development of provinces into contemporary administrative units of the state began early in the period of Swedish rule, over four hundred years ago. As the population has grown and the state administration has expanded, there has been a shift to even smaller territorial units, which has meant a constant increase in the number of provinces. As of 1969, the nation is divided into twelve provinces: Uusimaa, Turku and Pori, Aaland Islands, Häme, Kymi, Mikkeli, Kuopio, Vaasa, Oulu, Lapland, Keski-Suomi, and Northern Karelia.

In each province the general local authority, subordinate to the State Council and particularly its ministry of the interior, is the provincial government (lääninhallitus), headed by a governor and divided into a general department and a provincial treasury and accounting office. The division of labor between these two bodies is organized so that the latter considers primarily state property and state finances, as well as matters concerning fiscal accounts and bookkeeping; the former handles other matters under the jurisdiction of provincial government. A provincial counsellor is the office head of the provincial government and head of the general department; a provincial treasurer is head of the treasury and accounting office. Civil servant personnel include, in addition to these two individuals, a police inspector, a civil defense inspector, provincial secretaries, a bookkeeper, and a provincial auditor. Separate bureaus may also be set up in a provincial government.

In a provincial government matters are resolved on a one-man basis, following a procedure based on the principle of a monocratic office. In important matters decisions are made by the governor, following a report by a subordinate civil servant. If the governor is prevented from making a decision, matters under his jurisdiction are resolved by two rapporteurs, one of whom must usually be a department head. Less important matters can be delegated to a rapporteur or even a lower civil servant for resolution on his own responsibility.

As the general administrative authority, the provincial government must in all ways work for the best interests of the province and its population; with this purpose in mind, it must perform all tasks given to it by law or decree or otherwise considered under its jurisdiction. A provincial government is, first of all, the highest police authority in a province; in this capacity it supervises the preservation of law and security therein and directs police activity. Furthermore, it ensures that criminals are brought to trial; it provides official assistance when necessary to other authorities, and it handles other duties in its capacity as highest executive authority in the province. Measures by a provincial government extend to the area of state fiscal matters. It oversees the collection of taxes, provincial administration fees going to the state, and other revenues—insofar as the ministry of finance has not disposed of these tasks in some other fashion—and supervises the legal execution of state expenditures. Separate mention should be made of the supervisory duties of the provincial government. Administrative supervision focuses both on state officials who are subordinate to the provincial government and on self-governing communes. As detailed later, a provincial government must see to it that communal affairs are managed in accordance with laws and decrees and it must give directions to communal authorities when necessary.

Since local generalists and specialists work side by side in the same area independently of each other, it is impossible to avoid tense situations and difficulties in relations between the two types of officials. This phenomenon has increased in importance as the number of district officials in special administrative branches has increased and their jurisdiction expanded. It is understandable that the generalists—provincial governments—seek to preserve their right of supervision with respect to the different administrative branches, and that the specialists, for their part, try to achieve as independent a position as possible. The lack of contact makes systematic cooperative action, which in many respects is wanting, difficult to achieve among these different officials. Attention has been given to this unhealthy state of affairs, and in 1953 an attempt was made to ease the situation through a decree on cooperation between provincial and district administrative officials. As provided in this decree, each province now has a common discussion body of the officials mentioned above—a discussion organ led by the governor that strives for more effective cooperation as well as an increase in the planned character and uniformity of measures taken by a provincial government and the specialists. Permanent members of the discussion body are the manager in charge of construction, the head of public roads and waterways, the head of the surveying office, and the agricultural engineer. But other officials can be invited to its meetings, as can representatives of private organizations and economic experts.

It should be mentioned that a decision by a provincial government may generally be appealed before the Supreme Administrative Court. In some instances a complaint is lodged with the State Council, the court for disciplinary cases against government officials, or a court of appeals.

Law Enforcement Officers in Rural Areas. Provinces, as mentioned, are divided into counties, the significance of which became minimal after the office of county police commissioner was abolished in 1945; counties are divided into districts for rural law enforcement. The general administrative authority in such a district is the rural law enforcement officer (nimismies), who, in large districts, has an assistant. In 1965 there were two hundred forty-two rural law enforcement districts in Finland, which indicates that many such districts include several rural communes. All sorts of duties are performed by rural law enforcement officers; the duties cover police work and administration of justice, as well as actual administrative implementation. As police chief, the rural law enforcement officer ensures the maintenance of general order and security and directs police activity; subordinate to him are rural police constables. In the area of administration of law, he acts as the official prosecutor in a county court; in the sphere of implementation and distraint, he ensures that sentences and punishment are carried out and that taxes in arrears as well as other obligations to the community are discharged. A provincial government may entrust rural law enforcement officers with many other administrative tasks. In general, they execute orders from the provincial government and provide it with necessary information about local conditions and needs. Rural law enforcement officers should also display initiative in coordinating administration in different fields through cooperation with other such officers as well as with other state and communal officials.

City Administration. The general administrative authority for the state in cities, which lie outside the division into rural law enforcement districts, is the bench of magistrates.[1] This is a collegial body composed of a mayor and magistrates that handles general administrative matters, acts as distraining officer, and considers questions concerning city planning and construction. The bench of magistrates also has some judicial power: it can consider violations in the areas of "public order and economic matters" and it can hand down sentences for breaches of police order. In small cities the bench of magistrates and the city court have a common chairman and common members, but in larger cities the bench of magistrates has its own chairman, called a municipal mayor. A mayor is appointed by the Supreme Court from three names put forth by the city council. The election of magistrates is carried out by the council. In towns, corresponding to the bench of magistrates, a disciplinary court acts as the general authority. In cities a bailiff is the distraining officer; a city attorney is the official prosecutor before the bench of magistrates and before the city court. The police establishment maintains order.

Language Division. A consideration of territorial administrative divisions should include linguistic divisions, which, in a bilingual nation such as Finland, are very important. Communes are classified as unilingual or bilingual. A commune is unilingual if its entire population speaks the same language (Finnish or Swedish) or if the minority linguistic group accounts for less than 10 percent of the population; in other cases, or if the number of people speaking a second language is at least five thousand, a commune is bilingual. In 1965 forty-four of the nation's communes were Swedish-speaking and forty-seven bilingual. The working language of an official area smaller than a commune is determined in the same way: a self-governing area, which includes a number of communes, is considered unilingual if composed of communes speaking the same language. If the area includes communes which are Swedish-speaking and Finnish-speaking, or bilingual, the official language is considered to be the language of each commune in question. A change in the language relationship in a commune is a rigid matter; legislation stipulates that a bilingual cannot be transformed into a unilingual commune unless the number of people speaking the second language has dropped to eight percent. Every tenth year the State Council reviews the division on the basis of official statistics.

According to the Form of Government Act, every citizen is

1. Cities founded in 1959 or later are exceptions (laws of January 23, 1959, no. 20, and January 23, 1959, no. 21).

permitted to use his mother tongue, Finnish or Swedish, in court and before an administrative authority in pursuance of his own business or in a matter on which he is being heard. When turning to public authority otherwise in unilingual areas, the official language is that of the area in question, whereas in bilingual areas the language will be either Finnish or Swedish. Documents are prepared in the official language or, in bilingual areas, in the language used by the client. In the former instance, state officials of higher rank must append a translation if requested to do so by the client. Announcements and communiqués from the state and from communes are published in unilingual districts in the appropriate language and in bilingual districts in both languages.

The official language for officials is regulated separately. State officials in unilingual areas use the language of the area; state officials in areas that are bilingual or that include Swedish-speaking and Finnish-speaking, or bilingual, communes use the language of the majority in the area. In matters related to a document, however, the language of the document must be used.

Organization of Secondary Organs. Joined to the normal line organization of administration at various levels are a large number of secondary organs to perform staff duties: committees and commissions, discussion bodies, boards, and councils. Some of these assist officials in administrative activity and execute various planning, explanatory, and research tasks; others, in addition to those duties, handle and are responsible for administrative tasks given them on the basis of their own independent authority, which in some cases may be very broad indeed.

Forming their own group among these organs are the temporary committees and commissions set up by the State Council or the ministries. Their task is to investigate or prepare specific matters and to draw up proposals concerning them; when their work is finished, they pass out of existence. Committees and commissions are frequently established for a great variety of tasks: in 1965 alone, eleven printed and one hundred thirteen mimeographed committee reports were catalogued. Many committees and commissions execute preparatory work for legislation and make proposals in their reports concerning new laws, decrees, and State Council decisions. But the committee institution in Finland has not developed so far as, for example, that in Sweden.

There are great differences in terms of number of committee members, types of committees, and scope of activity. Some committees concern themselves with technical details of decisions already reached, while others prepare extensive plans for sweeping reforms in various areas. Since committees are generally not bound in their work by exact instructions when established, they have in the latter instance great power in the choice of alternative solutions. In schematic form, the different stages of work are: general familiarization with the problem and preliminary discussion; search for necessary information and explanations; detailed consideration of the matter and adoption of a position on the basis of material at hand and possibly on the basis of memoranda drawn up by a secretary; examination of a draft report drawn up by the secretary and final approval of a report. A completed report is left with the minister in whose area the matter falls; the committee or commission has done its work, and it becomes the duty of the State Council to initiate action.

Especially in the central administration, there are tens, perhaps even hundreds, of secondary organs similar to committees but permanent: committees, discussion bodies, boards, and councils. In April 1962 there were forty-three committees, commissions, and discussion bodies which had been set up either directly by the ministry for social affairs or on its recommendation, of which twenty-five were intended to be permanent; corresponding figures for the defense ministry at the same time were twenty-seven and thirteen. The composition and duties of some are determined in detail by decrees and regulations, but others function on the basis of a brief statement by the State Council or the ministry that establishes them, as in the case of temporary committees. These sorts of secondary organs, linked to the ministry of education, for example, are the state's scientific committees and the state boards on art, the council on universities, the state council for sports, the state board for work among youth, the Finnish department of the Nordic cultural committee, Finland's UNESCO committee, the state board for adult education, and the committee on school affairs. In the field covered by the ministry of communications and public works there are, for example, the employment council, the council on communications, the council for vocational guidance, the state building committee, an advisory body on matters related to job placement, and the water power commission.

Separate mention should be made of the economic councils, established by the State Council, which have existed since the 1920's under various names and with a changing membership. Their task has been to assist the entire State Council: they follow the development of economic conditions, prepare economic policy measures, and transmit proposals and statements to the State Council. In 1933 the government wanted to establish a permanent thirty-member economic council, but Parliament reacted unfavorably to this new "organ with constitutional significance"; the legislative proposal was defeated. In 1954 a decree was issued concerning an economic council, and in 1966 its position became stabilized in law. The council includes a chairman, as well as at least ten and no more than fourteen members. It must have at least two ministers, one of whom is the council chairman, and representatives from the economic organizations, institutes, or offices which best represent the field. With the exception of government representatives, the chairman and members are appointed for two years at a time. Another similar organ with far-reaching powers is the state planning commission.

Membership in these organs consists primarily of representatives from the state administrative offices and from interest organizations in different fields. The center of gravity varies in accordance with the action goals. A discussion body can be considered the normal type; its activity is merely of an explanatory and advisory nature, and consideration by it is not a prerequisite for resolution of a matter. The significance and effectiveness of activity depend a good deal on the official connected with the secondary organ. But there are also committees and boards which are charged with certain administrative duties and which exercise independent decision-making power: examples are the state's scientific committees and boards on art. In an extreme case, a committee at the level of central administration begins to remind one of a central office subordinate to a ministry.

From a general point of view, it is hoped that the organization of secondary organs will achieve a number of goals in state administration: it can help in bringing about cooperation among the administrative offices, in providing the administration with outside expertise handily and cheaply, in determining at an early date the positions of important interest groups and in accommodating them, and in increasing the authority of governmental decisions by making interest organizations partially responsible for the decisions.

Indirect Administration. Thus far only organization of direct state administration—administrative machinery formed by the state's own officials—has been touched upon. But, as mentioned earlier, when speaking of pressure groups there has been an effort over the last few decades to join to the administrative machinery various private bodies which practice administrative activity in a field carefully delineated by legislation. So that these bodies can perform their duties, the state entrusts them with public power and extends economic support, at the same time reserving the right of supervision of their activity. This organization of indirect administration, developed unsystematically over time, is very diffuse; it is not always easy to distinguish administrative activity carried out within this framework from private activity on one hand and direct state administration on the other.

THE CIVIL SERVICE

Individuals serving the state, generally called civil servants, can be divided into many groups. The core of the civil service consists of regular employees, who occupy permanent posts established by decree and who enjoy the rights of full-fledged civil servants. Employees not on a regular basis include the state's special and temporary civil servants, called fortuitous assistants, as well as individuals acting as substitutes. In terms of economic rights and the right to tenure, the latter groups are in a weaker position when compared with the regular civil service corps (the two categories included a total of about one hundred thousand employees in 1969). The following is primarily a consideration of the position of regular civil servants; a second approach could be based on education and position. In his study of the organization of civil servants, Väinö Luoma has divided the civil service into four groups on the basis of education: regular civil servants, service personnel, academic professionals, and special professionals.[2]

Appointment to a Post. Very explicit procedures for recruiting civil servants are set forth in laws and decrees, but in spite of this recruiting remains a question which evokes constant discussion and disagreement. The main principle is, of course, that a post should be filled by the person best able to handle it, in other words, by a person

2. Väinö Luoma, *Valtion virkamiesten järjestäytyminen Suomessa*, (Turku, 1962), I, 25–31.

who is most capable in terms of formal competence and substantive suitability. Conflicts arise from the fact that it is not easy to weigh the merits of applicants, and political factors are also related to the appointment of civil servants; it is particularly tempting for party-oriented officials making appointments to put party merits on an even keel with or even above substantive competence.

When considering the qualifications of an individual seeking a state post, attention must be given both to his formal competence and to other qualities considered essential for success in the post. The most common formal conditions for eligibility are Finnish citizenship (with a few rare exceptions), a good reputation, minimum age (generally twenty-one), appropriate studies and examinations, and linguistic skill. For many posts the necessary tests are carefully defined, whereas for other posts, even the highest ones, examinations are not a condition of eligibility. The nature and level of the required examinations vary, of course, with the character of the job. In Finland, as in Sweden, juridical examinations have long been the most common conditions of eligibility for high general administrative positions; personnel in the state administration have thus been strongly oriented in a legalistic direction.[3] However, as the administrative machinery expands, it appears that the role of individuals with a vocational education in different fields is increasing and that the structure of the civil service corps is slowly changing. There has been an attempt, especially after the Second World War, to expand the number of posts for individuals who have completed examinations in the social science fields. Professional expertise within the central administration is overwhelmingly concentrated in the central offices, whereas rapporteurs in the ministries above them are generally required to have legal training; this does not, of course, hold true in fields where central administration rests in a ministry. According to paragraph 29 of the Form of Government Act, the president has the power to grant exemptions from legal provisions, provided that the authority to make such an exception is embodied in a law. The State Council is empowered by paragraph 85 of the Form of Government Act to make exemptions concerning eligibility requirements prescribed by decree, except in the case of legal positions.

Formal eligibility requirements determine the minimum obligatory level before an appointee can be considered for a post. He must also

3. See, for example, Markku Kiviniemi and Kettil Bruun, "Suomen ja Ruotsin virkamieseliitti," *Sosiologia*, 1, no. 4 (1964), 162.

possess certain other qualities, more difficult to define in general terms, which make him suitable for the job; these factors are, in part, closely tied to the eligibility requirements listed above.

The basis for comparison of individuals seeking a job and possessing the necessary qualifications is found in paragraph 86 of the Form of Government Act, in the bases for promotion (skill, ability, and demonstrated civic responsibility). It is difficult to know exactly what is contained in these general statements: skill probably means intellectual competence as demonstrated through examinations and other achievements; ability probably means natural talents; civic responsibility probably means an irreproachable life and meritorious achievement in social activity.

Posts are usually filled through application, so that the official declaring a post open makes an appointment directly after the deadline for applications has passed or so that another, higher, official makes the appointment on the basis of a nomination or recommendation. An appointment based on a nomination occurs when an official who has declared a job open selects the three best qualified applicants and places them in a certain order, after which a higher official appoints one of them. The recommendation procedure differs from the above in that only one name is proposed for appointment to a post; in this case the official with appointive power is not bound by the recommendation. Concerning the official who makes an appointment, in general the president appoints individuals to the most important state posts; the Supreme Courts fill posts in the judiciary which are not subject to presidential appointment; the State Council and lower authorities, such as central offices and provincial governments, fill the other, less prestigious posts.

Political Merit. In the contemporary world, it is hardly possible in any country to avoid completely the spoils system, which became so well known years ago in the United States, and to divorce appointments completely from party politics. Politicization of administration long ago became part, as a general phenomenon, of the expansion of political democracy. In Finland, especially after the Second World War, it has been noted that the highest administrative posts—with respect to which parties have interests that need watching over—are often filled with an eye to an individual's party affiliation and his merits in the sphere of party politics. Complaints about this situation naturally come primarily from circles which have been excluded from leading policy positions. This is not, however, a new phenomenon in Finnish political life; politics in administration existed earlier, too. In part it has been only a question of change in the political and social structure of the highest civil servants, which is an understandable reflection of a corresponding change in structure that has occurred within Finland's political leadership. With respect to civil servants with permanent appointments the development proceeds more slowly. Probably no one can deny that party politics have also increased in administration after the Second World War, a phenomenon most clearly seen in the highest administrative posts of the state, which are filled by the president or by the State Council. Such appointments include, for example, governors, heads of central offices, the State Council's highest rapporteurs, members of the board of directors of the Bank of Finland, and positions on the boards of some large state establishments. It is more difficult to say to what degree political factors are influential in appointments made at the base of the administrative pyramid.

An attempt is made to give state administrative posts to members of one's own party as a reward for party service, and in part so that administrative activity can through their efforts be scrutinized. But, as Jansson has noted,[4] the politicization of high state posts does not always have to mean that an appointee lacks the substantive competence required for the appointment. On one hand, a normal civil service career may be part of his political activity, and on the other hand, political experience can in some posts nicely supplement experience which is purely administrative. It is, of course, a different matter if an official with appointive powers regularly gives preference to "politicians." In that case deserving civil servants have less chance for promotion, which in turn has an impact over time on the level of the civil service corps.

Salary and Retirement. The salary of state employees is regulated by law and decree. The core of a civil servant's salary is base pay. In accord with job responsibility and amount of work, as well as the skill and ability required for a job, base pay positions are divided into wage classes so that the lower positions are grouped in A-wage classes, of which there are thirty, and the higher positions in B-wage classes, of which there are eight. During the first half of 1969, the lowest annual base pay in the former group was 6,900 marks (there are

4. Jan-Magnus Jansson, *Frihet och jämlikhet* (Lovisa, 1952), pp. 460–461.

roughly 4.2 marks per dollar), and the the highest 23,700 marks; in the latter group corresponding figures were 38,000 marks and 65,800 marks. There are, in addition, twenty contractual wage classes. Some state posts which otherwise would be difficult to fill with individuals having the necessary high qualifications (primarily due to competition from the private sector) have been put on a contractual wage basis; in this case agreement is reached between the state and the appointee concerning wages. The total salary of civil servants in the A-wage classes can rise considerably above the base pay due to age increments and high cost of living supplements. Employees in these classes are given onc age increment at a time, after three, six, nine, twelve, and fifteen years of service; they may also receive a special supplement to cover relatively high costs of living in some communities. Some civil servants, moreover, are able to earn overtime as well as a personal wage increase.

The state competes with private employers for available labor, and it naturally seeks to staff its posts with individuals who are as competent as possible. Its position on the labor market has, however, been deteriorating due to the rigidity of the civil service wage system and the relatively low wages paid, particularly at the top levels. Only to a limited degree is it possible to avoid rigidity through the above-mentioned procedures of contractual wages and wage increases, and the fact that a civil servant has job security does not seem to have compensated fully for low wages—"a civil servant's loaf of bread is long but narrow." The discrepancy between wages paid for public and private work was narrowed in 1962, when there was a shift from a unified wage classification to the present A and B classes and when the salaries of some groups of civil servants, particularly at the highest levels, were raised substantially.

In accordance with a new pension law which came into force early in 1967, an individual having a contract with the state or serving in some comparable fashion is entitled to an old-age and disability pension. General requirements for receiving an old-age pension are that the beneficiary have at least four months of pension time (the time that a beneficiary, after reaching age twenty-three, has been continually—for at least four months—in uninterrupted service), that he be of pension age (normally sixty-three), and that his service be over. The amount of the pension is dependent on the length of pension time and on the size of salary received during the last years of service.

The Right to Tenure. One feature of the administrative systems in Finland and other Western democracies is that civil servants enjoy rather firm protection against dismissal from their jobs. However, with the general good in mind, it is not possible to guarantee civil servants an unconditional right to tenure; this is determined by the kind of letter of appointment that is issued for a particular post. A civil servant, for example, an officer, who is appointed by an "open letter" can be relieved of his post when the public interest so requires by a decision of the president. A civil servant appointed by a "job letter" (for example, police, rural law enforcement officers, and some other lower civil servants) can be relieved of his job by the official who made the appointment, when there is cause, and the civil servant may also lose his job through disciplinary procedure. An appointee to a regular state post usually receives a "letter of patent," which makes his dismissal much more difficult. He may be relieved of his job through disciplinary measures if, through his activity or his behavior either on or off the job or through dereliction of duty, it becomes clear that he is not worthy of the trust and respect demanded of his position; he may also be relieved of his job, through special administrative procedure, if unable to work. The right to tenure is most easily secured by judges. A court decision can oblige a judge to resign, even before retirement age in the event that he has for some reason or another lost his ability to work. All those belonging to the above-mentioned groups can, of course, lose their jobs by a court sentence for a crime; they are, furthermore, obliged to resign upon reaching the mandatory age for retirement, which generally is sixty-seven.

JUDICIARY

According to paragraph 5 of the Form of Government Act, Finnish citizens are equal before the law. This equality is sometimes imperfectly realized, but as a primary principle of the Finnish conception of rights it is an integral part of the permanent goals of the administration of law. Realization of the goal depends a great deal on the structure of the court system, on court procedures, and on the activity of judges.

Position of the Judiciary. Through the courts an attempt is made to provide citizens with legal protection. General provisions of law are applied to individual, concrete cases; and decisions, which are in consonance with the legal system created through legislation, are binding. In terms of the primary importance of judicial administration, an attempt is made through fundamental law to guarantee the judiciary independence from political organs—from Parliament, from the government, and from other officials—and from political change. It is expressly stated in the Form of Government Act that judicial power is exercised by independent courts. General higher and lower courts, as well as special courts, are regulated by law, and a Finnish citizen may be tried only in that court which has legal jurisdiction in the case. Courts must be permanent; temporary courts, whose task might be to consider certain individual cases or to try certain individuals, are forbidden (an exception to this principle was the establishment of a court for war responsibles after the Second World War). An effort has been made to strengthen the independence of the judiciary through the right of tenure for judges.

Judicial power in Finland is exercised by 1) general courts, 2) special courts, and 3) certain administrative officials, provincial courts, and the Supreme Administrative Court. The activity of courts and officials in the third group falls within the area of administrative law.

General Courts. General courts, where legal matters are regularly considered, handle civil and criminal matters and include, as courts of first instance, county courts in the countryside and municipal courts in the cities. Courts of appeals are courts of second instance, and the Supreme Court is the court of highest instance.

Lower courts in the countryside are organized so that the nation is divided (as of 1969) for work by county courts into seventy-three circuits, which are further divided into one hundred fifty-eight assizes. A county court holds sessions, or court, in the territory of a circuit's different assizes twice a year (autumn and spring courts of assizes) or more often (interim courts). The court is formed by a circuit judge and a jury composed of seven to twelve jurors. The judge is legally trained and is appointed by the Supreme Court. A jury is set up in every assize; any resident of the area who is at least twenty-five years of age and eligible for positions of communal trust may be elected to the jury. A vacancy is filled by the county court, for a three-year term, from a list of three names put forward by the communal council or a meeting of communal representatives. A jury of laymen, representing a knowledge of local conditions and "the healthy mind of a farmer," is designed to be of assistance and support to the judge, but it has not been considered desirable to entrust the jury with final decision-making power. The opinion held by the judge becomes the decision of the county court; a jury's viewpoint wins only in the event that it is a unanimous position against the judge.

There are several exceptions to the general rule that each city has its own municipal court. When an effort was made in the late 1950's to ease the formation of new cities, it was ruled that a new city does not necessarily have to set up a municipal court, but that it may continue as part of a circuit. Under certain circumstances this procedure may also be followed in older cities. The mayor is chairman of the municipal court, which includes the necessary number of magistrates. It has already been mentioned that as a rule the bench of magistrates and the municipal court are either wholly or partially made up of the same people; in some of the largest cities, however, they are completely divorced from each other. Of the magistrates, some are legally trained individuals (legal magistrates) and others are merely municipal magistrates. In cities where there are so many cases to be considered that it is impossible to deal with them in general session, a municipal court may be divided into departments with three judges constituting a quorum. Activity by a municipal court is, practically speaking, uninterrupted; when necessary it meets several times a week.

Above the lower courts are the courts of appeal, which may overrule a decision or sentence of a municipal or county court but which may also, as a court of first instance, consider some criminal matters. Furthermore, it is their duty to provide general supervision of the activity of lower courts. There are a total of four courts of appeal. The first was founded in Turku in 1623, the second in Vaasa in 1776, and a third in Viipuri in 1839. Since 1945 the latter has been in Kuopio as a court of appeals for Eastern Finland. In 1952 a court of appeals was set up in Helsinki, one section of which also functions as the supreme military tribunal. A court of appeals includes a president and justices, named by the president of the Republic. Other civil servants include a secretary, a public prosecutor, and prosecuting attorneys. Matters are considered in part in plenary session and in part (and primarily) in three-member sections.

Highest judicial power in legal matters is exercised by the Supreme Court. It can on appeal overturn rulings by courts of appeal and, in some cases, decisions of special courts. It has many other duties, such as supervision of the law as exercised by judges and distraining officials, the filling of certain positions within the judiciary, and the making of recommendations and statements regarding legislative questions. If the president is brought to trial for treason, or high treason, the matter is considered by the Supreme Court, which includes a president and, at the moment, twenty-three permanent justices, who must be fair-minded and legally trained and who must possess skill and experience in judicial work. The Supreme Court also functions, as a rule, in sections; only cases of the utmost importance in terms of principle are resolved in plenary session. The preparation of matters is handled by rapporteurs and court secretaries.

The normal procedure for consideration of a certain matter in a general court is that it begins in a lower court; a decision by a lower court may be appealed in a court of appeals, whose decision may in turn be appealed in the Supreme Court. There are, however, exceptions to this procedure. As mentioned, some matters are initiated directly in the proper court of appeals. The right of appeal before the Supreme Court is, moreover, not a general right; it is limited with respect to matters of little importance.

Special Courts. Along with general courts special courts exist to deal with designated matters in special areas. The high court of impeachment considers charges against a member of the State Council or the chancellor of justice, or a member of the Supreme Court or the Supreme Administrative Court, for illegality in the performance of his work. The president of the Supreme Court is chairman of the high court of impeachment; its members include the president of the Supreme Administrative Court, presidents of the courts of appeal, a law professor elected for four years by the law faculty of the University of Helsinki, and six other people chosen for four-year terms by Parliament's electors. A decision by the high court of impeachment is final; pardon can be granted only on the basis of a recommendation made by the court itself.

Other special courts include land partition courts (civil matters arising from land partition), military courts (criminal matters concerning personnel in the defense forces), the insurance court (conflicts concerning compensation for accidents occurring on the job), labor courts (civil matters involving mediation of labor contracts), water resources courts and the supreme court for water resources (civil and criminal matters deriving from the application of laws on water resources), and the prison court (matters concerning the placement of dangerous recidivists in special penal institutions and matters concerning crimes by youthful offenders).

Prosecution and Implementation. The nation's highest prosecutor, and the superior of other prosecutors, is the chancellor of justice. He has the right to take charge of a case in which there has already been an indictment, and he acts as prosecutor in the Supreme Court and in the high court of impeachment. A provincial prosecutor, and the superior of the general prosecutors in his area of jurisdiction, is the police inspector. Acting as prosecutor in a municipal court is the city attorney, in a county court the rural law enforcement officer, and in a court of appeals the public prosecutor. Special prosecutors include the official prosecutors of military courts, as well as the public prosecutor for the national board of customs. The ombudsman may prosecute in any court a case involving an offense committed by a civil servant in office. He may act as prosecutor in the high court of impeachment only in the event that a charge has arisen from a decision by Parliament.

General administrative officials are responsible for implementation of decisions and sentences. Punishment is carried out under the supervision of a provincial government, a bench of magistrates, and a rural law enforcement officer, as well as prison officials. The prison administration establishment is directed by the ministry of justice and, more specifically, by the latter's department of prison administration. In civil matters the office responsible for implementation in the countryside is the provincial government, in the cities the bench of magistrates; the distraining officer is the rural law enforcement officer and the city bailiff or some other individual designated to perform this duty.

Courts of Administrative Law. The organization of general law has been dealt with. Along with this organization there is machinery for administrative law, which seeks to protect citizens against public power—against decisions and measures of administrative officials. The question of developing this sort of legal protection has become even more important as the state has begun to an increasing degree to restrict through regulatory and protective measures an individual's freedom of activity and his life in general.

In contemporary administrative activity an effort is made to provide effective legal protection in many different ways, and so the system as a whole is rather complicated and difficult to explain. A basic distinction may be made between measures which are preventive, taken in advance, and measures which are repressive, or post-factum. Included in the first group are, for example, the binding of administration to well-defined forms of procedure, concern for maintaining a high-level civil service corps, permission for an individual involved in some subject to be heard during consideration of administrative matters, obligation to provide a rationale for decisions, and public access to general documents. The repressive machinery for providing legal protection includes measures that assist in rectifying an erroneous decision already made by an official and that help provide compensation for damage done. In essence, it is post-factum review occurring in the form of legal administrative activity that is generally the result of an administrative law complaint. There has been a strong effort in recent decades to develop this system; a significant step was the 1950 law concerning appeal in administrative matters, which made it possible to protest all decisions taken by administrative officials unless expressly forbidden to do so by law or decree.

The organization of the exercise of administrative law is rather complicated, and a detailed examination is neither possible nor necessary. In Finland there is a mixed system; complaints concerning decisions by administrative officials are considered by both the officials themselves and by general courts and special courts of administrative law. But development has clearly been in a direction away from internal control by the administrative machinery and toward more effective court control. At the highest level, exercise of administrative law is for the most part the responsibility of courts established expressly for this purpose, whereas consideration of complaints at lower levels is divided between administrative officials, special courts, and general courts.

A turning point was the establishment in 1918 of the Supreme Administrative Court as holder of highest judicial power in matters dealing with complaints concerning administrative law. Its authority is by nature general; all administrative law complaints not expressly reserved for consideration by other officials may reach the Court for resolution at the highest level. Complaints concerning decisions of the State Council, ministries, central offices, and other higher administrative authorities are directed to the Supreme Administrative Court unless special regulations provide that they be directed to some other official. Tax complaints, in particular, provide this Court, as well as lower officials charged with administration of the law, with much work. In addition, the Court supervises the exercise of law by lower officials in the sphere of administrative law. The Supreme Administrative Court includes a president and the necessary number of members (twenty-one in 1969). At least half the members must possess the qualifications of a judge; five members constitute a quorum. The Supreme Administrative Court generally carries out its work in sections. Rapporteurs and administrative secretaries handle presentation of the various matters.

The division of labor between the State Council and the Supreme Administrative Court is generally arranged so that the latter resolves legal questions and the former resolves questions whose outcome depends primarily upon consideration of appropriateness of a decision or measure. Complaints concerning matters of appointment, whether of a legal nature or not, are handled by the State Council; in these matters, however, the major question usually concerns consideration of the suitability of individuals seeking a particular post. Other complaints, too, are resolved at the highest level, sometimes by the State Council, sometimes by the Supreme Court.

The special court of administrative law is the supreme court for disciplinary cases against civil servants, which, at the highest level, considers complaints concerning loss of a job by a civil servant through disciplinary action. It includes five members, appointed for five years by the president of the Republic; the work they do in this court is incidental to their regular work—the number of cases is very small.

The avenues of appeal at lower levels are much more involved than in general matters concerning administration of law. The 1950 law on appeals distinguishes between three groups of administrative officials: 1) the State Council and its ministries, 2) higher administrative authorities (central offices, provincial governments, consistories, and other officials directly subordinate to the State Council), and 3) lower administrative officials, or officials subordinate to the higher administrative authorities. A legal complaint can be made concerning a decision of the State Council and of a ministry, whereas either a legal complaint or a complaint on the grounds of appropriateness can be made as the result of a decision by a higher or lower administrative authority. Only consideration of legal complaints is viewed as actual exercise of administrative law. The main rule (to which there are many exceptions) is that a complaint about a lower administrative authority be made to that higher administrative authority to whom the official who made the decision is subordinate; complaints concerning decisions of a higher authority, as well as decisions of the State Council and ministries, are usually made before the Supreme Administrative Court.

In this system, central offices and provincial courts occupy a key position in the sphere of lower-level administrative law. Prior to 1955 there were no special authorities in Finland for this task; it was handled within the framework of the ordinary organization of administration. But in 1955 a law established provincial courts in provincial governments, the task of which is to investigate and resolve administrative law complaints, as well as other administrative law matters under the jurisdiction of a provincial government and administrative matters assigned to them by decree for consideration. Large provincial governments have a number of provincial courts. In organizational terms they are not real courts; they are only departments of a provincial government, and their members are not in the position of judges. The chairman of this three-member court may be the governor, the provincial counselor, or the provincial treasurer; other members include the provincial assessor and the civil servant in the provincial government whose duty it is to present a matter under consideration to the provincial government. Legal matters are considered collegially, following court procedure; a decision may be appealed, generally in the Supreme Administrative Court.

X Communal Self-Government

THE DEVELOPMENT OF SELF-GOVERNMENT

The Basis of Self-Government. Well-developed local self-government is a fundamental part of the political system in Finland, as well as in other Nordic countries. Organized political life in these countries clearly began to develop on this basis. The roots of communal self-government extend all the way back to the tribal period in Finnish history. Even before Swedish rule came to Finland, a primitive kind of administrative organization had developed in the form of county assizes, where, in addition to legal matters, general administrative questions were considered. In time these questions were shifted more and more to the administrative machinery of the state and to parish meetings; the latter had the power to resolve matters concerning local congregations and were set up little by little in their own fashion without provisions of written law. Only in the seventeenth and eighteenth centuries was a conscious effort made to develop church administration of the parish through legislation. In this way it also bore the imprint of a peasant aristocracy, because only landowners were permitted to participate in a parish meeting. Parish meetings considered, in addition to actual congregational matters, many questions related to communal administration of the time, such as tasks connected with care for the poor, establishment and maintenance of seed banks, fire protection, education, and health and sanitation. The decree of 1852 concerning care for the poor was a significant step forward in the development of self-government in that every congregation was thereby obliged to establish a board for care of the poor, directed by a parish priest; the decree set forth more precise provisions than existed earlier concerning taxation for the collection of funds to cover expenditures related to care for the poor.

Another milestone in development was the 1858 decree on primary school education obliging congregations to establish beginning (two-year) schools as needed and which made possible the setting up of primary schools.

Over time, with growing demands, it became necessary to separate local secular from local church administration. In 1864 a decree concerning communal administration in the countryside was approved in the Diet, and it was ratified by the Russian emperor the following year. The law stipulated that the area of local self-government would be a commune, whose territory was formed by a congregation. Decision-making power in communal matters rested with the communal meeting, which was formed by all residents of the commune having the right to vote. Some authority could also be given to a council, but during the period of Russian rule councils were set up only in a few dozen communes; the executive organ was the communal board. Features of peasant aristocracy were preserved in communal administration. Since servants subject to wage regulation, vagabonds, and most women were disenfranchised, and since votes were weighted according to one's tax classification, decision-making power was retained by rich farmers. In 1898 a new communal law was passed that, for the most part, was similar to the previous one.

Communal administration of cities during the period of Swedish rule began to take shape in the middle of the fourteenth century, following German models, when King Magnus Eriksson issued a city law concerning the administration, construction, and planning of cities; for a long time this law, together with special rights granted cities, remained the basis of the privileged position enjoyed by cities. The general municipal meeting, as well as the council formed by mayors and magistrates, constituted the organ of administration and justice; later the council began to be called a bench of magistrates. In 1619 Gustavus Adolphus issued a decree concerning the administration of cities, but it was not until 1873 that a thorough legislative reform was achieved, when the estates approved a decree on communal administration in cities.

Toward the end of the period of autonomy, thorough legislative changes were planned for the administration of cities as well as of rural communes; it became possible to achieve these changes after the Russian Revolution. In 1917 communal laws for rural communes and cities were quickly passed; provisions in the laws were more detailed than before and more in accordance with the demands of the time, but they were, nonetheless, constructed on the old foundation. Universal and equal suffrage came into force, and the council institution became obligatory. The commune and congregation were made territorially independent of each other by a law of 1925 concerning a change in communal division. The 1917 communal laws were in force with only a few changes until 1948, when a new law touching on all forms of communal government was passed; it attempted to bring together the previously scattered provisions on communal administration, and at the same time it constituted an effort to make more uniform, insofar as possible, administration of cities and rural communes.

ORGANIZATION OF COMMUNAL ADMINISTRATION

Communal Forms. The Finnish system of local self-government includes three general communal forms: cities (kaupungit), towns (kauppalat), and rural communes (maalaiskunnat). They differ somewhat in administrative organization as well as in terms of number and character of tasks. Cities bear the greatest number of duties and economic burdens, but they are granted certain advantages not enjoyed by other communal forms. In 1969 there were 49 cities, 29 towns, and 443 rural communes in Finland. Helsinki is the largest city in population (497,000 residents) and Uusikaarlepyy the smallest (1,200 residents). Espoo is the largest town (population 75,000); and Helsinki is the largest of the rural communes (population 57,000). The State Council decides whether to set up or abolish a rural commune, whereas the president of the Republic makes that decision with regard to the formation of cities and towns. The State Council has the power of decision in matters concerning a change in communal division. After 1905, and for over fifty years, no new cities were established primarily because of the fact that towns, fearful of economic burdens and resultant increases in the level of taxation, opposed a shift to this communal form. New cities were granted certain easements in laws which came into force in 1959, and the result was that many large towns undertook steps to achieve city rights.

In addition to these communal forms, there are also a number of special communes, self-governing communities set up to accomplish limited tasks of a special nature. Examples include population center communities and assessment communes: the former are population centers located in the territory of and subordinate to rural communes, and they have been given a certain amount of independent administration in order to manage the internal affairs of a community (this communal form was found to be inappropriate, however, and by 1956 all these population center communities had been abolished). The practical significance of assessment communes is very little today, and there have already been several attempts to abolish them through legislative measures: an assessment commune includes owners of land and of establishments within a delineated territory of assessment, and its only organ is the assessment meeting, which considers minor economic matters. The communal law permits the establishment of communal districts within communes, but thus far no such organization has arisen through a special law or a decree, as required by the communal law. It had also been possible at one time to set up within the territory of rural communes dependent towns, whose relationship to the commune was roughly the same as that of the population center communities. The communal law in force today no longer recognizes this communal form; Ikaalinen however, was permitted to continue its activity as a dependent town.

Membership in a Commune. The basic membership of a commune consists of natural persons whose legal place of residence is the commune; in other words, individuals whose dwellings and homes are located in the commune and who are thus on the census registers. As full-fledged residents, they enjoy both the rights belonging to members of a commune and the accompanying burdensome duties. But juristic persons (companies, associations, institutions, and foundations) may also become members of a commune on the same basis. Furthermore, every natural or juristic person who owns or controls real property or who practices a trade or business in the commune is a communal member. Under these conditions, another commune and the state can also be members of a commune. A natural person may be a basic member in only one commune, but otherwise he, like a juristic person, can be part of the membership of two or even more communes.

Of the rights possessed solely by basic members, communal suffrage and eligibility for election to communal positions of trust should be mentioned. Closely connected with these rights is the duty to accept positions of communal trust. Among the rights and obligations shared by all members of a commune are, on one hand, the right to protest decisions of certain administrative organs of the commune and, on the other hand, the duty to pay taxes to the commune. In connection with payment of taxes, persons not included in the basic membership are probably aware of membership only through payment of taxes; they may in other respects have little or nothing to do with the commune.

Principles of Activity. Finland's Form of Government Act strives to achieve the principle of democracy in the activity of self-governing communities and seeks to bring all enfranchised citizens of an area into real self-government. It is, therefore, necessary to organize communal administration so that the impetus for a commune's activity comes from below, starting with the membership. As mentioned previously, in the 1917 communal laws there was a shift from direct democracy to a representative system, in accordance with which the members of a self-governing community elect a representative body which functions as a commune's decision-making organ and which determines the composition of executive organs. Members of a commune follow and supervise the activity of the representative body and it, in turn, supervises the activity of executive authorities. What prevails, therefore, is the same relationship of responsibility that exists in the political organization of the state.

The principle of democracy and responsibility in communal self-government is also emphasized by the fact that the administrative machinery of a commune is overwhelmingly in the hands of officials of trust, who perform their tasks as a civic duty. There are certain special features to such confidential tasks: an official of trust is always elected for a specified period of time; he is obliged to accept the work even though it may be contrary to his wishes unless he is prevented from doing so on legal grounds; he can lose his position of trust during a period of tenure only by a court decision; he does not receive an actual wage for his services, but he does receive some remuneration, such as payment for meetings. Some of the grounds for refusal regulated by law are unconditional, whereas others are subject to interpretation. In the former case, a candidate for a position of trust has an unconditional right to refuse to accept a public task; in the latter case, it is up to the communal council to decide whether or not the rationale advanced will be accepted.

Compared with these officials of trust, the number of communal civil servants is very small, especially in the rural communes. The civil servants differ in that they are selected for an indefinite period of time to a salaried position, usually their primary means of livelihood, following the submission of an application.

The communal institution of representation that exercises decision-making power is the communal council and the central executive organ is the communal board. Administrative tasks are also given to special committees, as well as to individual civil servants. Judicial power is exercised by a bench of magistrates in a city, by a disciplinary court in a town.

Communal Elections. The number of communal mandates fluctuates according to population as determined by a commune's census register. The smallest number of members on a council, in communes with no more than a thousand residents, is thirteen; the greatest number, in communes with over four hundred thousand residents, is seventy-seven. A council is chosen through direct and proportional elections, which are held every fourth year throughout the nation on the first Sunday and the following Monday of October. In general, every member of the commune who is a Finnish citizen, has reached age twenty before the election year, and is either on a commune's census register or eligible to be on it has the right to vote in these elections. A right to vote thus presupposes both membership in a commune and census registration. The grounds for loss of the right to vote are nearly the same as in state elections.

In general, every resident of a commune who is entitled to vote may be elected, with the exception of certain communal and state civil servants. A person who is elected may refuse council membership or some other communal position of trust if he has reached age sixty or has acted in the past four years as chairman of a council, a communal board, or a communal committee. As part of these unconditional grounds for refusal, no one is obliged to serve more than four years in the same position of trust. Examples of grounds for refusal subject to interpretation include sickness, family circumstances, professional work, and a public position or post.

Since communal elections follow the same principles as parliamentary elections, there is no need to discuss the election provisions. It need only be noted that communes naturally constitute the electoral districts (constituencies), and that a document signed by ten enfranchised members of a commune (or even three in the smallest communes) is sufficient for the formation of a voters association.

Worthy of note is the fact that party activity in communal elections differs significantly from the phenomenon as it relates to parliamentary elections. The campaign preceding communal elections is carried on within a smaller framework that is more local in character. Voitto Helander's enlightening study of the positions and behavior of council members in three communes in the southwestern part of Finland indicates that election activity in rural communes can be reduced to almost nothing. Half of the elected council members in the commune of Alastaro stated that on the eve of the last election they publicized their candidacy neither through newspapers, flyers, and pamphlets nor through election speeches. All those elected in the city commune of Turku and most in the town of Loimaa had at least conducted a newspaper campaign.[1] In the nomination of candidates, there is actually more activity by voters associations that have been formed on the basis of individual initiative than is the case for parliamentary elections; in the propaganda campaign more attention is given to local questions, questions that are from a national point of view perhaps "nonpolitical." It must, however, be noted that to an increasing degree party politics seems to be gaining ground in communal life, which means that the usual party lines are becoming more visible in the channeling of voters into different groups. In any event, communal elections do not have the great political importance that is attached to parliamentary elections; consequently communal elections are not able to depict so effectively party affiliations of the electorate, or changes in public opinion during periods between elections. Factors of most importance in determining the outcome of an election may be of a local character, which means that differences of opinion do not follow exactly the major political cleavages. But communal councils are not neutral in composition: with the exception of council members in the Aaland Islands, nearly all of the twelve thousand three hundred council members elected in 1964 could at least be identified in the collection of official statistics as belonging either to the socialist or nonsocialist grouping.

Of primary importance in communal elections is the relative strength of bourgeois and leftist candidates elected to communal

1. Voitto Helander, "Kunnallisvaltuutetun rooli," *Politiikka*, 7, no. 2 (1965), 27–28.

councils. That traditional division, which otherwise is obsolete and misleading in many respects, has thus retained its former significance at this level. This is especially true in the countryside, where the political struggle in communal life seems to be generally weaker and where social and political differences are often not so sharp as in population centers, cities, and towns. In many cases the candidate lists —or some of them—are merely bourgeois and sometimes merely leftist, which means that in an examination of election results it is not always possible to achieve a more exact differentiation on the basis of party lines. In official statistics it has been customary to draw a distinction only between bourgeoisie, leftists, and "others."[2] The weakness of party politics in many rural communes provides localism with a foothold, stimulating narrow-minded efforts which represent the local interests of different parts of a commune. An election campaign under such circumstances can be waged to a great extent on these terms, without a care for party lines. But, as mentioned, such phenomena have become rarer, and in cities and towns in particular, parties compete as separate groupings for support from the electorate. In some of the Communist-dominated communes in northern Finland, the decisive dividing line may also be between the People's Democrats and all other parties.

In some communes common understanding between the various groups may be so great that voting is not necessary. Under these circumstances the number of candidates is equal to the number of council members elected, so that the nominees can be declared elected without a vote. In 1964 this kind of election took place in nine rural communes, all of which were small island communes and, except for one, Swedish-speaking.

In an examination of statistics for communal elections during the period of independence, it is seen that a majority of ballots has always been cast for bourgeois candidate lists. This majority has, however, been sharply reduced since the prewar period, and in terms of the entire country, it exists only because of the rural communes: cities and towns are leftist in orientation. In the election of 1964 the bourgeois share of the vote in the nation as a whole, according to official statistics, was 50.1 percent; the percentage for the Left was 49.7 (People's Democrats 22.0, Social Democratic party

2. Now, however, reference is made by party to the number of votes won by the left and to all elected members of communal councils. Statistics since 1964 refer to socialist and nonsocialist parties.

Table 25. Bourgeois and leftist majorities in communal councils by province following 1964 communal elections

Province	Bourgeois majority			Leftist majority			Total number of communes
	Cities and towns	Rural communes	Total	Cities and towns	Rural communes	Total	
Uusimaa	6	22	28	7	11	18	46
Turku and Pori	–	79	79	9	28	37	116
Aaland Islands	1	15	16	–	–	–	16
Häme	–	32	32	9	18	27	59
Kymi	2	23	25	6	4	10	35
Mikkeli	–	22	22	4	4	8	30
Northern Karelia	1	11	12	2	7	9	21
Kuopio	–	23	23	3	3	6	29
Keski-Suomi	–	17	17	3	14	17	34
Vaasa	6	67	73	2	3	5	78
Oulu	1	42	43	3	10	13	56
Lapland	1	17	18	3	4	7	25
Entire country	18	370	388	51	106	157	545

Source: Official Statistics of Finland, ser. XXIX, B:2, table K (Helsinki: Valtioneuvoston kirjapaino, 1965), p. 20.

24.8, Social Democratic League 2.9, and other leftists 0.2 percent). The relative vote of the left in rural communes was only 43.1 percent, but in cities and towns it was 57.7. In accordance with the principle of proportionality, council seats are divided between the bourgeoisie and leftists roughly as these figures indicate. But it should be noted that the left is continually under-represented; this results from the fact that Social Democrats and People's Democrats participate in the elections almost everywhere as separate groupings, with their own election blocs.

The bourgeois majority of popular votes is not very great, but it is divided so evenly throughout the nation that over two-thirds of the communal councils have bourgeois majorities. As a result of the 1964 election, the bourgeoisie gained control of 388 and the left of 157 communes. A look at the different communal forms, however, shows the reverse relationship in towns, many of which are rather large industrial centers (see Table 25).

The percentage of communes with leftist majorities is especially great in the provinces of Häme and Keski-Suomi: a majority of elected council members in 1964 belonged to parties of the left in 46 percent of the communes in the former province and in 50 percent in the latter. Small pockets of communes with leftist majorities can also be found in the border area of Northern Karelia province, around Kajaani, and in the industrial areas of southern and south-western Finland. In the "bourgeois climatic area" of Vaasa province most communes have bourgeois majorities, as is also the case with most communes in Lapland province, where the social agrarianism of the Agrarian party has gained strong support. Completely different from other parts of the nation are the Aaland Islands, where it is difficult to detect party lines in the communal councils.[3]

Communal Council. The general name for the communal representative body is the communal council; depending on which communal form is taken, it is called a rural, city, or town council. A new council begins its period in office at the start of the calendar year following an election. The council annually elects its chairman, who calls and directs meetings, and one or two vice-chairmen. Generally a council meets when necessary, but in addition to these meetings the law requires sessions three times during the year. In a January

3. In Table 25, however, the councils for the Aaland Islands are considered bourgeois, taking exception to official statistics.

meeting the most important communal officials of trust are elected; in October at the latest, reports concerning activity in the previous year are examined, books are closed, members are elected to the taxation and examination committee, and a proposal is made concerning the level of taxation; finally, in December, a decision is made concerning the communal budget for the following year.

A quorum is constituted by the presence of at least two-thirds of the total number of elected council members. Since there are prescribed forms, moreover, for calling a session of the council, it must be determined at the beginning of a meeting that the council is legal and that a quorum is present. Meetings are regularly public. Before a matter can be brought up for resolution in a council, irrespective of the source of the initiative, the communal board must be given an opportunity to consider it. This procedure is designed to ease and speed up the work of a council and to promote more thorough consideration of matters. Only by a unanimous decision can a rural communal council take up an urgent matter for resolution without this sort of centralized preparation. Consideration of a subject by a council breaks down into a report, a discussion, and the making and implementation of a decision. The report is delivered by the council chairman, who also directs the discussion. If during the discussion proposals are made which differ from the proposal that is the basis for the consideration, the dispute is resolved by a vote. Following parliamentary voting procedure, ballots are cast on two proposals at a time until all have been voted on. As in the case of votes in Parliament, the vote is presented in such a way that one can respond either "yes" or "no." In elections which take place within a council, proportional representation is followed if two or more individuals are to be elected and if one-quarter of those participating in the election request it. Otherwise a plurality method is used.

In general, a simple majority is sufficient for the making of a decision, but in some of the most important matters a stipulated majority is required. For example, a two-thirds majority (two-thirds of the council members present) is required for the purchase, sale, and exchange of real estate, the formation and abolition of permanent funds, an increase to be collected through taxation, new appropriations or an increase in appropriations already granted, the taking out of a loan, and the setting up of a new position. As is apparent, the requirement for a stipulated majority is closely related to questions concerning economic management in a commune. Mention will be made later of cases in which a council decision comes into force only after it has been submitted to a state official, whose ratification is essential. There are a number of tasks of a special nature connected with the exercise by a council of highest communal decision-making power: most important are the issuance of communal regulations to be obeyed by members of a commune, as mentioned earlier, the exercise of communal economic power, the setting up of positions, the selection of communal officials of trust and highest civil servants, and the ratification of procedural rules and regulations for communal organs.

It has already been established that governmental activity by the state rests on a system of party government in which ruling power in actuality is in the hands of parties and is dependent on them. It is natural that the same basic features, though weakened and to a degree in different forms, are also found in communal administration. Elected council members organize themselves after an election more or less formally into political groups; the majority group seeks to preserve for itself the most important tasks and thus to influence as much as possible decisions to be made. However, depending on local conditions, there are different levels of party politics in communal administration. Differences among political groups in some councils may be rather small and may not have a decisive influence on the activity and composition of administrative organs in a commune; remaining in the background, activity by party groups gives way to competition between special territorial interests within a commune. In other cases the line of demarcation runs between bourgeois and leftist members of a council, when these two groups are rather united in opposition to each other. Finally, there is also a complete division according to party lines, in which case council groups correspond to party sections, functioning in the territory of a commune and represented in the council, and receive general orders from them. The first two types occur in rural communes; the third is characteristic of cities and towns, and it seems to have spread following the Second World War.

Helander's aforementioned research indicates that party work is a general stepping stone for election to posts of communal representation. Three out of every four members elected to the Turku council had previously worked for their parties at least at the local level, while in Loimaa and Alastaro this was true of only one out of two.

In other respects, too, Helander's research strengthens the general findings presented above concerning the varying character of politics in different types of communes. Half the members elected to city and town councils felt that in their work they represented the supporters of their own parties; the figure drops to one-fifth for members elected to rural communes. Representatives of this last communal form considered neighboring residents to be the most important group. The effort to achieve group unity in council activity was seen overwhelmingly as a positive phenomenon; individual, exceptional behavior was usually justified by those elected in cities in terms of personal conviction, whereas members of rural communal councils pointed to matters concerning their own particular neighborhood. In addition to communal form, party affiliation was also a basic variable regulating the behavior and opinions of elected council members.[4]

Communal Boards. In a rural commune the actual executive authority in charge of administrative tasks is the communal board, elected by the council, whose members—a chairman and at least five others—carry out their duties as a position of trust, just like council members. The chairman is in office four years, the members for only two. According to the 1948 communal law, it is now possible in a rural commune to bring a regular civil servant, a communal manager, into the administrative leadership who also acts as chairman of the communal board. Communal councils are permitted by law to establish such a position, but they are not obligated to do so; the State Council, however, has the power to order that the position of communal manager be established in a commune. By the end of 1966, such a position had been established in one hundred fifty-five communes. There has been a shift to this system mainly in communes which are large in terms of area and population, where it is felt that the centralization of local administration as well as flexible and appropriate management of affairs necessitate the presence in the communal board of a full-time civil servant with the proper training. The point of departure during consideration of the law was that it is difficult for an official of trust to have the necessary expertise and enough time to take care of public affairs when communal duties are increasing and branching out into even broader areas. An effort has been made to provide the communal manager with a strong position, so that he can carry out his duties independently and irrespective of

4. Helander, "Kunnallisvaltuutetun rooli."

temporary political changes in the body exercising decision-making power. Thus far, experience with the system is overwhelmingly favorable.

The communal body in a city is the city board, which has a city manager as chairman and at least four members. There may be, in addition, one or more deputy city managers, who serve as vice-chairmen. The city manager and the deputy city managers may not, however, constitute a majority on the city board. Members of the board are communal officials of trust who are elected for a year at a time; city managers, however, are permanent civil servants. With the aid of the provision mentioned above, it is hoped that decision-making power can be reserved on the board, too, for officials of trust. Administration of a town is directed, similarly, by a town board and a town manager.

Communal boards, assisted by the necessary committees and civil servants, handle routine administrative tasks, protect the common interests of the commune, prepare matters to be considered in the council, and implement decisions of the council. A board also directs the management of a commune's fiscal activity and, even though it is an organ subordinate to the council, supervises the legality of decisions made by the council. In principle, decision-making power in a commune rests with the council; but it should be noted that the line of demarcation between the exercise of decision-making power and of executive power is not entirely clear in communal administration. The communal board also makes final decisions in many important matters, and the council can, moreover, delegate some of its decision-making power to the board and even to a committee. But such a transferral of power cannot be made in matters which require a stipulated majority or which must by law be resolved by the council. Concerning implementation and review of the legality of decisions, it should be mentioned that if a communal board finds that a council decision is contrary to legal procedure or exceeds the authority of a council or is otherwise contrary to a law or decree, the board must refuse to implement the decision. If the council and board are in disagreement concerning the legality of a decision, the council may take the conflict to a provincial government for resolution.

The composition, duties, and authority of a communal board are set forth in rules for a communal board, which must be approved by the council and ratified either by the ministry of the interior for cities and towns or by the provincial government for rural communes. A council can fire the manager of a rural commune and a city or town manager. If a manager has been unable to carry out his duties for a period of one year due to illness or a physical disability, and if it appears that he will be unable in the future to carry on his duties, dismissal occurs without complications; dismissal on other grounds requires a three-quarters majority and ratification by a provincial government.

Committees and Personnel. The jurisdiction of a commune is so broad that a communal board is not able to manage the entire administration without help. Consequently, committees have been set up for different branches of administration, and the tasks of each are sharply defined and restricted. There are two types of committees, standing and voluntary. It is already apparent from the name that the establishment and authority of standing committees are determined by law; some of these committees are obligatory, whereas the setting up of others is dependent upon a decision by the council. The council freely determines the establishment and duties of voluntary committees. As communal government has expanded, the number of committees has also increased considerably; in a rural commune there may be as many as thirty and in a city even more. The most important standing committees are the committee for social affairs, the committee on health, the fire committee, a tax committee, a committee on investigations, a committee for roads, a construction committee, a primary school committee, a primary school board, a land settlement committee, a forestry committee, a temperance committee, a guardianship committee, an employment committee, and election boards. Voluntary committees set up in many communes include, for example, a committee for youth activities, a committee for sports and camping, a music committee, and a committee for industry.

Committee members are selected by the council for a specified period of time. There are, however, a number of standing committees which include some civil servants by virtue of their positions: for example, in the committee on health in a rural commune there is a communal doctor and a communal veterinarian. The communal board is obliged to select its chairman, or some member, as its representative on each committee.

Committees differ greatly with respect to position and jurisdiction, depending upon whether they are standing committees and permanent, or temporary voluntary organs in the machinery of communal administration. In general, the former function in their own field of specialization much more independently than the latter. Although a communal board supervises activity, many standing committees, practically speaking, carry out their duties independently of other communal organs. Examples of those which function independently are the committee for social affairs, the tax committee, and the committee on investigations. A communal board is expressly forbidden in communal law to interfere in decisions concerning matters which have been given by law or decree to committees for resolution. The board and its chairman otherwise have the right to request that a committee decision be examined by the board; if the board feels it cannot accept the decision for implementation, the board itself resolves the matter or returns it to a committee for reconsideration.

Within the framework of this swollen committee system, a large number of communal members are brought into communal activity through various tasks requiring special trust. Mention has already been made of the general position of officials of trust. In the sphere of communal administration, one naturally sees the same direction of development as in state administration: a constant increase in tasks and an expansion of the administrative machinery. This, in turn, means that it is no longer possible to manage the affairs of even a small commune merely with the assistance of officials of trust; it has been necessary to hire even more professional civil servants for work both in a commune's general central administration and in special fields of administration. The administrative machinery of large communes is consequently very complicated.

In principle a commune has great freedom with regard to its own civil servants. As mentioned, new positions may be created by the council. Communal rules and regulations cover the hiring and dismissal, as well as the activity, of civil servants. Working conditions and salary are set, and general provisions regarding procedures for filling posts are provided, insofar as they have not been regulated by law or decree, in communal rules dealing with public positions. Since uniformity among communes is desirable, however, an effort has been made to get them to follow as models the regulations drawn up by central organizations. In this way the legal position of communal civil servants has been made roughly equal in different parts of the country; as a whole, their rights and duties are the same as those for state civil servants, although in some respects (for example, the right of tenure) communal civil servants occupy a weaker position.

In many cases, however, the state is also interested in civil servant questions. Laws and decrees set forth provisions concerning the existence of jobs, as well as the positions, duties, and salaries of civil servants. This civil servant group, of particular interest to the state, includes, for example, health and medical personnel and primary school teachers. Appointments to some communal posts are made by state officials acting alone or with the assistance of communal organs. On the other hand, the state assumes part of the economic burden by participating in the payment of salaries for civil servants.

Communal Judicial Power. Earlier it was mentioned that in cities the bench of magistrates can be considered the organ exercising judicial power. It acts as a communal court in a city's economic and administrative matters. In towns the disciplinary court is the administrative court, although it has less authority than does the bench of magistrates—which, it should be noted, is not primarily a court; it is an authority, state rather than communal, which handles general administrative tasks.

COMMUNAL AUTHORITY AND DUTIES

Authority. The state through legislation sets the limits of communal self-government. They are described in a general way in the communal law: "In accordance with this law, and within limits otherwise established by law, a commune must handle common economic, public order, and other matters, insofar as existing laws and decrees do not specify that they be considered by an authority other than a communal official. Communal rights or tasks entrusted to a commune by law must not be transferred except on the basis of a law, and no new duties or tasks should in any other way be given to a commune." Clearly, the jurisdiction of a commune is by nature general. In addition to tasks defined as obligatory, communes may, if they so desire, assume the management of various tasks designed to improve conditions for the population, insofar as these tasks are not reserved for some other authority. Included under the economic matters mentioned in provisions of the law are questions concerning a commune's own economic management, measures which must be undertaken to raise funds and to pay for expenses incurred as a result of communal tasks. Special reference to public order matters should be considered somewhat dated today, since measures designed to maintain public order are of secondary importance in the activity of a commune now that preservation of order is primarily a concern of state officials; "other matters" covers tasks which are entrusted to communes through special laws, or which have been assumed voluntarily by a commune. In this last respect, the jurisdiction of a commune is nonetheless generally restricted so that a commune may not assume a duty reserved for some other authority and so that matters to be resolved by a communal official are of general concern to the commune. In practice, this last restriction means that a matter to be considered must—directly or indirectly—concern a commune's entire population, or at least a significant portion of it. One cannot, of course, draw an exact line for this situation; a decision must be reached separately for each individual case.

There are many different types of tasks to be handled by communes. Within a broad framework, they can be divided into four groups: 1) maintenance of order, 2) general communal tasks, 3) social tasks, and 4) business activity.

Maintenance of Order. Included in the first group are communal tasks related to administration of law; maintenance of police and fire departments; issuance of various communal regulations related to the maintenance of order; fire inspection; and supervision of construction work. General provisions concerning construction are included in a 1958 building law, according to which the utilization of territory is based on different types of plans: 1) a locality plan including a rough outline for the use of land in two or more communes, 2) a general plan depicting the main features for the use of land in cities and towns, 3) an urban plan including detailed provisions regarding the building and organizing of city land and land that belongs to a rural commune, and 4) a building plan containing provisions that concern the building and organizing of land belonging to a rural commune. More precise provisions with respect to construction are contained in a decree and in local building codes. Communal civil defense can be considered a security task belonging to this group.

General Communal Tasks. These include a number of services, through which effort is made to satisfy the needs of all communal residents, as well as to increase their comfort; the services are financed primarily by funds collected through taxation. Examples of such services are the construction and maintenance within a communal territory of highways, streets, market squares, and bridges; the organizing of public lighting and sanitation; the construction and maintenance of parks, playgrounds, swimming pools, water mains, and sewage networks. The growth in highway traffic during recent decades has greatly increased the tasks for communes in the area of highway maintenance and development. According to a new highway law passed in 1954, which came into force at the beginning of 1958, the state bears primary responsibility for the construction and care of public roads. The state alone is responsible for the upkeep of major highways, whereas expenses resulting from local roads are shared by the state and the communes. In densely populated communes, public authorities, along with private enterprise, have begun to enter the field of bus transportation. Communal transport facilities have been set up for this purpose in Helsinki, Turku, and Tampere. It is understandable that tasks included in this group are much broader in cities and towns than in rural communes, due to population density.

Social Tasks. Social services cover many different sorts of categories, of which the most important are educational and cultural work, health and medical care, social welfare, labor matters, and housing policy.

The field of educational and cultural work includes some of a commune's broadest tasks. First there is the primary school establishment, whose highest leadership and supervision, to be sure, rest with the state but which are nonetheless subordinate to communal administration. Communes are obliged to establish and maintain with state aid a sufficient number of primary schools. The state contributes to teachers' salaries, provides significant assistance to cover the costs of building primary schools, and covers a substantial part of other annual expenditures incurred by the primary school establishment. In addition to their legal obligations, communes have also tried voluntarily to further education and culture by creating and assisting junior high schools, various vocational schools, and institutes for workers, as well as by maintaining public libraries.

Communal duties in the field of health and medical care have increased over the years. Communes are obliged to support a city and communal doctor, a midwife and a specially trained nurse, and maternity and children's clinics; communes are also obliged to participate in the establishment and maintenance of hospitals. The committee on health, as the central health authority, supervises conformity with regulations on health care, follows the public health situation, and seeks in all ways possible to promote health care.

Social welfare from the outset was a communal duty; care for the poor has been one of the oldest forms of communal activity. Welfare, as it has expanded over time, has become more and more the concern of state officials, but communes still have a central role. They are obliged to give assistance to people who cannot make a living with their own resources or their own labor or with the help of relatives, to provide social protection for children and young people, and to organize assistance for vagrants and alcoholics. Measures connected with social welfare also include housekeeping help, care for invalids, care for relatives of military personnel, and housing loans.

In an effort to make more efficient and unify the administration of matters concerning the labor force, concern and supervision in this area was shifted in the early 1960's from communes to the state. State-led labor committees took the place of communal employment committees; organs concerned with vocational guidance and job procurement were also joined to the state organization. In anticipation of periods of unemployment, the state and communes are obliged to prepare advance plans for the creation of jobs and to be ready to implement them without delay. Every commune is obliged to place a predetermined number of workers in jobs of its own creation. For determination of the grounds on which this labor placement is apportioned, communes are divided according to their economic levels into ten classes. If it is not possible to provide all the unemployed with jobs, the question becomes one of paying unemployment compensation as a secondary method. These expenses, too, are shared by the state and the communes. Of the other questions related to labor matters, mention should be made of the fact that communes with enterprises subject to regulations concerning the protection of workers must pay one or more job inspectors, in addition to the state inspectors, to supervise observance of regulations.

In population centers, cities, and towns there has long been concern for land and real estate questions, but rural communes, too, especially after legislation having to do with the acquisition of land was strengthened, have shown an increasing awareness of these questions. Land settlement is primarily the concern of the state, but communes have also performed many different kinds of tasks in this area, both as land acquisition authorities acting independently and as mediators between private land recipients and state authorities.

Business Activity. According to the communal law, business activity designed purely for economic profit is not within the purview of a commune. A commune may not set up and maintain a commercial business and may not give a guarantee on behalf of a business enterprise. Communes do, however, practice extensive economic activity, which is permissible so long as its direct purpose is not the realization of profit. Communes have various technical institutions, such as establishments for electricity, gas, water, telephones, and transportation, which in terms of their purpose are for the general good and seek to fulfill the general needs of the communal population but which to a great extent are managed as business enterprises. Even closer to private enterprise are the communal slaughterhouses, saunas, hotels, and restaurants. In many coastal cities, harbors are important sources of communal revenue. Communes may also support industry if the products are used primarily for communal purposes. Examples of such industrial establishments include communal sawmills and brick factories.

COMMUNAL ECONOMY

Characteristic of Finnish territorial self-government is the fact that communes have their own fiscal administration, or monetary activity, which in principle they manage independently and for which they are responsible. The management of tasks connected with communal administration requires considerable funds, and a firm economic base is a necessary prerequisite for satisfactory fulfillment by the commune of its duties. Economic questions are, therefore, of central importance in communal politics. The extensiveness of the economy of communes, in comparison with the rest of the public economy, can be depicted in rough terms by noting that communal expenditures in recent years have amounted to almost fifty percent of state budgetary expenditures. Communes do not, however, have a completely free hand in the determination of their economy, since a substantial part of even communal expenditures is tied to law. And, in general, communes do not have so great a maneuverability in their financial and budgetary policy as does the state.

The basis of a commune's financial activity is a budget, which must be approved for each fiscal year (a fiscal year is a calendar year). The budget includes all expenditures and revenues anticipated for the next year, as well as any credit or debit for the previous year, divided into capital expenditure and expenditure proper and capital revenue and revenue proper. In accordance with the principle of a gross budget, all expenditures are recorded on the debit side of the budget, without subtracting revenue which might come from expenditures, and all revenue is included on the credit side without subtracting expenditures which might result from revenue. As far as communal business enterprises are concerned, however, only a surplus or deficit of an enterprise may be recorded in the budget. There are no detailed provisions in laws or decrees concerning the structure of communal budgets, but it has been possible with the aid of models prepared by central communal organizations to make the budgets almost wholly consistent. Revenues are divided by administrative branch into departments and expenditures into major classes. The budgetary presentation is prepared by the communal board, on the basis of proposals received from communal committees, and in the fall—no later than December 1—the board sends it to the council for consideration and approval. An approved budget is a directive binding on fiscal administration during a fiscal year.

Revenues. According to statistics, communal revenues in 1964, examined as a whole for all communes, can be broken down by source as in Table 26. This table shows that the primary source of revenue for communes is taxation; this income comes in turn almost entirely from a communal income tax. A communal tax, which every member of a commune is generally obliged to pay, differs in some respects from the state's income and property tax. In the first place, it is strictly an income tax; secondly it is a divided tax, the size of which is dependent for each individual on the size of the combined taxable income of all taxpayers and on the size of a commune's expenditures. The state's income and property tax is a fixed tax, the size of which is determined for an individual by his tax bracket, irrespective of other taxpayers. A third special feature of the

Table 26. Communal revenues, 1964

Revenue	Millions of marks	Percent
Tax revenues	1,577	54
Sale of goods and services	230	8
Net surplus of business enterprises	76	3
Other property revenues	190	6
Revenue transferrals	515	18
Loans	174	6
Sale of property	40	1
Other revenue	117	4
Total	2,919	100

Source: Taloudellinen katsaus 1966 (Helsinki: Valtioneuvoston kirjapaino, 1966), p. 70.

communal tax is its proportionality, which means that everyone must pay the same percentage of his income as a tax. A slight amount of progressiveness is brought to the tax by basic deductions from small incomes. Another deduction permitted by law is the child deduction, which concerns children and adopted children under sixteen years of age supported by a taxpayer and the size of which is determined within certain limits by the council.

Tax on personal income is paid to that commune in which the taxpayer lives; tax on income from property is paid to that commune where the property is located; tax on business and trade income is paid to that commune in which the occupation is practiced. All personal income is thus taxed in the same commune, whereas the same person or body may become a taxpayer in a number of communes on the basis of occupational and property income. Determination of the tax begins when the communal board, in preparing the budget, estimates how much money must be collected the following year through taxation; the sum is ratified by the council. Tax officials determine the amount of income on which each taxpayer must pay tax; each mark of taxable income constitutes a single tax unit. The size of the tax depends on the number of tax units and the value of each; the value is determined by dividing the amount to be collected through taxation by the total number of tax units for taxpayers in a commune. The value thus indicates how much a taxpayer must pay for each mark of taxable income, and the tax due is figured by multiplying the number of tax units by the value of a unit. Tax unit values naturally vary somewhat from one year to the next and from one commune to another; but, observed in lengthy perspective, they have in general been increasing. In 1966 the average value was 12.50 Finnish pennies. The communal tax is borne as a payroll deduction; these payments are deducted from the final tax, which is determined on the basis of a tax statement filed annually by a taxpayer.

The importance of other taxes in the communal economy is rather small; there are the communal dog tax, the communal inheritance tax or so-called percent of the poor people (paid as one-eighth of a percent of the total value of an estate) and a duty collected in cities with a customs office in order to support customs handling of imported goods. Along with taxes, communes gain revenue from payments made for use of communal establishments—harbors, hospitals, and certain educational institutions—and for measures taken by communal authorities.

The importance of earned income varies considerably, depending on the degree to which a commune has profit-making business enterprises, as well as agricultural and timber property. It should, however, be mentioned that the primary purpose of communal business activity is not economic gain, which means that an effort is made to keep the tax on business establishments within reasonable limits.

Communes would under no circumstances be able to manage their constantly increasing tasks without a system of extensive state assistance. From the table on communal revenue it is seen that revenue transferrals, the bulk of which come from the state, have great significance in the economy of communes. State aid is given for the maintenance of primary schools, communal educational institutions, vocational schools, workhouses, and public libraries, for the advancement of social welfare, public health, and sanitation, and for the prevention of unemployment.

Expenditures. If the total expenditures of communes are divided on the same basis as for revenues, the results found in Table 27 are reached. It is easy to see that consumer expenditures—mainly salaries and pensions, as well as the purchase of goods and services—are far and away the largest item of expenditure. Revenue transferrals, however, occurring as transferrals of purchasing power with no return, are much less important than in the state's economy. When

Table 27. Communal expenditures, 1964

Expenditure	Millions of marks	Percent
Salaries and pensions	887	30
Purchase of goods and services	511	17
Expenses for repairs and upkeep	122	4
Housing construction, new	277	9
Land and water construction; new harbors	250	9
Revenue transferrals	402	14
Interest and amortization on loans	142	5
Investment in communal business enterprises	139	5
Purchase of property and granting of loans	144	5
Other expenditures	56	2
Total	2,930	100

Source: Taloudellinen katsaus 1966 (Helsinki: Valtioneuvoston kirjapaino, 1966), p. 70.

examining communal expenditures by administrative branch, one finds that educational and cultural work, social welfare, and public health and sanitation are very large items of gross expenditure.

Fiscal Administration. General management of a commune's fiscal activity is a function of the communal board. In cities and towns a financial office exists to assist the board in the practical administration of monetary matters. In rural communes such an organ is not obligatory; funds and accounts can be handled in a commune's office. For the inspection of communal administration and accounts, the council selects for each calendar year at least four examiners who report to the communal board concerning steps taken in the course of their examination. The board passes the report on to the council for consideration, appending its own statement and perhaps other comments. In addition, the council may hire a permanent accountant, who carries on continual inspection and is directly subordinate to the council.

For purposes of taxation, a tax committee is established in every commune which determines both the communal tax and the state and church tax. After the determination of taxes, a tax register is drawn up; it includes information concerning the taxable income and property of taxpayers, as well as information concerning determined taxes, and it must be on public display for ten days. Complaints concerning taxation can be made to the committee on investigations. Its decision can be appealed to the provincial government, whose decision, in turn, can be appealed before the Supreme Administrative Court. In some cases it is a question of what is called a basic complaint, which means that the matter goes directly to the provincial government.

COMMUNAL COOPERATION

Finland's system of self-government is different from comparable systems in many other nations in that territorial self-government in Finland has gone no further than the communal level; a higher type of self-government, within a broader territorial framework, has not been organized, although the question has been discussed many times and proposals to this effect were made in the four-estate Diet. Such an arrangement has not seemed necessary in a small and sparsely settled nation like Finland, where rural communes are relatively large in size. But continued development of society has brought many far-reaching tasks into the purview of communal activity; they cannot appropriately or economically be handled by a single commune on its own and thus require, in one form or another, cooperation among many communes.

In practice the matter is organized so that communes are given an opportunity to cooperate for the realization of plans shared by two or more of them. As far back as 1865, a decree for rural communes included provisions concerning a common communal meeting, which exercised decision-making power on behalf of the communes. In the century since that date, cooperation has expanded greatly from that modest beginning and has assumed many facets. Especially important has been the development of public health care administration, which began in the 1930's. The system of communal cooperation in the 1960's has become a broad and intricate network; in general, it is based on voluntary action. The initiation of cooperation is up to the communes, although to a certain degree the coercive power of the state extends even to this area: on some questions cooperation is made mandatory by law. Forms of cooperation set forth in communal law are 1) a meeting of representatives from communes for consideration of common business, 2) a union of communes, and 3) agreements between communes and concordant decisions.

Cooperation between two or more communes for the realization of a common plan begins most naturally with a temporary meeting of communal representatives. A commune which desires cooperation with other communes makes a proposal to this effect, after which the communes in question select their representatives to a joint meeting. At the meeting discussion can be held and decisions made concerning common and uniform measures in certain matters; a decision can also be reached regarding the establishment and maintenance of a joint communal institution or enterprise. In accordance with earlier legislation it was once possible to designate the meeting of communal representatives as the administrative organ directing this endeavor, in which case the meeting became permanent; but in 1961, permanent meetings were removed from the forms of communal cooperation by a change in law. Meetings of representatives are most commonly called for consideration of questions related to the establishment of unions of communes.

A union of communes (kuntainliitto), which can be founded for the maintenance of a permanent joint enterprise or institution, is the most tightly organized and without doubt the most important form of cooperation in Finland today. It is primarily through unions of communes, which constitute independent juristic persons, that an effort is made to fill the void in the nation's administrative system arising from the absence of self-government at a higher level. A deficiency in this form of cooperation is, of course, the fact that the jurisdiction of a single union of communes is rather narrow; the union is generally established to handle only a single permanent undertaking. A union of communes must have basic rules including detailed provisions for administration and concerning the rationale for division among member communes of expenses incurred. The basic rules are submitted to a provincial government for ratification. The power of decision in a union of communes is exercised by the union council, to which the councils of the member communes select members for four years at a time. Administration is handled by a union board, selected by the union council, under which there may be committees charged with carrying out special tasks. A union council reaches independent decisions on matters concerning the union of communes, without inquiring as to the separate opinions of the members, unless otherwise stipulated in the basic rules of a union that has been established voluntarily.

There are no provisions in law with regard to the number of communes in a union, so a union may be set up by as few as two communes. There are, in all, about three hundred unions of communes.[5] A large portion of the unions maintain joint sanatoriums, mental hospitals, central hospitals, or other general hospitals, as well as educational institutions for vocational training; unions of communes are also established for the maintenance of workhouses and homes for the poor and aged. Communal membership is obligatory in unions that maintain central hospitals and that act in the fields of tuberculosis prevention and care for the mentally ill. Furthermore, the building code stipulates that locality unions must be set up on an equal footing with unions of communes for the purpose of planning. By establishing unions, communes have also sought to comply with a provision of a 1958 law concerning institutions for vocational training; the provision requires that communes have at their disposal a certain number of openings in vocational schools.

Joint communal matters are also managed with the aid of agreements and concordant decisions, which are relatively common. A typical example of the application of such a procedure is an agreement by which one commune grants another the right to use its hospital or some welfare institution. Of other forms of cooperation remaining outside communal legislation, mention should be made of associations, companies, or cooperatives that can be established by communes as independent juristic persons. In such instances they occupy the same position as any other natural or juristic person, and the same legal provisions are in force as would be the case generally for any similar activity. Most important of the associations between communes are the communal central organizations: the League of Rural Communes, the League of Finnish Cities, and the League of Swedish Rural Communes in Finland.

Experience shows that regional self-government can to a certain extent be redeemed through the forms of cooperation that have been considered, which rest mainly on the notion of volition. In the opinion of many communal workers, it will be possible in the future, too, to avoid administrative reform through development of the system of communal unions. The negative side of this system is that it is inchoate. Since the unions have come into being gradually,

5. In 1959 the number was 168. On an average there were 17 member communes in each union, and a commune's average membership was in 5 different unions; *Kuntien yhteistoimintakomitean I osamietintö* (*komiteanmietintö 1960:4*), pp. 11–12, app. 7.

one at a time, and since there is no unified plan with respect to territorial division, administrative divisions have become very confused. Also, since communal councils must select their representatives for many union councils, and since these gather only twice a year to consider reports and plans of the union boards, the ordinary communal servant does not have an opportunity to familiarize himself sufficiently with the matters in question, so that actual power rests to a great extent with the officials on the union board. Finally, there are difficulties within the framework of the system that arise from an equal sharing among communes of the economic burden.

COMMUNES AND THE STATE

In conjunction with the principle that the power of a self-governing community is based on a mandate from the state, the state checks, utilizing appropriate means, to ensure that tasks are managed well and in accordance with the law. Supervision of communes is by its general character legal supervision, in other words, examination of the legality of measures. Supervision of the appropriateness of decisions and measures is meant to take place only as an exception. Over time, however, the state has moved toward more regulation through legislative action of matters previously resolved independently by communes. As communal administration has become more extensive and more demanding, the state has considered it necessary to increase its supervision in order to ensure that communes are able to carry out their tasks satisfactorily and that measures taken by different self-governing communes are sufficiently consistent. As a condition for the economic aid which it extends, the state reserves for itself in many areas a special right of supervision with respect to the appropriateness of measures; to some degree, therefore, there has been a withdrawal from the principle of liberalism and decentralization according to which local self-government should be independent and responsible to itself, supervision remaining an exception and relating only to individual cases as legal supervision.

The general supervisory authority is the provincial government, which checks to see that communal matters are administered in accordance with laws and decrees, which gives instructions to communal officials, and which requires of them, when necessary, information and explanations. The ministry of the interior also has an important role, particularly in the supervision of communal decision-making power; supervision of the special administrative branches is carried out by that state official who has supreme leadership in the nation for the field in question.

Utilizing a division based on the degree of severity, the forms of state supervision can be grouped as follows: 1) provision of advice and instruction, 2) request for information, 3) state aid, 4) procedure of subordination, 5) procedure of complaint, 6) obligation to take certain steps, and 7) disbanding of a commune and its merging with another commune.

The procedures of subordination and complaint are in practice the most important forms of state supervision. The former means that in some cases a decision made by a communal official comes into force only after it has been submitted to some state official for examination and ratification. The higher official can examine not only the legality of a decision, but also its appropriateness. In general, a decision may either be ratified in the form presented or rejected; it cannot be altered. A great many matters must be submitted to a state official; as set forth in the communal law, general authorities with appropriate powers are the State Council, the ministry of the interior, and the provincial governments. Provisions about many other authorities with the power of review, especially ministries and central offices, are set forth in special laws; mention has already been made of this relationship of subordination within a commune, which affects decisions of committees.

More common is the procedure of complaint, utilization of which means that the legality of a decision made by a communal official may be brought before the appropriate state official for examination. Everyone, irrespective of communal membership, whose private rights are impinged upon by a decision, has the right to lodge a complaint; a complaint may, moreover, be made by any member of a commune on the grounds that a decision has been made following illegal procedures, that the official making a decision has exceeded his authority, or that a decision is otherwise contrary to a law or decree. Clearly, only a legal complaint is involved; a complaint cannot be made on the grounds that a decision is inappropriate. The procedure of subordination, therefore, is supervision coming from a state authority, from above, and is directed at the legality and appropriateness of activity by communes; the procedure of complaint, however, is legal supervision coming from below, from members of a commune, with the aid of which the members can guard not only their own interests but also the general interest of the commune. A decision of a communal council and board may be appealed before a provincial government. A decision of a provincial government may generally be appealed before the Supreme Administrative Court. However, an appeal concerning a council decision which is to be submitted to a state authority for ratification is made before that official to whom the matter must be submitted. A protest within a commune concerning a decision of a communal committee may be made to the communal board unless otherwise stipulated.

This communal complaint is only a secondary procedure for appeal, in that a general administrative-law complaint must be lodged when permissible. These forms of complaint differ in certain respects; a general complaint may be made only by a person whose rights or interests are directly affected by a decision, but it can also be based on grounds of appropriateness. The right to protest is more extensive in a communal complaint, but the grounds for complaint are more restricted.

As mentioned, the state to an increasing degree exercises supervision through economic assistance extended to communes. State aid is of primary importance to communes, and by attaching certain conditions to the aid it is possible for the state to guide development effectively in the desired direction, even in matters about which there have been no detailed provisions in legislation or decrees or in matters for which the communes are not directly responsible. In such cases pressure can be exerted by ending state aid, interrupting its payment, or calling for its repayment.

The state has, however, reserved for itself even more effective supervision in the event that a commune is not able to manage its economic affairs satisfactorily. A commune can be subjected to increased supervision if it has applied for and received state aid, as a loan or grant, in order to extricate itself from economic difficulties. A provision concerning increased supervision is announced by the State Council after it has heard from the communal council in question and from the provincial government. Supervision is carried out by a supervisor designated by the State Council, whose duty is to oversee the economic management of a commune and to ensure through his extensive powers that its economy returns to a stable foundation.

During the last two decades the relation between the state and the communes has gained importance. Before the Second World War communes were permitted to resolve their affairs relatively freely, within the framework of general provisions set forth in the communal law, but state leadership and dependency on the provisions of special laws have increased over time. Eino Waronen has characterized the course of development as follows: "Those tasks and duties for which a commune was responsible were primarily voluntary in earlier times, were based on a general provision in the communal law concerning the authority of a commune, and were fitted to local needs, no attempt having been made to standardize them for realization in all communes. But the situation is different today. Matters which may be resolved independently by communes have become fewer in number due to the fact that state power has extended legislation to new fields within the jurisdiction of communes."[6]

The development of special legislation restricts communes still more. As the economic and social activity of public communities has expanded, communes have through legislation been given many new tasks, the execution of which is regulated by detailed provisions and effective supervision. Their resolution requires an ever-expanding system of state assistance, which brings with it conditions and instructions limiting freedom of action. Under the exceptional circumstances which prevailed during and after the Second World War, state control extended even to small details such as communal payments and salaries for commune employees and workers.

Communal servants have not been wholly in favor of this development, and so certain areas of conflict between the state and the communes have arisen. It is held by some that, as the present development continues, communes will become organs of local administration for the state and communal self-government will thus become more apparent than real; in this connection the strong expression "a crisis in self-government" has been used.

There is no disagreement as to whether or not state supervision and dominance are generally useful, because it is well understood that expanding public action requires planning and uniformity in the decisions and measures taken by different authorities. The question concerns how far state leadership can go without infringing upon the principles of democratic self-government, how tasks should be divided between communes and the state, with an eye on expediency,

6. Eino Waronen, *Kunnallispolitiikan kysymyksiä* (Porvoo, WSOY, 1958), pp. 327–328.

and how the economic solvency of communes can be maintained in the face of increasing burdens. It is precisely this last question that has caused disagreement and evoked protests from communal servants, who feel that state authorities in placing new duties on communes do not pay sufficient attention to the question of whether or not communes are really able to support the resultant economic burdens.

XI Self-Government in the Aaland Islands

DEVELOPMENT OF THE AALAND ISLANDS QUESTION

The Aaland Islands region, formed by an archipelago off the mainland, is part of Finland, but regulation of its position and administration has been an international rather than an internal Finnish matter. Two factors account for the interest of several foreign powers in the Aaland Islands, which has resulted in the region's being brought before an international audience on numerous occasions: the militarily and strategically important position of the archipelago and the special linguistic and national character of its population. The former has led to demilitarization of the Islands, the latter to the granting of very broad self-government to the population. These two occurrences are not necessarily related; a consideration only of the latter follows, whereas the former will be discussed in a later chapter dealing with national defense.

In order to understand the special position of the region today, a brief look at events since the First World War is appropriate. Regional self-government and Swedishness have deep roots in the Aaland Islands, even though the region was joined to Finland administratively in the seventeenth century. For this reason it is not surprising that when Finland declared her independence and began to develop a system of government, demands were heard, based on the "right of self-determination for peoples," for joining the region to Sweden. Toward the end of 1917 a large mass petition was gathered in the Islands for transmission to Sweden, demonstrating that the vast majority of the adult population was in favor of joining Sweden. Early in February 1918, the Swedish king received a five-member delegation of Aaland Islanders who went to Stockholm to present the wish of the Islanders and determine the Swedish position. For understandable reasons, Sweden warmly supported the demands and proposed a popular referendum in the Islands. The Finnish government sharply rejected the demands, explaining that the Islands were an indivisible part of Finnish territory. But a strong popular movement for detachment of the region from Finland continued; its most important leaders were Julius Sundblom, a newspaper editor, and Carl Björkman, a lawyer. In June, on the initiative of the population itself, an illegal regional diet met. Early in 1919 a regional delegation led by Sundblom was sent to Paris to urge that the Aaland Islands question be put on the agenda of the Peace Conference.

Soon the Finnish government initiated steps to get the population of the Islands to give up its separatist efforts. In the fall of 1919 the government charged a commission with rapid drafting of a system of self-government for the Aaland Islands, and on May 6, 1920, a law was passed granting extensive autonomy to the population of the region. Events led in the summer to the arrest of Sundblom and Björkman, who were accused of treason.

The question thus came before the Council of the League of Nations for consideration, with the consent of Finland and Sweden. The Swedish government had earlier on numerous occasions requested the Great Powers to raise the question in international negotiations. Based on a statement made by the commission which investigated the matter, the Council in June 1921 publicly declared that the Aaland Islands belonged to Finland. At the same time, however, the Council proposed that the plenipotentiaries for Finland and Sweden agree on new guarantees for the Islands population, to preserve the Swedish language, ensure that land would remain in the hands of the original population, restrict the right to vote of those who move to the region, and lead to the appointment of a governor enjoying the confidence of the population. The plenipotentiaries agreed on some of the provisions which had been unanimously approved by the Council and were later incorporated in a law of guarantees passed on August 11, 1922, in Finland; the purpose of this law was to supplement the earlier law concerning self-government. A special provision was included (paragraph 6) regarding international guarantees for the preservation of concessions made to the region. This provision gave the League Council the right to supervise the application of the provisions of the law, and, connected with this, the government of the Republic was obliged to pass on to the Council—with its own comments appended

—those complaints which might be raised by the regional assembly of the Aaland Islands concerning application of the provisions of the law.

The question of reworking the regulations for the region came to the fore soon after the Second World War ended. The earlier laws on self-government did, to be sure, make possible the favorable development of conditions in the Aaland Islands, but they were not satisfactory in all respects. In particular, it was hoped in the Islands that there could be a more precise demarcation of jurisdiction between the state and the region. The first report by the government concerning this matter was made to Parliament in 1946, but six years elapsed before the question was finally settled. Consideration of the matter in Parliament was delayed to some extent by pressure from foreign powers. This time, too, certain foreign powers (Sweden and the Soviet Union) showed great interest in the resolution of the position of the Aaland Islands. Sweden emphasized that self-government for the Islands was not merely an internal Finnish matter and that the Geneva Agreement of 1921, which also imposed obligations on Finland with respect to Sweden, was still in force irrespective of the demise of the League of Nations and of agreements between Finland and the Soviet Union. Soviet presentations, insofar as information was released to the public, focused only on the abovementioned paragraph 6: the Soviet Union did not consider it desirable to preserve this paragraph in new legislation. The Finnish government had made such a proposal because the provision—although it had lost all real meaning—still had a certain symbolic value for the Aaland Islanders. To support its demand, the Soviet Union offered the somewhat peculiar rationale that an international guarantee limits Finnish sovereignty with respect to the Aaland Islands and is consequently in conflict with both the 1944 Armistice Agreement and the 1947 Peace Agreement. While the matter was under discussion in committee, Prime Minister Kekkonen recommended to Parliament that the point in question be stricken from the legislative proposal, and this was done.

After Parliament finally approved the new law on self-government the President, on December 28, 1951, ratified it. Seen as a whole, this law is built on the old foundation, even though many provisions of the earlier legislation were changed and made more precise. The law is supplemented by another law passed on the same day concerning the right of redemption on the Aaland Islands when real estate is transferred. Neither law can be altered or overturned without consent of the regional assembly of the Aaland Islands, and in such cases procedure for the legislation of fundamental law must be followed. These are, therefore, laws of the Finnish Republic, although they occupy a special position in that they may be changed only with the express consent of a self-governing community.

SYSTEM OF SELF-GOVERNMENT

In general, it can be said that the system of self-government in the Aaland Islands guarantees the population a position of rather extensive autonomy. Powers granted to local authorities are not limited merely to actual administration; they also extend to the field of legislation. The special position of the region is also brought home by the fact that details of the system of self-government are not determined in "state legislation." The issuance of regulations with respect to details is left up to the local representative body.

Institutions of Self-Government. A regional assembly (Swedish landsting), which includes thirty members chosen every third year by universal and proportional election, acts as the representative body. The assembly gathers yearly for its regular session, and, on an order by the president of the Republic, the governor can call it into special session; the president has the power to dissolve it and to call for a new election. The governor opens and closes the assembly and he passes on to it presidential proposals and communiqués. Actual administrative tasks are entrusted to a regional board (landskapsstyrelse), selected by the assembly, the head of which is called a lantråd. His activity is, in a sense, based on the principle of parliamentarism, since he remains in the post as long as he enjoys the confidence of the assembly. The other six members of the regional board are elected for three years at a time. In this respect, political life of the Aaland Islands is characterized by a preservation of continuity manifested by harmony and excellent mutual understanding in regional policy. Officials who are elected once are generally re-elected; Carl Björkman, for example, was lantråd for sixteen years, 1922–1938. There are departments in the regional board for different areas of administration: an office, a bureau for the preparation of laws, an accounting department, agricultural department, forestry department, department for roads, and department for historical sites.

Matters concerning state administration are handled by the governor and by the proper state authorities. The position of the governor is roughly the same as the position of other Finnish governors, but he has in addition certain special tasks connected with observance of the state's interests. Mention has already been made of his relationship to the regional assembly. He must prohibit implementation of a decision by an official of the regional administration if that decision exceeds the authority of an official, and he must report illegal measures by the lantråd or a member of the regional board to the chancellor of justice. The governor is appointed by the president of the Republic after agreement has been reached with the speaker of the regional assembly—or, if unanimity cannot be reached, after the assembly has submitted to him the names of five candidates. This procedure is designed to ensure that the appointed governor enjoys the confidence of the membership in the self-governing community. Certain tasks for advisers and experts are also entrusted to a special organ, the Aaland Islands commission, established for the equalization of taxes. Of its four members, two are appointed by the State Council and two by the regional assembly. The commission's chairman, who has regularly been the governor, is appointed by the president of the Republic.

Authority. The regional assembly has the right to pass regional laws on matters affecting the Aaland Islands which are not reserved in the law on self-government for general legislative organs of the state. State legislation includes fundamental laws, more precise legislation concerning fundamental rights, relations with foreign powers, general taxes and payments, criminal law, and most civil law, as well as the judicial establishment, social insurance, navigation, aviation, mail, telegraph, telephone, and radio. The regional assembly does, however, have the right of initiative in matters covered by state legislation if they concern only the Aaland Islands. Such legislative proposals are transmitted by the government to Parliament. The president has an unconditional right of veto with respect to laws approved by the regional assembly if after receiving an opinion on the matter from the Supreme Court and the Islands commission he "feels that a law approved by the regional assembly concerns matters covered by the state's legislative power, or concerns the internal or external security of the state."[1] It is not unusual for the Supreme Court to rule that the assembly has exceeded its power on a certain matter and for the Court to request that the law be dropped.

The division of administrative tasks into state matters and matters for self-government is determined on the basis described above. The regional board thus handles administration in those areas where legislative power belongs to the regional assembly. In paragraph 19 of the law on self-government there is special emphasis on the fact that administration of foreign affairs, of justice, of defense, administration concerned with state security, fiscal administration, and general supervision (insofar as it focuses on questions under the state's legislative power) of the educational establishment, which is under the jurisdiction of state authorities—all are subordinate to general administration by the state. Of the most important areas in administration of the region, mention should be made of health and hospital care, educational work, communications, administration of the region's fixed property and land settlement activity, administrative action concerning occupations, vocational education, housing, social welfare, participation in the maintenance of public order and security, conservation, and public enlightenment. Some of these areas are partially under state authority, partially under regional authority.

In addition to actual administrative activity, the regional board also has the right to issue decrees, based on a special power: the regional assembly can, when necessary, give it the right to issue provisions for implementation and application of a regional law by regional decree. A statement concerning the proposed decree must, however, first be sought from the Aaland Islands commission. Before the president or the State Council can issue decrees concerning matters under the state's legislative power that deal solely with the Aaland Islands, the regional board has an opportunity to express its opinion. An attempt has been made to achieve flexibility in the division of labor between state administration and administration of the region by ruling that it is possible with consent of the regional board to transfer to the regional administration for a specified period of time, or until further notice, tasks which are part of the state's general administration. The opposite also holds true.

1. *Ahvenanmaan itsehallintolaki § 14. Suomen Asetuskokoelma 1951 no. 670* (Helsinki: Valtioneuvoston kirjapaino, 1951), p. 1234.

Judicial power in legal matters on the Aaland Islands is exercised by state courts. Administrative law is carried out by the provincial government and other appropriate authorities; self-government of the region does not, therefore, extend to that area. Complaints may be lodged concerning work of the regional board in the same way they are lodged concerning decisions of a governor in similar circumstances.

Expenses resulting from self-government are borne by the region itself; with this in mind, it has been given a number of opportunities to seek the necessary monies. The region collects occupational and amusement taxes for itself, whereas elsewhere in Finland they go to the state. The regional assembly, which determines the annual budget, can also declare a special tax increase as part of a general taxation on income, as well as a special income tax to be collected only occasionally. The assembly can decide on payments resulting from the activity of regional authorities and on payments to be made for the use of regional establishments.

This revenue is not, however, sufficient to cover expenditures. Considering the fact that state expenditures with respect to the Aaland Islands have been reduced following the transferral of certain administrative branches to management by the region, it is considered reasonable to grant the region assistance from state funds. The amount of aid is determined by the Aaland Islands commission and final ratification is by the president. Execution of this tax equalization has often proven very awkward, and it has been a source of disagreement between the commission and the regional board.

Nationality Guarantees. The law on self-government provides special guarantees concerning preservation by the Aaland Islands population of its special national and linguistic character; the islanders were especially fearful during the years of struggle that in time the region would be Finnicized and absorbed into the mother country. Most important in this respect is the fact that the population on the Islands has its own "citizenship," called a native locality right. The regional board can on request grant this right to a Finnish citizen who has moved to the region and lived there for five years. Only individuals with this native locality right can participate in regional and communal elections; they also have certain privileges within the territory of the region, not shared by the rest of the state's population, regarding the practice of an occupation. In order to keep land ownership in the hands of the original population, it has been decreed that if real estate located on the Aaland Islands is sold to an individual who does not have the right of native locality or to a company whose board members do not all have this right or whose legal place of residence has not been the region for at least five years, the region and the commune on whose territory the real estate is located and a person having the right of native locality are permitted to redeem it. If agreement cannot be reached on the price, the right is enforced in accordance with prevailing prices. Preservation of the dominant position of the Swedish language has been attempted in many ways. The official language for state authorities is Swedish, and no one may be appointed to a state post in the region who lacks fluency. The region and the communes are not obliged to maintain anything but Swedish-language schools, and Finnish may not be taught in schools receiving assistance from the region and a commune without the latter's consent. In state educational institutions, too, the language of instruction is Swedish. Another special privilege is that individuals having the right of native locality are permitted to substitute service in civil administration for compulsory military service; until the matter is settled through legislation, therefore, the islanders are in actual fact freed from military service.

Party Activity. Political activity on the Aaland Islands is a creature by itself when viewed against the Finnish scene. Society on the Islands is united, without the economic, social, and national contrasts which might give birth to political struggle and intense competition for the electorate among groups striving for different goals. Party activity in the region has remained weak; until the Second World War it was, in fact, hardly noticeable. In this respect the Islands form an untouched idyl where today's political power struggle remains quite foreign.

Typical of political conditions in the region was the fact that in two elections to the regional assembly in the 1930's a Social Democratic list clearly flying the party's banners was included in a general election bloc with strictly bourgeois lists. At that time there were campaign fights of a sort, since many candidates were, in any event, competing for support of the electorate. But these fights were limited primarily to personal discussions, articles sent to the newspaper *Åland*, and modest campaign posters. Participation in elections is generally weak. Matts Dreijer, tongue in cheek, comments: "In the absence of social contrasts emphasized by catchwords and election slogans, the electorate thinks that Andersson may be as good as Pettersson and thus does something else in preference to gathering around the ballot box."[2]

Political activity after the Second World War picked up considerably as leftist groups gained strength and especially as the Communists began in earnest to seek a foothold in the region; but they have remained an insignificantly small minority. The majority sticks faithfully to the old "basic line" of the Aaland Islands; the Communists, like other new groupings, have not been able to change entirely the idyllic picture of politics on the Aaland Islands.

Elections to the regional assembly have also remained, in terms of party politics, an internal affair of the Islands. Active in the region is the large general electoral organization *Åländsk Samling*, which has undertaken the task of preparing for general elections and of increasing activity by the electorate and whose only counterweight is the small Communist grouping. In the 1967 election there were four election blocs within the Åländsk Samling, of which the largest, the agrarian-oriented group, won 20 seats in the regional assembly; the Social Liberals and Social Democrats received 4 seats, and two others, mainly a bourgeois grouping, a total of 6; the Communists failed to win representation. Approximately 14,700 people were entitled to vote, but only 54 percent did.

2. Matts Dreijer, *Ålands självstyrelse 25 år* (Mariehamn: Landstingets presidium, 1947), p. 180.

Part Three The System in Operation

XII Foreign Policy and the Conduct of Foreign Affairs

DECISION-MAKING IN FOREIGN AFFAIRS

Foreign policy is often considered a weak point in democracies. By this it is meant that the adaptation of democratic methods to the conduct of foreign affairs is one of the most difficult problems for a democratic system. The difficulty lies in the fact that two demands must be reconciled: the demand for an effective and appropriate policy and the demand for parliamentary supervision. But favoring one often means compromising the other. Indeed, one philosophy is that expressed by J. K. Paasikivi on the basis of his own lengthy experience as a political figure: "Foreign policy is much too difficult and complicated for resolution by the man in the street. Leaders must boldly assume responsibility and direct public opinion."[1]

The President of the Republic. Finland, like other democratic states, has retained a system inherited from the last century in accordance with which general authority in foreign policy questions rests with the head of state and the government. In addition to general parliamentary supervision, Parliament is permitted by the Constitution to exercise a decisive influence only with respect to matters mentioned explicitly. It has been noted earlier that in formal terms the relation between the president and the State Council in the field of foreign policy administration is not meant to be an exceptional one, although in practice it is precisely in this area that the president has become a political leader with significant personal influence and direct contact with representatives of foreign states. Though an effort has been made to follow common parliamentary procedures in the conduct of foreign policy with Western democracies, the forms of a presidential

1. J. K. Paasikivi, *Toimintani Moskovassa ja Suomessa 1939–41* (Porvoo: WSOY, 1958), p. 118.

system have been adopted in relations with some authoritarian countries. This is joined as either a cause or effect to the fact that after the Second World War examination of Finland's foreign policy line from abroad has focused on the most prominent political leaders, particularly the president. The prime minister and the foreign minister have, therefore, been overshadowed to a considerable degree in "summit diplomacy" by the president. Since the war the conduct of foreign affairs clearly has also strengthened the general position of the president.

Tasks which are important within the sphere of foreign policy administration include the resolution of war and peace, conclusion of agreements with foreign powers, recognition of new governments, appointment and reception of envoys, designation of special plenipotentiaries and delegations, and guidance and supervision of actions taken by representatives at international conferences and organizations. Insofar as international agreements are concerned, the president resolves in the State Council to begin negotiations. He designates the negotiators and, particularly in political matters, is generally active in the preparation of instructions and the examination of details included in agreements. He does not sign agreements, even though he may head negotiations for Finland; this is done by ministers with the proper authority or by civil servants in the administrative network for foreign affairs. Important agreements usually come into force only after they have been ratified by the heads of state and after documents of ratification have been exchanged. In this way it is possible to gain time for measures within a state, such as approval by Parliament. In addition to these formal and "official" measures, the head of state influences foreign relations in many other ways, for example, through his speeches and statements and through state visits including negotiations and discussions. Since the 1920's, an effort has been made to strengthen friendly relations with other Nordic countries through reciprocal state visits, and after the Second World War contact with the Soviet Union has been especially brisk. In the 1950's and 1960's Finnish heads of state, with their accompanying personnel, visited the Soviet Union—President Kekkonen has done so on many occasions. In addition to strengthening relations in general between the countries, these visits have also led to a number of concrete results. In negotiations during a 1955 visit agreement was reached on returning Porkkala, a military base leased to the Soviet Union, to Finland; in 1958 many questions concerned with economic cooperation were discussed; a nonstate visit in 1959 reduced tensions which had prevailed since the previous autumn; and, finally, in 1960 a customs agreement was concluded making it possible for Finland to join EFTA as an "associate member." President Kekkonen has also traveled to many Western countries, including some beyond Scandinavia. During these visits important political discussions have taken place, the results of which have often been contained in joint unsigned communiqués.

Parliament. The government's powerful rights in the conduct of foreign affairs are limited by some provisions of the Form of Government Act concerning the cooperation of Parliament in action taken. Questions to be considered in Parliament deal mainly with the most important agreements, which can be grouped as follows: 1) matters concerning war and peace, 2) agreements containing provisions which lie within the sphere of legislation, 3) agreements containing provisions which according to the Constitution otherwise require the consent of Parliament.

In paragraph 33 of the Form of Government Act it is stated that "the president resolves matters of war and peace with the consent of Parliament." This means that the president cannot declare war without the consent of Parliament or conclude a peace treaty before Parliament has approved it. Experience, however, has shown that in a small country like Finland Parliament usually does not have much choice in these matters. It could do nothing but approve the government's announcement in December 1939 and June 1941 that the nation was at war, as well as the peace treaty of March 1940 and the armistice of September 1944. As the Winter War came to an end, the situation was such that Parliament was given the peace treaty for consideration only after it had already come into force.

There was also consideration in Parliament of the 1948 Treaty of Friendship, Cooperation, and Mutual Assistance with the Soviet Union and of its extension in 1955; this procedure was based on the grounds that the treaty obligations were closely connected with the question of war and peace and that the treaty in other respects could decisively affect the fate of the nation. Likewise, Parliament in 1947 consented to Finland's joining the United Nations. In obvious conflict with the above provision of the Form of Government Act was the Ribbentrop Agreement, signed in June 1944, in which President Risto Ryti pledged, in order to achieve material aid from Germany for the Finnish front, not to negotiate a separate peace. This agreement was not given to Parliament for consideration; Ryti made it in his own name with the express purpose of leaving Parliament's hands free for future action following his resignation, which soon took place.

Category two of the above grouping deals with agreements which require, in accordance with the general division of labor between legislative and executive power, legislative measures by Parliament in order to be enforced. If the president and the State Council can issue the necessary provisions through decree, the cooperation of Parliament is not required.

Finally, Parliament must approve agreements containing matters which otherwise require, according to the Constitution, the consent of Parliament. Most generally this is a question of an agreement resulting in state expenditures, in which case Parliament must grant appropriations. Special mention is made in paragraph 3 of the Form of Government Act of the fact that the nation's borders can be changed only with the consent of Parliament, and paragraph 69 of the Diet Act requires that a proposal concerning a diminution of the nation's territory must have a two-thirds majority for approval. The first provision was applied when Parliament toward the end of 1955 approved the reunification of Porkkala with Finland.

Though in the cases mentioned an agreement absolutely must be given to Parliament for approval before ratification, the government can of course request parliamentary approval for other agreements as well. This frequently has happened, and the fact that the most important agreements are sent to Parliament for consideration without explicit obligation upon the government to do this can be considered a facet of parliamentary practice.

When an agreement requires legislative measures before enforcement, Parliament first approves the agreement and then the legislative provisions required. In this way Parliament participates in the making of an agreement, not just in the procedure by which it comes into force. Approval of the legislative provisions in question occurs through open, or blanket, law—a law passed in the usual legislative procedure which stipulates, without mentioning what parts of the agreement are concerned with the legislative sphere, that provisions of the agreement in this sphere are in force as law. Consideration of such a law cannot be postponed (in other words, put off until a new parliamentary election has been held).

Parliament's influence on foreign policy is not limited to consideration of international agreements; it can also exercise its various forms of legislative initiative toward this end. The government, too, can provide Parliament with special communiqués concerning foreign policy, which result in discussion and a decision by Parliament. Consideration of the budget, questions and interpellations, and an examination of the foreign policy section of the government's annual report, are all opportunities for a general exchange of opinions and the realization of parliamentary supervision. However, the nation's political position and the line that has been chosen mean that foreign policy questions are not central items on Parliament's agenda. In the Finnish Parliament, unlike parliaments of larger nations, there are no foreign policy discussions, and special questions under consideration rarely give cause for a broader exchange of opinion. The foreign policy section of the government's report is usually approved without lengthy speeches, and governments have reacted very niggardly with respect to special communiqués. Likewise, questions and motions by members of Parliament in the sphere of foreign policy are rather few in number.

The Foreign Affairs Committee. Continual parliamentary supervision of the conduct of foreign affairs takes place primarily through Parliament's committee on foreign affairs. The workload of this committee, which has at least nineteen members, is light, but the significance attached to it is shown by the fact that parties customarily choose their leading politicians as members. One of the committee's tasks is to prepare foreign policy matters coming before Parliament in the usual manner and to examine the foreign policy section of the government's report. But another task is more important in terms of examination: it must receive from the government "as often as circumstances require" a report on the development of foreign policy and on government measures in this field. The committee itself may take the initiative in order to receive a governmental report, and it may also (although it rarely seems to have done so) make a statement to the government concerning such a report.

It is perhaps through its committee on foreign affairs that Parliament is most concerned with foreign policy. From the committee's position and tasks it is evident that its purpose is to follow constantly the development of foreign policy and supervise consideration of important questions, beginning at the preparatory stage. A meeting of the committee can be called by the government even during a parliamentary recess. In general, however, there has been relatively little supervision and active intervention by the committee, and cooperation with the government has not always been smooth. Parliament complains that the government bypasses the committee and contacts it only for a post-factum explanation of events that have already taken place. On behalf of the government, however, it can be noted that the sensitive nature of many foreign policy questions requires a certain caution even in providing the committee with information: the silence of its members cannot be counted on and, indeed, secret information leaked out to the public during the war through the committee. On the other hand, it is evident that the committee itself has adopted a relatively passive attitude toward its duty as watchdog over the conduct of foreign affairs; it has focused most attention on the preparation of matters to be resolved by Parliament.

The government also has its own foreign affairs committee, established by law, which has had, particularly during the war years, great influence on foreign policy. For example, decisions on many of the most important questions during the Winter War were made wholly within this narrow circle.

The Ministry of Foreign Affairs and Representation Abroad. Actual administration of foreign affairs is centered in the ministry of foreign affairs, which is directed by the foreign minister assisted by a state secretary acting as office head. The ministry is divided into five departments: administrative, political, commercial, legal, and protocol. Most other ministries and central offices are also involved in one way or another with foreign relations, each in its own special field. The task of the ministry of foreign affairs is to supervise that activity of these various institutions which is carried on beyond Finland's borders and to ensure that in each instance the activity meshes with the general foreign policy line. Cooperation is not always without friction; difficulties arise particularly when it is felt that some office has acted too independently on important questions, bypassing the ministry of foreign affairs and the leadership in foreign policy.

Finnish relations with foreign states abroad are handled by diplomatic and consular representatives. Most important of the former are the ambassadors and ministers who head embassies or legations in other countries. The tasks of a diplomatic representative are to provide a channel for communications between the Finnish government and the government of the country in which he is located, gather information about political conditions and about the development of different fields, negotiate agreements and questions of mutual interest, promote commercial contacts, provide a general watch over Finnish interests, assist Finns traveling or living abroad, and preserve, in general, friendly relations between Finland and the country to which he is assigned.

The duties of consular representatives are in part the same, though they have certain special tasks in the field of commerce and shipping. Consuls are referred to as consul-generals, consuls, or vice-consuls. In addition to consuls sent from Finland, it is also permissible to designate as nonsalaried honorary consuls individuals living in a foreign country; the latter do not have to be Finnish citizens. An effort is made to place consuls in the largest cities of those countries with which Finland maintains constant and brisk economic relations. At the moment Finland does not have diplomatic relations with either West or East Germany, though permanent commercial delegations have been established in Cologne and Berlin to handle commercial, economic, and cultural relations; their counterparts from West and East Germany are in Helsinki.

Parties and Foreign Policy. The state's position in the arena of international politics and the nature of its internal power struggle determine how great a role foreign policy questions play in party activity and how sharp the disagreements are. In Finland, foreign policy does not occupy a central position in party programs or in public discussion; certain periods of domestic and foreign policy crisis, in which there was a sharpening of positions, have been natural exceptions to this general rule. During the first two decades of independence, Finland had to establish its international position and find a foreign policy line which would be most advantageous in terms of security. A certain amount of conflict between parties ensued and on occasion led to acrimonious clashes. But in general the period must be described as one of strong internal development; primary attention was focused on timely economic, social, and educational questions.

Finland's foreign policy position after the Second World War was sensitive and restricted, and the policy of neutrality was to a great extent passive. The result was a reservedness in the issuance of foreign policy statements, and foreign policy as a weapon in the domestic power struggle was eschewed. But as activity increased, discussion of the nation's foreign relations also became more lively. For the first time since 1945 foreign policy became a central topic in the domestic party struggle on the eve of the 1956 presidential election, when the Agrarian party attempted to make it the main issue of the election. The open crisis which prevailed in relations with the East during autumn 1958 caused an even broader discussion, lasting for a number of years, of relations with the Soviet Union. Brief mention should be made of the fact that during the interwar period the most consistent supporters of unconditional neutrality were the Social Democrats, who made their position clear immediately after they had recovered from defeat in the Civil War. They demanded peaceful neighborly relations with the Soviet Union, supported at an early date a closer association with Scandinavia, and, during the period of the Weimar Republic, also adopted a positive attitude toward Germany. The attitude of the other parties toward the Soviet Union, with the obvious exception of the Communists, was characterized by deep mistrust and outright animosity. Traditional sympathy toward Germany governed to a great extent the policy of the right and in part the policy of other bourgeois circles. The Swedish People's party was naturally the most clearly oriented toward Scandinavia, while the small Progressive party was probably the strongest supporter of contacts with the Anglo-Saxon world.

Since the Second World War there has prevailed among the parties great "official" unanimity concerning the main lines of foreign policy, which means that in this area no real struggles have occurred. All parties have declared their support for Finnish neutrality, the Paasikivi line, and Nordic cooperation. Most clearly differentiated from this common chorus are the People's Democrats, who demand a more consistent orientation toward the East—a multifaceted increase in contacts with the Soviet Union and with the People's Democracies. But it cannot be denied that, in individual instances, behind the official unanimity of other parties, too, there have been different notions concerning the details of foreign policy and application of the adopted general line. Jansson comments on this: "Support for our foreign policy is comparable to support for the Lutheran church. Ninety-five percent of the Finnish population belongs to the church, but represented within this group are all shades of opinion, from true believers to believers in name only and to the indifferent."[2] Differences of opinion have arisen primarily with respect to the handling of relations with the East. In general terms, the discussion has been a debate over which party or grouping has been most solidly behind the Paasikivi line and has best upheld his legacy. Since different parties and politicians evidently interpret that line slightly differently, the discussion has gotten nowhere. Because of the cautious and cloaked form in which statements are made, only a careful content analysis can reveal what the differences of interpretation really are. It can perhaps be said that some seek to give the Paasikivi line a far-reaching psychological interpretation, while others are satisfied with a less complicated legal interpretation. The latter position takes as its point of departure correct fulfillment of treaty obligations and consideration of Soviet strategic interests in Finland, whereas the former is based on psychological confidence —on what the Soviet Union thinks about Finland's official foreign policy, its politicians, and the entire nation.

Activity and participation by the public at large in foreign policy has been relatively weak, but the public obviously has given strong passive support to the actions of its political leaders and to results which have been achieved. In a 1964 poll commissioned by the planning committee for mental preparedness in national defense, about four-fifths of the respondents felt that Finland's foreign policy had in recent years been handled either "very" or "rather" well. About half were of the opinion that Finland's foreign policy leadership can influence her future "greatly" but, on the other hand, a substantial majority felt it unlikely that the country could remain neutral if a new world war should break out.[3]

THE MAIN LINES OF FINNISH FOREIGN POLICY

Neutrality. In a strictly legal interpretation, neutrality means that a state does not participate in a war between other states; it refrains from involvement, following certain fundamental rules. Such a definition in the contemporary world situation is too narrow. Neutrality affirmed thus does, to be sure, place certain international legal obligations on a state even during peacetime; but in any case, what emerges in practical politics is the political side of neutrality, a

2. Jan-Magnus Jansson, "Finlands östpolitik," *Nya Argus*, 51, no. 14 (1958), 207.
3. See "Mielipiteitä ulkopolitiikasta ja maanpuolustuksesta," *Sosiologia*, 2, no. 4 (1965), 194–196.

state's behavior, through which the preconditions for wartime neutrality and thus a state's security are continually created. Examined from this point of view, it is not possible to come up with any universal rules; every nation must fit its own policy to special circumstances shaped by geographic, historical, political, and strategic factors. The primary requirement is an unshakable desire for neutrality; the task of an appropriate policy launched on this basis is the creation and strengthening in a sensitive world situation of a climate characterized by psychological trust among close neighbors as well as states located further away.

The foreign policy of a small nation such as Finland must above all be a policy of national security the primary goal of which is to secure that nation's existence and freedom. One should be able in changing situations to choose the best means available to serve these purposes; a policy of neutrality is one such means. In a certain sense, the notion of Finnish neutrality can be traced back to the eighteenth century, to the activity of Finnish circles opposed to the war policy of Gustavus III; in any case it has had an important impact on the formation of foreign policy opinion for one hundred fifty years, since Finland in 1809 was joined to Russia.[4] Independent Finland pursued this goal from its early years and has charted its foreign policy line accordingly—groping at first and searching for direction, later with more purposefulness and more evident attention to the realities of world politics. To a degree, however, the official line is the result of efforts by strong domestic groups to pull in different directions, since parties disagree over location of the center of gravity in foreign policy.

Policy in the 1920's was in this respect still groping. It was characterized by a strongly emotional national-ideological distrust of and animosity toward Russia, as well as by fear of an attack from the Soviet Union. One of its concrete manifestations was the border state policy, favored in certain centrist circles and particularly by Foreign Minister Holsti, which did not, however, lead to the desired end. Only in the 1930's did a permanent foreign policy line begin to crystallize around the notion of neutrality. The nonaggression pact of 1932 between Finland and the Soviet Union was a turning point in that it was the first clear expression of Finland's desire to follow a policy of neutrality with respect to the East. Another important

4. G. A. Gripenberg, *Neutralitetstanken i Finlands politik* (Stockholm, 1960), pp. 9–10.

milestone was reached in 1935, when Prime Minister Kivimäki on December 5, in connection with consideration of the budget, presented a declaration in the form of a governmental communiqué emphasizing the importance of following a policy of genuine neutrality oriented toward Scandinavia. Parliament, parties, and the press were almost unanimous in approving this policy.

During the Second World War the special character of Finland's conflict with the Soviet Union was emphasized in many ways, and an effort was made to divorce Finland from the war between the Great Powers. Whatever one's opinion of this interpretation of the relationship, it did in any event receive recognition in that the United States refrained from declaring war on Finland and the demand for unconditional surrender was not extended to Finland.

After the war, in radically changed conditions, the question of the direction of foreign policy came to the forefront in an entirely new manner. Right after the war ended, it became necessary to improve relations with the Soviet Union, which was raised to a position of "most favored nation" in Finnish foreign policy. At the same time, the return to peace meant a more determined attachment to the neutrality line of the 1930's, which was found to be the foreign policy orientation corresponding best to the interests of the nation. This line has been strengthened over the years and an effort made to gain recognition of it from both Great Power blocs. Since the second half of the 1950's, Soviet leaders have on a number of occasions recognized without reserve Finnish neutrality and Finland's position as a nonaligned state. During his many state visits, President Kekkonen has made a special effort to gain recognition and approval from the Western states for this position and policy. The nation's foreign policy leadership has, in general, striven for inclusion by both Great Power blocs in the group of neutral countries along with, for example, Sweden and Austria.

The policy of neutrality in the years 1945–1955 was to a great extent passive; its basic notion was that Finland wanted to remain apart from conflicts of interest among the Great Powers and did not want to get involved in international disagreements. Finland avoids taking a stand in one direction or the other, particularly on questions resulting in disagreement between the Soviet Union and the United States; a good example is her attitude on the German question. It is clear that an effort was made, following this general guideline, to remain aloof from plans and alliances viewed by both sides in the cold war as directed against them. Finland did not join the Marshall Plan and has not sought membership in military or political organizations which have arisen at the initiative of the Western bloc. On the other hand, the Finnish government replied to a proposal made by the Soviet Union early in 1955 concerning the creation of a common security organization for Europe that Finland was willing to join provided that all European states approved the proposal. This did not happen, so Finland was not a party to the negotiations, which led to formation of the Warsaw Pact. Nevertheless, it is true that relations with the Soviet Union backed up with peace treaties and explicit defense agreements give a certain tone to Finnish neutrality.

Since the mid-1950's there has been a significant increase in activity as Finland, after having become a member of the United Nations and the Nordic Council, was able to participate on a broader scale in the different forms of international cooperation. In reporting on Finnish actions in the United Nations in 1958, the head of the political department of the ministry of foreign affairs, Minister Ralph Enckell (later named permanent representative to the United Nations) described this principle of active neutrality as follows: "We seek to avoid what might make difficult the maintenance of good relations with all countries, and especially with our neighbors. We also seek to eschew all measures which might cause conflicts or uphold and deepen them. Neither do we want to support decisions which from the outset clearly will not be abided by. We seek, on the contrary, to support all proposals which promote harmony and reduce conflicts and which have a real chance of being implemented."[5]

In contemporary Finnish foreign policy, one can distinguish within the framework of a general neutrality orientation certain main lines that are of critical importance in determination of Finland's international position. They are: 1) relations with the Soviet Union, 2) Nordic cooperation, 3) activity in the United Nations, and 4) efforts at economic cooperation. It must not, of course, be forgotten that Finland maintains political relations with many states on the globe and that she has very important commercial and cultural connections with many individual countries; these connections have their own special features, which cannot be covered in a brief exposition.

5. *Helsingin Sanomat*, Aug. 29, 1958.

Finland's Eastern Policy. The label which has come to be applied to Finland's postwar Eastern policy is the "Paasikivi line." Presupposing that Finland works actively for development of the best and most trustful relations possible with the Soviet Union, this line is *realpolitik*, free from ideological points of view, and its primary motive is that this line promotes the vital interests of both countries. Paasikivi described its principle in a 1955 newspaper interview:

> Although history does not always repeat itself, in spite of what one used to believe, it is, however, a fact that all the armed conflicts which Finland has had with Russia over 250 years have ended unhappily for our country, whereas, when meeting the Russians around the negotiating table, we have achieved many valuable results. In our history it has been necessary for the pen to rectify what has been caused by the sword . . . Good relations with Russia are now, and always will be, most important for Finland. This is determined by geography and history. We must think geographically in our foreign policy . . .[6]

The Paasikivi line is based on the notion that the Soviet Union as a Great Power is not interested in Finland as such, but only to the extent of concern for the security of her own northwestern border. Finnish security is consequently dependent on the security of her eastern neighbor; there is, therefore, an effort in relations with the Soviet Union to build a psychological atmosphere of trust, an effort to convince the Soviet Union that Finnish territory will never be used in preparations for an attack on the Soviet Union and that Finland is ready, if war should break out, to defend her own borders and to prevent possible attacks on the Soviet Union through Finnish territory.

Some circles immediately after the war considered the Paasikivi line opportunistic and dictated by force; at that time there was, in fact, no other possibility than to attempt to preserve the country's independence and freedom of political activity by seeking good relations with a recent opponent who had emerged victorious from the war. In time, however, the permanent value of this policy has become a more firmly established notion, as has the notion that the policy is not a wholly new or sudden orientation, but rather a consistent continuation of the foreign policy line begun in the 1930's —though only partially observed at that time. President Kekkonen's activity as the continuer and developer of Paasikivi's foreign policy

6. *Dagens Nyheter*, July 31, 1955.

has gained recognition in the label the "Paasikivi-Kekkonen line." As foreign policy activity has increased, the concept also seems to have expanded in that it describes more clearly than before the general international behavioral pattern of the country.

In a letter sent to President Paasikivi in February 1948, Generalissimo Stalin proposed—with reference to other agreements made by the Soviet Union at the same time—that negotiations be initiated concerning mutual assistance in the event of a possible attack by Germany. This resulted in the Treaty of Friendship, Cooperation, and Mutual Assistance signed by Finland and the Soviet Union in the spring. This mutual defense agreement covers a precisely defined area but nonetheless clearly expresses the principles of the Paasikivi line and the efforts of Finnish foreign policy: neutrality, as well as consideration of Soviet security interests and the development of friendly relations between the two countries. As far as Finland is concerned, the provisions that are psychologically most important are the affirmations of the country's neutrality and sovereignty. The treaty was concluded "taking into consideration Finland's effort to remain apart from the conflicts of interests among the Great Powers," and both parties to the treaty are bound "to observe the principle of mutual respect for sovereignty and independence, and noninterference in the internal affairs of the other state."

In terms of content, the treaty is quite narrow. Provisions concerning measures to be taken in the event of war or the threat of war are included in the first and second articles. If Finland, or the Soviet Union through Finnish territory, should become the object of armed attack by Germany or some other state in alliance with Germany, Finland will fight with all her strength to repulse the attack and to defend the inviolability of her territory. Action on Finnish territory will take place, when necessary, with the assistance of the Soviet Union or jointly with her. Agreement on aid "required by necessity" must be reached separately. The signatories agree to negotiate in the event that the threat of such a military attack is confirmed. There is no mention in the treaty of how confirmation of the threat of an attack will in practice be determined, but at least in Finland the article is interpreted as meaning mutual confirmation.

The treaty in question does, of course, restrict Finland's freedom of action, but compared with similar treaties concluded within the eastern bloc it is narrow in scope and weak. The treaty did, it is true, result from initiative by the Soviet Union, but some fundamental changes were made in the original draft on the basis of Finnish proposals. The machinery referred to by the military articles is put in motion only in the event that an armed attack threatens Finland or the Soviet Union through Finnish territory; in all military conflicts in which Finnish territory is not violated or threatened, the country can remain neutral. Explicit reference to Germany as the possible aggressor naturally stems from the fact that Germany in two world wars was Russia's chief enemy, and from the fact that the Germans during the Second World War used Finland as a base for attack. The obligation to negotiate is carefully restricted; it exists only when there has been confirmation of a threat of attack. It is important that the treaty does not extend into general political questions, since that could easily lead to a great reduction in the freedom to act in foreign policy. Finland defends her territory primarily with her own forces, and there is always separate agreement on the type and extent of aid necessary from the Soviet Union.

The treaty was originally concluded for ten years, but in 1955 it was extended for twenty years from that date; it is then in force for periods of five years in the absence of renunciation. In autumn 1961 the question of applying the military articles was unexpectedly raised. In its note of October 30 to the Finnish government, the Soviet government proposed—pointing to the rearmament of West Germany—consultation on measures to be taken for defense of both countries' borders on the basis of the threat of attack referred to in the treaty of assistance. In a later statement, it was said that the Soviet government requested the sending of a Finnish delegation to Moscow as soon as possible for negotiations. The series of events begun by the note ended, however, when the Soviet Union, as a result of talks between President Kekkonen and Prime Minister Khrushchev in Novosibirsk, agreed to defer the negotiations which had been proposed. This incident demonstrated that the treaty leaves room for interpretations by the other side that are even broader than perhaps was originally anticipated in Finnish circles. The sending of the note was a part of the tense world situation then prevailing and, to a degree, also part of the presidential election campaign, which was colored by the appearance of the Honka League as an effort to defeat President Kekkonen.

Only after conclusion of the Treaty of Friendship, Cooperation, and Mutual Assistance did cooperation between Finland and the Soviet Union take concrete shape. The treaty was an explicit call for continued development and strengthening of economic and cultural relations. One visible manifestation of the policy of cooperation is the expansion of commercial relations since the Second World War. In 1964, for example, trade with the Soviet Union rose to about 1,344 million marks and accounted for 15 percent of Finland's total foreign trade. The Soviet Union in that year was second to Great Britain as Finland's most important trading partner. As a point of comparison, in 1931–1935 the Soviet share of Finland's total trade averaged only 2.7 percent. In 1955 Finland and the Soviet Union concluded an agreement concerning scientific and technical cooperation. The forms of cooperation specified include an exchange of technical documents and scientific-technical information, invitations to experts to become acquainted with the achievements of both countries in the areas of industry and agriculture, an exchange of scholars, students, and lecturers, and the organization of scientific-technical negotiations.

The Soviet withdrawal in January 1956 from the naval base at Porkkala, which had been leased to the Soviet Union for fifty years in the 1944 Armistice Agreement, was generally considered a manifestation of growing trust in relations between the two neighbors in the spirit of the Paasikivi line. This event also strengthened the foundations of Finland's policy of neutrality. Soon afterwards the Soviet Union for the first time recognized Finnish neutrality without reservation. A later demonstration of the favorable trend in relations was an agreement signed in September 1962 in which the Soviet Union consented to rent to Finland the Soviet part of the Saimaa Canal.

Nordic Cooperation. In view of historical and geographic contacts, it is natural that a Scandinavian orientation is the second main line of Finnish foreign policy; but the fact that the Nordic nations do not form a wholly unified political group places certain limitations on cooperation. Finland has her own special position, and Norway, Denmark, and Iceland, for their part, are bound to the Western bloc through NATO. Only Sweden has sought to remain completely neutral and independent in world politics and has refrained from tying her hands through any sort of alliance. Under these circumstances it is natural that Finland has closest relations with Sweden, and that attention is focused above all on following her policy line. The Soviet Union in its own policy of security has been attentive to

Sweden's position of neutrality, and so it is considered important in Finland, too, that Sweden remain faithful to her neutral, alliance-free line.

Probably nowhere on the globe is there another group of states which has achieved such broad and close cooperation in various spheres of social life as the Nordic countries. What follows is a brief examination of the achievements and forms of cooperation visible only in the public sector; but it should be remembered that there are many other ties which are maintained between citizen organizations in political, economic, social, professional, and educational spheres, through which large numbers of private citizens are brought into cooperative work.

The most important and most tightly organized organ of cooperation between governments and parliaments is the Nordic Council, founded in 1952 by Sweden, Norway, Denmark, and Iceland. Finland became a member three years later, in autumn 1955; Soviet mistrust of the Council's purposes was the obstacle to earlier membership by Finland. According to paragraph 1 of the basic rules approved by the parliaments of the member nations, "The Nordic Council is the common organ of the Danish folketing, the Finnish eduskunta, the Icelandic alting, the Norwegian storting, and the Swedish riksdag, as well as the governments of these countries, in negotiating questions which concern cooperative action between all or some of these countries." The Council is therefore a territorial organization, the founding of which is permitted, and even recommended, in the Charter of the United Nations. The nature of the Nordic Council is apparent from paragraph 1: it is not a Nordic parliament capable of making decisions that are binding on the member states; it does no more than make proposals and recommendations.

Concerning the Council's jurisdiction, paragraph 10 of the basic rules merely states that it considers questions of common interest to the member nations. And there have been all sorts of questions on the agenda. But sensitive military questions, and foreign policy questions whose consideration would mean intervention in conflicts of interest among the Great Powers, have been excluded from the Council's jurisdiction. When becoming a member, Finland stipulated that her representatives would not participate in consideration of these matters if they should arise. Activity has been concentrated in the areas of economic, social, and educational life, where the Council seeks to achieve extensive coordination. Council action has led to the preparation of reports concerning conditions in member nations in various areas. The Council has also discussed the prerequisites for cooperation, taken cognizance of questions resulting in disagreements, and approved concrete recommendations to be passed on to the governments.

The basic rules of the Nordic Council are in content very narrow; they do not specify in detail the procedures to be followed by the organization and they do not put great obligations on the member states. A regular session, lasting about a week, is held in some capital every year. The Council has met in Helsinki three times (1957, 1962, 1967). The parliament of each nation selects members in its own way and for a period of time it favors; Iceland selects five members and the other four countries sixteen each, so that there are sixty-nine members in all. The governments also send as many representatives as they desire to sessions of the Council; the representatives participate in discussions but do not have voting rights. In some sessions there have been as many as thirty or forty ministers (the prime ministers are generally present). The role of ministers in the Council's work can be considered great when an attempt is made to achieve concrete results on individual matters. Every government and Council member has the right to make a motion. Committees, which handle the preparation of matters under question, can meet between sessions of the Council. Every member of the Council has one vote, which he is free to cast as he sees fit. On questions concerning only certain countries, the right to vote is restricted to members from those countries.

The Council has no central office, no common secretariat, and no other employees. The only permanent institution is a speakers council composed of a speaker and four deputy speakers chosen from members elected for each regular session and the interim period. Under the direction of this leadership, there is activity and cooperation among the secretariats of the various member nations.

The governments must at every regular session deliver a report on measures taken in implementation of recommendations made by the Council. During the first nine years of activity, up to the end of 1961, there were recommendations on a total of 241 matters. A study made early in 1962 showed that 125 (52 percent) were wholly or partially implemented or the goal achieved in some other way; 61 (25 percent) were about to be achieved or were under investigation; 55 (23 percent) were unrealized. Excluding internal matters of the Council, the largest number of implemented recommendations dealt with transportation and legal questions.[7] Outside the Council, cooperation among a state's officials and institutions is so broad and so complex that it is difficult to give an exhaustive account. At the governmental level, each country has a special minister for cooperation, mainly economic cooperation. The ministers of many administrative branches gather annually for negotiations; for example, meetings of the Nordic foreign ministers have a long tradition. Likewise, lower administrative authorities are in contact for discussion of common problems. Deserving of special mention is the Nordic Commission for Culture, founded in 1947 and functioning in the area of cultural life, which is subdivided into sections dealing with questions of science, schools, art, and public enlightenment.

One of the most important concrete results of Nordic cooperation has been the realization of uniformity in domestic legislation of the states in various fields. This work is facilitated by the fact that the countries in terms of their social structures and political systems are close to each other and by the fact that their legal systems are built on the same principles. Connected with this is cooperative action by police authorities in the prevention and solution of crimes. In the field of social policy, significant achievements have been realized in an effort to ensure that all Nordic citizens in any of the five countries enjoy the same social advantages that a single state has provided its own citizens. In 1954 a common Nordic labor market was created, which means freedom of movement by the labor force from one country to another. The transportation and communication fields are also examples of successful cooperative activity: Finland, Sweden, Norway, and Denmark form a common passport area, which means, on one hand, that citizens of these countries can move freely from one country to another without a passport and, on the other hand, that each country examines the passports of "foreigners" only at the outer borders of the area.

Cooperation also extends to international questions. Matters on the agenda of the United Nations General Assembly, for example, are discussed at annual meetings of the foreign ministers. It is relatively common that in their actions within international organizations these nations agree on joint presentations and common

7. *Nordiska Rådets verksamhet 1952–1961. Nordisk utredningsserie 1962: 8* (Stockholm, 1962), p. 329.

positions. An effort is made to win one seat for the Nordic nations, which is rotated among them, on leading organs of the various organizations. Thus Finland in 1957–1959 was a member of the U.N. Economic and Social Council and is at present (1969–1970) a nonpermanent member of the Security Council. The Helsinki Agreement of 1962 is, moreover, an outright obligation on the Nordic countries to negotiate questions of common interest arising in organizations and conferences.

Successful cooperation in economic life appears to be most difficult of realization. Of the major efforts in this direction, one need only mention that the plan prepared in the 1950's for a Nordic common market was dropped completely because of the birth of EFTA, and a joint program of development for the northern parts of Finland, Sweden, and Norway seems to have progressed very slowly. But recently, in the late 1960's, there has been a strengthening of efforts aimed at economic integration.

At the tenth session of the Nordic Council in Helsinki in 1962, a Nordic Agreement on Cooperation was approved; this constituted an attempt to gather together the hitherto scattered plans for action in different fields. In accordance with the established spirit of Nordic cooperation, this agreement does not seek uniformity of conditions through radical reforms and does not obligate member states with far-reaching commitments; it is more like a declarative statement of principle that, nonetheless, the contracting parties are considered duty-bound to observe. It was hoped that the agreement would ensure continued cooperation under Nordic banners in changing circumstances and would result in even broader efforts at territorial unification. The agreement includes a general plan for the preservation and development of cooperation in the legal, educational, social, and economic fields, as well as in transportation questions. Cooperation takes place, in accord with earlier practice, in ministerial meetings, within the framework of the Nordic Council and its different organs as outlined in the Council's basic rules, in special cooperative organs, or among appropriate authorities. The agreement came into force in 1962 after ratification by all participants.

Activity in the United Nations. Finland sought membership in the United Nations as far back as 1947, but because the question of membership had become a bone of contention between East and West, her application was not approved until December 14, 1955.

Earlier, some people had advanced the notion that it would be better for Finland to remain outside the U.N. in order to avoid political difficulties and for her own benefit; but experience shows that the advantages of membership outweigh the resulting difficulties. From the Finnish point of view, it was important that Finland, once she had become a member of the U.N., was freed from the position of a conquered "enemy state" and in this respect became the equal of other countries.

Membership in the United Nations brings, of course, not only rights, but also obligations—one of the most important of which is the obligation to participate, with armed force if necessary, in measures designed to preserve peace in accordance with decisions of the Security Council. Because the necessary military agreements have not been realized, this participation is on a voluntary basis. Finland has supported peace-keeping efforts of the U.N. in the Near and Middle East. In autumn 1956 a contingent of company strength was put at the U.N.'s disposal for supervisory work in the Suez as a result of the conflict there; and in spring 1964 a battalion was included in the Cyprus peace-keeping force. Likewise, Finnish officers were part of the inspection group sent by the United Nations to Lebanon for supervisory work during that nation's period of domestic turmoil in 1958. In October 1961, Finland placed two officers at U.N. disposal for inclusion in a group set up in Kashmir to police the armistice. Membership also brings economic burdens—which are not, however, very great.

Doubts concerning the desirability of Finland's becoming a United Nations member were based on the notion that Finnish delegates would frequently find themselves in a very difficult position since, as participants in a major political organization, they would have to take a stand on politically sensitive questions which had become matters of dispute between the Great Powers. In this respect Finland has strictly observed the foreign policy principles mentioned previously: she has carefully remained outside conflicts of interest among the Great Powers and has supported only those constructive proposals which have a good chance of being realized. Particularly on questions where there is sharp disagreement between the Soviet Union and the United States, Finland has abstained—which is, in a sense, a stand. In these cases it is possible to point out that the proposals are doomed from the very start; as there is no real chance of their being adopted there is no reason for Finland to support them.

It has thus been possible in international activity to join the principles of passive and active neutrality. Finland's delegates have consistently sought to make the Charter of the United Nations the basis for decision-making; they have repeatedly emphasized the importance of the organization as a forum for cooperation among nations and have sought to promote compromise solutions in questions involving strife. Following this line, Finland has not approved "moral condemnation" meted out in questions of great conflict, since it is felt that moral condemnation will merely aggravate existing problems.

Finland has her own independent line of action within the United Nations, and, on the basis of voting behavior in the General Assembly, it is not possible to place her firmly in any group of states. But if one wants to engage in this sort of pruning exercise, Finland should be seen as belonging primarily to the Nordic group, which generally represents thoughtfulness and moderation, as well as an effort to achieve conciliation in conflicts of political interest. Nordic cooperation extends, as mentioned, to United Nations policy, and, although these countries do not form a closely knit group in either a general scheme of international politics or in U.N. voting statistics, neither do they fall apart into groups with wholly contradictory opinions.

In addition to the main organization, there are some fifteen to twenty independent special organizations within the United Nations which have been founded through international agreements and are formally attached to the Economic and Social Council. The task of the latter body is to unify the activity of special organizations. Since the main organization seeks to achieve peace through political means, the special organizations attempt to strengthen the conditions for peace through practical assistance of a technical nature in various fields. This is a fundamental difference between the United Nations and the League of Nations. In the latter only one special organization, the International Labor Organization, supplemented the main political organization, and so the center of activity was clearly in the political sphere. The significance of political contacts after the Second World War has diminished proportionately, since practical action for the improvement of human conditions has assumed dimensions unanticipated in scope. Even before becoming a member of the U.N., Finland was able to participate in the activity of many special organizations, and in 1966 she was a member of the International

Atomic Energy Agency (IAEA) and of all thirteen special U.N. organizations. Connections with these organizations are handled by the proper ministry, central office, or special committee set up by the State Council.

Separate mention should be made of Finland's participation in international development programs. Most significant is the multilateral development assistance provided through the United Nations, its special organizations, and other international bodies. The U.N. Development Program (UNDP)—whose governing council includes Finland from 1968 to 1971—is the most important of these multination organizations. Finland participates in development assistance by granting annual appropriations in the budget, putting experts and administrative civil servants at the disposal of the U.N. and its special organizations, and placing foreign fellowship holders in Finland.

Bilateral development activity is conducted primarily within the framework of technical and economic agreements with certain countries—Tunisia, Peru, Ethiopia, and Tanzania—and joint Nordic projects. The best known of the latter is the Nordic Tanganyika center in Tanzania. The newest form of bilateral assistance consists of development groups financed through the budget; the first group, established by the foreign ministry and composed of twenty-two individuals, traveled to Tanzania in 1968 to provide educational and advisory services.

Finland's monetary contribution to development assistance was about 30 million marks in 1969; nearly three-fourths of this was multilateral in form and was utilized in development programs of international organizations.

Efforts at Economic Cooperation. Characteristic of postwar development within the Western economic area is a strong drive for economic cooperation designed to introduce more freedom in the organization of trade relations and payments. The exploratory work, lasting a number of years, concerned with the previously mentioned Nordic market was in most important respects completed in 1957. Implementation of the plan became impossible for a number of reasons, and in 1959, as Swedish, Norwegian, and Danish interest turned toward the realization of a broader West European system, the plan was dropped altogether. Once Great Britain, following the formation of the European Economic Community, had begun to seek a free trade area as a counterweight to the EEC, the European Free Trade Association (including Great Britain, Sweden, Norway, Denmark, Austria, Switzerland, and Portugal) came into being toward the end of 1959.

In this situation the prospects for continued and expanding Finnish exports seemed seriously weakened; from the outset, therefore, Finland was interested in the free trade area. EFTA membership was open to other nations, too, but direct membership for Finland presented many difficulties: an arrangement had to be found that would protect production and employment in certain weakly competitive areas during the transition period and that would be in harmony with the nation's other commercial obligations. Furthermore, consideration had to be given to the Soviet Union's generally negative attitude toward these sorts of groupings arising in the Western world. Lengthy negotiations with the Soviet Union and the EFTA nations resulted in an agreement that came into force on July 1, 1961, between Finland and the Free Trade Association. Finland did not join as a full member; the agreement provided for a new EFTA-Finland Association (EFA), within which Finland enjoys the same rights and obligations as exist for EFTA nations. Most important was the gradual reduction, according to a timetable, of import duties—except for purely fiscal duties—in trade between the member nations until tariffs would no longer exist. Contrary to the general provisions of the EFTA agreement concerning the abolition of quantitative restrictions on imports, Finland was permitted to retain the right to regulate imports of fuel, wheat, sugar, fertilizers, and cotton in order to protect Finnish-Soviet trade. To ensure flexible adaptation of production it was, moreover, agreed that a slower timetable would be applied with respect to certain goods (textiles, for example) as duties were done away with. Progress has been such that by the end of 1966 the member nations of EFTA abolished all remaining protective tariffs and quantitative restrictions on imports. In accord with her own agreement, Finland achieved the same goal by the end of 1967, with the exception of products covered by the special timetable.

The only administrative organ of EFTA is its joint council, where each nation and Finland has representatives. The permanent secretary is located in Geneva.

Late in the 1960's Finnish participation in international economic cooperation seemed to gain in both scope and depth. Illustrative of the first aspect is Finnish membership in the Organization for Economic Cooperation and Development (OECD), an advisory body with broad jurisdiction, which was sanctioned by Parliament in 1968; the second is manifested by a more purposeful effort to establish a Nordic customs union.

XIII National Defense

Since the end of the Second World War, the defense question in Finland has not been of much interest to the major parties; indeed, for a decade it was overshadowed by various economic and social questions, which is evident from budgetary appropriations for different needs. Only since the latter half of the 1950's has there been a significant strengthening of the military defense organization, as well as a development of economic and mental readiness and civil defense. Studies show that, in the light of official ideologies, the receptiveness of parties to national defense is clearly connected with the political dimension of right-left: the number of positive statements contained in party programs related to national defense is greatest on the right wing and diminishes as one moves left, until statements by the extreme left become negative. As far as the Communists are concerned, it should, of course, be noted that the question is one affecting their attitude toward the nation's present defense establishment.[1]

Before examining the organization of national defense, it is appropriate to look briefly at the external conditions within the framework of which the business of national defense is carried out. Consideration will not be given to natural conditions (population, wealth, geographic factors, and the possible character of a war scenario), but rather to those special duties and limitations on freedom of action imposed on Finland in agreements made with foreign countries.

1. For information concerning positions taken by the various parties and their supporters on national defense, see Antti Eskola, "Yhteiskunnan säilyttämistä ja puolustamista koskevat arvostukset," *Tiede ja Ase*, no. 20 (Helsinki, 1962), 5–90; Olavi Borg, "Puolueittemme ohjelmallinen asennoituminen puolustuslaitokseen ja maanpuolustukseen," Helsingin yliopiston yleisen valtio-opin laitoksen tutkimuksia, no. 2, 1963, mimeographed.

EXTERNAL CONDITIONS OF NATIONAL DEFENSE

Paris Peace Treaty. In an examination of the Finnish defense question, the following international treaties should be considered: the 1947 Paris Peace Treaty; the 1948 Finnish-Soviet Treaty of Friendship, Cooperation, and Mutual Assistance; the United Nations Charter; the 1921 Geneva agreement concerning the neutralization and nonfortification of the Aaland Islands; the 1940 Finnish-Soviet treaty concerning the Aaland Islands. Finland has also become a party to the 1963 partial nuclear test ban treaty, which, however, has only symbolic meaning in terms of the nation's military activity.

According to the Paris Peace Treaty, defense forces must be restricted to the execution of tasks of an internal nature and to local defense of borders. On this basis, the strength of the defense forces is limited so that the total strength of ground forces, including border and anti-aircraft troops, may not excede 34,400 men, the navy 4,500 men and a 10,000 total tonnage, the air force 3,000 men and 60 aircraft including aircraft of the fleet and the reserve. These manpower figures also include commissioned and noncommissioned officers and service personnel. Nuclear weapons, bombers equipped with internal bomb-carrying facilities, submarines, motor torpedo boats, and missiles are forbidden, as is excess war material (material unnecessary for the maintenance of defense forces permitted in the treaty). It is further stipulated in the treaty that military training may not be given to individuals who are not part of the defense forces. These military provisions can be changed through agreement between Finland and the other signatory nations or through agreement between Finland and the U.N. Security Council. Following the former procedure, it was possible in 1962 to achieve a new interpretation on one point in article 17 of the Paris Peace Treaty that was viewed in Finland as both militarily and politically significant. The treaty had completely forbidden missiles, which at that time meant weapons of attack. The development of weapons technology, however, has meant that certain missiles are necessary for effective defense. The Finnish government took the position that it cannot be contrary to the spirit and meaning of the treaty to interpret article 17 so that the phrase "self-propelled or guided projectiles" does not mean missiles of a strictly defensive type. Finland succeeded in winning the approval of the signatory powers on this point. The event was also seen by the foreign policy leadership as a significant demonstration of confidence in the policy of neutrality followed by Finland; sufficient defensive capacity is certainly one condition for the practice of a successful neutrality policy.

The U.N. Charter and the 1948 Defense Treaty. Military obligations upon Finland brought about through U.N. membership and the Treaty of Friendship, Cooperation, and Mutual Assistance with the Soviet Union have been mentioned. One need merely note that from a military point of view the latter is the more significant and that on the basis of obligations specified in the treaty the necessity of developing a defense establishment has been emphasized in recent years. In the event of an attack, Finland binds herself in the treaty to defend her territory on land, at sea, and in the air "with all the forces at her disposal." Discussion has centered on how the obligations imposed by the Treaty of Friendship, Cooperation, and Mutual Assistance can, if necessary, be fulfilled without violating the Paris Peace Treaty. Within the framework of limitations set by the latter, Finland's military forces would not be able to repulse or delay a major attack; mobilization of "all the forces at her disposal" would mean, in terms of numbers of troops, an increase in battle strength many times greater than the strength permitted by provisions of the Paris treaty. In the context of this book it is impossible to delve more deeply into this question or into the defense policy resulting from the Treaty of Friendship, Cooperation, and Mutual Assistance.

Agreements Concerning the Aaland Islands. For at least a hundred years the Aaland Islands question has had, from a military point of view, a significant "European interest." In the Paris Peace Agreement of 1856, after the Crimean War had ended, the Aaland Islands were declared a neutralized territory with a prohibition on the building of fortifications. In October 1921, many European powers concluded a new agreement in Geneva concerning neutralization of the Islands and the prohibition on fortifications; after the collapse of the security system of the League of Nations, however, the agreement lost much of its practical significance. At present the most important international document dealing with the military position of the Aaland Islands is the 1940 agreement with the Soviet Union obligating Finland to demilitarize the Islands, refrain from fortifying them, and refrain from placing them at the disposal of armed forces of other states. The agreement is explicit in defining the zone where construction of military and naval bases is forbidden. In order to ensure that the provisions of the agreement would be observed, the Soviet Union was given the right to have its own consular office on the Islands. The position of the archipelago is also mentioned in the Paris Peace Treaty; article 5 states that the Aaland Islands are to remain demilitarized in accordance with the prevalent situation. This clause is clearly a direct reference to the Finnish-Soviet treaty, which the Soviet Union wanted to remain in force.

DEFENSE FORCES

Defense forces include the defense and border establishments. According to a 1960 decree concerning the defense establishment, the general task of the defense forces in peacetime is to promote the nation's readiness for defense by providing military training and by emphasizing physical fitness and activity designed to increase the desire to defend one's country, to be otherwise prepared to defend the nation and protect neutrality, to defend the legal social order, and to participate in the maintenance of general order and security.

In defining wartime tasks, a certain caution is necessitated by the relatively modest technical level and size of the defense forces. The review committee on defense, which functioned during the years 1945–1949, wrote in its report:

> The task of Finland's defense forces is to create the military conditions necessary for the preservation of neutrality and necessary to remain aloof from war. At a minimum we must ensure that the nation, at least its vital areas, are not conquered by surprise attack, that life is not paralyzed, and that immediate mobilization cannot be prevented. If the nation in spite of all its efforts cannot remain neutral, if the nation is attacked, the goal of our defense forces is to win time and to create the conditions for, on one hand, receiving assistance, and, on the other hand, negotiations leading to peace.[2]

Military Duty. A defense establishment can be built on the basis of a professional, militia, or cadre system; in a country such as Finland under present conditions, the last is without doubt the best. In Finland there is a cadre system based on universal conscription and strengthened by a territorial system. This means that the core of the

2. "Puolustusrevisiokomitean mietintö n:o 2, komiteanmietintö 1949 n:o 22," mimeographed, pp. 22–23.

defense forces is formed by a regular salaried body of men serving in peacetime units, and every male citizen must participate in military training. The staffs of military provinces direct the training of units located within their own areas; a territorial organization formed by provinces and military districts handles the calling to duty of trainees and the supervision and the records of reserve personnel, as well as many tasks connected with mobilization.

"For the defense of the fatherland and the legal social order," every man meeting the necessary physical and mental requirements is subject to military duty from the beginning of the year during which he turns 17 until the end of the year he turns 60. During this period he is on active duty in the reserves or the militia. A youngster belongs to the militia, third class, from the year he reaches 17. Active service begins the year a young man becomes 20, and upon completion of this service he is transferred to the reserves. Upon reaching age 50, he is again put in the militia, now first class; but officers remain in the reserves until age 60, the highest officers even longer. The militia, second class, consists of individuals who for reasons of sickness or disability are not required to serve on active duty during peacetime. Active service lasts 240 days. Individuals who are trained to become reserve officers or noncommissioned officers or are trained for certain technical tasks must serve 330 days. Training is, therefore, shorter than in most countries. Restrictions in size imposed by the Paris Peace Treaty constitute a natural limit. Men in the reserves can be called for exercises for 40–100 days, depending upon position and task. For the most part, exercises in the postwar period have been organized only for a portion of the commissioned and noncommissioned corps.

In the event of mobilization, the reserves are the first to be called to duty, followed, if necessary, by the different age groupings in the militia; men who have reached age 50, however, can be called only with the consent of Parliament. When the defense forces are in a state of mobilization, men remain in service as long as necessary.

Along with the obligation to serve in the military, there is also a labor obligation of citizens. If during wartime it is temporarily necessary to build defense facilities and to perform other defense work, the military command is empowered by a 1930 law concerning a state of war to requisition labor for these tasks; in general, every physically able Finnish citizen is subject to conscription. Retention in this service generally may continue for 12 days at most, and a reasonable wage must be paid. In the 1942 law on labor obligation, which in part replaces the regulations mentioned above, citizens are required by various provisions, if a state of war should exist, to perform in accordance with their abilities and strength work which is important for national defense or for the population's well-being, or work necessary for the maintenance of the nation's economic life. A regular labor obligation affects individuals who have reached age 18 but who are not yet 55.

The Supreme Defense Command. The president of the Republic is the highest leader responsible for national defense. As commander-in-chief of the military forces, he possesses the highest decision-making power in matters dealing with the defense forces; as head of the Republic he also exercises considerable power in questions of national defense. He resolves matters of war and peace with the consent of Parliament, issues in the State Council the order for military mobilization, and determines when a state of war should be declared and ended. As the supreme executive authority, he directs national defense measures in all of the previously mentioned sectors.

In the last two wars a dualism was characteristic of Finland's military leadership because the president turned over the position of commander-in-chief, and with it supreme power in matters of military orders and appointments, to a soldier. Thus the military and political leaderships worked to a great degree separately and independently, partially unaware of each other, which of course caused all sorts of friction if not outright conflict. After the Second World War a number of steps were taken to develop the organizational leadership of national defense so that it would be better able to meet the demands of total war. An effort has been made to do away with the detachment of the military leadership and to increase the power and responsibility of the political leadership in military matters. In the new plans the point of departure seems to be that in the event of war breaking out, leadership will be concentrated in the hands of the president in all areas of total defense. He would thus also keep the position of commander-in-chief.

In a decree issued in 1957, a defense council was set up as the highest advisory and planning organ and as an advisory body to the president in matters dealing with national defense. The power of decision in the council is exercised by politicians; in addition to the minister of defense and the prime minister (who acts as chairman), the council includes other members of the State Council, but there are only two permanently represented professional soldiers, the commander of the defense forces and the chief of the general staff. The duties of the defense council are 1) to follow the military-political situation and plan the tasks of defense accordingly, 2) to examine basic defense plans for wartime contingencies and to comment on these plans as well as propose new measures, 3) to plan the financing of national defense, 4) to direct and coordinate defense preparations in different areas, 5) to comment on and make proposals concerning other matters designed to develop the nation's readiness for defense.

Leadership below the president is divided so that measures to be implemented in areas of civilian life—the sectors of political, economic, and psychological defense—are directed by the prime minister and the State Council, while the commander of the defense forces is responsible for military measures. He possesses, directly subordinate to the president, the power to issue military orders, and below him are the different parts and officials of the defense establishment. It is his duty to direct and supervise the preparation, development, and maintenance of defensive readiness of the forces, to ensure cooperation among the various parts of the defense forces and to ensure that leadership relations are appropriately organized, to consider and resolve military and personnel matters affecting the defense forces which are not a prerogative of the president or some other official, and to present to the president matters related to military commands and appointments. The staff of the commander of the defense forces is called a general staff; it also functions in economic and administrative matters as a central administrative office subordinate to the ministry of defense, the highest administrative authority of the defense forces.

The Defense Establishment. In addition to the highest organs of leadership already mentioned, the defense establishment during peacetime includes the ground forces, naval forces, air forces, training and certain other military institutions, supplies, military hospitals, and military courts. In 1966 the ground forces were reorganized so that the then existing staffs of three divisions and military provinces were unified, seven new military provinces becoming the largest areas of military administration. This step sought to simplify organization, to make leadership more effective by reducing the size of areas and by concentrating leadership in the hands of a single commander, and to unify in the most appropriate manner possible the fringes of military and civilian administration. Commanders of the military provinces direct both military districts and units within their territories. Their core consists of brigades, set up after the Second World War as small bodies suitable to Finnish conditions. The ground forces also include special units and formations. The naval and air forces have their own staffs, to which naval and air units are subordinate.

The Border Establishment. Separate from the defense establishment and subordinate to the ministry of the interior is the border establishment, which is responsible for guarding the nation's borders, for preventing the illegal transport of contraband and anything else unauthorized across the borders, for maintaining order and general security in territorial waters, and for carrying out police and customs inspection at sea. In the event of mobilization, the border establishment is joined to the regular defense forces. The border establishment includes a staff, which is a special department in the ministry of the interior, units located in the border areas, and the requisite training institutions. Its personnel normally consists of permanent state employees, as well as men and noncommissioned officers recruited on the basis of a contract; but men called to regular military duty are also trained and utilized in the border establishment.

CIVIL DEFENSE AND ECONOMIC/MENTAL PREPAREDNESS

Civil Defense. Civil defense before and during the Second World War was relatively well developed, considering the circumstances; it did not lag behind that in other countries. Civil defense work was carried out in many different forms both by the state and by voluntary citizen organizations. After the war it was almost completely forgotten for a decade, since most Finns showed little interest in it. The situation was quite different in Sweden, where civil defense has been of central importance in defense preparations. Finally—after individuals and certain organizations had begun voluntary civil defense work—the state undertook civil defense measures, the first notable result of which was passage in 1958 of a new civil defense law.

As stipulated in this law, the nation is divided into protection points and an area of supervision. The State Council can designate a population, industrial, transport, or other comparable center a protection point; the rest of the country becomes an area of supervision. During peacetime the following measures promoting civil defense readiness are to be undertaken: construction of protective shelters; drafting of plans for the transfer of population from protection points to other places; preparation of steps to promote wartime fire security, first aid, rubble clearing, and the appropriate organization of communications; provision of necessary equipment for civil defense; personnel training. Special attention is given to the construction of shelters in private and public buildings. The general division of labor is such that the state takes care of general planning and organization, advisory and enlightenment work and the training of key and special personnel; the commune takes care of civil defense measures necessary for residents within the communal territory; companies and private employers are responsible for the protection of people in their employ at the place of work and for the protection of their property.

Civil defense leadership rests with the ministry of the interior—with its department for civil defense matters, assisted by a special advisory organ on civil defense. Activity in the provinces is led and supervised by the provincial governments, which include special civil defense examiners. In communes with protection points there is a civil defense board, as well as a civilian defense head or director. In other communes the tasks of this board may be assumed by the communal board or by some other committee unless the ministry of the interior rules otherwise. Participation in civil defense work is generally on a voluntary basis during peacetime, but if war threatens or if a state of war has been declared, or if other weighty reasons exist, the State Council can require all citizens between the ages of 16 and 64 to participate in civil defense work. Along with the official organization, and closely connected with it, is Finland's Civil Defense Organization, which has played an important role in training.

Economic Readiness for Defense. Attention was first given to economic defense toward the end of the 1920's, when (in 1929) an economic defense council was set up to take care of the defense forces and civilian society through economic organization in the event of war. It was ten years after the Second World War before concrete steps were taken in this main branch of defense. Toward the end of

1955 the State Council established a planning committee for economic defense that included, in addition to a chairman, eighteen members representing different areas of economic life and industry, as well as different administrative branches of the state. The number of members was later increased (forty in 1965), and, when the members of sections are considered, it can be said that there are about three hundred people at work in the planning committee. The committee is subordinate to the ministry of commerce and industry; in 1960 its activity was established in law.

The planning committee is charged with investigative, planning, and organizational tasks necessary for development of the nation's economic-defense readiness, as well as for protection of the population's economic life and well-being during unusual conditions caused by war, the threat of war, or some other situation of unrest. The most important aspects of this work include the organization of production under normal conditions with an eye on defense, research activity concerning the possibility of replacing goods in short supply with others during times of crisis, and the drafting of plans dealing with stand-by stockpiles. In pursuance of these duties, the planning committee cooperates, insofar as it is necessary, with individuals in various occupations and with organizations they have formed, with communal authorities, and with state civilian and military authorities. To ensure uninterrupted work, a permanent office has been set up for the committee. Scientific research work connected with economic defense, as well as with other aspects of national defense, is directed by a scientific advisory body for national defense, established in 1961 by the State Council.

Nonmaterial Aspects of National Defense. A strong defensive will, a mental capacity to endure hardship, and a readiness for national defense are of special importance for small nations with limited material resources. The nonmaterial aspects of national defense were defined in a 1962 committee report as "the bringing together and strengthening of all the nonmaterial forces of a nation which are necessary in peacetime or wartime for the defense of the state's political independence, territorial inviolability, and the legal social order of Finnish democracy."[3] In terms of this sort of national defense, it is important that a common basis of motivation be found

3. "Henkisen maanpuolustuksen komitean mietintö n:o 1, komiteanmietintö 1962 n:o 72," mimeographed, p. 90.

—that those background factors can be affirmed and brought forward which make possible an understanding by all Finns of the significance of national defense. The basic values of Finnish democracy and neutrality of the state are seen as the primary factors influencing the nonmaterial basis of national defense. Means for promoting the realization of the established goal include citizen training, domestic and foreign information activity supporting neutrality and national defense, and research work, as well as public relations by the defense forces.

The organ that plans and directs this aspect of national defense is the planning committee for the nonmaterial aspects of national defense, subordinate to the ministry of defense, whose chairman and members are designated by the State Council for three years at a time. It is like the planning committee for economic defense, an organ resembling a permanent commission and made up of experts from various fields.

XIV National Fiscal Policy

State finances form one part, and the most important part, of the public economy; the second major part, communal finances, has already been dealt with in the chapter on communal politics. Increased intervention by the state in social matters has been characteristic in Finland, as elsewhere, during the last two or three decades. This, in turn, has resulted in a burgeoning of state finances. State expenditures in 1938 amounted to only 54 million marks, but by 1950 they had risen to 1,433 million and by 1965 to 6,821 million. In 1950 expenditures were thus 27 times, and in 1965 they were 126 times, as great as in 1938. The number of marks does not, of course, give a realistic picture of the situation because the growth in the sum of money is primarily a result of inflation. Perhaps the expansion of state finances is better revealed in a comparison of the state sector with the entire economy by examining the size of the state's share of the nation's entire returns from production. In 1938 state expenditures accounted for 18.3 percent of net national income; 22 years later this figure had risen to 34.5 percent. Corresponding figures for tax returns were 13.2 and 27.6 percent. State and communal taxes as a combined share of national income were 37.5 percent in 1960.

The real breakthrough in "welfare policy" occurred only after the Second World War. The enormous sums of money required for waging war naturally caused a growth in expenditures and a tightening of taxation, but later, when those exceptional expenditures were reduced state finances did not return to their previous status. Public funds were necessary to satisfy many economic and social needs which in part had been neglected during the war. It was, for example, necessary to construct an extensive system of price supports and to develop social welfare, as well as to expand the transportion network, hospitals and institutions for health care, and other public facilities.

The group of expenditures which has grown most since the war is that including income transfers, such as welfare payments, price supports and production subsidies, and interest on loans. A high level of employment and inflation has also played a role in making possible the expansion of expenditures; the former meant that unemployment expenditures were small, whereas the latter automatically increased the returns from a progressive income tax and reduced monetarily the burdens of fixed expenditures.

The growth in state expenditures has also meant, of course, a tightening of taxation, with respect both to direct and indirect taxes. A large portion of the increased expenditures has been financed by increasing indirect taxation. The relative significance of customs duties has, to be sure, decreased due to inflation, but a sales tax has risen to an even more important position as a source of revenue for the state.

The public economy in the modern state has become a real "tropical primeval forest with well concealed pitfalls."[1] It has become such an extensive and complicated system that even experts—to say nothing of less informed "mortals"—have difficulty understanding and controlling all its ramifications. The matter would be simpler if state finances could be confined merely to figures for the official budget, but such is not the case. A broad financial system has developed outside the economy of the budget, and within the framework of this system the proper authorities, exercising decision-making power, independently resolve matters concerning state finances. Grasping the general picture is further complicated by the involved relation between the state and the communes, as well as by the state's extensive business activity, not readily apparent from the budget. In this chapter, brief consideration will be given to some of the central questions of national fiscal policy: the state's expenditures and revenues, the national debt, the budget, and the organization of fiscal administration.

STATE REVENUES

The state collects a good four-fifths of its revenue through various taxes. It is, therefore, natural that decision-making power in this matter has been given to Parliament. In paragraph 61 of the Form

1. Allan Kankkunen, "Julkinen talous," *Taloudellisia selvityksiä 1958:I* (Helsinki: Suomen Pankin taloustieteellinen tutkimuslaitos, 1958), p. 26.

of Government Act it is stated: "Taxes, including customs duties, are regulated by law for a specified or unspecified period of time. This also holds for changing or dropping a former tax, as well as for general burdens." The basic principles behind payments made for documents and for action by officials must also be supported by law, as is the case for payments made for the use of the state's general facilities (postal, railroad, canal, hospital, and educational). In this instance, however, Parliament has not insisted upon its rights; in some cases—after determining the general grounds for taxation—Parliament has empowered the government to make detailed provisions concerning the amount of taxation. Such an enabling act must, of course, be passed in accordance with procedure followed for a fundamental law. In passing a tax law, the procedure followed is the same as for an ordinary law except that a proposal for a new or increased tax, for the continuation of a tax passed for a specified period of time, or for the contracting of a state loan cannot be delayed until a new election has been held. A proposal concerning a new or increased tax extending over a period longer than one year must be approved by a two-thirds majority on the third reading.

Tax System. It is customary to divide taxes on the basis of source into direct and indirect taxes. By far the most important of the direct taxes is the income and property tax made permanent by a law passed in 1920, which is collected regularly every year, in part in advance. There are really two different taxes involved, one collected on income, the other on property, but the sums are added together and considered a single tax. Individuals living in Finland, as well as various corporations, institutions, and foundations are subject to taxation; the state and its institutions, public law associations, and certain philanthropic bodies are exempt. The tax is levied according to net income received during the tax year, which means that expenses incurred through the pursuit and preservation of income are subtracted. The law also permits certain other deductions. Natural persons who must pay taxes are divided according to age, marital status, and obligation to provide sustenance into three tax classes, the first of which has the heaviest tax and the third the lightest. From income and property tax tables it is possible to determine how much tax each income group in the different tax classes must pay. For natural persons the tax is progressive, or increasing by degrees; in other words, the tax grows proportionately with an increase in income and property. In the collection of the income and property tax, as well as the communal tax, the church tax, and social security payments, the withholding principle is followed; an effort is made to withhold taxes as income is earned. Any balance due is collected through the filing of a tax statement, and possible overpayments are returned.

For the administration of taxation the country is divided into tax districts, each one of which has an office. In every commune there is a tax committee and a committee on investigations; in every province there is a provincial tax committee. After the tax office has completed preparations based on statements by taxpayers, it determines the tax. (Appeals were mentioned in the section on communal taxation.)

When compared with the income and property tax, the practical significance of a second direct tax, the inheritance and gift tax, is small. All who receive property as an inheritance, through a will or as a gift, must pay this tax. The inheritance tax is determined by a commune's inheritance tax committee on the basis of an assessment of the estate and the gift tax on the basis of a statement by the taxpayer. This tax, too, is progressive in nature. Another tax that can be considered direct is the social security and child allowance payments made by employers.

As far as indirect taxes are concerned, the best sources of revenue for the state are the sales tax, import levies, excise taxes (especially on tobacco), and the surplus of the State Alcohol Monopoly. The sales tax came into being in 1941 and since the end of the war has been the most lucrative of the indirect taxes. It can be realized in a number of different forms. Originally in Finland taxation was combined on finished products and retail trade, but in 1951 there was a shift to a purely production tax system. In 1964 the system was again reworked so that in principle the tax applies to the sale of all goods. Thus the taxpayer is a business entrepreneur who, in the form of business activity, prepares or sells, or only sells—who hires or performs labor in order to repair or alter goods. Some goods and services, however, are exempt from the sales tax. The rate of taxation is generally eleven percent. Sales tax offices carry out the taxation, and higher supervision, at the level of central administration, is provided by the sales tax office.

Customs duties on goods exported from Finland and on goods of foreign origin imported for sale are levied according to weight, number, size, or value. Export levies, which in the final analysis are borne by foreign consumers, are only collected for some separately designated commodities. Also included in indirect taxes are the stamp tax, which is paid by purchasing stamps for attachment to certain documents, and the automobile and motorcycle tax, which is paid to the state on the import of automobiles and motorcycles or collected from the manufacturer upon their first release to the public.

The state covers part of the expenditures incurred in the provision of services by collecting payments for use of its facilities. It is, of course, possible to deduct these payments from expenditures of the facilities in question, taking into consideration only net revenue or net expenditures. Payments differ from real taxes in that they are compensation for a specified service provided by the state.

Earned Income and Capital Revenue. The state receives some income in the same way private individuals do, and in terms of origin this earned income is much older than taxes. Earned income consists primarily of profits by business enterprises on one hand and of interest and dividends on the other hand, but it also can include certain special payments such as postal fees. The state has its own industrial activity and it owns large forest areas in eastern and northern Finland, the products of which are sold in quantity to private individuals. In 1964 the surplus of the state's forestry administration was about 44 million marks. Of the industrial establishments and other enterprises, some are directly owned by the state as administrative establishments and others are joint stock companies controlled by the state. According to information in the statistical yearbook, there were thirty-three of the latter in 1964, the largest of which were Enso-Gutzeit, Imatran Voima, Veitsiluoto, Outokumpu, Neste, Otanmäki, Valmet, Alkoholiliike, and Typpi Companies. When examining the returns from business activity by the state, it should be kept in mind that public enterprises are not always managed in accordance with strict business principles; enterprises running even in the red may be maintained for reasons of social policy and production.

Representative of capital revenue are funds received from the sale of property, repayment of loans, capital depreciation of business establishments, and loans taken out by the state.

Revenue Divided. The state receives a great part of its tax revenues from indirect taxation. This was the situation before the Second

World War, too, but the major emphasis over time has shifted from import levies to the sales tax. Customs before the war accounted for almost half of all tax revenues. But the great reduction in imports during the war years caused a sharp decline in returns from customs, and since increases in levies after the war did not match the increase in prices, the returns from these levies accounted in 1965 for only about eleven percent of the total sum of tax revenue. The sales tax has now become the single most important source of revenue for the state. It is very lucrative, in view of the fact that its returns automatically keep pace with the rise in prices and the growth of imports. Since 1948 it has in most years brought even more money to the state than the regular income and property tax. During and immediately after the war the share of direct taxes as a percentage of tax revenue was great, in part due to the reduction in customs revenue and in part to many extra taxes and a sharply progressive tax scale. Because extra taxes were done away with toward the end of the 1940's and the tax scale has been moderated several times, the significance of the income and property tax has diminished. Table 28 shows how state revenue was divided according to source in the years 1963, 1964, and 1965.

In order to clarify the categories in the table, it should be noted that the surplus of the state alcohol monopoly, as well as the income and property tax paid by it, is considered an indirect tax. The largest single group of taxlike revenue consists of payments made for child allowances (see Chapter XV). Other current revenue includes profits by business enterprises. Of direct taxes in 1965 the income and property tax accounted for 1,331 million marks; of indirect taxes, the sales tax accounted for 1,255 million marks, customs 522 million marks, and excise taxes 740 million marks.

STATE EXPENDITURES

In connection with the public economy it is often customary to speak of the law of expanding activity. State expenditures in Finland, like the expenditures of other public bodies, have shown continual growth that is not at all proportionate to the increase in population. Both world wars have played a role in hastening this course of development. The need for funds while waging war generally caused significant tax increases that in part remained permanent even after

Table 28. State budget revenues, 1963, 1964, 1965

Revenue	Millions of marks			Percentage		
	1963	1964	1965	1963	1964	1965
Direct taxes	865	1,257	1,357	19	22	20
Indirect taxes	2,255	2,748	3,092	49	48	45
Stamp tax and others	207	239	210	5	4	3
Taxlike revenue	388	446	520	8	8	8
Interest, dividends, shares	84	90	102	2	2	1
Other current revenue	167	231	275	4	4	4
Long-term loans	458	482	1,078	10	10	16
Other capital revenue	131	159	176	3	3	3
Total	4,555	5,752	6,810	100	101	100

Source: Taloudellinen katsaus, tables 14 (1965), 27 (1966) (Helsinki: Valtioneuvoston kirjapaino, 1965–1966).

military expenditures had been reduced with the return of peace. A reduction in expenditures for order and security has been accompanied by massive growth in cultural, social, and production expenditures. During the years right after the war, the state's economy was severely burdened by reparations to the Soviet Union and by compensation paid to Karelian refugees who were resettled in Finland. With the conclusion of these burdens, however, there was no significant relief; a continually expanding public social program has taken up the released funds. As mentioned earlier, the growth in total expenditures is to a great degree the result of an increase in revenue transfer expenditures. Revenue transfers pertain to the redistribution of funds collected from private individuals with certain economic and social goals in mind; they are, therefore, primarily grants made for various purposes, through which it is possible to equalize wealth and income differences in society. Revenue transfers can be compared with loans in aid, which the state today provides for many different purposes.

State expenditures can be grouped in a number of ways. According to the administrative grouping adopted in the budget, expenditures can be separated by branches of administration (see Table 33, page 408); in terms of practical needs this is an absolute necessity. Another possibility is to group expenditures from the perspective of the national economy, so that a division is reached like that in Table 29. Consumption expenditures include expenditures required for the maintenance of state activity: wages and pensions, repair and maintenance expenses, and the purchase of goods and services. Investment expenditures account for less than a fifth of total expenditures; they are either administrative investments (for example, in office buildings, schools, hospitals, and highways) or investments in state business enterprises covered by the budget. Investment expenditures also include state employment expenditures, insofar as they are intended for investment purposes.

Transfer expenditures, which account for almost half of all expenditures, include both real revenue transfers—the surrendering of funds for certain purposes with no compensation—and loans in aid from state funds. About a third of revenue transfers goes into social activity, child allowances, old-age assistance, and pensions and another third into support for production as well as price supports for provisions. In recent times agriculture has received, as production and price supports, eighty to ninety percent of revenue transfers in

Table 29. State budget expenditures, 1963, 1964, 1965

	Millions of marks			Percentage		
Expenditure	1963	1964	1965	1963	1964	1965
Consumption expenditures	1,327	1,522	1,693	27	27	25
Revenue transfers	2,014	2,396	2,747	42	42	40
Other current expenditures	255	303	369	5	5	5
Administrative investments	532	707	831	11	12	12
Investments in business enterprises	219	236	232	4	4	3
Disbursement of loans and other fiscal investments	284	331	538	6	6	8
Amortization of national debt	223	246	408	5	4	6
Total	4,854	5,741	6,818	100	100	99

Source: Taloudellinen katsaus, tables 15 (1965), 28 (1966) (Helsinki: Valtioneuvoston kirjapaino, 1965–1966).

this group. The major part of loans in aid, however, goes to commerce and industry.

State expenditures can be grouped in still a third way, by function. This classification is based on a distinction between order and security expenditures on one hand, and cultural, social, and production expenditures on the other. In the old budgetary classification, order and security expenditures would include actual expenditures of the ministries of defense, foreign affairs, and justice and their capital expenditures not productive of revenue, as well as expenditures of the ministry of the interior except for those of the medical establishment, which, with expenditures of the ministry of social affairs, are included in social expenditures. Cultural expenditures include those of the ministry of education; production expenditures, for the most part, include actual expenditures of the ministries of agriculture, communications and public works, and commerce and industry and their capital expenditures not productive of revenue. In Table 30 budgetary expenditures for the year 1964, except for amortization of the

Table 30. State budget expenditures by function, 1964

Expenditure	Millions of marks	Percent
Highest state organs and fiscal administration	118.0	2.5
Order and security expenditures	560.7	12.0
Cultural expenditures	653.4	14.0
Social expenditures	998.5	21.3
Production expenditures	969.7	20.7
Other items	1,377.7	29.5
Total	4,678.0	100.0

Source: Matti Leppo, *Kansantaloustieteen perusteet*, 4th ed. (Porvoo: WSOY, 1964), p. 86.

debt, are divided into categories on this basis. The category "other items" includes expenditures that are difficult to classify by function.

NATIONAL DEBT

In the earlier examination of state revenues and expenditures, it was seen that the state obtains some revenue through borrowing money at home and abroad and that one item on the side of expenditure is costs incurred as a result of the national debt, which in 1938 was only 37 million marks but by 1950 had risen to 1,357 million marks. This growth is striking, even though it was to a great degree a result of reduction in the value of money and a rise in foreign rates of exchange. Finland emerged from the war with an exceptionally small budgetary deficit; this situation generally causes an increase in the domestic debt in a corresponding amount.

It is customary to divide the national debt into 1) foreign and domestic debts and 2) long-term (consolidated) and short-term (floating) debts. Long-term domestic debts—actual state loans—are for the most part bond loans, whereas short-term loans are loans on promissory notes. Finland's national debt for the years 1938–1964, broken down into foreign and domestic debts, will be discussed in the following paragraphs on the basis of official statistics (see Table 31).

Table 31. National debt, 1938–1964

	Millions of marks		
Year	Foreign	Domestic	Total
1938	9	28	37
1945	199	656	855
1950	659	698	1,357
1955	616	751	1,367
1960	747	867	1,614
1964	1,187	1,817	3,004

Source: Statistical Yearbook of Finland 1965, table 227 (Helsinki: Tilastollinen päätoimisto, 1966), p. 221.

With the exception of a few years, the national debt has grown constantly during the period under examination. This phenomenon is typical, not only of Finland, but of all states at war and even neutral countries. It can in fact be argued that Finland has been relatively cautious in her loan policy, if, for example, the national debt is compared with national income. On the other hand, it is understandable that a state like Finland cannot assume such a large debt as some of the more developed nations can. At the conclusion of the Second World War, a major portion of the debt was domestic.

But since 1945 the foreign debt share has grown noticeably, and in 1964 it was 40 percent of the total.

Finally, it should be mentioned that the Form of Government Act requires the consent of Parliament before the state can contract a loan. The phrasing of the Constitution indicates that the taking out of a loan should proceed on the basis of a motion by the government. A state loan is decided not by law but by an empowering decision. Nevertheless, there is nothing to prevent the finance committee, for example, from making a motion during consideration of the budget for the contracting of a new loan by the state.

THE BUDGET, SPECIAL FUNDS, AND FISCAL ADMINISTRATION

The Budget. The budget period in Finland is a calendar year, meaning that the budget must be approved by the end of the previous year. The budget comes before Parliament for consideration each autumn, around September-October, but it has been subject since spring to much preparatory work among administrative officials and within the State Council. The first stage occurs when officials and institutions subordinate to the ministries and the State Council office draft their own appropriation proposals, in accordance with instructions from the ministry of finance, and send them to the proper ministries. There they are unified into proposals of the different ministries and the administrative branches subordinate to them and are, in turn, sent to the budget department of the ministry of finance for preparation of the final budget proposal. In financial matters even administrative officials easily function as pressure groups, each trying to satisfy as well as possible its own monetary needs; in the ministry of finance it has become necessary to negotiate with other ministries and to do some paring when considering the proposals. As an example: during the years 1948–1966 the final totals in the government's budget proposals were ten to thirty-five percent smaller than the figures in proposals by ministries. The proposal goes from the ministry of finance to the State Council, where it is considered in the committee on finance, in the evening school and other unofficial negotiations, and in the official plenary session. Finally, in the presidential session, a decision is made concerning transmission of the proposal to Parliament.

Initial parliamentary consideration of the budget proposal takes place during the third "reading" in the finance committee after parliamentary debate following submission of the proposal. After the committee's report has been tabled, the matter receives only a single consideration in plenary session; it is divided into a general and a detailed consideration. In the latter there is a presentation, first of expenditures and then of revenues, with supporting arguments appended, and, finally, of the general reasoning behind the proposal. If the report is not approved as presented—and this can hardly take place under normal conditions—the matter is returned to committee. If the committee suggests changes in decisions of Parliament, these proposals are either accepted or rejected in plenary session; the response of Parliament to the government's presentation is thus ready. The budget is published in the same way as a law passed by Parliament; it is signed by the president and approved by the minister of finance, after which it is published in a statute book.

Implementation of the budget, a responsibility of the government and of the administrative authorities subordinate to it, then commences. At the beginning of each fiscal year, the State Council office and the ministries must submit to the ministry of finance regulations on expenditures for offices, officials, institutions, and business enterprises, drafted in accordance with directives from the ministry of finance; the budget and the general thinking of Parliament about it must be strictly observed. The regulations are brought together in the ministry of finance and published as a thick book called a special estimate of expenditures, which is a detailed dissection of the budget for a given year. After a budget year has ended, inspection by Parliament of implementation of the budget—parliamentary auditing of the books—begins, lasting about two years. The length of a budget round (the time required for all stages of consideration of a single year's budget) is consequently close to four years.

Primary initiative with respect to the budget rests, in Finland as in most other modern states, with the government—which, as described above, prepares and submits its budget proposal to Parliament. Parliament participates in preparation of the budget by making amendments to the government's proposals, utilizing its own power of initiation. Proposals concerning addition to the budget of new appropriations, appropriations not included in the budgetary estimates, can be made by members of Parliament through fiscal bills, which must be submitted either at the beginning of a diet, during the period of general initiative, or a week after the budget presentation has been made. Fiscal bills are also sent to the finance committee, where they are considered, along with the budget proposal, in the fall. As already mentioned, the annual number of such bills is very great, but only a few of them result in action by Parliament; most are rejected outright (see Table 32).

Table 32. Appropriations requested in private member bills and approved by Parliament, 1954–1957

Year	Millions of old marks proposed in private member bills	Appropriations granted	
		Millions of old marks	Percent
1954	44,786.6	556.5	1.2
1955	55,292.5	449.1	0.8
1956	50,514.7	717.0	1.4
1957	53,817.2	708.5	1.3

Source: Jaakko Nousiainen, *Eduskunta aloitevallan käyttäjänä* (Porvoo: WSOY, 1961), p. 133.

Budgetary initiative by Parliament is indirectly limited in that appropriations approved in Parliament on the basis of a motion made during a diet are a conditional inclusion in the budget. The president has the power to determine whether or not this money will be used. During the first three decades of independence this budget veto did not have much practical significance, since it was very rare that conditional appropriations were rejected by the president. But since the 1950's the situation has changed. Conditional appropriations after 1955, for example, were left unratified most of the time; in 1963 the rejection figure was up to 89 percent.

When ratifying the budget, Parliament can alter the government's proposal even without making a motion; it can reduce or do away with appropriations included in the proposal or increase the amount so long as the increase does not fundamentally alter the purpose of the appropriations. In this respect, however, Parliament's freedom of action is restricted by an extensive system of committed or fixed expenditures. In any case, expenditures based on law or obligations of the state must be included in the budget, which means that Parliament's hands are tied.

The absence of political harmony between Parliament and the government, a feature of Finland's multiparty system, is clearly visible in consideration of the budget. There is a tendency for total budgetary expenditures to grow in Parliament, and the struggle of the minister of finance against additions to and increases in appropriations has become an almost annual occurrence. Even though Parliament does not make revolutionary changes in the government's presentation, the additions together can amount to a considerable sum of money. Research by Jussi Teljo in the 1920's and 1930's showed that Parliament generally sought to impede increases in "general expenditures"—items of expenditure required for the maintenance of order, the functioning of courts, and defense—while it promoted the growth of various "social expenditures." An understandable explanation of this phenomenon is that many social needs are familiar and close to members of Parliament, in addition to being a fundamental part of party programs, while the general needs just mentioned are more foreign to members of Parliament and to parties and do not evoke so much interest.[2]

During the course of a year, a number of changes are regularly made in the budget in the form of supplementary budgets. These result either from the fact that the government and Parliament fail at the outset, for political reasons, to construct the budget on a realistic basis or from the fact that the original estimates are no longer accurate due to changing conditions. There are at least two, usually more, supplementary budgets a year. Final expenditures during the years 1959–1965 were 3–17 percent greater than the sums set forth in the regular budgets for these years.

Table 33 shows the main lines of the budget. The revenue side is divided into general categories (GC), subcategories, and detailed points; the expenditure side is divided into major categories (MC), subcategories, and detailed points. Expenditures, as mentioned, are grouped according to an administrative principle; expenditures for the state's highest institutions are included in the first three major categories, followed by the various branches of administration, by ministries, and, finally, by a number of other expenditure categories.

In practice Finland has a gross budget, which includes all revenues and expenditures. But the net principle is followed with respect to state business institutions, as well as forestry and agriculture, which means that net revenues and expenditures are contained in the budget. Gross figures are given outside the columns.

2. Jussi Teljo, *Kansaneduskunta ja valtion tulo- ja menoarvio* (Jyväskylä, 1938), pp. 85–93.

Table 33. National budget, 1967

Expenditures by major category	Millions of marks	Revenue by general category	Millions of marks
President	0.8	Taxes and taxlike revenue	6,483.5
Parliament	11.2	Payments for use of state institutions	63.7
State Council and office of chancellor of justice	3.0	Miscellaneous revenue	306.0
State Council office	1.3	Revenue from interest and dividends	128.3
Ministry of foreign affairs	39.6	State business enterprises, forests, and farms	131.6
Ministry of justice	92.6	Loans	703.0
Ministry of the interior	958.4		
Ministry of finance	133.8		
Ministry of defense	439.5		
Ministry of education	963.4		
Ministry of agriculture	995.1		
Ministry of communications and public works	820.5		
Ministry of commerce and industry	421.8		
Ministry for social affairs	984.7		
General miscellaneous expenditures	499.1		
Pensions in some administrative fields	217.0		
National debt expenditures	850.4		
State business enterprises, forests, and farms	383.9		
Total	7,816.1	Total	7,816.1

Source: Asetuskokoelma 1966 no. 776 (Helsinki: Valtioneuvoston kirjapaino, 1966), pp. 1635–1734.

Appropriations included in expenditures are of three types: fixed, estimated, and transferable. Fixed appropriations may not be exceeded and must be used during the fiscal year. Some appropriations are based on estimates and under certain conditions may be exceeded if permission is granted by the State Council. Some long-term item of expenditure required, for example, by construction work can be recorded in the budget as transferable, which means that the appropriation may be wholly, or in part, transferred from the budget year for use at a later date.

State Funds. The largest portion of state finances is handled within the framework of the budget, but, as mentioned, there are a number of extrabudgetary "autonomous" funds whose revenue and expenditures are also included in total state revenues and expenditures. Utilization of such funds has become common since the end of the Second World War, for it is felt that in certain instances this permits greater flexibility in the management of affairs; it concerns utilization of certain revenue for purposes set forth explicitly. There are, in all, over fifteen hundred such funds; but most of them, for example, school fellowship funds, are without general significance. In 1966 the major extrabudgetary funds were the interior colonizations, import trade, standby stock, state railway renovations, post and telegraph renovations, and state grain store funds.

In the postwar years, significant sums of money have been transferred from the state budget to the interior colonizations fund. In 1965 the fund granted 61 million marks in loans for purposes connected with land settlement activity. In 1959 the import trade fund was set up, which seeks to protect imports by financing necessary purchases from abroad, as well as by compensating for price fluctuations in foreign trade. The standby stock fund was established to handle the stocking, through purchase, of raw materials and products considered necessary for the nation's economy and the population's well-being and health. The renovation funds are used by the board of administration of the state railways and the board of post and telegraph to finance repairs and new equipment necessitated by obsolescence and wear of assets in use. Within the framework of the state grain store fund, there is extensive sales and purchase activity in the area of grain products; the state grain fund has to do with purchases of domestic grain designed to maintain price stabilization, the import (exclusive rights) of foreign grain, the storing of grain, and the delivery of agricultural products to state institutions. Items transferred in 1965 through the state budget amounted, in all, to nearly 60 percent of the revenue of the special funds.

Fiscal Administration. Provisions concerning the management of state finances are contained in chapter 6 of the Form of Government

Act, from which it is apparent that an effort has been made to place highest authority in the hands of Parliament. The role of Parliament in economic management has already been noted in a number of connections. Parliament determines through legislation the collection of taxes, as well as the grounds for special payments and earned income; it also ratifies the annual budget and must consent before a state loan can be contracted.

Parliament also takes part in the supervision and examination of economic management. Parliamentary fiscal control is exercised primarily through state auditors; Parliament elects five auditors at each regular diet, to supervise observance of the budget and the "management and state of the national treasury," and examines their yearly reports. State auditors have the right to receive in pursuance of their duties all necessary official documents and reports, and to obtain these materials they are granted access to the offices and institutions in question. In their examination the auditors call attention to both the legality and appropriateness of fiscal management, and in their report they propose ways in which defects and bad practices can be corrected. Parliament then presents the suggestions which it has approved to the government. A second regular form of realizing parliamentary responsibility is examination of the report that the government is obliged to present to Parliament at every regular diet, concerning the management and state of the national treasury. The state balance sheet, published by the state treasury office, is transmitted to Parliament separately.

The highest executive fiscal authority is the State Council and, within that body, primarily the ministry of finance. The State Council must manage state finances in accordance with provisions and directions contained in existing laws and decrees, as well as in the budget. In general, the ministry of finance has jurisdiction over matters concerning the state budget, the nation's banking establishments, financial matters, taxation and economic development of the nation in accordance with demands of the national economy, and general statistics. The ministry has six departments: a general department, a budget department, a tax department, a department on the national economy, a department on wages, and a department on organization. Subordinate to the ministry of finance are the lower-level organs of fiscal administration such as the state treasury office, the national customs board, the excise office, the sales tax office, the mint, the inspection office for state finances, and the postal savings bank.

The state treasury office handles expenditures for the state and receives payments; manages the national debt and takes out loans for the state in accordance with its assumed powers; handles loans and investments by the state, as well as stocks and certain funds; supervises state currency in circulation; handles general bookkeeping; and draws up the state balance sheet. At the head of the office is an executive committee comprised of a director, two managers, and two department heads. The customs institution is charged with the collection of customs duties and other taxes and payments resulting from navigation and the exchange of goods with foreign nations. Subordinate to the customs board as organs of local administration and supervision are customs offices, bureaus, and stations. The excise office and sales tax office were founded to supervise the broad areas of taxation in question. The inspection office for state finances is an auditing institution whose duty is continual administrative inspection of the use of funds; in other words, it examines the legality and appropriateness of the way in which state finances are managed, as well as observance of the budget. Highest authority in the office is exercised by an inspection council. The organization of tax administration has already been mentioned.

The Bank of Finland. The Bank of Finland is a state bank which has the sole right to issue bank notes and whose task, as stated in its statutes, is "to keep Finland's monetary establishment on a firm and secure basis, as well as to promote and ease monetary transactions in the nation." The bank functions under the guarantee and in the care of Parliament and is subject to supervision by trustees elected by Parliament. Its administration is therefore within the jurisdiction of Parliament, not the State Council or the ministry of finance. The trustees have been entrusted with decision-making power in certain important monetary matters and matters concerning management of the bank; they determine its discount rate, ratify the fundamentals of the balance sheet, and make decisions concerning foreign credit, the granting to the bank's executive board of freedom from responsibility, and presentations to be made before Parliament or the State Council. The bank's executive board, whose chairman and at most four members are appointed by the president of the Republic following recommendation to the State Council by the trustees, is empowered to act in other matters.

The Bank of Finland is organized on the Swedish model as an

institution which to a great extent is independent of the government and Parliament. According to the interpretation adopted in practice, its executive board is not obliged to obey orders it might receive from the president or the State Council. Since activity for the most part is also beyond direct parliamentary power, the executive board is very independent both juridically and, depending upon its individual members, in actual fact when making decisions as to what measures should be adopted in a given situation in order best to manage the bank's affairs. The bank's leadership has strongly emphasized that institution's independent responsibility for the value of money and has expressed the opinion that a centralization of power in the hands of the government might mean an eclipse of monetary views in favor of short-sighted political goals. If the executive board seems to have acted in error, it is possible for the president to dismiss "as required by the general interest" those members who were appointed by open letter. The Bank of Finland, which directs one segment of economic policy, functions separately and is independent of the state's other economic leadership; this has on occasion given rise to serious disagreements between the government and the bank's executive board. Such was the case in 1957, when the bank wanted to maintain its own tight policy and refused to extend credit to the state that would have been used to ease payment difficulties. The government had no sanctions at its disposal, and so there was a temporary suspension of state payments.

XV Social Policy

THE EXTERNAL FRAMEWORK OF SOCIAL POLICY

Social Policy and Democracy. Social security and a reasonable standard of living are considered major indications of a welfare state. Because society abounds with social injustices which cannot be removed through the work of private citizens or of citizen organizations, there has been ever greater use of public power as a means of eradicating these inequities. But this conception of the obligations of society and the state has prevailed only during the present century. Still characteristic of the economic and political elite in Finland around the turn of the century was the old liberal notion that it is the responsibility of each individual to see to it that he and his family are able to get along in life. Little by little, however, comprehension grew of the fact that formal political equality and unrestricted economic competition are not able to bring people social security. There was, likewise, more receptivity to the idea that freedom in a democratic society is more a positive than a negative notion, and that it means more an opportunity for action than the absence of legal restrictions on action. Over time, and on this basis, there has developed—for the most part in spurts and without planning—the present system of social security, the construction of which has meant greater importance for public power and the costs of which have been assumed to a great extent by the state.

In Finland it has been the political and trade union movement of the workers which has worked most energetically for the removal of social wrongs and abuses. In the movement's early social program (during the period associated with the name of Viktor Julius von Wright) there were demands, at the 1893 Congress of Workers' Associations, for a ten-hour workday, free education and compulsory schooling, strengthening of land settlement activity and organization of relations concerned with land rental, and improvement in inspection of labor conditions. The first extensive reform program of the Social Democratic party dates back to 1906, when the workers were preparing on a broad front to take the path of parliamentary activity. In the social program prepared at the Oulu party congress in 1906 there were demands for an eight-hour workday, a general law protecting labor, development of labor protection for women and young people, strengthening of accident insurance and inspection of labor conditions, and adoption of health and old-age insurance. By the time of the Civil War, however, achievements in the field of social policy were very modest. In 1907 a law concerning work in bakeries was passed, and a law covering accidents was later made more inclusive. There was also regular organization of jobs for the unemployed in an effort to combat seasonal unemployment. But this was the extent of the reforms. Insofar as rural areas were concerned, the most important social question, the crofter question discussed in Chapter I, was wholly unresolved. A number of factors hindered the development of social legislation: the focusing of attention, once Russification had resumed, on defending Finland's rights against Russia; opposition from Russian governmental circles and diligent use by the Emperor of his unlimited veto right; lack of desire by bourgeois Finns and little interest in social questions; the class struggle position of Social Democrats, which worked against cooperation and compromise.

Finnish independence created new, much more favorable conditions for social reform work and it resulted in a stronger interest in social questions. The turning point was the year of revolution, 1917, when approval was given, in part due to extraparliamentary pressure, to an eight-hour workday and when decrees were issued concerning inspection of labor conditions and accident insurance. In terms of social reform work, conditions in the early 1920's were in many respects favorable. After the First World War a visible interest in social problems spread to all parts of the world, and these international awakenings also had an influence in Finland on legislation dealing with working conditions and the position of workers. Memories of the Civil War also served in many circles to increase the desire for reform. During this period the locus of political power was in the center, which was more favorably inclined than the right toward the demands for reform made by leftist parties and which also had its own social program. In some instances the Swedish People's party also backed proposals by Social Democrats in order to gain their support on language questions. Special attention was given in the 1920's to the development of labor legislation; in 1922 a law on contracts and one on labor regulations were passed, in 1923 a law on apprenticeship, in 1924 a law on collective agreements, in 1925 a law providing for mediation of labor disputes and one on accident insurance for workers, in 1926 a law on job placement, and in 1927 a law on inspection of labor conditions. There was also an effort to create, insofar as possible, a new system in the field of social welfare and health care. During this decade there was, moreover, an organization of a new field of administration—public social administration—which was necessitated by developing social work.

Both economic and political factors explain why the first years of the 1930's were very unproductive with respect to the development of social legislation. The impact of the world crisis extended to the Finnish economy. Exports declined substantially, prices fell, and unemployment soared. Under those conditions it was impossible to contemplate reforms that would increase state expenditures; it was enough to fight, through social work, the destruction wrought by the depression. Other influences on the course of development were the political crisis, the heightening of tensions between social classes, and the movement of policy even more to the right.

Around the middle of the decade healthier conditions were restored, and by the time of the Winter War significant reforms in various areas of social policy had been achieved. The Social Democrats, too, were given an opportunity to direct this work through the government. An effort was made to strengthen social security with the help of both social welfare and social insurance. In 1935 and 1939 significant changes were made in the law on accidents, and in 1937, with approval by Parliament of a national pension law, a far-reaching plan concerning compulsory old-age and disability insurance was realized. Employment protection and population questions became the new foci of social policy. As expanding market conditions increased job opportunities in the latter half of the 1930's, the question of unemployment was no longer so timely, although the unfortunate experiences of previous years necessitated at least the adoption in principle of some stand. In the light of modern economic theory, there was more and more comprehension of state and communal obligations with respect to providing job opportunities.

Population questions came to the forefront because of information concerning a declining birthrate and predictions of a slowdown and halt in population growth.

It is a known fact that social work reaches a peak in periods following great wars. In this respect the period following the Second World War was not an exception, for since 1945 there has been a particularly energetic effort to realize the welfare state. With the restoration of peace there were many important tasks for social policy: on one hand, the direct results of war had to be eliminated or at least mitigated, and, on the other hand, it was necessary to examine and amend earlier social legislation so that it would accord with prevailing conditions. Political factors assisted in advancing the development of social policy. The center of political gravity had shifted to the left, and for tactical reasons all parties became more interested in social problems. Social administration in the latter half of the 1940's was put to a hard test by the necessity of caring for and resettling Karelian refugees and having to provide compensation for losses suffered. In addition to handling the refugee question, there was also during these years an examination of legislation dealing particularly with industrial relations; and population problems, too, received more emphasis. In the 1950's primary attention was given to an extension of social welfare and to the question of unemployment, which by force of circumstances became the most important problem in economic and social policy. Finally, the 1960's have been marked by an effort to develop social insurance.

Social expenditures. Social expenditures can probably be regarded as a measure of social work and social security. The final sum of expenditures for 1964 was 2,107 million marks, according to information gathered by the social research office of the ministry for social affairs, of which the state accounted for 35 percent, communes 21 percent, employers 36 percent, and the population 8 percent. Of items close to or an integral part of social policy but not included in the statistics, work for the unemployed and support for housing construction should be mentioned. Examination of the growth of postwar expenditures in relation to population shows that social expenditures were 25 marks per resident in 1946, 165 marks in 1952, and 540 marks in 1965. The increase in the number of marks is, of course, partly a reflection of inflation, but the real increase has also been significant. The constant burgeoning of social expenditures has been possible due to the fact that national income has shown a corresponding increase. In the 1950's and 1960's social expenditures as a share of national income seem to have become fixed in the neighborhood of 10–12 percent, which, for the most part, corresponds to the level prevailing in the Nordic countries. In 1964 the major categories of social work, as a percentage of total expenditures, were as follows:

Old-age and disability	34 percent
Family and children	22
Health	26
War invalids and relatives of soldiers fallen in battle	6
Other social assistance	4
Industrial accidents	4
Unemployment	2
Tax deductions for children	2
Total	100 percent[1]

The largest single group of expenditures was for the system of national pensions, followed by general health and hospital care and the system of support for children (especially the allowances for all children under age sixteen).

Insofar as social expenditures by the state are concerned, that share of total state expenditures has grown significantly: in 1946 it was 5 percent but in 1964 it was 15. Social expenditures of the communes in 1964 accounted for 32 percent of total expenditures financed through communal taxation.

Social Administration. The highest authority for planning, inspection, and supervision in the field of social administration is the ministry for social affairs, to which, early in 1923, the central office social board (founded in 1917) was joined. The ministry, which is one of the State Council's broadest offices, is divided into general, labor, welfare and population, temperance and alcohol, forestry wages, insurance, health, and research departments, as well as an extraordinary department on prices. Tasks connected with social work are also handled by many other central administrative authorities, such as the ministries of justice, communications and public works,

1. *Sosiaalinen Aikakauskirja*, no. 6 (1966), 347–354.

and commerce and industry and the national health board and board of schools. Of the lower social authorities subordinate to the ministry for social affairs, mention should be made of the district inspectors of social welfare in the provinces, whose duty it is to follow the development of social welfare and to obtain information concerning its necessity and causes, to supervise welfare activity in the communes, and to give advice and instructions to communal officials. Provincial governments, and police authorities subordinate to them, also have important duties in the field of social administration. Other bodies subject to supervision by the ministry for social affairs include the communal organs of social administration, as well as the many social and labor market organizations, and the organizations in the fields of temperance and welfare, which have been entrusted by the state with public administration tasks. Because there are many such citizen organizations assisting in the management of social welfare as provided for in law, there is extensive utilization in social work of indirect administrative activity.

In practice, most welfare activity is carried out within a communal framework in such a way that the state shares in its costs and also directs and supervises welfare procedures. The most important communal social authority is the committee for social affairs; in general, one such committee must exist in every commune, although in some of the smallest communes the communal board can handle the tasks involved. The committee directs the administration of social welfare in a commune and cooperates with those voluntary organizations whose activity is a part of general welfare work. Social work is also dealt with by a number of other committees, both voluntary and standing, such as the health, hospital, temperance, school, and vocational training committees. In communes with over four thousand residents there must also be a director or a secretary for social affairs to handle the committee's tasks of preparation and implementation. Since the 1920's the number of salaried civil servants in communal social administration has increased greatly.

LABOR RELATIONS AND THE PROTECTION OF WORKERS

Legislation concerned with labor relations includes a large number of laws regulating the legal relationship between employers and workers. The first provisions in this area, following the realization of freedom to choose one's occupation, came into being at the end of the last century, but the real shaping of legislation on labor relations occurred during the first decade of independence.

Labor Contracts and Apprenticeship Agreements. A 1922 law concerning labor contracts includes general provisions with regard to labor relations. The law imposes—within, of course, the framework of legislation and collective agreements—some restrictions on labor contracts, which are otherwise freely negotiated; the purpose of the restrictions is to protect the position of the workers, who are the weaker participant on the labor market. It is stipulated that if a labor contract is negotiated for a specified period of time, that time may be no longer than three years, and the period of notice may not exceed six months. Obligatory provisions are stipulated with respect to payment of salaries, fringe benefits, withholdings from salary, piece-rate work, sick pay, and labor certificates.

An apprenticeship agreement is made by a person under twenty-one who goes to work for a tradesman to learn a profession. The apprenticeship period varies from two to four years, at the end of which the apprentice undergoes an examination. If the sample of his work is approved, he receives a certificate showing that he is an accredited worker. Interest in apprenticeship agreements has not been especially great. Employers avoid them because they carry certain obligations, and workers avoid them because they do not want to tie themselves down for many years to the same employer; besides, ordinary workers are often better paid.

Collective Agreements. Steps were begun in 1907 to develop through legislation a system of collective agreements; the office charged with preparing laws and decrees was given the task of drawing up a proposal on the matter. It was not until 1924, however, that the first law on collective agreements was realized. During its first twenty years of existence the law had very little practical significance; the system of collective agreements in Finland before the Second World War had not reached the level of the other Nordic countries. The major explanation was to be found in the negative stand of employers, who did not want to recognize trade union organizations as spokesmen for the workers and consequently avoided collective agreements. On the other hand, especially in the 1920's, cooperation was made difficult by the politicization of the trade union movement and by its internal splits. This disputed question was resolved only under wartime conditions. In an agreement on cooperation made in 1940, the "January Agreement," the Confederation of Finnish Employers (STK) and the Confederation of Finnish Trade Unions committed themselves to bargain collectively on all labor market questions, and in a general agreement of 1944 the employers consented in principle to accept a system of collective agreements as the common basis for labor relations. In 1946 the law on collective agreements was reworked to fit contemporary circumstances; almost the entire STK labor market was then covered by collective agreements.

This law stipulates that a collective agreement is an agreement between one or more employers or registered associations of employers on one hand, and one or more registered associations of workers on the other hand, and the agreement concerns those conditions which must be met in labor contracts and relations. Collective agreements usually cover wages, hours, vacations, job regulations, the position of representatives appointed by the workers, and other working conditions. The agreements are usually made for a year at a time, and the contracting partners are generally an employers' union and the corresponding trade union. Collective agreements are national in scope, and workers who are not organized normally enjoy the benefits accruing from these agreements. When agreements are renewed the general direction, particularly with respect to wages, is set through bargaining that involves the major industrial fields, for example, the metal and pulp-and-paper industries. But the confederations have also played an active role in collective agreement policy by concluding among themselves general agreements, or broad agreements, that set forth guidelines and sometimes effectively tie the hands of member bodies.

Concerning implementation of wage and collective agreements, it should be mentioned that trusted representatives are elected by trade union sections at the place of work to represent them, to supervise observance of the agreements, to convey the complaints and wishes of the workers to employers, and to represent workers in negotiations. There is also a second type of trusted representative in labor legislation, but the tasks of the two types are generally placed in the hands of a single person. Legal matters of dispute deriving from collective agreements are considered and resolved by a special court, the labor court, established in 1947.

Mediation of Labor Disputes. Included in the principles affecting labor in a democratic system is the right of workers to stop work and go on strike, following certain prescribed forms, and the right of employers to close their places of work. Since the occurrence of widespread strikes around the turn of the century, work stoppages caused by mass labor disputes have occurred regularly, mostly during periods of economic well-being and political unrest when workers have the most to gain and disputes are most easily intensified. In this respect the postwar peaks were 1950 and the year of the general strike, 1956, when nearly seven million workdays were lost due to work stoppages.

Because labor tranquility is important from the viewpoint of the entire national economy and society, the state has undertaken steps to prevent and reduce labor confrontations. Of particular importance in situations of national crisis is the uninterrupted flow of production; strikes and lockouts were forbidden by law during the war. But there has also been an effort during peacetime to strengthen the system of mediation of labor disputes, especially in recent years because of experiences connected with the 1956 general strike. In accordance with a 1962 law on mediation of labor disputes, there is a full-time national mediator and five part-time district mediators, in addition to which the ministry for social affairs can designate temporary mediators or mediation boards.

The national mediator seeks in cooperation with labor market organizations to promote good relations between employers and workers, as well as between their organizations. It is also his job to act at the request of both sides as chairman in collective agreement negotiations, to begin mediation in labor disputes having national significance, and to oversee the district mediators. A mediator must constantly follow the development of labor relations in his area of jurisdiction, and he must begin mediation after he has been informed of a dispute which could lead to a work stoppage. The disputants are obliged to attend negotiations set up by the mediator, or to send their representatives, and to provide the mediator with information which he considers necessary. Neither side, however, is bound to mediation proposals which may be made.

Freedom of action by the disputants is limited in two respects. There can be no work stoppage unless two weeks notice has been given to the opposing side and to the mediator of labor disputes. If it is felt that an intended work stoppage, or its extension, will affect society's vital activity or will significantly endanger the general interest, the ministry for social affairs can, in order to provide sufficient time for mediation, forbid a work stoppage or its extension for up to fourteen days from the moment that the existence of a labor conflict is announced.

Production Committees. After the Second World War, when an increase in industrial production and labor productivity was made necessary by, for example, war reparations and a desire for foreign trade, the state made an effort to develop industrial democracy and thereby increase cooperation between employers and employees. It was felt that it would be advantageous for production and labor productivity if workers were given information on questions concerning the enterprise and if they could negotiate such questions with their employers. A law passed in 1946 and reworked three years later provides for the establishment of an advisory organ, a production committee, formed by representatives of the employer, workers, and salaried employees in all industrial establishments where at least a hundred twenty thousand work hours (with the exception of overtime) are performed annually. The committee's task is to consider questions concerning the economy of an enterprise, production efficiency, and labor procedures, as well as to further harmonious relations between an employer and his workers. The production committees have not, however, been of much assistance in realizing industrial democracy.

Protection of Workers. The provision in the Form of Government Act concerning protection of the labor force has put an outright obligation on the government and Parliament to undertake legislative steps to further the protection of workers. The most important provisions in this area deal with general labor security, special protection for women and minors, work hours, annual vacations, and the observance of laws and decrees. Some general legislative provisions follow.

The 1917 law on an 8-hour day was obsolete in conditions after the Second World War, and so in 1946 a new law was passed, the law on work hours, which covered many more groups of workers. Nevertheless, even today many areas of work such as agricultural work, forestry work and logging, domestic work, and temporary odd jobs are not affected by regulations on work hours. There are at most

8 hours of work a day and 47 a week. In some special areas, such as rail and motor transportation, hospitals, hotels and restaurants, and art and amusement establishments, where working hours are arranged within the framework of a period longer than a day or a week, there are at most 141 hours in a 3-week period. The law on working hours also includes provisions about overtime, night work, and rest periods. Working conditions in commercial businesses and offices and hours for domestic help are regulated in special laws passed in 1946 and 1949, and work by seamen is regulated in a 1961 law. There are separate provisions concerning protection on the question of hours for children and young people, as well as women. Following the example of leading industrial nations, an effort is now being made in Finland to shift to a 5-day, 40-hour work week. With this in mind, approval was given in 1965 to changes in the law on work hours; but the changes do not become fully effective until early 1970.

A worker's annual vacation with pay is determined by the length of time he has been at a particular job. In general, he is entitled to one-and-a-half vacation days for each calendar month, increased to two days if the relationship with his employer has continued for ten years. The normal lengths of annual vacations are thus three weeks and one month. The vacation must usually be given as a whole during the period from May to September, and an employer does not have the right to keep an employee at work during this vacation period. It has now become customary for production establishments to close down completely for several weeks in midsummer and to give all workers their vacation at the same time. State civil servants and educators are in a more favorable position with respect to vacation benefits; the former normally have a one-month vacation and, after long service, a month and a half.

Accident and health protection has many different provisions at various levels, beginning with general legislation and ending with directives in effect for various industrial and occupational fields and at private production establishments. To ensure that provisions concerning the protection of workers are observed, there are job inspectors subordinate to the ministry for social affairs who, in addition to the ministry's chief inspector and deputy chief inspector, can be divided into five groups: male, female, and deputy inspectors, inspectors experienced as workers and recommended by labor organizations, and communal job inspectors. Taken separately, state job inspectors number about fifty. For consideration of questions arising in the application of laws concerning the protection of workers, there was founded in 1946, subordinate to the ministry for social affairs, a labor council whose members are appointed by the State Council for three years at a time. The decisions and statements of the council, comprised for the most part of individuals representing employer and worker organizations, have often had great importance in the interpretation of laws.

SOCIAL SECURITY

Social Welfare. As already mentioned, there was a continued expansion of social policy in the 1950's—especially in the field of social welfare. On one hand, there was legislative reform work designed to fill in gaps from the prewar period; on the other, there was a strengthening of practical welfare organization by such actions as the construction of new welfare facilities in various areas. Characteristic of social welfare is the fact that it is not directed at large numbers and that it is free. The right to receive welfare and compensation is an individual matter; in other words, necessity and kind of welfare measures are considered in each case on a personal basis and compulsion is resorted to only in extremity. Contemporary welfare policy is a conscious effort to strengthen welfare measures which are preventive and serve to increase the self-reliance of recipients. As an actual welfare need is met, there is a simultaneous effort to eliminate permanently the causes of the need.

The 1956 law on welfare assistance, which resulted in a reworking of welfare regulations for the poor, points explicitly at both actual and preventive welfare assistance. It can now be extended to people with limited resources, as well as to the penniless; in addition to care and sustenance that is an absolute necessity, welfare assistance also includes other support which serves to promote the health, well-being, and self-reliance of a recipient and his family. An effort is made to provide welfare assistance primarily in the form of aid at home. Insofar as institutional care is concerned, communes are obligated to build not only communal homes but also welfare institutions for individuals in need of special care.

The heart of social welfare activity is formed by measures provided for in laws on child protection, alcoholics, and vagrants, along with the system of welfare assistance. In accordance with the law on child protection, a commune's committee on social affairs must undertake steps of varying intensity with respect to a child who has not received or is in danger of failing to receive the necessary training and care. Protective supervision and custody are actual forms of care, whereas preventive measures include support for training at home and supervision of care for foster children, as well as protection for children and young people from improper sources of income (for example, prostitution and work injurious to one's health). Special provisions provide care for children born out of wedlock or of divorced parents, children of the mentally retarded, and children who are misfits in society, relatives of men serving in the military, or crippled.

An effort is made to cure alcoholism through care in the form of guidance and warnings, placement under temperance supervision, or, as an extreme measure, institutionalization. A warning and supervision are the first measures with respect to vagrant care, too; stiffer measures consist of dispatch to a workhouse or compulsory labor.

Social Insurance. Social welfare activity is complemented by social insurance, the development of which is heavily emphasized by modern social policy. In many respects it has turned out to be the more appropriate system; the negative side of social welfare is that its application on a broad scale is difficult, since each individual case must be examined separately—in addition to which it may, because of its nature as care for the poor, offend an individual's sense of self-respect. This feature is absent in social insurance, which is a realization of social justice based on the mutual solidarity of society's members. Insurance based on forced savings secures health and ability to get along for some people through payments made by the masses. In practice, however, popular insurance is today more like a system of social assistance than a system of real insurance.

Social insurance is utilized to cope with need resulting from accidents, illness, old age, disability, and unemployment. Finland's system of insurance has developed more slowly than in many other developed nations, reflecting both economic factors and opposition from political groups. Thus far accident insurance, health insurance, old-age and disability insurance, and job pension insurance are universal and compulsory.

The law on accident insurance, approved in 1948, provides job accident compensation not only for physical laborers but also for white-collar workers, workers in positions of public law, and students in certain educational establishments and courses. Only the self-employed, family members of employers, and individuals engaged in work of very short duration are not covered by insurance. A state civil servant is protected against an accident (defined as an injury received by a worker on the job or under circumstances resulting from his work) by special laws. Occupational diseases are also covered by insurance. An individual is compensated for an accident or an occupational disease in the form of health care, a per diem allowance, an annuity, and a disability allowance. The costs are borne by employers and the insurance provided by domestic insurance companies. Compensation for military accidents is arranged through special provisions included in the law on military disability.

Compulsory health insurance, which became fully effective in the beginning of 1967, covers all persons living in Finland and seeks to compensate for the loss of earned income and for expenses incurred as a result of illness, as well as pregnancy and birth. Compensation is paid for doctors' fees, medicines, travel expenses, laboratory tests, and expenses resulting from care by a nurse or midwife. The amount of per diem allowance is determined by earned income. The system has two special characteristics: full compensation for expenses is not provided; daily hospital fees are excluded from coverage. The insured, the state, and employers participate in the financing of the system, and the national pensions institution and local health insurance offices are charged with its administration.

A law on national pensions, which was passed in 1937 and became effective in 1939, provides for old-age and disability insurance. It was reworked in 1956 in order to guarantee citizens even greater security, and insurance was extended to the aged and disabled who were not entitled to a pension on the basis of the earlier law. Payment of premiums begins at age sixteen; employers also share in the costs, by making a pension payment equal to a set percentage of the wages of their workers, as do the state and communes. An old-age pension is paid to everyone who has reached age sixty-five and a disability pension to those who are physically unable to work but do not yet receive an old-age pension. Normal pension payments may be increased by a special support increment, the receipt and size of which depend on the size of an individual's income, his obligations to provide sustenance, and the local costs of living. In addition to old-age and disability pensions, old-age support may be given to unmarried women aged sixty to sixty-four who have no income or only a small one. A separate effort has been made to improve the position of pension recipients living in difficult economic circumstances by providing certain supplemental allowances, such as the allowance for wives, the allowance for children (lapsikorotus), a support allowance, and a disability allowance.

The new law on national pensions also changed the previous arrangement in that it put an end to the banking of funds coming to the national pensions institution; funds collected are now used directly in the payment of pensions. It was thus possible to increase pension amounts, but they are still not sufficiently high to guarantee the well-being of the aged and disabled. In September 1966 the average old-age pension was 132 marks a month; pensions for the permanently disabled averaged 141 marks and old-age support 88. The basic pension allotments are financed by premiums paid by the insured and by employers and through interest received by the national pensions institution, whereas the supplemental allowances are financed through contributions by the state and communes. Since there is no sort of comparability between premiums paid by the insured and pensions received, this is not really an insurance system, but rather a system of social security financed by taxlike payments.

Implementation of the insurance program is handled by the national pensions institution; its highest administrative organs are trustees elected by Parliament and a board and an enlarged board whose members are designated by the State Council. The field organization is made up of district directors and communal pension offices.

A sweeping social reform, a system of labor pensions, was realized in a law enforced in 1962 stipulating that employers must take out pension insurance for their workers from a pension fund or pension foundation or from an insurance company; this means that employers must provide their workers with sufficient security against old age and disability, supplemental to national pensions. Old-age pensions begin when a worker has reached age sixty-five, and the amount is determined by salary and number of years in service. A full pension is 40 percent of a worker's salary, which comes with forty years of service. A worker retains his pension benefits when he changes jobs, so the final pension can consist of pensions earned in the service of many employers. In computing disability pensions, a worker can include time remaining before eligibility for an old-age pension.

Special laws deal with pension security for individuals in jobs of short duration, for example, in forestry, agricultural, construction, and harbor work. In 1967 family pensions were joined to the system of labor pensions; payments are made to the widow and children of a deceased worker. The central organ of the system is the pension security center, which in its administration includes representatives of the state, as well as organizations of employers and workers. Pension security for state civil servants and their survivors is organized separately.

Unemployment. In the postwar period the balance between demand for and supply of labor has at times been badly shaken, and mass unemployment threatens to become a permanent phenomenon in certain areas. The situation was especially difficult in the late 1950's; a peak was reached in the early months of 1959, when there were nearly 100,000 people on the registers of unemployed. To be sure, only 19,000 were really without work because the others were put to work by labor force authorities. But, on the other hand, it has not been possible to measure the total extent of unemployment through use of the registers. Unemployment is heavily concentrated in the underdeveloped (eastern and northern) parts of the nation, and it has a very seasonal nature as well as being easily subject to change in the light of market conditions. But the crux of the matter seems to be structural weakness in the economy, demonstrated by the fact that even in good years there is unemployment in the winter, when the unemployed are put to work on public projects. In terms of structural unemployment, the core of the problem is that the small farmers in northern Finland are not able to get along on the basis of their land and they have insufficient opportunity to earn a living otherwise.

Since unemployment has achieved such great proportions, it is clear that its prevention must be part of the state's general economic policy. Of central importance in unemployment policy are the correctly timed public works arranged by the state and communes, as well as a preventive market policy whose component parts are foreign trade and currency policy, credit policy, fiscal policy, and policy in support of investment activity.

Long-range management of the unemployment question requires reorganizations of the entire economic structure, development of industry in appropriate directions, and rational management of land settlement activity. Of the labor and social measures aimed at preventing unemployment or mitigating its effects, mention should be made of the strengthening of professional education and choice of profession and the organizing of job placement, as well as unemployment insurance and assistance.

Through free job placement an effort is made to put prospective employees in contact with prospective employers and thus to reduce frictional unemployment. This task was once primarily the responsibility of the communes, but since the beginning of 1961 there has been a shift to a system of centralized state leadership, and job placement is now a function of state job emplacement offices. A private association may also be given permission to act in this sphere, however. The extent of public job placement is depicted by the fact that in 1964 there were as clients a total of 566,000 people seeking work and 384,000 job vacancies, of which 321,000 were filled. In a sense, job placement includes guidance on choice of profession (which since the 1950's has been noticeably strengthened), an effort to direct young people to fields of work where labor is needed and where it seems likely that the nature of a job and a youngster's inclinations can be matched.

Unemployment insurance in Finland has developed within the framework of voluntary unemployment funds that have been founded by trade unions and enjoy state support. These funds do not have major significance in the mitigation of unemployment effects because they have been few in number and include as members only a small portion of salaried workers. In the early 1960's an effort was made to shift to a system of unemployment insurance for the entire nation; the government submitted proposals to Parliament, but after the trade union movement and employer circles had reached agreement on an expansion of the voluntary system of funds, Parliament dropped the proposals and in 1960 was content to amend earlier legislation. An attempt was made to strengthen the activity of funds by increasing the maximum amounts of assistance, by increasing financial assistance from the state, and, above all, by requiring employers to make unemployment insurance payments (one-fifth of one per cent of the wage bill) to a central unemployment fund. This system was supplemented by the adoption of unemployment compensation (financial assistance paid from state funds to individuals on unemployment registers for whom there are no jobs and who consequently need economic support).

Administration of labor policy is divided primarily between the ministry of communications and public works and the ministry for social affairs. The department of labor force problems, a part of the communications ministry, handles matters of labor force policy proper, employment policy, job placement, and guidance in choice of profession; labor relations, wages, and the protection of workers are within the jurisdiction of the ministry for social affairs.

Population Policy. Population policy, brought into being by the threat of a diminishing population, seeks to influence through indirect means population development; its measures are directed at support for family formation, improvement in the health and well-being of newly born children and their mothers, and amelioration of family expenses. Examples of social assistance in this area are maternity care, household help, family allowances, and child allowances (lapsilisä).

A part of maternity care is called maternity assistance and is provided in money or in kind to all who seek it within a specified time. Expectant mothers are from the early stages of pregnancy obliged to undergo examination and seek advice from a doctor, midwife, or maternity clinic. Closely connected with care for mothers and children is temporary household help, arranged when a mother is unable to take care of her family due to childbirth, illness, exhaustion, or another compelling reason. The state extends assistance to communes if they decide to establish posts for communal domestic helpers.

Assistance granted on the basis of the law on family allowances comes from state funds and goes to poor families in which there are at least four (or, if the chief provider for the family is deceased or permanently disabled, two) children under sixteen years of age. Of much greater importance, however, is the child allowance, for sustenance and education, provided for all children under sixteen regardless of parental income and wealth. In 1967 the allowance for the first child was 198 marks, for the second 234, and for each remaining child 282 marks per year. Generally it is the mother of the child who is entitled to receive the child allowance, although a commune's committee on social affairs can rule payment to some other person; if obvious misuse of the allowance is discovered, the committee can take possession of the money and use it in a way advantageous to the child. Child allowances are for the most part financed through payments made by employers. Expenditures in

1963 resulting from child allowances were about 282 million marks, and, practically speaking, employers bore all the costs. In 1961 special child allowances came into being that can be paid, under certain conditions and in addition to the general child allowance, to a child for whom special economic support is a necessity to ensure subsistence, care, and education. Continuation of schooling or studies means that it is possible to receive special child allowances until age twenty. In its entirety, the system of child allowances results in a significant bridging of income levels both in terms of different population groups and geographical areas.

Housing Policy. The severe housing crisis which has prevailed since the Second World War has lifted housing policy to a more central position than ever in social work. Since it was impossible to eliminate the housing shortage through construction based purely on private enterprise, production began to be supported through disbursement of low interest-rate loans from state funds. In the latter half of the 1940's primary emphasis was given to the countryside, where the level of housing was raised considerably through state support based on a land acquisition law and other related laws. Since the 1950's, however, the population centers have been in the limelight. In 1949 previously diffuse regulations were codified in Arava (national housing board) legislation; this legislation, in turn, was reworked first in 1953 and then in 1966 by a law on housing construction.

In accordance with the newest law, there is disbursement from state funds—in order to promote housing development and improve housing conditions—of housing loans, primary and supplemental; guarantees are given; payments are made for additional interest, increases resulting from inflation and early remissions of interest; and research funds are provided. A loan can be granted from available appropriations for the construction of a rented apartment house, a cooperative apartment house, a private home, or a building in which individuals have purchased apartment space. For the first two types of housing, the maximum loan permitted is 60 percent of the approved value, for the latter two it is 40 percent. The longest periods permitted for repayment of loans are forty-five and twenty-five years respectively. Interest rates vary from 1 to 3 percent; the low rate is the real advantage gained by those who take out a loan. Special provisions establish certain maximum and minimum quality specifications for the construction of housing. For example, an apartment may not be larger than one hundred twenty square meters. All in all, state supported housing has fundamentally reduced the housing problem, has improved the quality of apartments, and has made possible an end to rental regulations. The present problem seems to be that a significant number of Arava apartments are too small for family living.

An effort has been made through special law to ensure that families with children are able to live so that housing expenditures do not exceed what is considered to be a reasonable portion of a family's income. It is, therefore, possible to grant poor families living in rented apartments with children a housing supplement that amounts to 20–70 percent of rent and heating costs. Activity specified in the law on housing and in the law concerning housing supplements for families with children is the responsibility of a housing board, which is a central office body subordinate to the ministry of communications and public works.

Supplementary Readings Index

Supplementary Readings, by Chapter

CHAPTER I. THE STRUCTURE OF FINNISH SOCIETY

Lento, Reino. *Väestö ja hyvinvointi*. Porvoo: WSOY, 1956.

Lindman, Sven. "The Concept of 'Nationality' in Swedish-Finnish Political Thought," *Annales Academiae regiae scientiarum Upsaliensis*, vol. VIII. Stockholm: Almqvist & Wiksell, 1964, pp. 8–20.

Mead, W. R. *An Economic Geography of the Scandinavian States and Finland*. London: University of London Press, 1958.

Modeen, Gunnar. *Finlands befolkning*. Helsingfors: Söderström & Co., 1953.

Sariola, Sakari. "Defining Social Class in Two Finnish Communities," *Transactions of the Westermarck Society*, vol. II. Åbo: Westermarck Society, pp. 134–157.

Stenius, Göran, ed. *Introduction to Finland 1963*. Porvoo: WSOY, 1963.

CHAPTER II. POLITICAL PARTIES

Allardt, Erik. "Facteurs économiques et sociaux du vote à gauche en Finlande," *Cahiers de sociologie economique*, no. 6 (May 1962), 258–266.

——— "Social Sources of Finnish Communism: Traditional and Emerging Radicalism," *International Journal of Comparative Sociology*, 5, no. 1 (March 1964), 49–72.

——— "Structural Cleavages in Finnish Politics," Helsingin yliopiston sosiologian laitoksen tutkimuksia, no. 6, 1961 (mimeographed).

Allardt, Erik, and Pertti Pesonen. "Citizen Participation in Political Life in Finland," *International Social Science Journal*, 12, no. 1 (1960), 27–39.

——— "Cleavages in Finnish Politics," in Seymour M. Lipset and Stein Rokkan, eds., *Party Systems and Voter Alignments*. New York: The Free Press, 1967, pp. 325–366.

Billington, James H. "Finland," in Cyril E. Black and Thomas P. Thornton, eds., *Communism and Revolution: The Strategic Uses of Political Violence*. Princeton: Princeton University Press, 1964, pp. 117–144.

Bonsdorff, Göran von. *Samlingspartiet*. Lovisa: Söderström & Co., 1947.

——— *Studier rörande den moderna liberalismen i de nordiska länderna*. Ekenäs: Ekenäs Tryckeri Aktiebolag, 1954.

——— *Suomen poliittiset puolueet*. Helsinki: Tammi, 1957.

——— *Svenska folkpartiet I*. Helsingfors: Söderström & Co., 1956.

Borg, Olavi. "Basic Dimensions of Finnish Party Ideologies: A Factor Analytical Study," *Scandinavian Political Studies*, vol. I. Helsinki: Political Science Associations in Denmark, Finland, Norway, and Sweden, 1966, pp. 94–117.

——— "Monipuoluejärjestelmän ideologisten peruserojen kuvaamisesta," *Politiikka*, 5, no. 1 (1963), 1–13.

——— *Suomen puolueet ja puolueohjelmat 1880–1964*. Porvoo: WSOY, 1965.

——— *Suomen puolueideologiat*. Vammala: WSOY, 1964.

Colliander, Rafael. *Svenska folkpartiet i Finland 1906–1926*. Helsingfors: Tidningsaktiebolaget Nylands Tryckeri, 1926.

Flemming, Tarja, Marja Nikkari, and Esko Niskanen. *Turun poliittiset yhdistykset*. Turku: Turun yliopiston valtio-opin laitos, eripainossarja A, no. 1, 1961.

Hakalehto, Ilkka. *Suomen kommunistinen puolue ja sen vaikutus poliittiseen ja ammatilliseen työväenliikkeeseen 1918–1928*. Porvoo: WSOY, 1966.

Hodgson, John H. *Communism in Finland: A History and Interpretation*. Princeton: Princeton University Press, 1967.

——— "The Finnish Communist Party," Slavic Review, 29, no. 1 (March 1970), 70–85.

——— "Finnland," in C. D. Kernig, ed., *Die Kommunistischen Parteien der Welt* (*Sowjetsystem und Demokratische Gesellschaft. Sonderband*). Freiburg, Basel, Vienna: Herder, 1969. Pages 189–200.

Inkilä, Arvo. *Kansamme eheyttämisen puolesta*. Helsinki: Kansallinen edistyspuolue, 1945.

Kipinästä tuli syttyi. Muistiinpanoja Suomen kommunistisen puolueen 40-vuotistaipaleelta, 3rd ed. Helsinki: Yhteistyö, 1958.

Krosby, Hans Peter. "The Communist Power Bid in Finland in 1948," *Political Science Quarterly*, 75, no. 2 (June 1960), 229–243.

Kymmenvuotias liitto. Suomen kansan demokraattinen liitto. Helsinki: SKDL, 1954.

Laine, Y. K. *Suomen poliittisen työväenliikkeen historia*, vols. I–III. Helsinki: Tammi, 1945–1946.

Lindman, Sven. *Partistudier 1–3*. Åbo: Acta Academiae Aboensis, Humaniora XXII 4, 1957.

Matti, Bengt. "Finland," in William E. Griffith, ed., *Communism in Europe*, vol. II. Cambridge, Mass.: M.I.T. Press, 1966, pp. 371–410.

Nousiainen, Jaakko. *Kommunismi Kuopion läänissä*. Joensuu: Pohjois-Karjalan Kirjapaino Oy, 1956.

——— *Puolueet puntarissa*, 2nd ed. Helsinki: Kirjayhtymä, 1959.

Nyholm, Pekka. *Suomen eduskuntaryhmien koheesio vuosien 1948–1951 vaalikaudella ja vuoden 1954 valtiopäivillä*. Helsinki: Finska Vetenskaps-Societeten, 1961.

Oittinen, R. H. *Työväenkysymys ja työväenliike Suomessa*, 2nd ed. Turku: Tammi, 1953.

Paasivirta, Juhani. *Suomen poliittisen työväenliikkeen kehitys*. Porvoo: WSOY, 1949.

Pesonen, Pertti. *An Election in Finland: Party Activities and Voter Reactions*. New Haven: Yale University Press, 1968.

——— *Valitsijamiesvaalien ylioppilasäänestäjät*. Vammala: Tammi, 1958.

Rantala, Onni. *Konservatiivinen puolueyhteisö*. Vammala: Vammalan Kirjapaino Oy, 1956.

——— *Konservatiivinen ja radikaalinen asennoituminen*. Tampere: Tampereen Kirjapaino-Osakeyhtiö, 1960.

——— *Konservatismi ja sen kannattajat*. Tampere: Tammi, 1960.

——— "The Political Regions in Finland," *Scandinavian Political Studies*, vol. II. Helsinki: Political Science Associations in Denmark, Finland, Norway and Sweden, 1967, pp. 117–140.

Rintala, Marvin. "An Image of European Politics: The People's Patriotic Movement," *Journal of Central European Affairs*, 22, no. 3 (October 1962), 308–316.
——— "The Problems of Generations in Finnish Communism," *The American Slavic and East European Review*, 17, no. 2 (April 1958), 190–202.
——— *Three Generations: The Extreme Right Wing in Finnish Politics*. Bloomington: Indiana University Press, 1962.
Routavaara, Akseli. *Kolme vuosikymmentä Kansallisen kokoomuspuolueen vaiheita*. Helsinki: Kansallisen Kokoomuspuolueen Keskusliitto, 1949.
Sänkiaho, Risto. *Puolueiden alueellinen kannatus Uudenmaan läänissä*. Helsinki: Finska Vetenskaps-Societeten, 1968.
Soikkanen, Hannu. *Sosialismin tulo Suomeen*. Porvoo: WSOY, 1961.
Suomen sosialidemokraattinen työväenliike 1899–1949. Helsinki: Suomen sosialidemokraattinen puolue, 1949.
Teljo, Jussi. *Suomen valtioelämän murros 1905–1908*. Porvoo: WSOY, 1949.

CHAPTER III. PRESSURE GROUPS

Galenson, Walter. "The Labor Movement and Industrial Relations," in Henning Friis, ed., *Scandinavia between East and West*. Ithaca: Cornell University Press, 1950, pp. 113–138.
Hetemäki, Päiviö. "Työnantajajärjestöt," *Oma maa*, vol. III. Porvoo: WSOY, 1958, pp. 19–33.
Huuska, Väinö. *Etujärjestöjen painostuspolitiikka Suomessa*. Porvoo: WSOY, 1968.
——— "Maataloustuottaja- ja työmarkkinajärjestöjen poliittisesta toiminnasta Suomessa 1950-luvulla," *Politiikka*, 7, no. 3 (1965), 1–23.
——— "SAK: n toiminta painostusryhmänä 1950-luvulla," pts. 1–2, *Politiikka*, 4, no. 1–2 (1962), 1–33, 85–111.
Knoellinger, Carl Erik. *Labor in Finland*. Cambridge, Mass.: Harvard University Press, 1960.
Korpela, E. J. "Maataloustuottajain järjestäytyminen," *Oma maa*, vol. X. Porvoo: WSOY, 1961, pp. 236–243.
Krusius-Ahrenberg, Lolo. *Kring intresserepresentationen i vår riksdag*. Meddelanden från ekonomisk-socialvetenskapliga institutionen vid Svenska Handelshögskolan, no. 4. Helsingfors: Svenska Handelshögskolan, 1955.
——— "The Political Power of Economic and Labor-Market Organizations: a Dilemma of Finnish Democracy," in Henry W. Ehrmann, ed., *Interest Groups on Four Continents*. Pittsburgh: University of Pittsburgh Press, 1960, pp. 33–59.
——— "Synpunkter på intresseorganisationernas politiska frammarsch," *Vår syn*, vol. III. Tammerfors: Söderström & Co., 1957, pp. 93–129.
Kuuskoski, Reino. "Yksilön oikeus, järjestöjen valta ja valtion etu," *Suomalaisen kansanvallan kehitys*. Porvoo: WSOY, 1956, pp. 316–327.
Luoma, Väinö. *Valtion virkamiesten järjestäytyminen Suomessa I–II*. Turku: Virkamiesliiton julkaisuja no. 8, 1962.
Noponen, Martti. *Kansanedustajien sosiaalinen tausta Suomessa*. Porvoo: WSOY, 1964.
Teljo, Jussi. "Painostusryhmät ja painostuspolitiikka," *Sosialistinen Aikakauslehti*, no. 11–12 (1953), pp. 416–420.
Waris, Heikki. "Suomen ammattiyhdistysliike," *Oma maa*, vol. X. Porvoo: WSOY, 1961, pp. 280–295.

CHAPTER IV. THE PRESS

Aho, Lauri. "Suomen lehdistö," *Oma maa*, vol. I. Porvoo: WSOY, 1958, pp. 223–237.

Grönvik, Axel. *The Character of the Finnish Press*. Helsinki: Työväen Kirjapaino, 1953.

Levikintarkastus Oy—Ab Upplagekontroll. "Levikkitiedot vuosilta 1962–1965" (mimeographed).

Mårtenson, Gunnar. *Oy Suomen Tietotoimisto—Finska Notisbyrån Ab—1887–1962*. Helsinki: Sanoma Osakeyhtiö, 1962.

Nordenstreng, Kaarle, and Osmo A. Wiio. "Some Effects of Radio and Television on Candidate and Party Images," *Scandinavian Political Studies*, vol. II. Helsinki: Political Science Associations in Denmark, Finland, Norway and Sweden, 1967, pp. 223–244.

Nousiainen, Jaakko. *Tutkimus eräiden sanomalehtien vaalipropagandasta vuoden 1956 presidentinvaaleissa*. Vammala: Acta Politica. Edidit Institutum Politicum Universistatis Helsingiensis, fasc. 1, 1958.

Qvist, Martti. *Lukemisharrastus*. Hämeenlinna: Karisto, 1960.

Rantala, Onni. "Suomen puoluelehdistön kehityksestä ja merkityksestä," *Politiikka*, 6, no. 1 (1964), 13–43.

Routavaara, Akseli. *Suomen sanomalehdistö 1771–1932*. Helsinki: Suomalaisen Kirjallisuuden Seura, 1935.

Steinby, Torsten. *Suomen sanomalehdistö*. Porvoo: WSOY, 1963.

Vehmas, Raino. *Sanomalehtiemme ulkomaanaineisto*. Turku: Institute of Sociology, Turku University, ser. B: 10, 1964.

CHAPTER V. FINLAND'S CONSTITUTION

Brotherus, K. R. *Suomen valtiollisen järjestysmuodon kehitys*, 3rd ed. Porvoo: WSOY, 1963.

Constitution Act and Parliament Act of Finland. Helsinki: Ministry for Foreign Affairs, 1967.

Democracy in Finland: Studies in Politics and Government. Helsinki: Finnish Political Science Association, 1960.

Erich, R. *Suomen valtio-oikeus*, vols. I–II. Helsinki: Tietosanakirja Oy, 1924–1925.

Jansson, Jan-Magnus. "Finland och de mänskliga rättigheterna," *Vår syn*, vol. III. Tammerfors: Söderström & Co., 1957, pp. 63–92.

——— *Grundlagsutskottets funktioner vid riksdagarna 1939–1952*. Helsingfors: Finska Vetenskaps-Societeten, 1954.

——— "Die Verfassungsentwicklung in Finnland seit dem Jahre 1939," *Jahrbuch des öffentlichen rechts*, NS, vol. VI. Tübingen: J. C. B. Mohr, 1957, pp. 285–318.

Jutikkala, Eino, and Kauko Pirinen. *A History of Finland*. New York: Frederick A. Praeger, 1962.

Kastari, Paavo. "Constitutional Protection of Civil Rights in Finland," *Democracy in Finland*. Helsinki: Finnish Political Science Association, 1960, pp. 58–73.

——— "The Historical Background of Finnish Constitutional Ideas," *Scandinavian Studies in Law*, vol. VII. Stockholm: Almqvist & Wiksell, 1963.

Merikoski, V. *Laillisuusvalvonta Suomen oikeusjärjestyksessä*. Vammala: Lainopillisen ylioppilastiedekunnan kustannustoimikunta, 1953.

——— "The Realization of the Equality of the National Languages in Finland," *Democracy in Finland*. Helsinki: Finnish Political Science Association, 1960.
Sipponen, Kauko. "Valtiovallan kolmijako I–III," *Politiikka*, 3, no. 3 (1961), 129–145; 3, no. 4 (1961), 174–203; 4, no. 1 (1962), 34–68.
Tammio, E. H. I. *Lain säätäminen itsenäisessä Suomessa*. Vammala: WSOY, 1948.
Uotila, Jaakko, ed. *The Finnish Legal System*. Helsinki: Union of Finnish Lawyers Publishing Company, 1966.

CHAPTER VI. PARLIAMENT

Allardt, Erik. *Social struktur och politisk aktivitet*. Helsingfors: Söderström & Co., 1956.
Allardt, Erik, and Kettil Bruun. "Characteristics of the Finnish Non-Voter," *Transactions of the Westermarck Society*, vol. III. Copenhagen: Ejnar Munksgaard, 1956.
Brotherus, K. R. *Suomen valtiollisen järjestysmuodon kehitys*, 3rd ed. Porvoo: WSOY, 1963.
Jansson, Jan-Magnus. *Grundlagsutskottets funktioner vid riksdagarna 1939–1952*. Helsingfors: Finska Vetenskaps-Societeten, 1954.
Kastari, Paavo. *Eduskunnan hajoitus Suomen oikeuden mukaan*. Vammala: Suomalainen Lakimiesten Yhdistys, 1940.
——— "The Parliamentary Ombudsman: His Functions, Position, and Relations to the Chancellor of Justice in Finland," *International Review of Administrative Sciences*, 28, no. 4 (1962), 391–398.
Kekkonen, Urho. "Eduskuntatyön rationalisoimisesta Suomessa," *Valtiotieteellisen Yhdistyksen vuosikirja 1948–1949*. Vammala: Valtiotieteellinen Yhdistys, 1949, pp. 5–25.
Krusius-Ahrenberg, L., and M. Kull. *Kring frågan om en reform av vårt proportionella valsätt: Meddelanden från ekonomisk-socialvetenskapliga institutionen vid Svenska Handelshögskolan*, no. 1. Helsingfors: Svenska Handelshögskolan, 1954.
Lindman, Sven. "Eduskunnan aseman muuttuminen 1917–1919," *Suomen kansanedustuslaitoksen historia*, vol. VI. Helsinki: Eduskunnan historiakomitea, 1968.
Mäkinen, Eino, ed. *The Finnish Parliament*. Helsinki: The Finnish Parliament, 1957.
Noponen, Martti. *Kansanedustajien sosiaalinen tausta Suomessa*. Porvoo: WSOY, 1964.
Noponen, Martti, and Pertti Pesonen. "The Legislative Career in Finland," in Erik Allardt and Yrjö Littunen, eds., *Cleavages, Ideologies and Party Systems*. Turku: Westermarck Society, 1964, pp. 441–463.
Nousiainen, Jaakko. *Eduskunta aloitevallan käyttäjänä*. Porvoo: WSOY, 1961.
Nyholm, Pekka. *Maatalouden ryhmäetu eduskunnassa vuosien 1930–39 ja 1945–51 vaalikausina*. Pieksämäki: Jyväskylän Kasvatusopillinen Korkeakoulu, 1965.
——— *Suomen eduskuntaryhmien koheesio vuosien 1948–1951 vaalikaudella ja vuoden 1954 valtiopäivillä*. Helsinki: Finska Vetenskaps-Societeten, 1961.
Pesonen, Pertti. *An Election in Finland: Party Activities and Voter Reactions*. New Haven: Yale University Press, 1968.
——— "Vaaliliittoyhteistyön vaikutus eduskuntaryhmien voimasuhteisiin," *Politiikka*, 7, no. 1 (1965), 1–21.
Salervo, Olavi. "Eduskunnan puhemiehen asema ja tehtävä Suomessa," *K-A. Fagerholm, mies ja työkenttä*. Helsinki: Tammi, 1961, pp. 75–85.

Seitkari, O. "Edustuslaitoksen uudistus 1906," *Suomen kansanedustuslaitoksen historia*, vol. V. Helsinki: Eduskunnan historiakomitea, 1958, pp. 7–162.
Sipponen, Kauko. "Some Aspects of the Delegation of Legislative Power in Finland," *Scandinavian Studies in Law*, vol. IX. Uppsala: Almqvist & Wiksell, 1965, pp. 159–176.
Tammio, E. H. I. *Lain säätäminen itsenäisessä Suomessa*. Vammala: WSOY, 1948.
Törnudd, Klaus. *The Electoral System of Finland*. London: Hugh Evelyn, 1968.
Tuominen, Uuno. "Autonomian ajan yksikamarinen eduskunta 1907–1916," *Suomen kansanedustuslaitoksen historia*, vol. V. Helsinki: Eduskunnan historiakomitea, 1958, pp. 163–411.

CHAPTER VII. THE PRESIDENT OF THE REPUBLIC AND THE STATE COUNCIL

Björksten, S. R. *Statsrådet i Finland från konstitutionell synpunkt*. Åbo: Söderström & Co., 1929.
Hirvikallio, Paavo. *Tasavallan presidentin vaalit Suomessa 1919–1950*. Porvoo: WSOY, 1958.
Jyränki, Antero. "Yhdysvaltain ja Suomen presidentin aseman vertailua," *Politiikka*, 4, no. 4 (1962), 208–244.
Kastari, Paavo. "Ministereitten kannanottojen ja lausuntojen merkityksestä tasavallan presidentin ratkaistessa asioita valtioneuvostossa," *Valtiotieteellisen Yhdistyksen vuosikirja 1941*. Vammala: Valtiotieteellinen Yhdistys, 1941, pp. 39–63.
——— "Ministerivaliokuntia koskevia näkökohtia," *Valtiotieteellisen Yhdistyksen vuosikirja 1947*. Vammala: Valtiotieteellinen Yhdistys, 1947, pp. 92–108.
——— *La présidence de la République en Finlande*. Neuchâtel: Editions de la Baconnière, 1962.
——— "Tasavallan presidentin asemaa koskevia näkökohtia," *Lakimies*, 58 (1960), 675–709.
Lindman, Sven. *Notes on the Presidential Elections in Finland*. Åbo: Åbo Akademi, 1951.
——— *Studier över parlamentarismens tillämpning i Finland 1919–1926*. Åbo: Åbo Akademi, 1937.
Pesonen, Pertti. *Valitsijamiesvaalien ylioppilasäänestäjät*. Vammala: Tammi, 1958.
Prokuraattori—oikeuskansleri 1809–1959. Juhlajulkaisu. Helsinki: Valtioneuvoston kirjapaino, 1959.
Tarkiainen, Tuttu. *Tasavallan presidentin asema Suomen parlamenttaarisessa hallitusjärjestelmässä*. Jyväskylä: Gummerus, 1938.
Teljo, Jussi. "Valtionpäämiehen asema Suomessa," *Suomalainen Suomi*, September, 1937, pp. 343–356.
Uotila, Jaakko. *Päätösvallan siirtäminen Suomen valtionhallinnossa*. Vammala: Suomalainen Lakimiesyhdistys, 1963.

CHAPTER VIII. PARLIAMENTARISM

Bellquist, E. C. "Finland: Democracy in Travail," *Western Political Quarterly*, 2, no. 2 (June 1949), 217–227.
Bonsdorff, Göran von. *Suomen poliittiset puolueet*. Helsinki: Tammi, 1957.

Kuusisto, A. A. "Parliamentary Crises and Presidential Governments in Finland," *Parliamentary Affairs*, 11, no. 3 (Summer 1958), 341–349.

Lindman, Sven. "Begreppet parlamentarism," *Historisk tidskrift för Finland*, 39 (1954), 126–133.

——— *De homogena partiregeringarna i Finland 1926–1928*, vols. I–II. Åbo: Åbo Akademi, 1940–1941.

——— *Parlamentarismens införande i Finlands statsförfattning*. Uppsala: Almqvist & Wiksell, 1935.

——— *Studier över parlamentarismens tillämpning i Finland 1919–1926*. Åbo: Åbo Akademi, 1937.

Nousiainen, Jaakko. "Näkökohtia 1950-luvun parlamentarismista Suomessa," *Historica I, Studia Historica Jyväskyläensia I*. Pieksämäki: Jyväskylän Kasvatusopillinen Korkeakoulu, 1962, pp. 453–475.

Ståhlberg, K. J. *Parlamentarismi Suomen valtiosäännössä*. Helsinki: Otava, 1927.

Tarkiainen, Tuttu. "Suomalainen parlamentarismi," *Oma maa*, vol. I. Porvoo: WSOY, 1958, pp. 268–280.

——— *Tasavallan presidentin asema Suomen parlamenttaarisessa hallitusjärjestelmässä*. Jyväskylä: Gummerus, 1938.

CHAPTER IX. THE BUREAUCRACY AND ADMINISTRATION OF LAW

Hyvönen, J. T. *Mietintö virasto- ja virkamiesoloista (komiteanmietintö 1928: 15)*. Helsinki: Valtioneuvoston kirjapaino, 1928.

Jansson, Jan-Magnus. "Language Legislation," in Jaakko Uotila, ed., *The Finnish Legal System*. Helsinki: Union of Finnish Lawyers Publishing Company, 1966, pp. 55–68.

Kastari, Paavo. "Ministeriöiden ja valtioneuvoston toiminnan rationalisoimisesta," *Lakimies*, 45 (1947), 31–61.

Koskimies, M. E. *Hallintokoneistomme*. Helsinki: Otava, 1950.

Kuuskoski, Reino. "The Administrative System and Legal Safeguards in Administration," in Jaakko Uotila, ed., *The Finnish Legal System*. Helsinki: Union of Finnish Lawyers Publishing Company, 1966, pp. 89–102.

Luoma, Väinö. *Valtion virkamiesten järjestäytyminen Suomessa*, vols. I–II. Turku: Virkamiesliitto, 1962.

Merikoski, V. *Hallinto-oikeuden oikeussuojajärjestelmä*, vols. I–II. Vammala: Suomalainen Lakimiesyhdistys, 1959, 1961.

——— *Laillisuusvalvonta Suomen oikeusjärjestyksessä*. Vammala: Suomalainen Lakimiesyhdistys, 1953.

——— *Suomen julkisoikeus pääpiirteittäin*, vols. I (3rd ed.), II (2nd ed.). Porvoo: WSOY, 1966, 1964.

Nousiainen, Jaakko. "Talousneuvostojen rakenteesta ja tehtävistä Suomessa," *Politiikka*, 6, no. 2 (1964), 67–97.

Paavilainen, Väinö. *Valtakunnansuunnittelu Suomessa*. Helsinki: Valtakunnansuunnittelutoimisto, 1963.

Palmgren, Bo, and Carl-Hendrik Lundell. "Court Organization and Procedure," in Jaakko Uotila, ed., *The Finnish Legal System*. Helsinki: Union of Finnish Lawyers Publishing Company, 1966, pp. 69–88.

Pesonen, Pertti. *Tiede ja opetusministeriö*. Helsinki: Valtioneuvoston kirjapaino, 1961.

Uotila, Jaakko. "Improving Public Administration in Finland," *Revue internationale des sciences administratives*, 27, no. 1 (1961), 65–70.

——— *Päätösvallan siirtäminen Suomen valtionhallinnossa.* Vammala: Suomalainen Lakimiesyhdistys, 1963.

Valtionhallinnon organisaation uudistamiskomitean mietintö I. Periaatemietintö (komiteanmietintö 1958:5). Helsinki: Valtioneuvoston kirjapaino, 1958.

CHAPTER X. COMMUNAL SELF-GOVERNMENT

Eskola, Aarne. *Local Self-Government and Municipal Law in Finland.* Helsinki: Finnish Association of Rural Municipalities, 1968.

Hannus, Arno. *Kunnallislain uudet säännökset kuntien yhteistoiminnasta.* Porvoo: Suomalainen Lakimiesyhdistys, 1961.

Hannus, Arno, and Reino Kuuskoski. *Kunnallislaki*, 5th ed. Porvoo: WSOY, 1965.

Helander, Voitto. "Kunnallisvaltuutetun rooli," *Politiikka*, 7, no. 2 (1965), 19–43.

Holopainen, Toivo. "Puolueiden vaikutus kunnallishallinnossa ja niiden suhtautuminen eräisiin kunnallisiin peruskysymyksiin," *Politiikka*, 3, no. 3 (1961), 113–128.

Ikkala, Olli. *Kunnan yleinen toimivalta.* Vammala: Suomalainen Lakimiesyhdistys, 1959.

Itkonen, Rieti, and Pirkko Valliniemi. *Kunnallismiehen käsikirja*, 5th ed. Porvoo: WSOY, 1955.

Kuntien yhteistoimintakomitean I ja II osamietintö (komiteanmietintö 1960:4 ja 1963:1). Helsinki: Valtioneuvoston kirjapaino, 1960, 1963.

Kuuskoski, Reino. *Suomen kunnallisoikeus pääpiirteittäin.* Porvoo: WSOY, 1966.

Larma, Otto, Aarne Eskola, and L. O. Johanson. *Kunnallisasiain käsikirja*, 3rd ed. Helsinki: Kirjayhtymä, 1961.

Lindman, Sven, ed. *Problems in Finnish Local Government.* Åbo: Institutet för samhällsforskning upprätthållet av Statsvetenskapliga fakulteten vid Åbo Akademi, 1964.

Modeen, Tore. *Det kommunala förtroendeuppdraget.* Åbo: Åbo Akademi, 1962.

Pystynen, Erkki. *Kunnan suuruus kunnallishallinnossa.* Helsinki: Maalaiskuntien Liiton kirjapaino, 1965.

Rekola, Esko. *Kunnallisverotuksen pääpiirteet*, 2nd ed. Porvoo: WSOY, 1957.

Rytkölä, Olavi. *Finnisches Gemeindeverwaltungsrecht.* Helsinki: Der Finnische Juristenverein, 1961.

——— "Self-Government," in Jaakko Uotila, ed., *The Finnish Legal System.* Helsinki: Union of Finnish Lawyers Publishing Company, 1966, pp. 103–117.

Soikkanen, Hannu. *Kunnallinen itsehallinto kansanvallan perusta. Maalaiskuntien itsehallinnon historia.* Helsinki: Maalaiskuntien Liitto, 1966.

Suomen kaupunkiliitto 1912–1962: Juhlajulkaisu. Helsinki: Suomen Kaupunkiliitto, 1962.

Waronen, Eino. *Kunnallispolitiikan kysymyksiä.* Porvoo: WSOY, 1958.

CHAPTER XI. SELF-GOVERNMENT IN THE AALAND ISLANDS

Barros, James. *The Aland Islands Question: Its Settlement by the League of Nations.* New Haven: Yale University Press, 1968.

Castrén, Erik. "Die Entmilitarisierung und Neutralisierung der Ålandinseln," in F. A. Heydte, ed., *Wölkerrecht und rechtliches Weltbild.* Wien: Springer-Verlag, pp. 107–116.

Dreijer, Matts. *Ålands självstyrelse 25 år, Festskrift.* Mariehamn: Landstingets presidium, 1947.

Palmstierna, Carl-Fredrik. "Ålandsfrågan 1918–1951," *Världspolitikens dagsfrågor,* no. 4, 1951. Stockholm: Utrikespolitiska institutet, 1951.

Suontausta, Tauno. "La situation juridique des îles d'Aland," *Zeitschrift für ausländisches öffentlichen Recht und Völkerrecht,* 13 (1951), 741–752.

CHAPTER XII. FOREIGN POLICY AND THE CONDUCT OF FOREIGN AFFAIRS

Ahava, Teini. "Pohjoismainen lakiyhteistyö," *Lakimies,* 56 (1958), 711–727.

Anderson, Stanley V. "The Nordic Council and the 1962 Helsinki Agreement," *Nordisk Tidskrift for International Ret,* 34 (1964), 278–300.

——— *The Nordic Council: A Study of Scandinavian Regionalism.* Seattle: University of Washington Press, 1967.

Bonsdorff, Göran von. "Regional Cooperation of the Nordic Countries," *Cooperation and Conflict,* 1, no. 1 (1965), 32–38.

Fagerholm, K-A. "Finland in the Nordic Family Circle," in Urho Toivola, ed., *Introduction to Finland 1960.* Porvoo: WSOY, 1960.

Finnish Foreign Policy. Vammala: Finnish Political Science Association, 1963.

Gripenberg, G. A. *Neutralitetstanken i Finlands politik.* Stockholm: Lindqvists Förlag, 1960.

Halme, Veikko. *Suomi ja maailmantalous toisen maailmansodan jälkeen,* 2nd ed. Helsinki: Tammi, 1962.

Hodgson, John H. "The Finnish Communist Party and Neutrality," *Government and Opposition,* 2, no. 2 (January–April 1967), 269–287.

——— "The Paasikivi Line," *American Slavic and East European Review,* 18, no. 2 (April 1959), 145–173.

——— "Postwar Finnish Foreign Policy: Institutions and Personalities," *Western Political Quarterly,* 15, no. 1 (March 1962), 80–92.

Holsti, K. J. "Strategy and Techniques of Influence in Soviet-Finnish Relations," *Western Political Quarterly,* 17, no. 1 (March 1964), 63–82.

Ilvessalo, Jaakko. "Suomi ja Yhdistyneiden Kansakuntien suuret pulmakysymykset," *Politiikka,* 3, no. 4 (1961) 161–173.

Jakobson, Max. *Aspects of Finnish Foreign Policy since the Second World War.* London: Hugh Evelyn, 1968.

——— *The Diplomacy of the Winter War.* Cambridge, Mass.: Harvard University Press, 1961.

Killinen, K. *Puolueettomuuden miekka.* Porvoo: WSOY, 1964.

Korhonen, Keijo. *Ydinaseettomat vyöhykkeet maailmanpolitiikassa.* Helsinki: Tammi, 1966.

Kuusisto, Allan. "The Paasikivi Line in Finland's Foreign Policy," *Western Political Quarterly,* 12, no. 1 (March 1959), 37–49.

Lundin, C. Leonard. *Finland in the Second World War.* Bloomington: Indiana University Press, 1957.

Nordiska Rådets verksamhet 1952–1961: Nordisk utredningsserie 1962:8. Stockholm: Nordiska rådets sekretariat, 1962.

Ørvik, Nils. *Europe's Northern Cap and the Soviet Union.* Cambridge, Mass.: Harvard University Press, 1963.

Paasivirta, Juhani. *L'administration des affaires étrangères et la politique extérieure de la Finlande depuis le début de l'indépendance nationale en 1917 jusqu'à la guerre russo-finlandaise de 1939–1940.* Turku: Turun yliopisto, 1966.

——— *The Victors in World War I and Finland: Finland's Relations with the British, French and United States Governments in 1918–1919.* Helsinki: Suomen historiallinen seura, 1965.

Törngren, Ralf. "The Neutrality of Finland," *Foreign Affairs*, 39, no. 4 (July 1961), 601–609.

Törnudd, Klaus. *Suomi ja Yhdistyneet Kansakunnat.* Helsinki: Tammi, 1967.

Upton, Anthony F. *Finland in Crisis, 1940–1941: A Study in Small-Power Politics.* London: Faber, 1964.

Wendt, F. *The Nordic Council and Co-operation in Scandinavia.* Copenhagen: Munksgaard, 1959.

CHAPTER XIII. NATIONAL DEFENSE

Borg, Olavi. "Puolueittemme ohjelmallinen asennoituminen puolustuslaitokseen ja maanpuolustukseen," Helsingin yliopiston yleisen valtio-opin laitoksen tutkimuksia, no. 2, 1963, (mimeographed.)

Eskola, Antti. "Yhteiskunnan säilyttämistä ja puolustamista koskevat arvostukset," *Tiede ja Ase*, no. 20. Helsinki: Suomen sotatieteellinen seura, 1962, pp. 5–90.

Halsti, Wolf H. *Suomen puolustuskysymys.* Kuopio: Kivi, 1954.

Killinen, K. *Demokratia ja totaalinen sota.* Porvoo: WSOY, 1956.

——— *Puolueettomuuden miekka.* Porvoo: WSOY, 1964.

——— "The Relation between the Political and the Military Direction in Finland," *Democracy in Finland.* Helsinki: Finnish Political Science Association, 1960, pp. 74–80.

Suontausta, Tauno. "Ålands rättsliga ställning," *Statsvetenskaplig Tidskrift*, 54 (1951), 241–252.

Tervasmäki, V. *Eduskuntaryhmät ja maanpuolustus valtiopäivillä 1917–1939.* Mikkeli: WSOY, 1964.

CHAPTER XIV. NATIONAL FISCAL POLICY

Andersson, Edward. "Taxation in Finland," in Jaakko Uotila, ed., *The Finnish Legal System.* Helsinki: Union of Finnish Lawyers Publishing Company, 1966, pp. 225–235.

Dahmén, Erik. *Ekonomisk utveckling och ekonomisk politik i Finland.* Helsingfors: Finlands Banks institut för ekonomisk forskning, 1963.

Frederickson, J. William. "The Economic Recovery of Finland since World War II," *Journal of Political Economy*, 68, no. 1 (1960), 17–36.

Kastari, Paavo. *Suomen Pankin erikoisasema valtiokoneistossa.* Vammala: Suomalainen Lakimiesyhdistys, 1955.

Leppo, Matti. *Päätäntävallan ja vastuun ongelma inflaation torjuntatyössä.* Helsinki: Institutum oeconomicum Universitatis Helsingiensis, 1958.

Melin, Ingvar S. "Public Enterprises in Finland," *Bank of Finland: Monthly Bulletin*, 38, no. 3 (March 1964), 18–22.

Nousiainen, Jaakko. *Eduskunta aloitevallan käyttäjänä.* Porvoo: WSOY, 1961.

Paalanen, Erkki. *Valtion kassa- ja tilinpitojärjestelmä*, 2nd ed. Vammala: Lainopillisen ylioppilas-tiedekunnan kustannustoimikunta, 1961.

Purhonen, Eino. *Eduskunnan budjettivalta.* Vammala: Suomalainen Lakimiesyhdistys, 1961.

Teljo, Jussi. *Kansaneduskunta ja valtion tulo- ja menoarvio.* Jyväskylä: Gummerus, 1938.

Törnqvist, Erik. "Long-Term Budgetary Planning," *Bank of Finland: Monthly Bulletin,* 40, no. 1. (January 1966), 18–22.

Tuominen, Heikki. "Development of the Finnish Budgetary System," *Bank of Finland: Monthly Bulletin,* 42, no. 6 (June 1968), 18–22.

CHAPTER XV. SOCIAL POLICY

Knoellinger, Carl Erik. *Labor in Finland.* Cambridge, Mass.: Harvard University Press, 1960.

Kuusi, Pekka. *Social Policy for the Sixties. A Plan for Finland.* Kuopio: Finnish Social Policy Association, 1964.

Nieminen, Armas. *Mitä on sosiaalipolitiikka?* Porvoo: WSOY, 1955.

Oittinen, R. H. *Työväenkysymys ja työväenliike Suomessa,* 2nd ed. Turku: Tammi, 1953.

Piirainen, Veikko. *Suomalaisen sosiaaliturva.* Hämeenlinna: Karisto, 1964.

Pulkkinen, Terho. *Työttömyyden levinneisyys.* Helsinki: WSOY, 1956.

Rinne, Raf. "Industrial Relations in Post-War Finland," *International Labour Review,* 89, no. 5 (May 1964), 461–481.

Sundberg, Heimer. "Social Security," in Jaakko Uotila, ed., *The Finnish Legal System.* Helsinki: Union of Finnish Lawyers Publishing Company, 1966, pp. 205–223.

Suviranta, Antti. "Labour Law," in Jaakko Uotila, ed., *The Finnish Legal System.* Helsinki: Union of Finnish Lawyers Publishing Company, 1966, pp. 193–203.

Waris, Heikki. *Suomalaisen yhteiskunnan sosiaalipolitiikka,* 4th ed. Porvoo: WSOY, 1968.

Index

Aaland Islands, 6, 44, 69, 147; and electoral system, 163; voter turnout in, 176; government of, 292–294; communal elections in, 321; and detachment movement, 345–347; agreements concerning, 383, 384–385
Aamulehti, 136
Åbo Underrättelser, 137
Academic Socialist Society, 26
Academy of Finland, 202–203
Act of Union and Security, 146
Agence France Presse, 141
Agrarian (Center) party, 30, 31, 32–33, 254, 255; development of, 23–24, 27, 28, 35–36; becomes Center party, 27, 90; strength of, 32, 34–35, 42–44, 256; preference for, by social class, 46–47; membership of, 55–56; structural differences in, 67–70; ideology and programs of, 89–92, 100; and electoral system, 165–166, 171; members of Parliament from, 178, 179, 189; parliamentary group of, 187; parliamentary work of, 210–211; and presidential elections, 217–219, 222, 223, 224; Cabinet members from, 260–261; and foreign policy, 364. *See also* Center party
Agreements, and labor relations, 419–420
Aitio, Paavo, 223
Akava (Council of Academic Cooperation), 118, 119
AKAVA (Council of the Academic Professions), 118
Åland-paper, 137, 352–353
Åländsk Samling, 353
Alkio, Santeri, 23, 80
Allardt, Erik, 46n, 58n22, 221; on support base, 48; on political divisions, 50; on voter turnout, 176, 177n13,n15
Andrén, Nils, 135
Appeals, and presidential decisions, 250
Appointments, presidential, 232–233
Arava (national housing board), 431
Armistice Agreement, 347, 372
Association of Finnish Cities, 119
Association of Finnish Metal Industries, 107
Association of Rural Communities, 119
Association of the Self-Employed, 109
Association of White-Collar Labor (HTY), 117
Association of Wholesalers, 109

Bank Committee, 208
Bank of Finland: under parliamentary scrutiny, 208; as civil servants, 302; functions of, 411–412
Bilingualism, *see* Swedish-speaking population
Björkman, Carl, 346, 348
Boards: Communal, 324–326, 336; city, 325
Bonsdorff, Göran von, 30, 258n
Borg, Olavi, 81n, 85n57, 100, 382n; on party groupings, 31–32; on Finnish Rural party, 88–89
Borgåbladet, 137
Brotherus, K. R., 245n
Bruun, Kettil, 177n13, 300n

Cabinets: types of, 258–260; parties in, 260–266; formation of, 266–270; and Parliament, 270–271, 277–279; resignation of, 271–274; and the president, 275–276
Cajander, A. K., 229, 248; Cabinets of, 238, 254, 259; and formation of Coalition, 255; appointed prime minister, 270
Campaign activities, 168–173
Castrén, K., government of, 214, 273

Center party, 29, 30, 72–73, 170; changes from Agrarian to, 27, 90; support for, 44, 47, 50–51; membership of, 56–57, 58; electoral organization of, 62, 64, 76–77; central leadership of, 65–67; finances of, 74–75; parliamentary group of, 77, 78–79, 122–124, 186; ideology and programs of, 89–92, 100; and the press, 134–135, 136, 137, 141. *See also* Agrarian (Center) party
Central Association of Swedish Agricultural Producers, 111
Central Chamber of Commerce of Finland, 109
Central League of Social Democratic Youth, 71
Central offices, 290–291
Central Organization of Finnish Cooperatives (SOK), 109, 122
Chancellor of justice, 308; duties of, 206–207, 250–251; appointed by president, 232
Chemical Confederation, 108
Christian Democratic Group, 71
Christian Workers' League, 33
Circulation Examination Company, 133
Civil Defense Organization, 390
Civil servants: types of, 299; qualifications of, 300–301; and the spoils system, 301–302; salary and retirement of, 302–303; right to tenure of, 304; communal, 327–328
Civil War (1918), 24, 25, 30, 232
Coalition party, *see* National Coalition party
Coalitions, types of, 258–259
Colliander, Rafael, 69n36, 95n73
Committees, 191–194; foreign affairs, 249, 361–362; finance, 249–250; and commissions, 296–297; communal, 326–328; social affairs, 418; production, 422
Communal: organizations, 62–64; elections, 317–321; committees, 326–328
Communes, defined, 292; unilingual or bilingual, 295
Communists, *see* Finnish Communist party
Confederation of Agricultural Producers (MTK), 110–111; and Center party, 125; strike by, 128
Confederation of Agricultural Societies, 112
Confederation of Commerce Employers (LK), 108, 109–110
Confederation of Consumer Cooperatives (KK), 109, 122
Confederation of Finnish Employers (STK), 108, 420
Confederation of Finnish Technical Salaried Employees, 118
Confederation of Finnish Trade Unions (SAK), 103–104, 119, 420; membership of, 112, 113, 114; of 1930, 112–116; of 1960, 114; and representation in parties, 124; and pressure politics, 127–128; and the press, 138
Confederation of Finnish Wood Processing Industries, 107
Confederation of Handicrafts and Small Industry, 108
Confederation of Retailing, 109
Confederation of Salaried Employees and Civil Servants (TVK), 117, 118, 119
Confederation of Small Farmers (PVK), 111
Confederation of Taxpayers, 122
Confederation of White-Collar Labor (HTK), 117, 118
Congress of Workers' Associations, 413–414
Constitutional-Finnish Minded party, 20–21
Council of Academic Cooperation (Akava), 118, 119
Council of the Academic Professions (AKAVA), 118
Court: general, 305–307; special, 307–308; Supreme, 305, 306–307, 309–310

Danielson-Kalmari, J. R., 21
Defense council, 387–388; functions of, 232; duties of, 388
Democratic League of Finnish Women, 60, 71
Democratic Youth League of Finland, 71
Demokraattinen Lehtipalvelu (DPL), 141
Denmark: and NATO, 372; and Nordic Council, 373–376; and EFTA, 379–380
Deutsche Presse-Agentur, 141
d'Hondt method, of determination of election results, 165, 166
Diet, 188–189; four-estate, 19, 21, 160; Act (VJ), 147, 148, 154, 160, 190, 204
District organizations, 64–65
Dreijer, Matts, 353
Duverger, Maurice, 22, 34, 55, 145, 274; on electoral campaigns, 172

Education League of the Workers, 73
EFA, EFTA, *see* European Free Trade Association
Ehrmann, Henry W., 101n
Elections: general, 39; parliamentary, 39, 173–177; presidential, 217–220; communal, 317–321

Electoral system, 162–168, 214–217
Employer Association of the Countryside, 108, 112
Employer Association of Finnish Metal Industries, 108
Employer Association of Finnish Wood Processing Industries, 108
Enckell, Carl, 279
Enckell, Ralph, on neutrality, 368
Enne, Yrjö, 61n26
"Era of Freedom," 19
Erich Cabinet, 254
Erkko family, 137
Eskola, Antti, 382n
Etelä-Pohjanmaa, 23, 48
Etelä-Saimaa, 137
Etelä-Suomen Sanomat, 137
European Free Trade Association (EFTA), 359, 376, 379–380; -Finland Association (EFA), 380
"Evening school," 248–249

Fagerholm, K. A., 219, 221, 222; Cabinet of, 255, 257, 268, 271, 273; "red earth government" of, 256
Farmers' party, 69
Federation of Finnish Industries, 107
Fieandt, Rainer von, 256, 259; Cabinet of, 205, 260
Finnish Broadcasting Corporation, 141; under parliamentary supervision, 208
Finnish Communist party (SKP), 26, 28, 30, 61, 73; support for, 10, 36–37, 52; formation of, 25; as part of opposition, 31, 266; strength of, 42–43, 54; preference for, by social class, 47, 48–50; membership of, 57, 58, 60; ideology and programs of, compared with SKDL, 61, 81–85, 100; central leadership of, 65–67; structural differences in, 70; parliamentary group of, 79–80; and the press, 135, 138; and presidential elections, 222; imprisonment of members of Parliament, 229; and government cooperation, 254, 255; in Aaland Islands, 353
Finnish Labor party, 21
Finnish News Agency (STT), 141
Finnish party, 19, 20, 23, 24. *See also* National Coalition party
Finnish People's Democratic League (SKDL), 26, 32, 76, 124, 211; in mid-1960's, 29; support for, 51; membership of, 57, 60; organizational structure of, 60–63, 64, 65, 66; party activity of, 72–73; parliamentary group of, 79–80, 187–188; ideology and programs of, 81–85, 100; and the press, 138; and electoral system, 167; and presidential elections, 219, 222
Finnish People's party, 165–166; formation of, 27, 92; becomes Liberal People's party, 27–28; ideology of, 32, 92–94, 100; preference for, by social class, 47; organization of, 77, 124; and electoral system, 167; members of Parliament from, 178; and presidential elections, 219–220, 222; Cabinet members from, 261. *See also* Liberal People's party
Finnish Rural party, 34; in mid-1960's, 29; membership of, 56; number of organizations, 62, 64; ideology and programs of, 88–89; and presidential elections, 223
Finnish Social Democratic party, *see* Social Democratic party
Finnish Women's Democratic League, 26
Flemming, Tarja, 75n48
Foreign affairs committee, 249, 361–362
Foreign policy, 230–231
Foreign Trade Association, 109
Form of Government Act (HM), 145–150, 151–160 *passim*
Forssa party congress, 21
Forssa program, 85
Freudenthal, A. O., 20
Friedrich Karl, Prince, 146
Fund-raising, 74–75

Gartz, Åke, 279
General Group of Finnish Employers, 108
Germany: and Ribbentrop Agreement, 359–360; and diplomatic relations, 363; and Finnish parties, 364; as possible aggressor, 370, 371
Great Britain: trade with Finland, 372; and EFTA, 379–380
Greek Orthodox church, 6
Gripenberg, G. A., 366n
Gustavus Adolphus, 3, 313
Gustavus Vasa, 3
Gustavus III, 366

Hackzell's government, 278
Häme province, 44; population of, 4, 8, 12; government of, 292–294; communal elections in, 321
Hämeen Yhteistyö, 138
Heberle, Rudolf, 28
Heckscher, Gunnar, 105
Helander, Voitto, 318, 323–324
Helsingin Sanomat, 137, 139

Helsinki, 44; newspapers of, 136–140; court of appeals in, 306
Helsinki Agreement of 1962, 376
Hermanson, Robert, 160, 237
High Court of Impeachment, 147
Hirvikallio, Paavo, 215
Holsti, Rudolf, 273–274, 366
Honka, Olavi, 223
Honka-league, 222–223, 371
Housing policy, 431–432
Hufvudstadsbladet, 134, 137
Huopalahti, 159n2–160
Huuska, Väinö, 130n; and pressure politics, 125n, 127
Hynninen, P. J., 279

Iceland: and NATO, 372; and Nordic Council, 373–376
IKL, *see* People's Patriotic Movement
Ilkka, 137
Ilomantsi, 44
Ilta-Sanomat, 137
Ingman Cabinet, 254, 258, 273
Insurance, social, 425–428
International Atomic Energy Agency (IAEA), 378–379
Interpellations, 204–206; and Cabinet resignations, 271–272

Jacobstads Tidning, 137
Janhunen, Matti, 82
Jansson, Jan-Magnus, 302; on exceptional laws, 201–202; on foreign policy, 364–365
"January Agreement," 420
John III, 3
Johteinen, Taisto, 83n55
Joint Committee of Finnish Employers, 108
Jutikkala, Eino, 50n

Kajaani, 44
Kaleva, 137
Kallio, Kyösti, 222, 224, 225, 235; Cabinets of, 25, 205, 254, 255; and Communist members of Parliament, 229
Kankkunen, Allan, 394n
Kansan Lehti, *Sana*, *Tahto*, and *Uutiset*, 138
Karelia, *see* Northern Karelia
Kari, J. K., 267
Karjalainen, Ahti, 90n66, 121
Karjalainen coalition, 257
Karjalainen, 136
Karjalan Maa, 134
Kastari, Paavo, 207n24; on fundamental rights, 153; on laws, 202; on the president, 236–237, 239
Kauppila, Erkki, 70n
Kekkonen, Urho, 80, 202, 238, 347; in presidential elections, 219–226; Cabinets of, 230, 255, 273; leadership of, 240; resignation request of, 272; as prime minister, 279; visits to other countries, 358–359, 367; and "Paasikivi-Kekkonen line," 369–370; talks with Khrushchev, 371
Kemi riots, 232
Keskisuomalainen, 137
Keski-Suomi province, 292–294, 321
Keskustapuolueen Sanomakeskus, 141
Khrushchev, Nikita, 371
Kilpi, Eino, 221, 222
Kivimäki Cabinet, 254–255, 258, 278, 367
Kiviniemi, Markku, 300n
Knoellinger, Carl Erik, 104n, 112n
Kotonen, Anton, resignation of, 210
Krusius-Ahrenberg, Lolo, 122–124; on pressure groups, 101–102
Kuluttaja, 121
Kuopio province, 46, 51; newspapers in, 137, 138; government of, 292–294; court of appeals in, 306
Kuusinen, Hertta, 82
Kuuskoski, Reino, Cabinet of, 257, 259, 260
Kymen Sanomat, 134
Kymi province, 44, 51, 54; government of, 292–294

Lagerroth, Fredrik, 147
Länsi-Savo, 137
Lapland province, 44, 46, 51, 69; population of, 4, 5, 12; voter turnout in, 176; government of, 292–294; communal elections in, 321
Lappeenranta, newspapers in, 137, 138
League of Coalition Party Women, 71
League of Coalition Party Youth, 71
League of Finland's Small Farmers, 112
League of Finnish Cities, 339
League of Finnish Comradely Associations, 26
League of Independents, 27
League of Industrial Entrepreneurs, 108
League of Liberals, 34, 92, 222
League of Rural Communes, 339
League of Small Farmers (PVL), 111–112
League of Swedish Rural Communes in Finland, 339
League of the Young Center, 71
Legislation, 195–203; initiation of, 195–198; first, second, and third readings of, 199–200; passage or rejection of, 201, 202–203; exceptional laws, 201–202

Lehdistön Sanomapalvelu (LSP), 141
Lehto Cabinet, 257, 260
Leino, Yrjö, 274
Leskinen, Väinö, 27, 270
"Leskinens," 27
Liberal party, 20
Liberal People's party, 29, 34, 62, 64; formation of, 27–28; support for, 44; membership of, 57; central leadership of, 65–67; finances of, 75; and electoral system, 76, 167; parliamentary group of, 78; ideology and programs of, 92–94; and the press, 132–133, 134; and propaganda, 172–173. *See also* Finnish People's party
Liberal Youth League, 71
Lindman, Sven, 73n44, 92n68, 225; on Swedish People's party, 96n; on parliamentarism, 267
Lipset, Seymour Martin, 37, 48n16
Littunen, Yrjö, 48n16
Loimaa, 318
Luoma, Väinö, 112n, 117; on the civil service, 299
Lutheran church, 6, 364–365

Maakansa, 137
Maaseudun Tulevaisuus, 120
Magnus Eriksson, 313
Mannerheim, C. Gustaf, 146, 216, 226, 231–232
Mantere government, 229, 254, 273
Mäntsälä Revolt, 232
Marshall Plan, 368
Mechelin, Leo, 20, 21, 267; resignation of, 204
Meyer, Poul, 159n1
Meynaud, Jean, 106n
Miettunen, Martti, 257
Mikkeli province, 44; government of, 292–294
Military duty, 385–387
Ministry of agriculture, 243, 287; areas of jurisdiction for, 285–286; expenditures of, 402
Ministry of commerce and industry, 243, 287; areas of jurisdiction for, 286; expenditures of, 402; tasks of, concerning social work, 417–418
Ministry of communications and public works, 243, 287, 288, 297; areas of jurisdiction for, 286; expenditures of, 402; tasks of, connected with social work, 417; administration of labor policy, 430
Ministry of defense, 243; areas of jurisdiction for, 285; expenditures of, 402
Ministry of education, 243, 287, 297; areas of jurisdiction for, 285; expenditures of, 402
Ministry of finance, 243, 293; areas of jurisdiction for, 285; and the budget, 404, 405; and fiscal administration, 410
Ministry of foreign affairs, 243, 287, 289, 362–363; areas of jurisdiction for, 285; expenditures of, 402
Ministry of the interior, 243, 288, 292, 340–341; areas of jurisdiction for, 285; and civil defense, 390; expenditures of, 402
Ministry of justice, 243, 268; areas of jurisdiction for, 285; expenditures of, 402; duties of, connected with social work, 417
Ministry for social affairs, 243, 287, 289, 422; areas of jurisdiction for, 286; expenditures of, 402; duties of, 417–418; and protection of workers, 423, 424; administration of labor policy, 430
Montesquieu, 148, 149
MTK, *see* Confederation of Agricultural Producers

National Coalition party, 25–26, 29, 30, 31–33, 165–166, 211; formation of, 24; and conservatism, 28; strength of, 39–42; support for, 44, 47–48; membership of, 55–60 *passim*; organizations of, 62–65; central leadership of, 65–67; structural differences in, 67–70; party activity of, 72–73, 173; finances of, 75; ideology and programs of, 32, 96–100; and the press, 134–135, 136, 141; and electoral system, 76–77, 167; nomination of candidates, 170; ministers of Parliament from, 179; parliamentary group of, 78, 122–124, 186, 187, 188; and presidential elections, 217–220, 222, 223; Cabinet members from, 261–266
National Pensions Institute, 208
National Progressive party, 24, 25
NATO, 372
Neutrality, 364, 365–368
Nieminen, Armas, 15
Nikkari, Marja, 75n48
Niskanen, Esko, 75n48
Noponen, Martti, 124, 179, 184n
Nordic Agreement on Cooperation, 376
Nordic Commission for Culture, 375
Nordic Council, 373–376
Nordic Tanganyika center, 379
Northern Karelia, 23; population of, 8, 12; refugees, 13, 400, 416; Social

Northern Karelia—Continued
Democratic majority in, 54; government of, 292–294; communal elections in, 321
Norway: and NATO, 372; and Nordic Council, 373–376; and EFTA, 379–380
Nya Pressen, 137
Nyholm, Pekka, 38n, 48n15; and parliamentary voting, 32; on party divisions, 51; on parliamentary groups, 187–188

Occupational structure, 9–15; changes in, 12–15
"Old Finland," 3
Old Finnish party, 20–21, 23, 24, 39, 50. *See also* National Coalition party
Ombudsman, 206–207
Organization for Economic Cooperation and Development (OECD), 381
Oulu province, 44, 46, 51, 69; population of, 4, 5, 8, 12; and Small Farmers' party, 33; newspapers in, 137, 138; voter turnout in, 176; government of, 292–294

Paasikivi, J. K., 233, 240, 270; memoirs of, 22; and presidential elections, 219, 222, 224, 225, 226; Cabinets of, 255; on foreign policy, 357
Paasikivi government, 273, 274
Paasikivi line, 364, 365, 369–372
Paasio, Rafael, 223
Paasivirta, Juhani, 69n38
Päivän Sanomat, 138
Palmen, E. G., 21
Paris Peace Agreement (1856), concerning Aaland Islands, 384
Paris Peace Treaty (1947), 347, 383–384, 385
Pekkala, Mauno, 222, 268; Cabinet of, 255
Pensions, 426–428
People's Democratic party, *see* Finnish People's Democratic League (SKDL)
People's party, *see* Finnish People's party
People's Patriotic Movement (IKL), 25–26, 255
Pesonen, Pertti, 48n16, 58n22, 177n15, 220; 1958 study of Tampere, 32, 141; *An Election in Finland*, 58n23, 136n, 137n, 139n, 171n, 173n11, 177n14
Pessi, Ville, 62
Pirkka, 121
Plenary session, 247–248
Pohjanmaa, 6, 23, 44
Pohjanmaan Kansa, 138
Pohjois-Häme, party membership in, 58, 59
Pohjois-Karjala, *see* Northern Karelia
Pohjois-Savo, 44, 46, 54
Pohjolan Sanomat, 137
Pohjolan Työ, 138
Population: density of, 3–4; by sex and age, 4–5; linguistic duality of, 5–6; religious breakdown of, 6; educational level of, 6–7; urban and rural, 7–8; policy for development of, 430–431
Pori, *see* Turku and Pori province
Porkkala, 268; military base at, 358, 372; reunification of, 360
Poverty, influence of, on political opinion, 52
President: his relations with Cabinet, 275–276; and State administration, 282; and foreign affairs, 357–359; as commander-in-chief of military, 387–388
Procopé, Hjalmar J., 279
Progressive party, 92, 254, 255; becomes Finnish People's party, 26–27; and liberalism, 28; People's party merges with, 33; strength of, 39–42; membership of, 55, 56; and the press, 136–137; and electoral system, 167; ministers of Parliament from, 178; parliamentary group of, 187; and presidential elections, 217–219, 222; Cabinet members from, 261; and foreign policy, 364
Propaganda, 139–140; use of, by pressure groups, 120–121, 126; during campaign, 172–173
Provinces, development of, 292
Publications, political, 73–74, 120–121

Qvist, Martti, 140

Rantala, Onni, 28n, 67n, 71n, 97n; on political division, 47; on party membership, 56n, 58, 60n, 63n33; and party finances, 75n48; 1956 study by, 170; on Coalition party activity, 173, 186n, 188n18
Rauhala, Urho, 15
"Red earth government," 256
Relander, Lauri, 224, 225, 229, 269, 273
Religious factors, and political behavior, 6
Reuters, 141
Ribbentrop Agreement, 359
Rights, fundamental, 150–155
Rokkan, Stein, 48n16
Roos, John E., 159–160n2
Routavaara, Akseli, 55
Rural party, *see* Finnish Rural party
Russification, 20–24 *passim*, 39, 131, 145–146, 149, 414. *See also* Soviet Union
Rydman, Eero, 221, 222

Ryti, Risto, 231, 240, 359–360; resignation of, 216; and presidential elections, 219, 222, 226

Saimaa Canal, 372
Saimaan Sanomat, 138
SAJ, *see* Trade Union Organization
SAK, *see* Confederation of Finnish Trade Unions
Satakunnan Kansa, 136
Satakunnan Työ, 138
Satakunta, 170; Coalition party activity in, 56, 58, 59, 173
Savon Sanomat, 137
School of Midwifery case, 252
Seamen's Union, 129
Seppänen, Paavo, 131n1
SKDL, *see* Finnish People's Democratic League
Skog, Emil, 27, 223
"Skogs," 27, 113
SKP, *see* Finnish Communist party
Small Farmers party, 165–166; formation of, 33; and electoral system, 167; and presidential elections, 222
Snellman, J. V., 19, 20
Social classes: and party preference, 8–9, 46–48; occupations of, 15–18
Social Democratic Central League of Women, 71
Social Democratic League of Workers and Small Farmers (TPSL), 27, 87–88; in mid-1960's, 29; formation of, 34, 69; number of organizations, 62, 64; leadership of, 66; structural differences in, 68; finances of, 74–75; and elections, 165–166, 167, 171, 219, 321
Social Democratic party, 21–36 *passim*, 125, 171, 414; ideology and programs of, 28, 29–30, 80, 85–88, 100; strength of, 42–43, 54; support for, 44–46, 47, 48–50; membership of, 55; organizational structure of, 60, 62–65; leadership of, 65–67, 256, 257; structural differences of, 70; party activity of, 72–73; finances of, 74–75; and electoral system, 76–77, 165–167; parliamentary group of, 79, 186, 187; and the press, 134–135, 137–138, 141; nomination of candidates, 169; members of Parliament from, 178, 184, 189; parliamentary work of, 210–211; and presidential elections, 219–220, 222, 223; and government responsibility, 254, 255; Cabinet members from, 261; and communal elections, 319–321; on Aaland Islands, 352–353; and foreign policy, 364
Social Democratic Women's League of Finland, 71
Social Democratic Youth League of Finland, 71
Social reform, development of, 413–416
Social services, communal, 330–332
Socialist League of Students, 60
Socialist Unity party, 26
Socialist Worker's party of Finland, 25
SOK (Central Organization of Finnish Cooperatives), 109, 122
Soviet Union: visits to, by Finnish presidents, 358; and Treaty of Friendship, Cooperation, and Mutual Assistance, 359, 370–372; and Finnish parties, 364; and Paasikivi line, 365, 369–370; and Finnish neutrality, 366–368; and trade with Finland, 372; and Finnish abstention in U.N., 377; and EFTA, 380. *See also* Russification
Spoils system, 301–302
Ståhlberg, K. J., 25, 229, 237, 270; as leader of Young Finns, 21, 24; proposal of his constitutional committee, 145, 146, 148, 253–254; and presidential elections, 214, 215, 219, 222, 225; as first president, 238; leadership of, 240; and Cabinet resignations, 273
Stalin, Joseph, letter to Paasikivi, 370
State Alcohol Monopoly, 396, 398
Strike, general (1956), 232, 421; as political pressure, 128–129
Sukselainen, V. J., 186, 256, 260n, 268n; Cabinets of, 205, 257
Sundblom, Julius, 346
Sunila Cabinets, 205, 235, 254
Suomenmaa, 137
Suomen Sosialidemokraatti, 138
Suometar, 136
Svinhufvud, P. E., 202, 214, 229, 235, 238; as leader of Young Finns, 21, 24; and presidential elections, 215, 219, 222, 225; leadership of, 240; Cabinet of, 254
Sweden: neutrality of, 372–373; and Nordic Council, 373–376; and EFTA, 379–380
Swedish Association of Women, 71
Swedish Cooperative Association, 109
Swedish Left party, 33–34
Swedish party, 19–20
Swedish People's party, 24, 29, 173, 255, 415; formation of, 22–23; ideology and programs of, 32, 94–96, 100; strength of, 42, 44, 176; preference for, by social class, 47; membership of, 55, 57; organizations of, 62, 64; leadership of, 65–67; structural differences in, 67–70;

Swedish People's Party—Continued
finances of, 75; and electoral system, 76–77, 167; parliamentary group of, 78, 122–124, 186, 187; and the press, 134, 135, 137; and presidential elections, 217, 219, 222, 223; Cabinet members from, 266; and foreign policy, 364
Swedish-speaking population, 6, 42, 295–296; party preference of, 47; and the press, 135–136; frequency of voting of, 176; and representatives in government, 266; in Aaland Islands, 351–352
Swedish Workers' League of Finland, 71
Swedish Youth, 71

Tampere: Pesonen's study of, 32; party membership of, 58; newspapers in, 136, 138
Tanner, Väinö, 25, 80, 222, 254, 271
Tarkiainen, Tuttu, 225; on the presidency, 237–238
Taxes, 393–395; communal, 333–335, 336–337; direct, 395–396, 398; indirect, 395, 396–397, 398; sales, importance of, 398
Teljo, Jussi, 120n; on first party groups, 22; on expenditures, 407
Textile Council, 108
Törngren, Ralf, 221, 222, 279; resignation of, 268, 270
TPSL, *see* Social Democratic League of Workers and Small Farmers
Trade Union Organization (SAJ), 113, 119, 125; membership of, 114
Trade unions, 112–119
Treaty of Friendship, Cooperation, and Mutual Assistance, 359, 370–372, 383, 384
Tulenheimo Cabinet, 254
Tuomioja, Sakari, 221, 222, 230; Cabinet of, 255, 258, 259
Turku and Pori province, 44; population density of, 4, 12; newspapers in, 136, 137, 138; election blocs of, 165–166; government of, 292–294; court of appeals in, 306; city commune of, 318
Turun Sanomat, 137
Työkansan Sanomat, 138
Työväen Sanomalehtien Tietotoimisto (TST), 141

Unemployment, 428–430
Union of Civil Servants, 117
Union of Communal Civil Servants, 117
Union of communes, 338–339
Union of Finnish Architects, 119
Union of Finnish Doctors, 119
Union of Finnish Teachers, 117
Union of Nurses, 117
United Nations: Finnish membership in, 376–379; Charter, 383, 384
United Nations Development Program (UNDP), 379
United States, and Finnish abstention in U.N., 377
Uusi Aika, 138
Uusimaa province, 44; population of, 4, 6, 8, 12; government of, 292–294
Uusi Suometar, 136
Uusi Suomi, 136
Uutiskeskus (UK), 141

Vaasa province, 44; conservative outlook of, 54; newspapers in, 136, 137, 138; government of, 292–294; court of appeals in, 306; communal elections in, 321
Vaasa, 136
Väisänen, Matti, 222
Vapaa Sana, 138, 139
Vasabladet, 137
Västra Nyland, 137
Vennamo, Veikko, 34, 223
Vennola Cabinet, 274
Viipuri province, 3; court of appeals in, 306
Virkkunen, Matti, 223
Virolainen, Johannes, 279; on rural outlook, 89
Voting turnout, 174–177

Waris, Heikki, 15
Waronen, Eino, 343
Warsaw Pact, 368
Welfare, 424–425
Women: drawn into party activity, 70–71; voting frequency of, 176–177
Women of the Center Party, 71
Women of the Liberal People's Party, 71
Work day, 8-hour, 422–423
Work stoppages, 421–422
Worker, protection of, 422–424
Wrede, R. A., 21
Wright, Viktor Julius von, 21, 413
Wright period, 21

"Years of frost," 20
Yhteisvoimin, 121
Young Finnish party, 20–21, 23, 56; becomes National Progressive party, 24; strength of, 39
Youth, drawn into party activity, 70–71
Yrjö-Koskinen, Yrjö Sakari, 19, 21